Oxford Readings in Classical Studies
Vergil's Georgics

Edited by
KATHARINA VOLK

OXFORD
UNIVERSITY PRESS

Great Clarendon Street, Oxford OX2 6DP
Oxford University Press is a department of the University of Oxford.
It furthers the University's objective of excellence in research, scholarship,
and education by publishing worldwide in
Oxford New York
Auckland Cape Town Dar es Salaam Hong Kong Karachi
Kuala Lumpur Madrid Melbourne Mexico City Nairobi
New Delhi Shanghai Taipei Toronto
With offices in
Argentina Austria Brazil Chile Czech Republic France Greece
Guatemala Hungary Italy Japan Poland Portugal Singapore
South Korea Switzerland Thailand Turkey Ukraine Vietnam

Oxford is a registered trade mark of Oxford University Press
in the UK and in certain other countries

Published in the United States
by Oxford University Press Inc., New York

© Oxford University Press 2008

The moral rights of the author have been asserted
Database right Oxford University Press (maker)

First published 2008

All rights reserved. No part of this publication may be reproduced,
stored in a retrieval system, or transmitted, in any form or by any means,
without the prior permission in writing of Oxford University Press,
or as expressly permitted by law, or under terms agreed with the appropriate
reprographics rights organization. Enquiries concerning reproduction
outside the scope of the above should be sent to the Rights Department,
Oxford University Press, at the address above

You must not circulate this book in any other binding or cover
and you must impose the same condition on any acquirer

British Library Cataloguing in Publication Data
Data available

Library of Congress Cataloging-in-Publication Data
Vergil's Georgics / edited by Katharina Volk.
p. cm.—(Oxford readings in classical studies)
Includes bibliographical references and index.
ISBN 978–0–19–954294–9 ISBN 978–0–19–954293–2
1. Virgil. Georgica. 2. Didactic poetry, Latin—History and criticism.
3. Virgil—knowledge—Literature. 4. Allusions in Literature. 5. Rome—In literature.
I. Volk, Katharina, 1969–
PA6804.G4V47 2008
873'.01—dc22   2008009943

Typeset by SPI Publisher Services, Pondicherry, India
Printed in Great Britain
on acid-free paper by
Biddles Ltd., King's Lynn, Norfolk

ISBN 978–0–19–954293–2 (Hbk.)   978–0–19–954294–9 (Pbk.)

1 3 5 7 9 10 8 6 4 2

OXFORD READINGS IN CLASSICAL STUDIES

The series provides students and scholars with a representative selection of the best and most influential articles on a particular author, work, or subject. No single school or style of approach is privileged: the aim is to offer a broad overview of scholarship, to cover a wide variety of topics, and to illustrate a diversity of critical methods. The collections are particularly valuable for their inclusion of many important essays which are normally difficult to obtain and for the first-ever translations of some of the pieces. Many articles are thoroughly revised and updated by their authors or are provided with addenda taking account of recent work. Each volume includes an authoritative and wide-ranging introduction by the editor surveying the scholarly tradition and considering alternative approaches. This pulls the individual articles together, setting all the pieces included in their historical and cultural contexts and exploring significant connections between them from the perspective of contemporary scholarship. All foreign languages (including Greek and Latin) are translated to make the texts easily accessible to those without detailed linguistic knowledge.

OXFORD READINGS IN CLASSICAL STUDIES

Homer's *Iliad*
Edited by Douglas L. Cairns

Virgil's *Aeneid*
Edited by S. J. Harrison

The Roman Novel
Edited by S. J. Harrison

Euripides
Edited by Judith Mossman

Aristophanes
Edited by Erich Segal

Greek Tragedy
Edited by Erich Segal

Menander, Plautus, and Terence
Edited by Erich Segal

The Greek Novel
Edited by Simon Swain

Ancient Literary Criticism
Edited by Andrew Laird

Aeschylus
Edited by Michael Lloyd

Ovid
Edited by Peter E. Knox

The Attic Orators
Edited by Edwin Carawan

Lucretius
Edited by Monica R. Gale

Catullus
Edited by Julia Haig Gaisser

Vergil's *Eclogues*
Edited by Katharina Volk

All available in paperback

Preface

This volume was originally conceived as one half of a collection of *Oxford Readings* on both the *Eclogues* and the *Georgics*, but was later deemed capable of standing on its own. It is a special pleasure to acknowledge those who have sweetened the *labor* that has gone into this publication and without whose help I would not have been able to see it to completion. My thanks go to Hilary O'Shea for initiating the project and to Jenny Wagstaffe and the staff at Oxford University Press for their assistance in the book's production. Niklas Holzberg, Bob Kaster, Jim Zetzel, and the anonymous referees gave me helpful suggestions for the choice of articles; I am also grateful to Niklas for letting me use his invaluable bibliographies (see Introduction, note 3) and to Jim for his comments on the Introduction. Thanks to a generous grant from the Stanwood Cockey Lodge Fund (Columbia University), I was able to employ a research assistant, Kristin Robbins, whom I thank for her wonderful job in compiling and editing the papers and bibliography.

More than to anyone else, I am indebted to the authors. In addition to agreeing to have their articles reprinted, they made themselves available to answer queries, make revisions, and either provide themselves, or discuss and correct, the English translations of Latin and Greek passages. I am delighted to have been able to gather such a distinguished group of Vergilians between covers; this truly is their volume.

KV

New York
September 2007

Contents

1. Introduction: Scholarly Approaches to the *Georgics* since the 1970s 1
   Katharina Volk
2. Agriculture and the *Georgics* 14
   M. S. Spurr
3. Prose into Poetry: Tradition and Meaning in Virgil's *Georgics* 43
   Richard F. Thomas
4. Authorial Rhetoric in Virgil's *Georgics* 81
   Richard Rutherford
5. Virgil's Metamorphoses: Myth and Allusion in the *Georgics* 94
   Monica R. Gale
6. *Labor Improbus* 128
   Richard Jenkyns
7. Italian Virgil and the Idea of Rome 138
   Michael C. J. Putnam
8. Cosmology and National Epic in the *Georgics* (*Georgics* 2.458–3.48) 161
   Philip Hardie
9. Pindar and the Proem to the Third *Georgic* 182
   L. P. Wilkinson
10. Callimachus, the *Victoria Berenices*, and Roman Poetry 189
    Richard F. Thomas
11. The Fourth *Georgic*, Virgil and Rome 225
    Jasper Griffin

Bibliography 249
Acknowledgements 266
Index of passages cited 267

1

Introduction: Scholarly Approaches to the *Georgics* since the 1970s

Katharina Volk

SORTES VERGILIANAE: TRENDS IN VERGILIAN SCHOLARSHIP

To an extent unparalleled by any other text from Graeco-Roman antiquity, the works of Vergil have been considered capable of producing meaning.[1] Their status as an engine of unlimited signification finds its emblem in the *sortes Vergilianae*, the practice (attested from the second century AD onward) of consulting Vergil's poems as an oracle by opening the text at random and interpreting the first verse chanced on as pertaining to the consultant's situation.[2] While modern critics typically approach Vergil in a less haphazard fashion, the variety of divergent interpretations at which they are able to arrive, and the ways in which these interpretations respond to the enquirers' own intellectual and ideological concerns, attest to the poet's continuing

---

[1] This introduction has a counterpart in that of this book's 'sister volume', *Oxford Readings in Classical Studies: Vergil's 'Eclogues'*. I originally wrote a single introduction to what was supposed to be a single volume on both works. When the Press decided to publish two separate books instead, I had the task of splitting up the introduction as well, which explains the identical structure of the two chapters, as well as the overlap in the first section. Readers interested in how the trends in Vergilian scholarship described here play out in the *Eclogues* are invited to consult the other volume.

[2] On the *sortes Vergilianae*, see briefly Comparetti 1997: 47–8, as well as Martindale 1997: 6, who likewise considers the practice emblematic of approaches to Vergil in general.

appeal as a provider of meaningful answers to a multitude of different questions.

The resultant lack of consensus in Vergilian scholarship has—especially in recent, poststructuralist times—been viewed as a positive thing, with the inherent openness and polysemy of Vergil's works being regarded as indicative of their quality. To take just a few examples, S. J. Harrison concludes the introduction to his 1990 *Oxford Readings in Vergil's 'Aeneid'* with the observation that 'the volume and variety of recent criticism is a tribute to the continuing literary interest and stature of the *Aeneid*', a work that, in the same sentence, he characterizes as 'great poetry' (20). Also that year, Christine G. Perkell predicted that future scholarship on the *Eclogues* would 'deemphasize the notion of a proper understanding, of a correct reading, in favor of opening up the text, of acknowledging ambiguities and not simplifying complexities' (1990: 47). As for the *Georgics*, Philip Hardie's remark about the story of Aristaeus—that 'to insist on a single interpretation may be to do violence to this polymorphous and Protean text' (1998: 45)—could easily be extended to the poem as a whole, about which Hardie concludes that 'many contemporary readers are left feeling that this is a text with more problems than answers' (52). However, the very elusiveness of the work contributes to its greatness, as maintained, among others, by William W. Batstone, who writes that 'the diversity of compelling interpretations is part of the *Georgics*' larger value and meaning' (1997: 125).

If the ability to produce divergent readings is thus, by general consensus, an intrinsic feature of Vergil's poetry, and if the extant interpretations of his works are as many as the leaves blown about in the Sibyl's cave, giving an overview of Vergilian scholarship is a daunting task, one that might appear doomed from the start. Fortunately, though, my purpose in the following pages is rather more circumscribed. Since the present volume is concerned with the *Georgics* only, works on the *Aeneid* and *Eclogues* appear only in supporting roles. Likewise, since the papers collected here date exclusively from 1970 onward, my discussion of Vergilian criticism is similarly restricted to the last 37 years. The starting date of 1970 is somewhat arbitrary and was chosen on the assumption that scholarship from the last third of a century or so may still be considered vaguely contemporary. However, beginning with the 1970s also makes a certain amount of sense since that decade saw a number of important new impulses in the study of the *Georgics*, ones that have continued to influence scholarship.[3]

In one way or another, the *Georgics* has always stood in the shadow of Vergil's other poems, especially the *Aeneid*. An example of a genre halfway between the lowly and the sublime and a work of the poet's mid-career, the poem has often been regarded as 'transitional' (thus C. G. Hardie 1971), a mere way-station on the path to the epic masterpiece in which Vergil's life and work culminated—according to the teleological view of the poet's career that is found in the *Vitae* and still colours perceptions of the Vergilian *oeuvre* today.[4] While the georgic mode enjoyed occasional periods of popularity at various points in the history of Western literature, it has long been unfashionable, and if poems about farming do not hold much appeal for the general public, professional classicists, too, tend to eye them with a certain suspicion. As a result, the *Georgics* are studied in colleges and universities far less frequently than the *Aeneid* (and probably the *Eclogues* as well), and scholarly publications on Vergil's epic far outnumber those on his didactic poem. In addition, the very methodologies and approaches critics bring to bear on the *Georgics* are often ones first developed in the study of the *Aeneid* (this is true especially of the 'Harvard School' pessimistic approach), a fact that neatly illustrates the poem's secondary status.

This is not to say, however, that there has not been considerable work done on the *Georgics*. The last thirty or 50 years have seen the publication of major commentaries (Erren 1985–2003, R. F. Thomas 1988, Mynors 1990) and numerous books and articles, which are

---

[3] For scholarship on the *Georgics*, see Suerbaum 1980 as well as the more up-to-date and extensive bibliography compiled by Niklas Holzberg (available online at <www.psms.homepage.t-online.de/georgicabib.html> (2003)). In addition, the journal *Vergilius* publishes an annual Vergilian bibliography. Recent monographs on Vergil, all with discussion of and bibliography on the *Georgics*, include P. R. Hardie 1998 (the best general introduction to the poet), La Penna 2005, Holzberg 2006, and von Albrecht 2006. Two 'companions' to Vergil, Horsfall (ed.) 1995 and Martindale (ed.) 1997, provide articles on individual works and other topics of interest. Finally, the *Enciclopedia Virgiliana* (1985–90) contains a wealth of information on all things Vergilian.

[4] On Vergil's career, see Lipking 1981: 76–93, Theodorakopoulos 1997, and Volk 2002: 152–6.

representative of both Vergilian scholarship (in all its variety and with all its controversies) and the general developments and advances of Latin literary studies in the late twentieth and early twenty-first centuries. While the multiplicity of approaches and results makes it difficult to give even a broad overview or construct a simple narrative, it nevertheless seems to me possible to discern two principal strands in the interpretation of Vergil's work in general and of the *Georgics* in particular, strands that are not infrequently intertwined but are nevertheless markedly different.

The first trend involves readings that might be called 'ideological'. By this I mean approaches predicated on the idea that Vergil's poems are designed to 'convey a message' (Putnam 1970: 4 on the *Eclogues*), which the critic endeavours to uncover. This message may be seen to concern the social and political situation of the work's composition, the poet's own poetry or poetry in general, or (quite frequently) human life and the human condition—or any combination of these and similar issues. As is well known, critical assessments of Vergil's position on such matters have varied considerably over the past decades. While the poet was traditionally credited with a positive or 'optimistic' attitude, not only toward the georgic life presented in his poem, but also concerning the political ascendancy of Octavian reflected more obliquely in his text, scholars starting in the 1970s began increasingly to detect deep ambivalence and even downright 'pessimism' in the *Georgics*.[5] This type of approach was clearly influenced by the 'Harvard School' or 'two-voices' pessimistic criticism of the *Aeneid*, which was going strong already in the 1960s[6] but left its mark on the study of Vergil's earlier poems with

---

[5] The division of ideological readings of Vergil into 'optimistic' and 'pessimistic' is overly simplistic and has been criticized, e.g. by R. F. Thomas 1990: 64–5, who prefers 'Augustan' and 'ambivalent' instead (Thomas also points out, in 64 n. 1, that the designation 'Harvard School' is less than appropriate for a critical trend shared by scholars from many universities). For the sake of convenience, however, I shall stick with these terms. As for Thomas's preferred 'ambivalent', it seems to me that there is a wide spectrum of readings that detect some form of ambivalence in Vergil's text. As P. R. Hardie 1998: 51 writes, such interpretations are 'more often than not' ultimately pessimistic (since ambivalence is experienced as disruptive); however, a number of scholars maintain that Vergilian poetry (especially the *Georgics*) is indeed characterized by an (uneasy) balance, in which positive and negative aspects exist side by side, without either one being privileged.

[6] Generally on the 'Harvard School', see Serpa 1987: 76–88; on pessimistic interpretations of the *Aeneid*, see S. J. Harrison 1990: 5–6.

characteristic delay.[7] Ideological readings since this paradigm shift have concentrated on determining the nuances of Vergil's optimism or pessimism, often concluding that the poet's texts are characterized by a deep and deliberate ambiguity, which mirrors the complexity of the world and of human life as represented in the poems. It should be pointed out, however, that recent years have seen a reassessment of Vergil's political stance especially and that, in a kind of New Augustanism, scholars these days are again much more inclined to see the poems as reflecting positively on Octavian and his politics.[8]

The second approach might be labelled 'literary' and characterizes a wide variety of studies that examine the *Georgics* primarily as works of literature. These include discussions of the poem's didactic genre, a notorious problem since 'didactic poetry' is, to some extent at least, an anachronistic construct that was not recognized as a proper genre in antiquity. Another major field of interest—in Latin studies in general and in Vergilian scholarship in particular—has been intertextuality and the ways in which poems allude to and position themselves vis-à-vis their models. In this context, much attention has been paid to the influence on the *Georgics* of Lucretius and Callimachus. Finally, critics have focused on questions of poetics, that is, on how Vergil in the *Georgics* presents his own endeavour and ambition and how he undertakes to inscribe his own efforts into a literary tradition.

As mentioned above, these two approaches are not mutually exclusive. Ideological readings frequently concern themselves with the role of the poet, while primarily literary studies may have much to say about the poem's political or more generally philososphical

---

[7] This trajectory can be traced nicely in the monographs of Michael C. J. Putnam, one of the most eminent representatives of the 'Harvard School': only after his first book on the *Aeneid* (1965) did he tackle the *Eclogues* (1970) and only later still the *Georgics* (1979).

[8] See e.g. one of the most recent monographs on Vergil, Holzberg 2006. Already in 1990, Richard F. Thomas (1990: 65; with reference to Don Fowler) detected an Augustan backlash to the 'Harvard School' approach, but it would appear that his New Augustans are simply old Augustans who resist the contemporary shift to pessimism. By contrast, today's New Augustans, such as Holzberg, have gone through the pessimists' school, are attuned to the complexities and ambivalences of Vergil, but still conclude that the poet projects a largely positive image of Octavian (and of whatever else is at stake).

outlook. Still, not only do many works of Vergilian criticism fall fairly clearly into the one category or the other, but there has also been, over the past few decades, a kind of metapoetic turn, a shift away from reading Vergil for his message and toward studying him for his poetics. Practitioners of present-day *sortes Vergilianae* are thus less likely to ask 'What do these poems tell us about life?' than 'What do these poems tell us about poetry?' The following overview of scholarship on the *Georgics* will further illuminate this tendency.

THE *GEORGICS*

Hailed as the 'best poem of the best poet' (Dryden), the *Georgics* is a work unlike any other, one whose very generic affiliation causes puzzlement. What kind of text is this? It is possible to classify the work as didactic (a genre that is itself ill-defined; see Volk 2002: 25–68), and scholars have isolated and examined various features typical of the genre: Schiesaro 1993, Rutherford 1995 (reprinted in this volume), and Gibson 1997 focus on addresses to the student; Schindler 2000: 150–215 treats the similes (see also Briggs 1980 on similes in the *Aeneid* that are based on passages in the *Georgics*); Volk 2002: 119–56 discusses the work's (typically didactic) poetic self-consciousness; Schiesaro 1997 attempts to unravel its underlying epistemology; and P. R. Hardie 2004 traces the theme of education throughout the poem.[9] There is, however, a near-complete scholarly consensus that 'Virgil's poem is didactic only in appearance' (R. F. Thomas 1988: 1.24), that is, that the work is intended not to teach agriculture to farmers but rather to convey a larger message.[10] Thus, Effe 1977: 80–97 considers the *Georgics* representative of what he calls the 'transparent' type of didactic poetry, in which the poet purports to teach one thing but really wants to get across another.

---

[9] For more general discussions of the *Georgics* as didactic, see Effe 1977: 80–97 and Dalzell 1996: 104–31.

[10] Against this majority opinion, Spurr 1986 (reprinted in this volume) views the *Georgics* as indeed applicable to contemporary agriculture.

Introduction

The larger message of the poem is typically believed to concern, in one way or another, 'the life of man in this world' (Parry 1972: 36; Putnam 1979: 15 describes the *Georgics* as 'one grand trope for life itself'), but scholars have differed sharply on what the poet's take on this issue might be. Looking back over the last few decades, we see the familiar development from optimism to pessimism and/or ambiguity and then back to a new form of optimism. According to the optimists (e.g. Otis 1964: 144–214, Klingner 1963 = 1967: 175–363, and Buchheit 1972), the *Georgics* celebrates the dignity of labour and of agricultural life, as well as the endeavours of Octavian, which might lead to a new Golden Age in Italy. By contrast, in the view of the pessimists (especially Putnam 1979, Boyle 1986: 36–84, Ross 1987, and R. F. Thomas 1988), Vergil draws attention to the harsh realities of life in the Iron Age, the futility of human toil, and the problems and uncertainties surrounding the rise of Octavian. Some scholars (e.g. Miles 1980, Perkell 1989, Nelson 1998, and Gale 2000), rather than coming down on one side or the other, maintain that the poem exhibits a stance of profound ambiguity: the *Georgics* shows both the positive and negative aspects of existence and thus reflects the complexities of the real world. In recent years, the pendulum has begun to swing back toward a (cautious) optimism (e.g. Cramer 1989, Lee 1996, Schäfer 1996, Heckel 1998, Morgan 1999, and Nappa 2005), with critics again discerning a positive attitude to Octavian, who in one interpretation (Nappa 2005; compare also Lee 1996, Heckel 1998, P. R. Hardie 2004: 106–11, and Holzberg 2006: 51–6) is seen as a student meant to profit from Vergil's poem (viewed as a kind of 'mirror of princes'). What optimists and pessimists share is the conviction that the *Georgics* carries a deeply significant message for mankind; critics who detect a lighter side in the poem (e.g. Dalzell 1996: 118–25) or who resist reading it symbolically as expressive of a coherent world-view (e.g. Jenkyns 1998: 295–386 and already Wilkinson 1969) remain a minority.

The larger metapoetic turn in Vergilian (and Latin) scholarship has left its mark on studies on the *Georgics* as well. In addition to discussions of the poem's genre (see above), there has been particular interest in its intertextual relations with various poetic models.[11] The standard

---

[11] For Vergil's use of prose sources, see R. F. Thomas 1987 (reprinted in this volume) as well as Horsfall 1995 (on Cato via Cicero).

point of reference is Farrell 1991, which examines Vergil's reworking of Hesiod, Aratus, Callimachus, Lucretius, and Homer and shows how the poet shifts from one model to the next in the course of the work. Schäfer 1996 and Gale 2000 treat the crucial influence of Lucretius (compare also Schiesaro 1997), while Richard F. Thomas has dedicated a number of publications to Vergil's Callimacheanism (R. F. Thomas 1983 (reprinted in this volume), 1985, 1993, and 1998; see also 1988 *passim*). Cadili 2002 examines Vergil's debt to Hellenistic encomiastic poetry; Hollis 1996 detects an allusion to the third-century poet Rhianus in the sphragis; and S. J. Harrison 2004 explores intertextuality with Nicander.

Vergil's creative use of mythological themes in the *Georgics* is the topic of Gale 1995 (reprinted in this volume). The prominent trope of the Golden Age in particular has been much discussed; see especially the monograph of Johnston 1980, as well as now Perkell 2002.

Treatments of individual passages are found in many of the monographs mentioned above (in particular, Putnam 1979, Miles 1980, and Nappa 2005 offer close readings of the entire poem). Gigante (ed.) 1982 contains interpretations of the four books by different authors. In addition, I single out the following, without attempting to be comprehensive.

As for Book 1, Batstone 1988 offers close readings of 1.1–5 and 43–6, exemplifying the methodology of reader-response criticism, while Adler 1983 discusses the invocation to the agricultural gods and Octavian in relation to the rest of the poem. The so-called 'theodicy' (1.118–159) with its central concept of *labor improbus* (145–6) has been much scrutinized and used as the keystone especially for pessimistic or ambivalent interpretations (see, for example, Perkell 1986); Jenkyns 1993 (reprinted in this volume) lays out the issues at stake before presenting his own reading. The finale of Book 1 is treated by Lyne 1974; Kaster 2002 examines the role of *invidia*; and Dewar 1988 and 1990 connects the image of the chariot out of control with the madness of Orestes as described by Aeschylus.

Apropos of the simile in 2.273–87, which compares the arrangement of vines to armies arrayed for battle, Betensky 1979 reflects on the use of military imagery throughout the *Georgics*; this topic is discussed further in Carilli 1986, Glei 1991: 277–86, and Heckel 1998.

On the ambiguities of the *laudes Italiae* and the praise of country life at the end of the second *Georgic*, see Putnam 1975 (reprinted in this volume).

The finale of Book 2, with its synkrisis of the (Lucretian) *felix* who understands the causes of things and the (Vergilian) *fortunatus* who knows the country gods, is discussed by Clay 1976, Barchiesi 1982 (see also 1981 on the figure of Dike), and Kronenberg 2000; P. R. Hardie 1986: 33–51 (reprinted in this volume) and Nelis 2004 treat the passage together with the beginning of Book 3. A. Hardie 2002/3 discusses the theme of initiation into the mysteries in the invocation to the Muses and elsewhere in the poem.

The third proem raises a number of issues and has been the object of many studies. Controversy surrounds the question of whether the epinician tone of the passage owes more to Pindar (thus Wilkinson 1970 (reprinted in this volume) and Balot 1998) or to Callimachus (thus R. F. Thomas 1983 (reprinted in this volume) and 1998; see also 1999: 9–10 n. 13). Kraggerud 1998 discusses the issue of the new poem (the *Aeneid*?) announced in the proem.

Vergil's anthropomorphizing description of the animals in Book 3, which in particular highlights the destructiveness of love, is the topic of Miles 1975, Gale 1991, and Knox 1992. D. West 1979 compares the Noric plague at the end of the book with the Athenian plague in Lucretius; E. L. Harrison 1979 argues in favour of understanding the disaster as the punishment of a community that has lost the *pax deorum*; and Clare 1995 throws light on the mention of Chiron and Melampus.

The episode of the old gardener in Book 4 is illuminated, from various angles, by Clay 1981, Perkell 1981, R. F. Thomas 1992, Thibodeau 2001, S. J. Harrison 2004, and Johnson 2004; Marasco 1990 and Leigh 1994 discuss Servius' note on the designation of the *senex* as *Corycius*.

The enigmatic myth of Aristaeus with its inset story of Orpheus and Eurydice has given rise to many divergent interpretations and has served to back up both optimistic and pessimistic views, depending on whether prominence is given to the sucess of Aristaeus or the failure of Orpheus. J. Griffin 1979 (reprinted in this volume) provides a *historia quaestionis* in addition to his own interpretation; see also Crabbe 1977 (on intertextuality with Catullus 64), Perutelli 1980,

Bettini 1981 (with a Proppian analysis of fairy-tale motifs), Neumeister 1982, Nadeau 1984, Conte 1986: 130–40 and 1998, Habinek 1990 (on the *bugonia* as an aetion for animal sacrifice, with a response by R. F. Thomas 1991), Lee 1996, and Morgan 1999. The question of the *laudes Galli* and the supposed revision of the *Georgics* is reopened by Hermes 1980, Jocelyn 1984, Jacobson 1984, and Lefèvre 1986; the last two authors suggest that the Orpheus story replaced the praise of Gallus (that Orpheus is specifically meant to represent Gallus is believed by, among others, Domenicucci 1985 and Gagliardi 2003: 61–114). W. S. Anderson 1982 compares Vergil's treatment of Orpheus with that of Ovid in the *Metamorphoses*.

Unlike the *Eclogues* and the *Aeneid*, the *Georgics* did not function as a major intertext for large parts of European literary history, and its reception has therefore been less extensively studied (the best overview remains Wilkinson 1970: 217–313, and see now von Albrecht 2006: 98–106). Note Christmann 1982 on the reception in antiquity, as well as Ziolkowski 1993 on modernist reactions. For echoes of the Orpheus story, see Segal 1989: 155–98.

THE PRESENT VOLUME

The papers in this volume have been chosen with the purpose of creating an anthology that will serve as an introduction to scholarship on the *Georgics* since 1970. Two main considerations have directed my choices. First, wanting to represent a wide variety of approaches, I have included scholars with different styles and different critical convictions, whose views on the texts they treat vary considerably. Second, I have aimed to cover major topics of contemporary research on the *Georgics* while also highlighting prominent passages. Of course, there is no way to do so comprehensively, and, out of considerations of space, I have not been able to include contributions on every famous episode.[12]

---

[12] Just as the views of Vergil's work expressed in the ten papers vary considerably, so too do the authors differ over the correct way to spell the poet's name. Should it be *Vergil* or *Virgil*? To preserve the individuality of the contributions, no attempt has been made to unify the spelling.

The volume opens with M. S. Spurr's 'Agriculture and the *Georgics*' (1986), a paper that challenges a number of conventional ideas about the poem. Spurr argues that Vergil's agricultural advice, while selective, is not unreliable; that it concerns not the subsistence peasant farmer, but the villa estate; and that there is no evidence for a deterioration of Italian farming in the period of the Civil Wars. He concludes that the *Georgics* is a serious work of agricultural instruction in line with the prose treatises of Cato, Varro, and Columella.

Vergil's poetic transformation of his prose sources, especially Varro and Theophrastus, is the topic of Richard F. Thomas's 'Prose into Poetry: Tradition and Meaning in Virgil's *Georgics*' (1987). Thomas describes the poet's methods of reshaping his prosaic material (which include suppression, expansion, distortion, and the use of similes and mythological examples) and shows how through his artful treatment of the science of agriculture, Vergil is able to convey a larger vision of human endeavour.

In 'Authorial Rhetoric in Virgil's *Georgics*' (1995), Richard Rutherford considers Vergil's self-presentation as both teacher and poet. Discussing the speaker's interactions with his various addressees, his rhetorical strategies for establishing authority, and his reflections on his own task and on the status of his work, Rutherford stresses the complexity of Vergil's poetic project and of the didactic persona he has constructed for himself.

The didacticism of the *Georgics* owes much to Lucretius, but Vergil can also be shown in many ways to be reacting against his poetic predecessor. Monica R. Gale compares the two poets' treatments of myth in 'Virgil's Metamorphoses: Myth and Allusion in the *Georgics*' (1995), demonstrating how Vergil effectively rewrites Lucretius by conflating Lucretian and non-Lucretian accounts; remythologizing where Lucretius rationalized; and dwelling on metamorphoses and monsters, phenomena his model ridiculed as impossible.

These more general discussions of the poem are followed by a number of papers about specific passages. Richard Jenkyns in '*Labor Improbus*' (1993) revisits the 'theodicy' in Book 1, concentrating in particular on lines 145–6. Arguing in favour of a progressive interpretation and against the pessimistic readings of Richard F. Thomas and others, Jenkyns nevertheless stresses the negative connotations of *improbus* and suggests that Vergil's tone is one of 'wry, dour irony' when he describes human toil as, in effect, 'hard work, dammit'.

In 'Italian Virgil and the Idea of Rome' (1975), Michael C. J. Putnam contemplates the ironies inherent in Vergil's praises of Italy and of country life in *Georgics* 2, with a comparative look at some passages in the *Aeneid*. Rather than straightforwardly celebratory, the poet's text is shown to be profoundly ambiguous and full of hints at the darker side of Rome's domination and, more generally, the 'stimulus of power and its effects on the minds and deeds of men'.

Examining the finale of *Georgics* 2 together with the proem of *Georgics* 3, Philip Hardie in 'Cosmology and National Epic in the *Georgics* (*Georgics* 2.458–3.48)' (1986) discusses how after the *recusatio* in Book 2, where Vergil first considers but ultimately rejects a cosmological poem in the style of his admired model Lucretius, the poet in Book 3 turns to nationalistic epic in praise of Augustus. This extended reflection on the right poetic 'path' is held together by a number of interrelated metaphors (many indebted to Lucretius), which Hardie treats in detail.

The epinician elements of the third proem (in which Vergil imagines himself as driving a hundred chariots on the banks of the Mincius and instituting Greek-style games) is the topic of the following two papers. L. P. Wilkinson's 'Pindar and the Proem to the Third *Georgic*' (1970) argues for the pervasive influence of Pindar (a poet popular in Rome at the time of the *Georgics*' composition), pointing to the references to actual chariot-racing and also to Vergil's use of the architectural metaphor for poetry (a favorite of Pindar) in the description of the marble temple that the poet announces he will build.

By contrast, in 'Callimachus, the *Victoria Berenices*, and Roman Poetry' (1983), Richard F. Thomas suggests that Callimachus' *Victoria Berenices* (an epinician passage from the beginning of *Aetia* 3 surviving in fragmentary form and first published in 1977) is the central model for the proem. Thomas traces in detail the echoes of Callimachus' text not only in the *Georgics*, but also in Propertius 3.1 and Statius, *Silvae* 3.1. He then uses evidence from the Roman texts to draw conclusions about the original form of Callimachus' victory song, whose central mythological panel may have been presented as an ecphrasis of an embroidered cloth (similarly to Catullus 64).

Finally, Jasper Griffin in 'The Fourth *Georgic*, Virgil and Rome' (1979) ponders the significance of the fourth book and the relationship of the discussion of the bees to the epyllion of Aristaeus and Orpheus. The juxtaposition of the collective state of bees (who lack love and art but whose race lives on eternally) with the individual Orpheus (who despite his dedication to love and art suffers and must die) is expressive of Vergil's misgivings about Roman imperialism and its costs, misgivings that the poet would go on to explore further in the *Aeneid*.

2

Agriculture and the *Georgics*

M. S. Spurr

'As writes our Virgil, concerned more with what made the best poetry than with complete accuracy, since his object was to delight his readers rather than to instruct farmers.'[1]

Seneca passed this judgement on the *Georgics* after witnessing certain agricultural practices where he was staying (at Liternum on the north-west coast of Campania), which appeared to disagree with a statement of Virgil's (*G*. 2.58). He then proceeded to mention another Virgilian agricultural error (*G*. 1.215–16), selected from 'all the others' (*alia omnia*) that he says he could have discussed, in order to drive his point home.

While it may be that Petrarch and some other humanists adopted Virgil as their agricultural guide, recent scholarship has accepted Seneca's judgement. Thus two influential modern commentators (whom the English-speaking student is likely to read early in his research on the *Georgics*) describe it as 'pertinent' or 'wise'.[2] They consider the agricultural content to be something of a defective surface, which covers symbolic depths: 'the intellectual didactic material is,

---

This paper first appeared in 1986 and is reprinted here virtually unchanged.

[1] Seneca *Ep*. 86.15 *ut ait Vergilius noster, qui non quid verissime, sed quid decentissime diceretur aspexit, nec agricolas docere voluit, sed legentes delectare*.

[2] 'Pertinent': Wilkinson 1982*a*: 322. This article, which contains Wilkinson's latest thoughts on the *Georgics* (others are to be found in his recent translation of the poem for Penguin Classics), is by no means a mere summary of his earlier book, Wilkinson 1969. There (p. 15) he referred to Seneca's comment as 'obvious'. 'Wise': R. D. Williams 1983: x. (This is the most recent English edition of the *Georgics*.) For Petrarch's use of the *Georgics* as a practical handbook: Wilkinson 1969: 290–1.

Agriculture and the Georgics

at surface level, the subject of the poem; but the real subject is emotional or indeed spiritual.'[3] This means that, as readers of the *Georgics*, we must 'eradicate from our minds any lingering notions that the poem is utilitarian'.[4] Instead the poem can be seen to 'convey the essence of a way of life, hard and sometimes tragic, but regular and often rewarding'. What that life might be is defined more precisely: 'there was a feeling abroad among thinking people, reflected also by Horace, that a simple, Sabine-type, peasant life was happier and morally healthier.'[5] We are reminded that 'the district Virgil knew best, the Po valley and the surroundings of Naples, happened to be the ones where the small holder (*colonus*) still flourished.'[6] And as the student continues to read through the recent and growing literature on the *Georgics*, he or she will also inevitably come across some version of the further view that Virgil, whether or not following some 'official line' was concerned about 'the desecration of the countryside during periods of war', and 'the poem is therefore related to...the urgent desirability of restoring Italian agriculture'.[7]

In what appears to be a climate of considerable renewed interest in the *Georgics*, it will be worth while to step back a moment from the symbolic depths, which are being explored with ever increasing interpretative skill and imagination,[8] to consider some of the readily accepted generalizations that regard the *superficies*: Virgil's supposed agricultural inaccuracy, his supposed description of the

---

[3] R. D. Williams 1983: x. (It is not clear why he chooses to describe the didactic material as 'intellectual'.)
[4] Putnam 1979: 7.
[5] Wilkinson 1982*a*: 323 and 320.
[6] Wilkinson 1982*a*: 320, cf. 1969: 54. See also Quinn 1979: 134, who assumes that Virgil is describing the world of the small subsistence fanner.
[7] R. D. Williams 1983: x–xi.
[8] See for example the review of recent studies of the *Georgics* by Gransden 1982 and especially J. Griffin 1981. For the development of the now orthodox literary approach to the *Georgics*: Otis 1964: 145: 'It is only very recently that some critics— I think especially of Burck, Klingner and Büchner—have refused to treat Virgil with such naiveté (*sc.* reading the *Georgics* as a poem about agriculture) and have tried to penetrate the deeper meaning of the poem...'. He provides bibliographical details on the history of interpretation of the *Georgics* in Appendix 6, p. 407. See also Wilkinson 1969: 71 ff. and 314–15. Readers of *Greece & Rome* have been well served with articles on the *Georgics*: cf. the contributions of Jermyn 1949 and 1951; an early article by Wilkinson (1950); and more recently J. Griffin 1979.

small subsistence farm and the supposed ruin of Italian agriculture. This is not to suggest that the search for a profounder significance is in any way mistaken. But if the poem is to succeed as a unified whole, both surface and depth (even if that distinction does not turn out to be largely illusory), must be accorded due appreciation.

SENECA THE AGRICULTURALIST?

In his eighty-sixth moral letter to Lucilius, then, Seneca reports on a demonstration, by the new owner of Scipio Africanus' old estate, of the speedy establishment, or perhaps restoration, of an olive plantation. Two methods to this end are discussed, both of which are apparently new to Seneca. In his view they contradict Virgil's statement (*G.* 2.58) that newly planted trees will grow so slowly that they will provide shade not for the farmer himself but for his grandchildren. To take the second method first (*Ep.* 86.19), on examination it turns out to be nothing other than a crude form of propagation by the planting out of olive cuttings from the parent tree, which is discussed by the three major prose agricultural writers, Cato, Varro, and Columella.[9] Whereas they advise the careful planting of cuttings in a well-tended nursery in preparation for future transplanting into an olive grove, Aegialus, Seneca's host, cuts vigorous young branches from the parent tree and plants them directly in the olive grove.[10] In fact, Columella mentions in passing (and thus with no hint that the technique is new) this cruder method as one way of propagating fruit trees (5.10.6–9) but apparently not olives, which are treated with greater care. From the agricultural point of view, Aegialus' technique

---

[9] The only very approximate dates that we have of the publication of the three agricultural treatises are: first half of the second century BC (Cato), second half of the first century BC (Varro) and middle of the first century AD (Columella). Columella (3.3.3) mentions Seneca as the owner of exceptionally productive vineyards near Nomentum. Seneca may have been one of Columella's patrons, although that need not mean that Seneca ever read his or any other available agricultural manual. See: M.T. Griffin 1976: 290–1.

[10] We know that Aegialus, a freedman, gained a considerable reputation for successful farming near Liternum (Pliny, *HN* 14.49).

would be no quicker, as regards the eventual establishment of the oliveyard, and would certainly be less secure of success.[11]

The first demonstration on which Seneca reports (*Ep.* 86.17–18) is even more agriculturally dubious and is also confusingly described. It appears that Aegialus selected certain mature trees, pruned them with extreme severity, cut off their roots and then replanted them deep in the earth. This seems scarcely credible. Severe pruning is sometimes practised these days in order to rejuvenate an old or damaged tree but the treatment does not include transplanting.[12] In both cases Aegialus carefully stamped down the earth around the freshly transplanted trees or cuttings, an agricultural 'hint' for which Seneca shows his admiration. Had either he or Aegialus read their Cato they would have realized that this technique was at least some two hundred years old, and that, moreover, Cato's reason for doing so contained more agricultural sense than Seneca's own explanation.[13] One further curiosity concerns the season for this transplanting. It would seem that Seneca witnessed it during late June, whereas the agricultural writers (in tune with modern advice) advise transplanting in spring.[14]

Thus rather than passively accept Seneca's criticism of Virgil's agricultural inaccuracy, we should begin to have grave misgivings about his own agricultural knowledge. Moreover, when the context of *Georgics* 2.58 is examined, we might legitimately begin also to

---

[11] Cf. Food and Agriculture Organization of the United Nations 1973: 27–8.

[12] Yet it is quite possible that Virgil himself refers to this supposedly new method at *Georgics* 2.30–1 (and see note *ad loc.* in Conington and Nettleship 1898). The poet expresses his astonishment that such a replanting system could work—*mirabile dictu*. One further difficulty in comprehending Seneca is caused by textual corruption (*Ep.* 86.14), where he is describing what sort of olives are treated in this way. The usual reading of editors appears to mean that the olives are healthy and productive. It would seem senseless then to prune so radically and then transplant.

[13] Seneca speaks of keeping the cold and wind from the roots. Cato advises the firming of the soil around the roots at 28.2; 49.1. A serious danger is that otherwise the roots will become waterlogged when it rains: ibid. 61.2.

[14] Ancient agricultural advice: Cato 40.1; Varro 1.30; Columella 5.9.6–7. Modern advice: Food and Agriculture Organization of the United Nations 1973: 27–8. Modern, yet traditional, practice is also to transplant cuttings (usually into a nursery) immediately after the winter pruning. Virgil perhaps alludes to this by his stress on *putator* 'pruner' (*G.* 2.28).

doubt his knowledge of Virgil, since he has misleadingly removed the line *tarda venit seris factura nepotibus umbram* from its context. Not only does it refer to arboriculture in general (and not to olives in particular), but it actually belongs to what Virgil is telling us not to do, namely the growing of trees from seed, since that method takes too long. Therefore, Virgil instructs, olives should be propagated from cuttings (*G*. 2.63).[15]

Nor should Seneca's second agricultural example, to prove his point about Virgil's inaccuracy, inspire greater confidence. He reports that in late June near Liternum he saw beans being harvested and millet being sown. Virgil, Seneca reminds us, had included both among spring-sown crops (*G*. 1.215–16). Yet the truth of the matter is that millet can be sown either in the spring or summer. Moreover, from other ancient evidence, it would appear that in fertile parts of Campania (of which Liternum was one) millet was a particularly prized crop, which could be sown in the early summer in order to fit into a three-fold annual rotation pattern.[16] To be complete, Virgil should have said that millet was *either* a spring *or* summer crop, although it is true to say that most commonly, in Italy, it was sown in the spring. Seneca's observation, on the other hand, again reveals more about his, than Virgil's, agricultural ignorance.[17]

VIRGIL'S SELECTIVITY

We must therefore beware against charging Virgil with agricultural inaccuracy.[18] Nevertheless it does seem that Virgil is selective in his

[15] Varro had clearly stated that in the case of slow-growing trees, such as the olive, it takes too long to grow them from seed and thus advises propagation from cuttings (1.41.6). Virgil makes exactly the same point, but Seneca misunderstands.

[16] Cf. Spurr 1983.

[17] It would seem also that Seneca is disputing Virgil's statement that beans were a spring crop. Yet, where winters were severe (inland hill and mountain zones and the Po valley), they had to be spring-sown. In warmer areas there was a choice, although it was generally acknowledged that spring-sown yielded less than autumn-sown beans (Columella 2.10.9). Pliny the Elder considered, rightly perhaps, that Virgil was thinking particularly of the Po valley (*HN* 18.120).

[18] There are, in fact, only very few real agricultural 'mistakes' in the *Georgics*: he is incorrect to state that repeated ploughing of poor soils causes loss of moisture, as

treatment. Thus it has been stated that the *Georgics* would be useless as a guide to agriculture for the novice farmer. This argument then proceeds to the conclusion again that, if the didactic material is of no real help, the meaning or significance of the poem must lie elsewhere.[19]

This selectivity is in contrast, it has been argued, with the agricultural prose writers: 'But what strikes one particularly on comparison with Varro, or still more with Columella, is what Virgil selects to treat, and how much he decides to omit.' As an example of this, Wilkinson proceeds: 'Book 2 is nearly all devoted to the vine: there are only a few lines on the equally important olive, and other trees receive the most cursory treatment.' And in a later work he remarks (again on the slight treatment of olives): 'Nothing could make it clearer that the *Georgics* is a poem, not an exhaustive handbook.'[20] Compare:

[Olives are given so few lines because] Virgil wishes to leave behind his series of precepts about the work which the farmer must do and to give a picture of Nature's unaided contributions to human welfare. The great theme of the whole work is the balance between the bounty of Nature and the toil of man...[21]

Caution is again necessary, since much of this is misdirected. After treating vines in some 130 lines (*G.* 2.259–419 with a digression at 2.315–45), Virgil does appear to give olives short shrift (*G.* 2.420–5).

R. D. Williams 1983 points out in his note on 1.70, following White 1967/8. But it is not usually explained that this was what was generally believed at the time (Columella 2.4.11; Pliny, *HN* 18.242), and thus the error can hardly be ascribed just to Virgil. Other mistakes: pear trees can not bear apples, nor plum trees cornels, after grafting (2.33–4; but again a shared error: cf. Varro 1.40.5). He recounts wondrously how mares in Asia Minor are impregnated by wind (3.269–75) but even Columella was prepared to credit similar stories (6.27.7). In Book 4 the queen bee is a *rex*, and Virgil advocates *Bugonia* as an effective method of reproducing bees. Yet, again, both were common, if not universal, ancient misconceptions. The female sex of the queen bee was only decisively proved in the mid-18th century: K. Thomas 1983: 62 n.

[19] See for example, Kramer 1979. (This is one of the new works reviewed by J. Griffin 1979, who incidentally approves of Seneca's judgement on Virgil.) See also Otis 1964: 148.
[20] Wilkinson 1969: 67–8 and 1982*b*: 95.
[21] R. D. Williams 1983: 172.

But before we assign a deeper significance to this we should understand the simple agricultural fact that, for the Romans at least, olives could succeed with very little cultivation. According to Columella, the olive was the best of all trees precisely because it produced such goodness with the minimum of care (5.8.1). Whereas he wrote two and a half books on viticulture (books 3.1–5.7), he advised on olives in two short sections of one book (5.8–9). Thus one could almost invert the argument to say that had Virgil in the second book been describing 'the bounty of Nature' the olive, with all its essential uses for mankind compared to the little expenditure of effort necessary for its cultivation, should have received a lengthy encomium. Instead it is clear that Virgil's treatment of the olive was in proportion to its perceived agricultural needs.

Further on the general question of selectivity, even a rapid glance at the pages of Cato's *De agricultura* or Varro's *De re rustica* will reveal that the prose writers also were highly selective. Cato's treatise appears to be an incomplete and random assemblage of agricultural precepts and while Varro's work exhibits a much greater (too much, some modern commentators complain) logical organization of material, it could never be described as a comprehensive farming manual.[22] To concentrate for a moment on Varro will be particularly valid, since his treatise appeared only a few years before the *Georgics* and certainly influenced Virgil, perhaps considerably. In book 1, which deals with agriculture proper, in the middle of a discussion of various soils Varro includes, illogically, an excursus on different methods of staking and supporting vines (1.8). Then, later, towards the end of the book where he discusses harvesting, he mentions briefly with what grapes one should begin the grape harvest (1.54.1) but then jumps immediately to the pressing (1.54.2–3); while for olives, he provides some details on the olive picking but says almost nothing about the pressing (1.55).

To account for this selectivity, and for what often seems, according to our present standards at least, to be a lack of logical organization

---

[22] See Rawson 1978: 14–15. For a review of previous judgements on the worth of Varro's treatment, whether from the agricultural or compositional point of view: Skydsgaard 1968: 89 ff.

of material, is not easy.[23] One thing, however, is surely clear: these treatises were not written for novice farmers. Instead they presumed that their readers already possessed considerable agricultural knowledge and close acquaintance with the varying climatic and topographical conditions in Italy. On opening his discussion of vines Pliny could say that he took common knowledge for granted and would address himself only to matters which required clarification (*HN* 17.8).

Thus criticism that Virgil's didactic material is too selective to be of practical use is out of place. The concept of the 'novice farmer' is a modern one. It should rather be understood that the selectivity of the *Georgics* fits the tradition of the agricultural handbook. Of course it is important to remember that Virgil was also writing in the tradition of didactic poetry and selectivity is apparent in Hesiod, the first extant writer in that genre.[24]

Furthermore, complaints of an unsystematic or illogical organization of material would surely have surprised Virgil's contemporaries. Instead, one could argue, Virgil's division of his subject into four books represented a considerable achievement, if not advance, in rational composition. And all commentators draw attention to the orderly and compact way in which Virgil presents the subject of each of his four books in the opening four lines of the poem.

Finally, for an interesting clue as to how the Roman reader of an agricultural treatise could derive the maximum practical benefit from a superficially disordered work, we can turn to Varro (3.2.13). He describes a certain Seius who made large profits from the specialized breeding (*pastio villatica*) of dormice, thrushes, pigeons etc. desired by the urban market. Seius' success was ascribed to the fact that he had collected together all the relevant comments, hitherto 'scattered and unsystematic' (*separatim ac dispersim*), in the available agricultural manuals. Absence of systematic treatment, then, was the rule rather than the exception. But that did not necessarily damage the utility of the didactic material.

---

[23] Rawson 1978 argues that Latin Prose composition on a systematic basis, of the sort now taken for granted, was a gradual development, certainly not complete by Varro's time, although he contributed significantly to its progress. Thus to judge work of that period by later ideals is unjustified.
[24] See M. L. West 1978: 53 ff.; 252–3.

Given this necessary correction of the orthodox view of Virgil's selectivity, nevertheless it will be true to say that one criterion of this selection process was his desire to keep his readers entertained. There is a clear hint of this in *Georgics* 1.75–6, where Virgil appears to anticipate a certain unwillingness of his audience to listen to 'humdrum tasks' (*tenuisque curas*). He proceeds to describe otherwise possibly dull details on the construction of the threshing floor in a particularly poetic way. However, it is most important to realize that this 'honeying of the cup' does not signify any distortion of the agricultural accuracy.[25] Prose manuals of agriculture (and of other technical subjects) sought also to entertain the reader lest he become bored and not wish to continue, but this does not detract from their informative worth. There can be no doubt that Virgil wished to 'delight his readers', in Seneca's phrase: but to equate that with agricultural inaccuracy could not be more incorrect. By 'delighting', a writer makes his didactic material all the more memorable.

LITERARY BORROWING

To quantify how much of the agricultural content of the *Georgics* is Virgil's own and how much is derived from other sources is probably impossible. Thus Wilkinson expresses extreme diffidence in attempting to confront the problem.[26] It will bear on the question of Virgil's agricultural reliability if one believes that he borrowed substantially from Greek sources and thus incorporated material incompatable with rural Italy.

Yet is this a real problem? Does it matter that Virgil followed a work by Aratus on weather signs or by Eratosthenes on the zones of heaven? Reactions of animals and birds at the prospect of rain,

---

[25] Thus, too, when Lucretius says (1.926–50) that he uses poetry to enliven and make palatable the dry reasoning of philosophy, as doctors honey the cup that contains medicine, he does not mean that he will thereby sacrifice the serious didactic content to poetic imagination. Poetic digressions and 'purple passages' enhance the directly informative sections and make them more effective.

[26] Wilkinson 1969: 223–5 and 1982*b*: 31–2.

phases of the moon, and indication of weather from the sun surely fitted both Greece (or Egypt) and Italy?[27] Or if Virgil adheres to Theophrastus' botanical analysis of the vine, we can surely accept that vines in Greece were similar to those in Italy.

But we can go further than this. While it can be shown that Virgil derives details from Theophrastus' highly technical discussion of plant propagation, he clearly seeks to organize what was in his source an abstract account into advice of a practical nature. Thus, as has been seen above, he rejects the propagation of trees by self-sowing from seeds and instead prescribes layering for vines and cuttings for olives (*G.* 2.56 ff.). When he comes to mention the varieties of vines (2.89 ff.), he makes a clear distinction between Italian vines and those from the eastern Mediterranean. Regarding wines, Virgil singles out, at the head of his list, Italian varieties: Falernian and Aminean are included, while, interestingly, the less well-known Rhaetic, from Cisalpine Gaul, is his first choice. This seems to reflect the poet's personal preferences, based on his own experience (2.94–7).[28]

It is this Italian emphasis which is so obvious in the poem and which should dispel any doubts about an imagined distorting dependence on Greek sources. Following his review of wines, Virgil invites the reader 'to cast his eyes abroad' (2.113) and refers in turn to cultivation in Arabia, Egypt, India, China, and Persia (2.113–35). The reason for this excursus is soon made clear: 'none of these places could rival Italy...'; and thirty lines praising Italy, and mentioning specifically places from the Northern lakes to Campania, bear out his statement. He concludes the passage with: 'I sing the song of Ascra throughout the Roman towns' (2.176). As every student knows, that is an open reference to Hesiod; but Virgil would have been surprised were it to be understood as anything more than homage to the

---

[27] For a detailed account of Virgil's adaption of the works of Aratus, Eratosthenes, and Theophrastus: Wilkinson 1969: 234 ff., 242 ff. Some have worried that the rooks which Virgil describes (following Aratus) were uncommon in Italy but see Royds 1918: 40–1.

[28] Wilkinson 1969: 245: 'But there is no known predecessor to Virgil's selective and discriminating list, and it may of course represent his own taste. At any rate he has diverged here from Theophrastus...'. The fullest ancient account of Italian wines is given by Pliny the Elder (*HN* 14.20–76). Varro's comment on Theophrastus is noteworthy: 'His books are more suited to philosophy students than farmers' (1.5.2).

founder of the genre of didactic agricultural poetry. Certainly it should not be taken to signify that Virgil borrowed more than the minimum amount of agricultural detail from Hesiod: Virgil does, after all, sing his poem throughout the *Roman* towns. Again, it can be added, the prose agricultural writers also used Greek sources but with a judicious independence derived from their own knowledge of Italian agriculture.[29] Indicative of their independence is Pliny's comment that the agricultural information of the greatly celebrated Carthaginian agronomist, Mago, was really applicable only to North Africa (*HN* 17.128).

An important feature of this reassuringly Italian emphasis is Virgil's characteristic method of involving the reader and himself in the agricultural content of the poem. This does not simply fit well with the generally prescriptive (e.g. in the use of imperatives) tradition of the agricultural prose writers, or just reflect a didactic poetic technique of Lucretius. Rather it provides the effect of direct personal observation. This begins immediately after the invocation at the opening of the first book with the *mihi* of line 45. It is helped by phrases such as *quid dicam* (1.104) and *ecce* (1.108) and is referred to most clearly in *vidi* (1.193, 197), *saepe ego... vidi* (1.316–18) and *memini me... vidisse* (4.125–7). This sense of autopsy appears also in the way in which Virgil backs up a general precept with a concrete Italian example, such as Mantua's river meadows (2.198–9), or fertile soil near Capua and between Vesuvius and the sea (2.222–3). It is also apparent in those particular details which bespeak a local agricultural knowledge, such as the choice of Rhaetian wine (see above); of the oak as a supporting tree for vines in an *arbustum* (2.290 ff.), which is much more unusual than the elm (1.2; 2.361), but might have been selected, since, as we know from Pliny (*HN* 17.201), it was a tree used for this purpose north of the Po; of the scattering of ash as manure, or dust on ripening grapes, or the sowing of beans in the spring, all of which practices, again, were perhaps common in the Transpadane region of Virgil's boyhood (*HN* 17.49; 18.120).

---

[29] For their use of sources: Gummerus 1906. For Varro in particular: Skydsgaard 1968, White 1973.

PEASANT FARM OR VILLA?

Without notable exception, modern commentators assume that Virgil was describing the work on a small farm. Yet ancient readers of the *Georgics* would have entertained no doubt that Virgil, like Cato and Varro before him, and Columella later, was writing primarily about a rich man's estate. Just a few agricultural considerations will suffice to demonstrate this, perhaps to some, disturbing revelation; and these can even be taken from the first book, which deals with cereal farming, the usual preserve of the subsistence peasant farmer, according to conventional modern views of the agricultural development in Italy during the later Republic and early Empire.[30]

The first agricultural advice, which comes after the invocation to rural deities and Octavian, is to break up the land in early spring with a plough drawn by oxen (1.43 ff.). That the land was to be ploughed in spring means that it has been allowed to lie fallow during the autumn and winter and is to be sown either later in spring or, more likely, in the following autumn. This is clearly a technique adopted on a farm where the cultivator is not constrained to use all his land each year in order to subsist. Moreover, the use of a team of oxen signifies a considerable acreage under pasturage or fodder crops, rather than under crops solely for the human household. While a plough drawn by an ass might be common enough on a small farm, oxen are the mark of a larger estate.[31]

As an alternative to fallowing, Virgil continues (1.71), the farmer should consider a rotation pattern (1.74–5), and for this, especially in poorer soil, a rich manuring will be necessary (1.80). While some simple rotation of grain and beans was probably practised even on the peasant farm, the variety of rotation crops, which include fodder

---

[30] The conventional view is that, as a consequence of the growth of slave-staffed villa estates and the eradication of the peasantry in the second century BC onwards, cereal cultivation was replaced by the cultivation of vines and olives. See for example: A. J. Toynbee 1965: 247 ff., 286 ff. and *passim*.

[31] Pliny the Elder said that one of the main functions of asses was ploughing (*HN* 8.167). Economical to feed (Columella 7.1.2), the ass would have been inexpensive and its forage not difficult to find even on the least prosperous peasant farm.

crops, prescribed by Virgil, and the abundance of manure necessary for success, again belong to the larger estate.[32]

The conclusion that the poet is envisaging a large farm is further borne out by the element of choice, that the farmer is supposed to have, of what to plant where. Thus the 'micro-climates' of the different sectors of the farm are to be carefully considered (1.50–61); and the long excursus on choice of soils refers not only to regions the length and breadth of Italy but also to the varieties of soil to be found on the one (large) property (2.177–258). Once the right soil has been chosen and worked by the plough—which might mean the bringing under cultivation of part of the farm hitherto left as woodland (1.50–1; 2.203 ff.: a luxury not open to the subsistence cultivator)—the remaining clods of earth must be pulverized and then the field levelled with a wicker-work harrow (1.95). The harrow was included among the equipment of the villa estate by Varro; and Columella was later to advise its use in careful preparation of a field to be sown as pasture.[33]

A mark of rational agriculture is careful seed selection. The best seeds must be chosen from the previous harvest and stored separately for a later sowing. Varro, and later Columella, emphasized this, and Virgil draws attention to it with *vidi* (1.197). Otherwise the crop will degenerate. Again, however, this element of choice was more characteristic of the large farmer, since the peasant would grow a mixed field of cereals, either as the result of careless seed-selection or from scarcity of the right sort of seed.[34] With all this careful agriculture practised on rich soil, it is not surprising that the crop could run the risk of being too abundant and thus prone to wind-flattening (1.111). One precaution was to allow sheep into the cereal fields while the crop was still

---

[32] Cato and Varro both concern themselves with rotation patterns but do not treat all the possibilities envisaged by Virgil. This could indicate Virgil's own experience. Pliny noted Virgil's advice on fallowing but remarked that this was possible only on a large enough farm. Otherwise a rudimentary rotation system should be adopted (*HN* 18.187). No doubt many small holders continued to grow grain year after year on the same land, with resulting low yields.

[33] Varro 1.23.5 refers to the making of such a harrow (a 'drag' would be a better term, since it is mentioned by Virgil and Columella (2.17.4) as an implement only for levelling ploughed fields), without describing its use. See White 1967: 147. Virgil's reference to its function may again be the result of personal knowledge.

[34] Spurr 1983: 9.

in leaf, before the ear had emerged (1.112–13). This practice was explained in greater detail later by Pliny (*HN* 18.161), and can probably be understood as another of Virgil's own observations. A possible danger to the crop during its later development is thus avoided and, instead, is transformed into a positive benefit for the animals of the farm, since such special pasture is highly nutritious. Elsewhere Virgil recommends that calves be fattened on it (3.176). All this, which refers to a well-integrated system of cereal and livestock again is surely more likely on the rich man's farm.[35]

Other, increasingly obvious, considerations will serve to confirm this hypothesis. Although Virgil says very little about harvesting (Varro had treated the matter in depth at 1.50), threshing does receive attention. Construction of the threshing floor (1.178–9) signifies something more permanent than a patch of hardened ground, which was what at most, it can be assumed, the poor cultivator used for the purpose.[36] The threshing process could then be carried out with sledges and drags (1.164), both of which were part of the equipment of the villa estate (Varro 1.52; 1.22.1), drawn by oxen. It could also be effected by driving horses around the threshing floor (3.133), a technique not mentioned elsewhere in the extant literature before Columella (2.20.4). Since horses were in no way essential to cereal cultivation, their presence can only indicate the largest of Roman arable estates, which had enough land given over to pasture and fodder crops to breed and maintain such status-associated animals.[37] On such a farm will be seen Virgil's oxen drawing wagons filled with grain (2.205–6), and the granaries will burst (1.49; 2.518). The subsistence cultivator, who would have kept his hard-won

---

[35] Various other references to fencing sown fields (e.g. 1.270–1; 2.436) show that Virgil was considering a farm with a combination of cereal cultivation and livestock farming. The livestock provides manure for various crop rotations (1.80) and in return will need forage crops and pasture. Fences will have to be constructed as part of the livestock management—to keep the animals in, or out of, fields at different times.

[36] Pliny, *HN* 18.295 and Columella 2.19.2.

[37] A convenient summary of the reasons for horse breeding is found in Varro 2.7.15: cavalry, carriages, racing and breeding. Cf. Virgil 3.72–208. They were not employed for ploughing until the Middle Ages: Parain 1966: 142 ff. Virgil's long passage on horses in Book 3 is probably the most obvious proof that his work concerns the agriculture of the upper classes.

grain in a heap inside his house (cf. *Moretum* 15–16), is again far from sight.[38]

It should therefore be accepted that Virgil follows the agricultural handbook tradition in this too, and so the agricultural material of the *Georgics* concerns principally the villa estate. 'Principally', since Virgil, like the agricultural writers, especially Varro and later Columella, with his Italian-wide purview, clearly does not limit himself to just one ideal farm. Instead he envisages a range of possible villa estates and even, on occasion, the small farm. In this way the reader can come to understand the variety (and complexity) of the agricultural reality of Roman Italy.

To take an example from Columella, while not straying from the immediately foregoing discussion: his advice on threshing clearly refers to arable farms of various sizes. Largest were those where horses were available; next down the scale were those estates which could dispose of enough oxen, but no horses, to trample the grain; then come comparatively smaller estates with only 'a few teams of oxen', *pauca iuga* (but we should remember that a 200-*iugera* arable farm required two *iuga*: Columella 2.12.7; so a farm of some considerable size is still being envisaged), which utilized threshing sledges and drags. Otherwise, if the ears of grain only were harvested, they could be threshed with sticks during the winter when food was required, or could be trodden by *pecudes*. This more general term for 'animals', most probably indicates the ubiquitous ass or mule, rather than oxen or horses, and so the last two alternatives probably refer to small-scale cereal cultivation at subsistence level. Thus in this passage it can be seen how Columella rapidly surveys a wide range of types of arable farming.

This range is noticeable also in Virgil. Firstly by comparison with Columella, we can assume that when he refers to horses threshing the grain (3.133), he envisages a very large estate; while in Book 1, a smaller estate (but of at least 200 *iugera*), which uses oxen and threshing sledges, is in mind. As regards various *modes* of arable farming on the large estate, in Book 1 he appears to describe a

---

[38] It has recently been argued that the originator of the agricultural didactic poem, Hesiod, was a wealthy peasant: Millet 1984, but comparison will show that Virgil's farming was carried out on a much larger scale.

Agriculture and the Georgics

specialized cereal farm where burning off of the stubble can be practised (1.84 ff.); while elsewhere he refers to an *arbustum* (which signifies mixed cultivation of cereals with orchard trees, olives, or vines supported on trees, in the same field), where burning of the stubble would be clearly impossible.[39]

In a description of death caused by plague, farming without oxen is vividly depicted: 'Thus men break up the earth with mattocks and dig in crops with their own fingernails' (3.534–5). Yet this might not be far from normal agricultural practice for the poor peasant cultivator, as we can glean from passing references in other writers, and so Virgil's description derives its power from reality.[40] Happier, certainly, was the gardener in the vicinity of Tarentum, who had put his plot of land, however small, to profitable use (4.125–46). Flowers were always in demand in towns and so, with the money from their sale, he no doubt purchased, rather than cultivated, his basic foods.[41] It is possible too that the beekeeper elsewhere in Book 4 owned only sufficient land for successful honey production. Varro (3.6.10) had described profitable apiculture carried out by two brothers of his acquaintance on a one-*iugerum* plot. Like the Tarentine gardener (who also kept bees, 4.139–41), they were involved in a type of highly specialized farming dependent on a flourishing urban market. Most small cultivators in Roman Italy, however, must have practised mixed farming in an attempt to produce as many of their basic needs as possible themselves. A more typical scene is perhaps alluded to in Book 1.291–6, where Virgil seems to describe a poor peasant or tenant farmer and his wife.

But elsewhere, it must now be emphasized, Virgil refers to varieties of the villa estate. Thus the well-known line: 'Praise huge estates but cultivate a small one' (*laudato ingentia rura | exiguum colito*, 2.412–13), is not a recommendation of the peasant way of life but refers to relative sizes of the villa estate. 'Huge estates' were those which could not be cultivated in the intensive mode advised throughout the *Georgics*, since the amount of land was too great for

---

[39] e.g. 2.416.
[40] e.g. Strabo 5.2.1; Pliny, *HN* 18.178; Hor. *Carm.* 3.6.38–9.
[41] Flowers: Cato 8.2; Varro 1.16.3; Columella 10.308; It is clear that the *dapibus inemptis* (4.133) of Virgil's gardener refer only to fruits and vegetables. He must have purchased grain and wine, for which we are told his land was unsuited.

the available labour force. Columella significantly cited Virgil's words while referring disparagingly to the *amplissima veterata* (1.3.10) of enormous estates which included a large acreage of unworked land. These were the infamous *latifundia* criticized by Pliny, who also refers for support to Virgil here (*HN* 18.35). What all the agricultural prose writers, and Virgil with them, considered to be ideal was the villa estate cultivated well and intensively.

This revelation, that the *Georgics* describe primarily the rich man's farm, while being highly important in itself also rids us of the old conundrum of why, if his audience consisted of the rich and educated class, did Virgil write about peasant cultivators. The various attempted solutions to the puzzle—that Virgil was looking back nostalgically to Rome's peasant origins, or that he looked forward to some supposed Augustan policy of agricultural restoration based on the small cultivator, or even that he participated in a 'feeling of thinking people that a simple peasant life was happier and morally healthier' (see n. 5 above)—will all become redundant. Several symbolic interpretations of the poem will then also necessarily appear misdirected. Virgil was a realist who wrote about the Italy of his own time for his own class. The conventional misconception derives partly from the ancient biographical tradition, which conceived of Virgil as the son of a peasant farmer or poor potter. Cautious scholars no longer accept this, although the tradition is still reflected uncritically in some modern editions.[42] He was instead more likely to have belonged to a rich landowning family. One apparent reading of the Life of Virgil compiled by Probus, that his father's land was of sufficient size to settle sixty veterans, may not have been far from the truth.[43] As the son of a wealthy landowner he naturally wrote

---

[42] e.g. R. D. Williams 1983: vii.
[43] Brunt 1971: 329; C. G. Hardie 1970: 1123. If the reading *sexaginta veterani* is credited, and if the veterans received an average of 35 iugera apiece (Keppie 1983: 90), then Virgil's father was a rich man. Not all the 2,000-odd *iugera* would have been included in one farm. Instead the pattern of landholding was to own several estates, of, perhaps, ca. 200 *iugera* (Varro 1.19.1), often in the same area. An example often cited is Sextus Roscius of Ameria in Umbria, who owned thirteen farms in the Tiber Valley in the vicinity of his home town: Cic. *Rosc. Am.* 15; 20. A poem sometimes ascribed to Virgil, *Catalepton* 8, speaks of his father missing Mantua and Cremona after his expropriation. Perhaps his estates were located in the territories of both towns.

about the type of farming he knew best. One objection to all this is that slaves are not discussed in the *Georgics*. Villa estates were staffed by slaves and thus omission of this topic is taken to confirm the view that Virgil's subject is the subsistence cultivator.

Most of Italy consisted of rough upland pasture exploited for absentee landlords of huge estates by slaves under a bailiff, not by those to whom the poem is addressed: farmers working a smallholding with their own hands... nevertheless the deliberate exclusion of slavery from the *Georgics* can only be seen as highly significant: the contrast with the contemporary assumptions of Varro, a large landowner, is striking.[44]

This article has instead shown that there is no contrast with Varro's assumptions. Virgil's lack of any direct discussion of slavery can only be seen as an example of his selectivity. There was nothing inherently poetic about agricultural slavery and thus it was an obvious choice for suppression. By convention also, slaves did not appear in serious literature. If Virgil's own *Eclogues* are an important exception to this, that is because they belong not to reality but to the 'imaginary world of ideas'.[45] Moreover, it is most important to observe that Varro, and later Columella, once they had discussed that section of the farm's *instrumentum*, 'equipment' (as Varro defined slaves), make very little direct mention of them thereafter. Their presence is instead tacitly assumed and the landowner-reader is addressed and advised throughout in the second person singular. That is to say, were the 'slavery sections' omitted from the works of the prose writers, the agricultural instructions could conceivably (but of course mistakenly) be understood as directed at a peasant cultivator.

Thus we should rather take it for granted that the workforce of the *Georgics* included slaves as the farm's core of staff, although, again as the agricultural prose writers make clear, a villa estate would also

---

[44] Wilkinson 1982*b*: 22–3. It can be noted here that Wilkinson's attempt to back up the conventional notions with the statement that in the Po valley and the Naples area the small holder still flourished (n. 6 above) is, as it stands, misleading. Archaeological surveys over the last fifteen years have shown it is likely that small farms remained numerous throughout many areas of Italy. And we know too from archaeology that there were plenty of agricultural villas in the Po valley and Campania. The point of departure for such evidence remains the important article of Frederiksen 1970/1.

[45] G. Williams 1968: 294–5, 303 ff.

employ free men as hired labourers, on a regular basis, or as extra help at harvest time and for other heavy tasks, and as well might lease out part of its land to tenant farmers. It is probable that the considerable workforce several times alluded to in the *Georgics* was also drawn from all these sources of labour.[46]

DESECRATION OF THE ITALIAN COUNTRYSIDE AND THE RUIN OF AGRICULTURE

[The poem] contains passages in praise of Octavian (the future Emperor Augustus) which indicate poignantly the longing of the Romans for an end to the civil wars and the return of peace. For Virgil this longing was focused on the desecration of the countryside during periods of war, and the poem is therefore related to the political and social needs of the time, to the urgent desirability of restoring Italian agriculture.

Thus Williams voices a traditional, and traditionally vague, view of the *Georgics*.[47] Yet it is difficult to comprehend how the recent civil wars could have desecrated the Italian countryside in any significant

---

[46] Varro 1.17 for slaves, hired labourers and (probably) tenant farmers. Cf. Columella 1.7. References in the *Georgics* to labour include: 1.210 *exercete viri* which will refer to ploughmen, either slave or hired; 1.259 ff. the sort of tasks that can be done by the various members of the workforce (cf. *alii*, 1.264), which resemble the prose writers' admonitions to keep the labourers always at work, even if the weather is too bad to go out: e.g. Cato, 2.3; 39.2. Work can be done after dark (Cato 37.3, Columella 11.2.90) and before light (Varro 1.36) in winter. Besides not working, another danger was that the agricultural slave might run away, even from the most vigilant owner's estate (Cato 2.2) and this is referred to by Virgil at 1.287. 1.291–2 perhaps refer to a tenant couple (and the Hesiodic *nudus ara, sere nudus*, 1.299, suits such a picture), whereas the reapers of 1.316 were probably a mixture of slaves and hired labourers (cf. Varro 1.17.3). Slave girls to carry out the spinning (1.390) came under the supervision of the slave bailiff's female partner, as Columella later made clear (12.3.6). The planting of vines was (and is) a very hard job, because the earth must be dug to a depth of up to four feet, depending on the nature of the terrain (Columella 3.13.8). It was probably usual to hire labourers for this operation, since Columella refers to a *conductor*, a 'contractor' (3.13.12). Thus Virgil's reference to the establishment of a vineyard with 'much expense' (*multa mercede*, 2.62) should be taken literally. Yet the 'digger' referred to at 2.264 is probably a slave, as is the *vinitor* (2.417). A vinedresser was a skilled and valued slave, but a *fossor* also could be skilled (thus the formula *optimus fossor*, Columella 11.1.12). The division of labour on a slave-staffed villa estate was quite marked (see especially Columella ibid.).

[47] R. D. Williams 1983: x–xi.

way. In 49 BC Caesar crossed the Rubicon and sped down the Adriatic coast, careful not to alienate people *en route*. At the time landowners were only worried about the safety of their farms, as Cicero complains, and were not preoccupied with politics. The fact that the tide of feeling throughout Italy turned rapidly in Caesar's favour shows that he did not interfere with agriculture apart from requisitioning local grain on taking up his siege position at Corfinium. Pompey conscripted some slave shepherds in Apulia. Neither act could have had much effect on Italian agriculture.[48]

Indeed, were one to think back over Roman history, no war on Italian soil could have been more deleterious to Italian agriculture than the Second Punic War, when Hannibal ravaged the countryside for some sixteen years. At least one important modern historical work has considered that period to be a major turning point in the development (and decline) of traditional Italian agriculture.[49] Yet a careful examination of the sources demonstrates that destruction was limited to certain areas only and, in any case, an occupying army has to eat and so must beware wholesale desecration.[50] Moreover, it was not easy permanently to ruin the countryside. Pliny recounts a story (*HN* 18.182), which shows how difficult it was to destroy an emergent cereal crop. Olives, as was noted earlier, are very hardy; and to ensure the end of a vineyard, complete eradication followed by burning is necessary, as Columella's instructions for the clearing out of an old vineyard demonstrate (3.11.4).

Nor should the resourcefulness of the Italian peasant be underestimated. Cereal yields, with or without war, fluctuated enormously from year to year. Peasants would have been inured to hardship and a precarious existence. To supplement or even replace cultivated crops in times of shortage, recourse could be had to many wild plants, even acorns, and hunting. These alternative sources of sustenance have to be emphasized, because modern historians rarely take them into consideration.[51]

Again, to argue or assume (as is sometimes done) that, with her husband on military campaign and with children to support, the Italian peasant woman was unable to cope with the family farm, is

---

[48] Caesar, *B Civ.* 1.18.4; 1.24.2.
[49] A. J. Toynbee 1965: *passim*.
[50] Brunt 1971: 269–77.
[51] On alternative sources of food see the chapter 'Wild and Cultivated Plants' in Frayn 1979 (pp. 57–72). Virgil mentions hunting: 1.271, 307–9; and refers to collection of berries, and sometimes acorns, as food: 1.305–6; 1.148; 1.159.

a generalization of little worth. Varro, with a certain admiration, describes how he had seen Illyrian women 'carrying logs of firewood and children at the breast at the same time', and continues, 'this shows that *our* women who, after giving birth, lie for days under mosquito nets are worthless and contemptible' (2.10.8). The personal pronoun *nostrae* surely refers only to women of the upper, and urbanized, classes. It is clear, too, from occasional remarks by the agricultural prose writers, that children could be usefully employed in farming.[52]

There can, however, be no glossing over the effects of warfare on the individual or local scale. Farms and villages could be abandoned and burned, and people killed. And women and children would not be able permanently to replace male labour. Yet to generalize about the wholesale decline of Italian agriculture, or about profound changes to the rural economy as the result of warfare, shows little awareness of the agricultural reality and underestimates the tenacity of the peasant. A further important point is that the permanent workforce on the villa estate was made up of slaves, who were not, under normal circumstances, enrolled in the army. Thus conscription for military campaigns would not seriously interrupt work on the large farm.

With such general considerations in mind, some further events of the civil war period can be briefly examined before turning once more to the text of the *Georgics*. Such scene painting as Lucan's deserted Italian towns, crumbling houses and abandoned and overgrown fields, as a direct result of the war between Caesar and Pompey must be, then, attributed to poetic licence (*B Civ.* 1.24 ff.). Yet our main historical sources are also prone to exaggeration. Famine began to oppress Rome, because grain importation by sea was blocked by Sextus Pompey and because Italian agriculture was ruined by the 'wars' (Appian, *B Civ.* 5.18). Now the extent of inland Italy which fed Rome was very limited. It was a fact about the ancient world that, since land transport was so costly, a town's productive agricultural territory was necessarily confined. Each area had to be self-sufficient, unless it enjoyed easy access to the sea (as did Rome), where transport was much less expensive. Thus if it is true that because of war Rome was unable to procure supplies from its hinterland, this

---

[52] Children's work could include: vine trimming, cutting back ferns, hen keeping (Columella 11.2.44; 2.2.13; 8.2.7) and shepherding (Varro 2.10.1).

cannot be taken to show that Italian agriculture as a whole had been interrupted. Moreover, since Sextus Pompey's blockade continued for the best part of six years (42–36 BC), and Rome did not starve, it is probably a considerable exaggeration even that agriculture within the city's *territorium* had failed.

But, in any case, what were the 'wars' to which Appian referred? His previous account concentrates on Antony's siege of Mutina in Cisalpine Gaul (*B Civ.* 3.49 ff.). Yet this campaign was clearly very localized. Then he describes the proscriptions by the newly-formed second triumvirate (42 BC). Many rich enemies of Antony, Lepidus, and Octavian were killed, or fled to join Sextus Pompey, and their properties were seized (ibid. 4.5 ff.). Yet new owners took over their estates and agriculture continued productively, as we can deduce from the report that the beneficiaries from the proscriptions were alarmed for their new lands when a truce was made with Sextus Pompey in 39 BC (ibid. 5.74).

Otherwise that treaty was greeted with rejoicing in Rome and Italy, since, according to Appian, it heralded the end of a variety of ills, including the desertion of slaves, the cessation of agriculture, and, especially, famine. But Sextus Pompey's blockade of grain supplies could only have affected Rome and perhaps one or two coastal cities unable to be fed completely from their territories, not the whole of Italy. Appian states that Sextus also made raids on the coasts of Italy; but raids are by definition localized and temporary affairs and were also resisted by Octavian.[53]

Perhaps the desertion of slaves was more pertinent. This would affect the villa estate, Virgil's central subject. Yet it cannot be determined whether the 30,000 slaves who crewed Pompey's fleet and were captured by Octavian in 36 BC, were agricultural slaves.[54] From Appian's account they would seem to have been a mixture of both

---

[53] Appian, *B Civ.* 5.19; 56 (raids in the south of Italy). After Octavian recovered Sardinia he 'strengthened the coast of Italy with many garrisons' (ibid. 5.80). Even if, as Cicero said in another context, merely the threat of hostile attack caused men to flee their fields (*De imp. Cn. Pomp.* 16), that would mean only a very temporary setback for agriculture.

[54] The figures comes from *Res Gestae* (25.1) and may well be exaggerated, since Augustus represents the war against Sextus Pompey as a war entirely against slaves and pirates.

urban and rural, mainly from the eighteen most flourishing towns of Italy, whose land had been promised to the triumvirs' veterans (*B Civ.* 4.85). A number also came from Sicily (ibid. 5.13). Again, therefore, it cannot be right to generalize from this about Italy's agriculture.

It was when the news came out that the land of the eighteen finest Italian towns was under threat of confiscation that Lucius Antonius, the triumvir's brother, began to make political capital out of the discontent against Octavian. Those destined to lose land were joined by others who feared similar treatment. 'Thus almost the whole of Italy rose up', in Appian's words, against Octavian (ibid. 5.27). But that again is certain exaggeration, which perhaps stemmed originally from Lucius' anti-Octavian propaganda. From Appian's account we hear that Octavian's enemies were soon confined mainly to one town, Perusia, and dealt with rapidly and effectively in the winter of 41/40 BC (ibid. 5.33 ff.). 'So ended the war which had promised to be long drawn out and most harsh to Italy' (ibid. 5.49). But as it was, its effects could not have been far reaching.

Those rich landowners, anxious about their properties, who joined Lucius, did not, we must assume, destroy their own vines, olives, and livestock. In the autumn of 41 BC, when the crisis was reaching a head, it is possible that, in the uncertainty many of them did not sow cereals, especially if they had sufficient supplies in their granaries from previous years. But a year's fallow in some areas could not have had a lasting deleterious effect on Italian agriculture. Indeed, of those originally threatened with confiscation, senators certainly were later excused (Dio 48.8.5), and many other influential men succeeded in retaining their lands. If in the end small holders suffered from confiscation as much as, if not more than the rich, the allotment of their land to veterans meant only the replacing of one set of small cultivators with another—and not the destruction of agriculture.[55]

After distribution to veterans, there is no evidence of a diminution in prosperity of the areas concerned. It used to be thought that the newly settled veteran was likely to fail as a farmer and that the land he

---

[55] Brunt 1971: 330–434. Brunt believes that the Perusine War was more widespread than is argued here (cf. 290–1). But the only other hard evidence is the sacking of Sentinum and the capitulation of Nursia, small towns in comparison with Perusia (Dio 48.13).

took over declined rapidly in productivity; but recent studies have done much to dispel such preconceptions, which were based mainly on the understandable laments of the dispossessed shepherds in the *Eclogues*.[56] In the *Res Gestae* Augustus, looking back over his reign with historical perspective, could state that his various veteran settlement programmes had been a success (28; cf. 15.3; 16.1). Despite the tone of self-glorification, there is no substantial evidence to counter or disprove his statement. Italian agriculture, especially as practised by the rich, continued to flourish.

It has been necessary to explore in some detail these events of the confused period of the civil wars in order to demonstrate the fragile basis of traditional generalizations about the effects of war on the Italian countryside and agriculture. Virgil, it has been argued above, described the contemporary Italian scene in the *Georgics*, with special emphasis on the villa estate. Thus we should expect to find by and large a portrayal of flourishing agriculture. And we do.

Nothing could be clearer than the *laus Italiae* in Book 2 (136–76). Especially worthy of a note is the praise of Italian cities (2.155–7), which is corrective of Lucan's bleak view, or of any exaggerations that might be based on the distribution to veterans of lands belonging to Italy's finest *oppida*. Varro also had spoken in such glowing terms in his treatise on agriculture published in the mid-thirties BC: 'You who have travelled through many lands; have you ever seen any land more fully cultivated than Italy?... What useful product is there which does not only grow but also flourish in Italy? What emmer wheat shall I compare to that of Campania, what bread wheat to that of Apulia, what wine to Falernian, what oil to Venafran?' (1.2.3, 6). Of course, Varro, like Virgil, wrote from the standpoint of the rich echelons of society and he described principally the continued success of the villa estates. But there can now be no doubt that his eulogistic appreciation found recognizable reflection in the contemporary agricultural situation.[57]

---

[56] For a typical comment about the failure of veterans as farmers: Wilkinson 1982a: 320. On contemporary laments see, for example, R. D. Williams 1983: 95 *ad Eclogue* 1.70–2; Keppie 1983: 101.

[57] To explain Varro's enthusiasm some commentators consider that his praise of Italy belongs to a much earlier draft of the work, since they believe in an agricultural crisis in the thirties BC. See Heurgon 1978: 105. Editors of Virgil will point out that

Virgil's encomium of Italy (2.136–76) throws into high relief in a sustained fashion what is always latent, and often obvious, throughout the *Georgics*. In fact the flimsy case for desecration of the Italian countryside rests ultimately on one short passage, which occurs at the end of Book 1 among the catalogue of troubles which followed from the assassination of Julius Caesar.

> ... to the plough no due honour is given, fields are unkempt since the farmers have been taken away and curved sickles are transformed into straight hard swords.
>
> (1.506–8)

In particular he lays emphasis on the wretched state of Italian farming, contrasting the miserable conditions of the battle-ravaged countryside (506–8) with the potential beauty and glory of ordered agriculture, the theme with which so much of this book has been concerned.[58]

But the context of Virgil's emotive words is the whole world, not Italy. As a result of Caesar's death, according to the poetic hyperbole, wars rage throughout the world from East (the Euphrates) to the West (Germany).

Williams is right to call these references to wars indefinite,[59] but he is wrong to specify Italy as the country where agriculture was ruined. When Virgil writes 'the whole world is in arms, neighbouring cities everywhere fight with each other, nowhere is due respect given to the plough', that is a generalized and highly emotional statement and every element of it indefinite. It comes as a climax of a poetic 'heaping-up' of laments, which had included among other wonders a list of portents (469–88). It cannot be taken as a realistic picture of the state of Italy's, or any other nation's, agriculture. Clearly indicative, however, of the conventional and inverted interpretation of this passage is Williams's reference to the other agricultural

---

the *laus Italiae* was a well-established traditional literary feature which had nothing to do with reality. A recent acute study shows, perhaps rightly, that the passage contains some pessimistic elements in the form of moral admonition against violence and the pursuit of luxury: R. F. Thomas 1982a: 39 ff. But such moralising is also part of the agricultural manual tradition (see n. 65 below).

[58] R. D. Williams 1983: 156. Cf. the long-standing unchallenged words of Page 1974: 242, 'The words admirably connect the whole lament for the ruin of Italy with the subject of the *Georgics*'.

[59] R. D. Williams 1983: 156 (*ad* 1.509).

description of Book 1, apart from this short passage, as 'potential' rather than real.

RESTORATION OF ITALIAN AGRICULTURE

It used to be thought that Octavian/Augustus was interested in the restoration of Italian agriculture and thus that Virgil was following some official directive in writing the *Georgics*. Such a policy might then be hinted at in Virgil's reference to Maecenas' 'commands' (3.41). However, it has since been pointed out by historians that Augustus did very little to help Italian agriculture.[60] Thus interpretation has changed, Maecenas' *iussa* are toned down, and the writing of the *Georgics* has less to do with agriculture than with restoration of Roman morality:

> The attunement of the *Georgics* to future Augustan policy was more moral than agricultural. Nor need we press the words 'your behest, no easy one, Maecenas' (3.41): whatever encouragement may have come from the statesman, its inspiration is clearly literary and personal...[61]

This is a clear case, it would seem, of a historical argument's effect on literary interpretation. Yet then how can we account for Horace's attribution of the prosperity of Italian agriculture to Augustus in the last poem of Book 4 of the *Odes*? Was it merely an indication of imperial propaganda, which some critics discern more clearly in Book 4 than in the previous three books, akin perhaps to the partisan historical account of Velleius Paterculus; or was it even a verbal anticipation of the *Ara Pacis*?[62]

The truth, however, is less extreme. Firstly, Italian agriculture did not, as has been argued, require restoration. Thus Augustus did not

---

[60] e.g. A. H. M. Jones 1970: 142–3.
[61] Wilkinson 1982a: 320.
[62] Hor. *Carm.* 4.15.5: *fruges et agris rettulit uberes*; cf. Vell. Pat. 2.89.4. The *Ara Pacis* was dedicated in 13 BC (the year in which it is quite conceivable that Horace wrote 4.15), although not 'opened' until 9 BC. For an interpretation of the monument as a piece of Augustan propaganda: Weinstock 1960; cf. J. M. C. Toynbee 1961: 153–6. For Horace as propagandist: Brink 1982: 523 ff.

need to put into effect an agricultural 'policy' in the same explicit way as he introduced moral reform. Yet it is wrong, on the other hand, to deny completely that he fostered the continuation and growth of Italian agricultural prosperity already in existence.

During his reign Augustus established, or re-established some 40 veteran colonies and settled other veterans in many *municipia* in Italy. Imperial money flowed into these towns to construct public buildings, theatres, and such important utilitarian structures as aqueducts. Augustus understood the key to a successful Italian rural economy: prosperous towns that stimulated the agricultural productivity of their *territoria*. He also repaved roads, built and repaired bridges. Transport of produce was thus facilitated, no doubt helped also by the campaign against brigandage.[63] In these ways Augustus was concerned to increase the well-being of rural Italy; but they were the sort of methods which could only succeed in an already flourishing situation. Agriculture was already in full swing in Italy and Augustus did not have to intervene in any direct way as, for example, he did in Egypt, where he set soldiers to clean out irrigation canals.[64] Thus Horace's or Velleius Paterculus' attribution of agricultural prosperity to Augustus can be seen as pardonable exaggeration with a core of truth. Had Virgil lived longer and written the *Georgics* later, his *laudes Italiae* would have glowed with even greater enthusiasm.

CONCLUSION

Virgil ensured that his agricultural information was correct. Accuracy of detail contributes largely to the realistic picture of

---

[63] On Augustus' settlement of veterans see: Brunt 1971: 326 ff. and Keppie 1983: 115 ff. for works of public utility, including roads. The campaign against brigandage: Suet. *Aug.* 32.1.

[64] Suet. *Aug* 18.2. After continual difficulties with the grain supply to Rome, Augustus reached a settlement which suited grain merchants, the Roman poor, and arable farmers (*aratores*). In the context, the 'farmers' were surely Italian and local to Rome, and it could have been that the cultivation of cereals in the environs of the city was declining because of growing imports. Although the precise details are unclear, it does seem that, in this local and particular case only, Augustus intervened directly in Italian agriculture: Suet. *Aug.* 42.

the Italian countryside as a whole. Thus can be understood the otherwise perplexing fact that the later agricultural prose writers, Pliny and Columella, cite Virgil, even more often than Cato or Varro, as a source of agricultural knowledge. No doubt Columella hoped to make his long work more entertaining and literary by the inclusion of excerpts from the *Georgics*, but that cannot explain the seriousness with which Virgil's authority is adduced; and Pliny cites Virgil without quoting the relevant verses, and thus does not seem so interested in literary adornment. Columella once points out (4.11.1), from his own considerable experience, that Virgil was mistaken, but is careful to show that the error was shared by earlier prose writers as well. Then again, as noted above, Virgil provides valuable new information, and his originality in these cases seems reinforced by Columella's observation (3.10.20) that some sound Virgilian advice occurs in no other written source. We must assume that estate owners who read the prose treatises also considered Virgil a reliable source of agricultural information.

But practicality apart, there are other important reasons to accept and attend seriously to the precise agricultural content of the *Georgics*. Only thus, as has been pointed out, can be kept in check some of the more fanciful and generalized overall interpretations of the poem. Dismissal of the agriculture liberates a dangerously wide-ranging hunt for symbolic meaning. Instead 'surface' and 'depth' must work (and be considered) together, if the poem is to succeed as a unified whole.

Virgil certainly explored, in no necessarily consistent way, the varied symbolic associations which the countryside evoked in the poetry of the time. These associations are given more credibility and vitality in the *Georgics* than in other Augustan poems, since they depend on, and grow out of a realistic, rather than idealized, view of the countryside and agricultural activities. Moreover, several of these topics such as the historical-moralising tradition of praising the past, when Rome was supposedly self-sufficient, not reliant on imported foodstuffs, when urban avarice, sloth, and luxury did not exist, and when ancestral moral and religious values were focused in the countryside belong also to the tradition of the agricultural prose writers, as always an important key to the correct understanding of the *Georgics*.[65]

Then, too, another cogent reason for closer attention to the agricultural detail of the poem lies in the proper appreciation of how Virgil succeeds in bringing to life very precise agricultural terms. In other words, it is the very ability to incorporate technical terms and turn them into poetry, which makes the poem so astonishing. This appears constantly but is rarely recognized. In lines 97–8 of Book 1, for example, *proscindere* is the technical term for the first ploughing (see Varro 1.29.2), and *in obliquum* refers knowledgeably to the tilting of the plough (Columella 2.2.25; Pliny, *HN* 18.178). These two terms are interwoven with words which personify the earth, *suscitat* and *terga*; while the whole hard job of breaking the compact soil is emphasized by 's', 'c' and 't' sounds. It is the startling poetry at this immediate level, which is often neglected during the search for deeper meanings.

In conclusion we can return to reconsider and recast Seneca's judgement of the *Georgics*. Virgil did not sacrifice accuracy to audience delectation. Instead it is that very agricultural accuracy which gives life and strength to the poem *and* (therefore) delight to its readers.[66]

[65] Cato, *praef.*: farming is better than all other pursuits, as our ancestors rightly judged. Varro 1.13.6–7: modestly-sized agricultural villas are better (as our ancestors thought) than luxurious and parasitic suburban villas; 1.69.3: violence is endemic in the city of Rome; 2 *praef.*: luxury and idleness in towns; Rome relies on imports; farmers have left their land for the easy life at Rome; 3.1.1–5: the country is sacred to the gods and country life more noble and traditional. All these moral topics are dealt with also by Pliny, *HN* 1.1–22, and in the long preface of Columella.

[66] I should like to thank Malcolm Davies and Elizabeth Rawson for their valuable criticism of an earlier draft of this article.

3

Prose into Poetry: Tradition and Meaning in Virgil's *Georgics*

Richard F. Thomas

It is difficult fully to appreciate the audacity of Virgil's enterprise in writing the *Georgics*. A new poet of the second generation, heir to the urbane attitudes and refined poetics of Callimachus and Catullus, he set out to produce a poem which at least purported to teach subjects completely alien to the higher literary tradition which was his heritage: sheep-dipping, soil-testing, irrigation, and manuring were to provide the terms and the metaphors for issues ultimately not dissimilar to those which had concerned him in the *Eclogues* and which would continue to occupy him in the *Aeneid*.

Virgil knew and did not know the countryside, much as the nature-walker or even the kitchen vegetable-gardener knows and does not know the realities of dendrology and horticulture. Love of or empathy with the country is not equivalent to knowledge, and we should be careful of romanticizing or idealizing.[1] By Virgil's day Roman agriculture had become a science, many of its precepts

---

This paper is based on a Loeb Classical Lecture given at Harvard University in May 1986. It was first published in 1987 and reprinted in R. F. Thomas 1999: 142–72, and it appears here virtually unchanged except for the addition of translations of the Greek and Latin passages by Katharina Volk.

[1] Although there has at times been skepticism about Virgil's science in the *Georgics*, it is fair to say that throughout the ages, from Columella on, his practical knowledge has been overrated—a natural result of the reverence towards his poetic genius; cf. Wilkinson 1969: 270–313.

not essentially unlike those of today:[2] through observation and experiment the Romans knew that graft compatibility depended at least on stock and scion being intrafamilial and preferably intrageneric; somehow they had hit upon the fact that the rotation of wheat crops with legumes brought about what we know as nitrogen-fixation and revitalized the soil; and they knew that some trees were better propagated from seed, others through cultivated means. These topics are the scientific basis of the *Georgics*,[3] and for information on them Virgil for the most part did not consult the memories of his early years in Mantua or information imparted to him by his father, but rather the agricultural treatises of Greece and Rome.

In 37 BC, or possibly 36, shortly before Virgil began writing the *Georgics*, Varro published his *Res Rusticae*.[4] The timing was extremely felicitous. Virgil could doubtless have drawn from other works now virtually or completely lost, such as the Latin translation of Mago the Carthaginian, which, according to Varro, was commissioned by the senate,[5] or the treatises of Tremelius Scrofa and Licinius Stolo, participants in the dialogue of Varro,[6] but Varro's work in particular held obvious attractions for Virgil, perhaps because it was the first agricultural treatise in Latin with literary, rather than just instructional, pretensions. It is fair to say that without the *Res Rusticae*, the *Georgics* would have looked very different; the overall theme and many of the details of Virgil's poem are firmly based on Varro's work. The same must be said on the Greek side about the works of Theophrastus, chiefly the *Historia Plantarum*, and to a lesser extent the *De Causis Plantarum*. The studies of P. Jahn[7] and W. Mitsdörffer[8] prove beyond

---

[2] The works of K. D. White, particularly White 1970, establish the reasonably sophisticated state of agricultural knowledge in Virgil's time.

[3] Whether or not Virgil consistently adheres to scientific truth, or even correctly understands it, is of course another matter; see below.

[4] There is no good reason, on internal or external grounds, to doubt the information given in the *Lives* of Donatus and Servius that the *Georgics* took Virgil seven years to produce and was completed in 29 BC.

[5] See *Rust.* 1.1.10; cf. also Mahaffy 1890; V. Lundström 1897.

[6] The fragments of such writings down to the time of Varro are most conveniently available in Speranza 1974.

[7] Jahn 1903.

[8] Mitsdörffer 1938/9.

any doubt that Virgil used Theophrastus directly—indeed, there is even an instance (2.131) where his adaptation reflects a false manuscript reading in the *Historia Plantarum*, a reading which otherwise survives only in a citation of Theophrastus by Athenaeus.

The problem confronted by Virgil may be simply put: how does a poem like the *Georgics*, whether or not we concur with Dryden's judgment of it as 'the best poem of the best poet', emerge at least as a candidate for such a status when it has as its foundation some of the most functional and mundane prose of ancient literature? No other poem in Greek or Latin even confronts, let alone overcomes, such a challenge. The technical poetry of Alexandria is precisely what it seems to be, namely the poetic reshaping of didactic or otherwise specialized information resulting in a literature which retains that specialized thrust and whose meaning, albeit expressed with learning and elegance, is all on the surface and is not in any appreciable way distinct from the meaning of its prose sources. This is one of the reasons why the *Phaenomena* of Aratus and the poetry of Nicander can never be considered great; the idiosyncrasies of subject matter are not accommodated to any particular literary aim, beyond the characteristically Alexandrian aim of putting into poetry that which had previously been outside the range of poetry. The same holds true for the Latin translations of Aratus, for Manilius' *Astronomica*, and for all such poems which bear a superficial resemblance to the *Georgics*. Even the *De Rerum Natura*, although Lucretius sought constantly to invigorate scientific and philosophical material with passages of a higher and more lyrical mood, is in the final analysis equivalent to the sum of its parts; there is little beneath the surface.[9]

I propose, then, to examine the *Georgics* from the point of view of its technical, prose background, observing the variety of ways in which Virgil integrates this material into his poem, and attempting to define how it is that the poem not only transcends the sum of its own parts, but how those parts themselves transcend the parts of the technical models on which they are based and of which they at times

---

[9] There are those who feel that Lucretius' poem is more cryptic and metaphorical than it is generally acknowledged to be, but theirs is a view which I find difficult to accept in any pervasive sense.

seem mere 'translations'.[10] The examples will be somewhat selective, but the categories in which they are placed are generally representative. I have also completely ignored the so-called digressions and passages indebted to higher forms of literature;[11] with his prose sources Virgil confronts distinct problems and devises different procedures of integration. I hope it will emerge, however, that in the *Georgics* the poetic status of passages rooted in more mundane models is ultimately equal to, and as important as, that of the more conventionally 'poetic' sections.[12]

I

First, on the levels of structure and style, Virgil constantly reshapes his more technical material. In both of these features his practice may be seen as 'compensatory'; there are, for instance, several examples of numerical patterns, which seem to be concentrated not in the more literary sections, but precisely in the technical parts. At the beginning of the second book, on the propagation, variety, and habitat of trees (1–135), Virgil presents the technical material in blocks of 26 lines each (9–34, 47–72, 83–108, 109–35[13]), separated off by units of eight (1–8), twelve (35–46), and ten (73–82) lines. Eight lines on soil preparation prior to planting (2.346–53) are followed by eight on cultivation after planting (2.354–61). Or, at 3.384–413, three technical passages on wool, milk, and dogs, which provide a transition from the accounts of Libya and Scythia to the treatment of the snake and plague, each receive ten lines. Passages on the selection of cattle

---

[10] A number of critics have collected Virgil's sources: Jahn 1903; Mitsdörffer 1938/9; Knoche 1877; Morsch 1878; van Wageningen 1888; Rostagno 1888—the genre, *Quellenforschung*, is recognizable. There have also been sporadic studies which go beyond mere collection, notably Jermyn 1954; Wilkinson 1969: 56–68. There has, however, been no study of Virgil's general method of adapting his prose sources.

[11] For Virgil's method of reference to poetry, see R. F. Thomas 1986.

[12] In spite of the admonitions of Klingner and others the *Georgics* still tends to be viewed as a bipartite poem, alternating between the 'technical' (i.e. 'dull' or 'unimportant') and the 'lyrical' (i.e. 'interesting' or 'meaningful'); as long as this distinction is maintained the poem will continue to be misunderstood.

[13] Line 129 is an interpolation.

(3.49–71) and on the selection of horses (3.72–94) each extend over 23 lines and find numerical as well as thematic recapitulation later in the same book, when the plague strikes down first the horse (498–514, seventeen lines), then the ox (515–30, sixteen lines). Such patterns may seem unimportant, but they indicate Virgil's sense of the burden imposed by his subject; material previously outside the realm of poetry is given a visual elegance through structural ordering.

In style, as in structure, similar compensation occurs; features such as anaphora, the tricolon *abundans*, chiastic arrangement, or artfully devised word order appear in the technical sections as frequently as or more frequently than in the 'digressions'. The result is the imposition of a stylistic unity, a feature which again distinguishes this poem from one such as the *De Rerum Natura*, which tends to alternate between two styles.[14] 'Style' is always difficult to define, but when, as is often the case with the *Georgics*, we have the prose model and the Virgilian version, then it is at least possible to appreciate the differences. One instance of compensatory elegance may represent Virgil's general practice. At 3.322–38 he treats the summer pasturing of sheep and goats:

> at vero Zephyris cum laeta vocantibus aestas
> in saltus utrumque gregem atque in pascua mittet,
> Luciferi primo cum sidere frigida rura
> carpamus, dum mane novum, dum gramina canent,   325
> et ros in tenera pecori gratissimus herba.
> inde ubi quarta sitim caeli collegerit hora
> et cantu querulae rumpent arbusta cicadae,
> ad puteos aut alta greges ad stagna iubebo
> currentem ilignis potare canalibus undam;   330
> aestibus at mediis umbrosam exquirere vallem,
> sicubi magna Iovis antiquo robore quercus
> ingentis tendat ramos, aut sicubi nigrum
> ilicibus crebris sacra nemus accubet umbra;
> tum tenuis dare rursus aquas et pascere rursus   335
> solis ad occasum, cum frigidus aëra Vesper
> temperat et saltus reficit iam roscida luna,
> litoraque alcyonen resonant, acalanthida dumi.

---

[14] On alternation as a feature of Lucretian style see Kenney 1971: 14–29.

But when at the Zephyrs' call joyous summer sends each flock to glade and pasture, let us hasten to cool fields at the rising of the morning star, when the day is young and the grass is white with frost and the dew on the tender blades is most pleasing to animals. Then, when the sky's fourth hour has heightened their thirst and the plaintive cicadas burst the bushes with their song, I will order the flocks to wells or to deep standing pools, to drink the water running in oaken channels. But in the midday heat I will have them seek out a shady valley, where either the great oak of Jove with ancient wood spreads out its enormous branches, or where a grove with sacred shade lies dark with many holm-oaks; then again give them clear water and pasture them until sunset, when the cold evening star cools the air and the dewy moon already refreshens the glades, and when the shores resound with the kingfisher, the bushes with the finch.

By and large Virgil's instructions are technically sound, derived as they are from Varro, *Rust.* 2.2.10–11:

eaeque [sc. oves] ibi, ubi pascuntur in eadem regione, tamen temporibus distinguntur, aestate quod cum prima luce exeunt pastum, propterea quod tunc herba roscida meridianam, quae est aridior, iucunditate praestat. sole exorto potum propellunt, ut redintegrantes rursus ad pastum alacriores faciant. (11) circiter meridianos aestus, dum defervescant, sub umbriferas rupes et arbores patulas subigunt, quaad refrigeratur. aere vespertino rursus pascunt ad solis occasum...ab occasu parvo intervallo interposito ad bibendum appellunt et rursus pascunt, quaad contenebravit; iterum enim tum iucunditas in herba redintegrabit.

And where they pasture in one and the same area, there is nevertheless a distinction according to the seasons, in summer in as far as they leave for pasture at sunrise, for the reason that the dewy grass of that hour is more pleasing than that of midday, which is drier. Once the sun has risen they make them drink so that by refreshing them, they make them in turn keener on the grazing. During the midday heat, they lead them underneath shady rocks and spreading trees, in order to cool them down, until it gets colder. In the evening air they pasture them again until sunset...after the sun has set and a short while has passed, they call them to drink again and make them graze again, until it grows dark; for then the pleasantness of the grass will refresh them.

But there is a world of difference between the two. Although Virgil has more or less faithfully transmitted the information of Varro,[15] his actual diction coincides only in the use of the common phrase *solis*

---

[15] There can be no doubt that Virgil is working closely with Varro at this point; earlier in the same section (*Rust.* 2.2.4) Varro was against rams with black or

ad occasum (for Varro's *ad solis occasum*), and he has reworked the instructions into one of the most exquisite passages in the poem. After specifying the season in the opening line he presents the four periods of the day in four lines each, thereby depicting the structure of the shepherd's day through the structural neatness of the passage.[16] Varro's *sole exorto* has become an evocative and descriptive couplet, marked by elevation of the temporal expression and by an elegant and vivid anaphora:

> Luciferi primo cum sidere frigida rura
> carpamus, dum mane novum, dum gramina canent.
> (*G.* 3.324–5)

For Varro's *tunc herba roscida meridianam... iucunditate praestat*, Virgil borrowed a line from the *Eclogues*, appropriately evoking his own poetic pastoral world: 326, *et ros in tenera pecori gratissimus herba* (=*Ecl.* 8.15, with *et* for *cum*). This evocation is to have a far from superficial significance a little later in the book, when the heat associated with the pastoral existence becomes excessive and turns into the parched setting of the snake and of plague, as the pastoral world, no longer a functioning world for Virgil, meets its destruction. The welcome shade, pleasing pasture, and refreshing streams of the lines are all to lose their appeal and their salutary pastoral function:

> non umbrae altorum nemorum, non mollia possunt
> prata movere animum, non qui per saxa volutus
> purior electro campum petit amnis.   (*G.* 3.520–2)

Neither the shade of lofty groves nor the soft meadows can touch his heart, nor the stream which, clearer than amber, rolls over rocks towards the plain.

Next Varro's *circiter meridianos aestus... sub umbriferas rupes... subigunt* generates first line 331, *aestibus at mediis umbrosam exquirere vallem*, then the further elaboration of *umbrosam* over three artful lines, shaped again by anaphora—of *sicubi*—and closed by the key word *umbra*:

spotted tongues since they will produce offspring with the same markings. Virgil without authority compresses this into a warning against rams with black tongues (*G.* 3.287–90)—they produce lambs with dark spots.

[16] To achieve this structural elegance, and perhaps for the sake of compression, Virgil omits one of Varro's feeding times, that which occurs after sunset (*ab occasu*). He was also concerned to give the passage a typical pastoral closing, occurring *at* sunset.

> sicubi magna Iovis antiquo robore quercus
> ingentis tendat ramos, aut sicubi nigrum
> ilicibus crebris sacra nemus accubet umbra.   (G. 3.332–4)

The whole passage ends on a sonorous note with the line *litoraque alcyonen resonant, acalanthida dumi*, modelled again on a line from the *Eclogues*, which in the same way uses alliteration to reflect the sense of the verb *resonare*:

> sole sub *ardenti* resonant *arbusta* cicadis.   (*Ecl.* 2.13)

Under the burning sun the bushes resound with cicadas.

In effect the technical passage of Varro has become a bucolic poem of 17 lines, elegantly structured and self-contained, but at the same time setting up a contrast with one of the chief themes of *Georgics* 3—the subsequent annihilation of pastoral existence.[17]

Virgil's procedure in these lines, particularly his very purposeful evocation of the world of pastoral (a world distinct from that of real shepherding as it is represented in Varro), amounts to something more than mere embellishment, but it is true to say that his developments are in part stylistic, what we would expect of many poets drawing from such a source. The same sort of attention and elevation may be found in Aratus and Lucretius. It will now be useful to go beyond stylistic and compositional features and observe the ways in which Virgil actually transforms and appropriates the content of these models. His practice may best be looked at in a sort of ascending order of categories, beginning with small-scale alteration and proceeding to the ways in which, across entire books, he re-interprets his tradition.

II

First there is the matter of tone or sensibility. Much of the material in Theophrastus and Varro is of necessity earthy; that is a natural result of discussing the realities of the earth. Virgil consistently either *refines*

---

[17] For a detailed study of the fate of the pastoral existence in *Georgics* 3 see Ross 1987: 149–87.

or *suppresses* such material, and I think the motives for this refinement lie in his own sensibility rather than in any proto-Augustan sense of restraint; it is worth remembering that the blunt realities of the *Res Rusticae* were produced shortly before Virgil began working on the *Georgics* and that the crudities of Horace's *Epodes* 8 and 12 were also a product of the thirties.

First, on a small scale but in telling fashion, Virgil through euphemism or vagueness avoids certain unpleasant realities. So in his adaptation of Theophrastus' account of the medicinal value of the citron or 'Persian apple' (*Hist. pl.* 4.4.2), he renders the blunt information that it serves as an emetic (δοθὲν γὰρ ἐν οἴνῳ διακόπτει τὴν κοιλίαν καὶ ἐξάγει τὸ φάρμακον, 'taken in wine it upsets the intestine and drives out the poison') with the vague words *membris agit atra venena* ('it drives dark poison from the limbs', 2.130)—the specific reference to the effects on the intestine is simply omitted. Or, at 3.251, Varro's explicit recommendation for overcoming the bashfulness of stallions (*Rust.* 2.7.8, *ab locis equae nares equi tangunt*, 'they smear the mare's discharge on the nostrils of the stallion') is generalized by Virgil to the more acceptable *si tantum notas odor attulit auras* ('if only the scent has brought the familiar breezes')—the details are left to the imagination.[18] It is in fact a remarkable achievement, if one looks at *Georgics* 3 from the vantage point of the second book of the *Res Rusticae*, that Virgil, while choosing for his major theme *amor* in the animal world, at the same time completely avoided the crude realities of that theme. Where Virgil does get his hands dirty, he does so either with apologetic self-consciousness, as in the prescription to manure at 1.79–80 (*arida tantum | ne saturare*

---

[18] The same development occurs in Virgil's adaptation of a poetic source at 4.415–31. At *Od.* 4.441–6 Homer dwells on the stench of the seals among which Menelaus hides prior to ambushing Proteus (cf. 441–2, τεῖρε γὰρ αἰνῶς | φωκάων ἁλιοτρεφέων ὀλοώτατος ὀδμή, 'for the horrible smell of the seaborn seals vexed us terribly'); so bad is it that Eidothea puts ambrosia under their nostrils. In Virgil's adaptation Cyrene also spreads ambrosia about Aristaeus, but its function has nothing to do with the odor of the seals (415–8, *liquidum ambrosiae diffundit odorem... atque habilis membris venit vigor*, 'she pours out the liquid fragrance of ambrosia... and supple strength came to his limbs'); that phenomenon is confined to a descriptive line which comes subsequently and which avoids comment on the effect of the odor (431, *exsultans rorem late dispergit amarum*, 'gambolling, they spread the unpleasant liquid far and wide').

fimo pingui pudeat solo, 'just do not be ashamed to fertilize dry soil with rich dung'), or else the poetry itself compensates for and elevates the theme; as Addison remarked: 'he delivers the meanest precepts with a kind of grandeur, he breaks the clods and tosses the dung with an air of gracefulness.'[19]

On a larger scale, under the same heading of *suppression*, Virgil simply ignored certain technically important but poetically inappropriate themes treated by his sources. The end of Varro's treatise is naturally profit. As he says to Fundania at the outset: *quare, quoniam emisti fundum, quem bene colendo fructuosum cum facere velis, meque ut id mihi habeam curare roges, experiar* ('therefore, since you have bought an estate, which you wish to make profitable through good management, and have asked me to make this my concern, I will make an attempt', *Rust*. 1.1.2)—it is his very reason (at least purportedly) for writing the work; and the motive of profit is mentioned on virtually every page. I have been able to find only one reference in the *Georgics* to this central topic, at 3.306–7, where Virgil points out that there is a profit to be made from goat hair. In the same breath, however, he seems to compensate for the reference by introducing the subject of the fleeces of Miletus, whose costliness is a topos in higher literature, namely in Aristophanes (*Lys*. 729; *Ran*. 543–5) and Theocritus (*Id*. 15.126)—thereby making the reference primarily literary rather than merely functional.

The basis of every Roman farm, regardless of its size, was its manpower, and its manpower was, of course, provided chiefly by slaves. Cato, in discussing the requirements for a vineyard of 100 *iugera*, speaks of slaves, wine-presses, and vats in precisely the same tone, and Varro, having treated the breeding of pigs (*ad feturam verres duobus mensibus ante secernendi*, 'as regards breeding, the boars are to be separated out two months ahead of time', 2.4.7), will later in the same book begin a discussion of the breeding of herdsmen in precisely the same style, with precisely the same formula: *quod ad feturam humanam pertinet pastorum*, 'as regards the breeding of herdsmen', 2.10.6. The modern reader is somewhat jolted, as he is when reading Cato's recommendation that the farmer economize by selling off

---

[19] Cf. Wilkinson 1969: 299–300 for the eighteenth century's admiration of Virgil's skill in this matter.

worn-out oxen, blemished sheep, old wagons, old tools, old slaves, sick slaves, and whatever else is superfluous (*et siquid aliut supersit*, 1.2.7). Virgil's reaction, and this is not necessarily a projection of modern sensibility, is similar to ours, for, in spite of the central position of the slave laborer, the only reference to farm workers in the *Georgics* is in the idealized passage at the end of the second book, where the staff, referred to as the farmer's *socii* (a ridiculous notion if, as is clearly the case, it is intended to include all the workers), enjoy a rustic picnic, gathered around the wine bowl and engaged in athletic contests.

At *Rust.* 2.4.3 Tremelius Scrofa, whose cognomen has qualified him to lead the discussion on pigs,[20] asks: *quis enim fundum colit nostrum, quin sues habeat?* ('for who of us manages an estate who does not keep pigs?'). Indeed Varro devotes more space to pigs than to any other animal.[21] But pig-farming clearly created the same reaction (deserved or not) in Virgil as in us, for his answer to Scrofa's question is a clear *non ego*—he does not mention pigs at all as a technical subject;[22] and the same goes for asses and mules, which are likewise important on the Roman farm. This is partly because the horse and the ox can be ennobled and, as will be observed below, can be approximated to man—a boundary which the pig cannot cross without comic effect. But in part the motive is simply refinement: the pig simply does not belong in Virgil's poetic world.

In each of these instances it is not sufficient to say that the themes are merely unpoetic, for soil-testing and drainage are also by nature unpoetic, but Virgil treats them, for they can be made metaphorical of issues, such as elemental imbalance, which have implications outside the world of the farmer. It is, however, the case that the realities of pig-farming and slavery offend a certain sensibility, and what distinguishes this poem from all other agricultural literature in

---

[20] Cf. 2.4.1 *Scrofam potissimum de ea re dicere oportere cognomen eius significat* ('his name shows that Scrofa is the one who should speak about this topic'). Similarly 'Vaccius' leads the discussion of cattle (2.5.2), 'Appius' of bees, and so on.

[21] Pigs receive 22 paragraphs; sheep come next with 20, while cattle are given 18.

[22] At 3.248 and 255–6 boars are mentioned along with other animals affected by *amor*, and at 497 they suffocate from the plague, but Virgil avoids all discussion of selection, breeding, care, etc.

Greek and Latin is in large part that that sensibility is shared by the poet and by us.

III

The reverse of suppression is *selectivity*, or *promotion*, and it is by means of this feature that Virgil's poem really acquires its meaning. For the time being we will look only at small instances, where Virgil chooses a technical detail or theme and expands it or presents particular bias, with the result that it is transformed, taking on meaning and assuming significance completely absent from the source. This is a process which occurs throughout the poem and which may in effect be seen as Virgil's *modus operandi* in his use of the technical tradition. In the well-known passage at 1.118–49 Virgil defined the cultural setting of the poem: the golden Saturnian age has passed; that of Jupiter and *labor*, in which things can and do go wrong, is now in effect. A few lines later he gives instructions on preparing the threshing floor:

> possum multa tibi veterum praecepta referre,
> ni refugis tenuisque piget cognoscere curas.
> area cum primis ingenti aequanda cylindro
> et vertenda manu et creta solidanda tenaci,
> ne subeant herbae neu pulvere victa fatiscat.   180
> tum variae inludunt pestes: saepe exiguus mus
> sub terris posuitque domos atque horrea fecit,
> aut oculis capti fodere cubilia talpae,
> inventusque cavis bufo et quae plurima terrae
> monstra ferunt, populatque ingentem farris acervum   185
> curculio atque inopi metuens formica senectae.   (*G.* 1.176–86)

I can tell you many ancient precepts, if you do not shrink back and are loath to learn such trivial cares. First, the threshing floor must be flattened with a huge roller, kneaded by hand, and made solid with binding chalk, lest weeds take root or, turning to dust, it open up. Then various pests mock you: often the tiny mouse makes its home under the ground and constructs its storehouse, or sightless moles dig out their bedrooms. In hollows the toad is found and all the countless monsters that are born of the earth, and the weevil ravages the enormous heap of grain, as does the ant which fears a destitute old age.

The words *veterum praecepta* point to a technical source.[23] Now both Cato and Varro had described the preparation of the threshing floor, and a glance at their versions shows just how inferior Virgil's precepts are from any instructional point of view:

aream sic facito. locum ubi facies confodito. postea amurca conspargito bene sinitoque conbibat. postea conminuito glebas bene. deinde coaequato et paviculis verberato. postea denuo amurca conspargito sinitoque arescat. si ita feceris neque formicae nocebunt neque herbae nascentur. (Cato *Agr.* 91)

Make a threshing floor in the following way. Dig up the area where you are going to make it. Then sprinkle it with *amurca* and wait for it to be absorbed. Then break up the clods of earth. Afterwards level it and beat it with rammers. Then sprinkle it again with *amurca* and let it dry. If you do it in this way, neither will ants harm it nor will weeds grow.

aream, ubi frumentum teratur, sic facito. confodiatur minute terra, amurca bene conspargatur et conbibat quam plurimum. conminuito terram et cylindro aut pavicula coaequato. ubi coaequata erit, neque formicae molestae erunt, et cum pluerit, lutum non erit. (Cato *Agr.* 129)

Make the threshing floor, where wheat is to be ground, in the following way. Let the earth be dug up diligently, be sprinkled with *amurca*, and allowed to absorb as much as possible. Break up the earth and level it with a roller or rammer. Once it is leveled, ants will not be a problem, nor will it turn to mud when it rains.

aream esse oportet in agro sublimiori loco, quam perflare possit ventus; hanc esse modicam pro magnitudine segetis, potissimum rotundam et mediam paulo extumidam, ut, si pluerit, non consistat aqua et quam brevissimo itinere extra aream defluere possit; omne porro brevissimum in rotundo e medio ad extremum. solida terra pavita, maxime si est argilla, ne, aestu peminosa <si sit>, in rimis eius grana oblitescant et recipient aquam et ostia aperiant muribus ac formicis. itaque amurca solent perfundere, ea enim herbarum et formicarum et talparum venenum. (2) quidam aream ut habeant soldam, muniunt lapide aut etiam faciunt pavimentum. nonnulli etiam tegunt areas, ut in Bagiennis, quod ibi saepe id temporis anni oriuntur nimbi. ubi ea retecta et loca calda, prope aream faciundum umbracula, quo succedant homines in aestu tempore meridiano. (Varro *Rust.* 1.51.1–2)

---

[23] In fact they effectively constitute a footnote, as does the phrase *more patrum* at 3.177.

The threshing floor should be in a more elevated place, so that the wind can blow through it. It should be appropriate to the size of the arable land, ideally round, and a little bit higher in the middle, so that when it rains, the water does not collect but is able to flow out of the threshing floor on the shortest possible way; for in a circle, the path from the middle to the border is the shortest. It should consist of solid, leveled earth—especially if it is of potter's clay—so that, when it is cracked in the summer, grains do not hide in its cracks and attract water and open up paths for mice and ants. Therefore they are accustomed to sprinkle it with *amurca*, which is poison to weeds, ants, and moles. In order to have a solid threshing floor some people fortify it with stones or even pave it. Some even roof their threshing floors, as among the Bagienni, because there it often rains at that time of year. Where it is uncovered and the area is hot, one should put up awnings next to the threshing floor to which the people can retire in the midday heat of summer.

Varro's threshing floor in particular is a reasonably complex thing; he prescribes position, exposure, size, and shape, treats the need for elevation of the center, discusses the material and construction, and recommends in some cases the building of a roof to protect it. Virgil, however, confines his practical advice to an elegant couplet, marked by a tricolon *decrescens*, and shaped by three gerundives which refer to the three parts of the task:

>   area cum primis ingenti aequanda cylindro
>   et vertenda manu et creta solidanda tenaci.   (*G.* 1.178–9)

The verb *solidare*[24] self-consciously reflects the functional theme; it seems not to be otherwise found before Vitruvius and is always used in technical contexts. What concerns Virgil, beyond giving this technical flavor, is not the actual construction—a threshing floor built on the basis of this information would be defective—but the reason for the construction and the care which is entailed: to keep out pests. For Cato there is a danger from weeds, ants, and water, for Varro weeds, ants, moles, and water, and in both authors these are mentioned briefly. Virgil has completely inverted the focus of his models, devoting lines to a slightly different and expanded list of these *pestes*: the mouse, the mole, the toad, the weevil, and the ant. And he has omitted what is in reality the greatest threat to the

---

[24] Cf. Varro's *solida terra pavita*.

Tradition and Meaning in Virgil's Georgics

threshing floor, the inanimate threat posed by moisture. Nor are the creatures enumerated merely what they seem, that is, insects or animals. They represent rather the forces which attack man's works in the age of Jupiter, for the words *tum variae inludunt pestes* (181) clearly recall the statement 35 lines earlier (*tum variae venere artes*, 'then the various arts arrived', 145), describing the advent, after Saturn's departure, of the phenomena associated with *labor*. The magnified importance of these creatures, and their new status, completely absent from the accounts of Cato and Varro, are confirmed at 184–5, where Virgil describes them as *quae plurima terrae | monstra ferunt* ('all the countless monsters that are born of the earth'). Now *monstrum* is not a light word in Latin—in fact it appears here for the first time of such apparently innocuous creatures. Virgil used it with a purpose, for these 'earth-born monsters', which threaten Jupiter's threshing floor, will be recalled on the level of myth one hundred lines later, where the assault of the Giants, now directed against the mythical, rather than the agricultural, realm of Jupiter, is treated:

> tum partu Terra nefando
> Coeumque Iapetumque creat saevumque Typhoea
> et coniuratos caelum rescindere fratres.   (*G.* 1.278–80)

Then in monstrous labor Earth brings forth Coeus and Iapetus and savage Typhoeus, and the brothers conspiring to tear down heaven.

All this, then, from Cato's straightforward *si ita feceris, neque formicae nocebunt neque herbae nascentur*. For Virgil, insects, moles, and toads have become a destructive force operating on a scale no longer recognizable from the technical tradition and contributing to one of the major themes of the poem—that of nature's resurgence against the works of agricultural man.[25] In fact, some of Virgil's most important motifs and metaphors are prompted by such minute and technically uncomplicated themes in the prose tradition. One noteworthy instance is to be found in *Georgics* 3. In the second book of the *Res Rusticae*, under the heading of pasturing, Varro mentions

---

[25] At *Fast.* 5.35–6 Ovid seems to accommodate both references in the *Georgics*: *Terra feros partus, immania monstra, Gigantas | edidit ausuros in Iovis ire domum* ('the Earth brought forth savage offspring, enormous monsters, giants that dared to attack the abode of Jupiter').

the practice of some herdsmen who keep their cattle shut up in their pens to keep them from being bothered by the gadfly:

> eas pasci oportet locis viridibus et aquosis. cavere oportet ne aut angustius stent aut feriantur aut concurrent. itaque quod eas aestate tabani concitare solent et bestiolae quaedam minutae sub cauda ali, ne concitentur, aliqui solent includere saeptis. (*Rust.* 2.5.14)

> One should pasture them in green and watery places. One should take care that they do not stand together too closely or hit each other or collide. And because in the summer gadflies typically vex them and certain tiny animals live under their tails, some are accustomed to shut them up in their pens.

Virgil was to develop the potential of this piece of straightforward information:

>   saltibus in vacuis pascunt et plena secundum
>   flumina, muscus ubi et viridissima gramine ripa,
>   speluncaeque tegant et saxea procubet umbra.   145
>   est lucos Silari circa ilicibusque virentem
>   plurimus Alburnum volitans, cui nomen asilo
>   Romanum est, oestrum Grai vertere vocantes,
>   asper, acerba sonans, quo tota exterrita silvis
>   diffugiunt armenta; furit mugitibus aether   150
>   concussus silvaeque et sicci ripa Tanagri.
>   hoc quondam monstro horribilis exercuit iras
>   Inachiae Iuno pestem meditata iuvencae.
>   hunc quoque (nam mediis fervoribus acrior instat)
>   arcebis gravido pecori, armentaque pasces   155
>   sole recens orto aut noctem ducentibus astris.   (*G.* 3.143–56)

They pasture them in open glades and next to brimming rivers, where there is moss and the bank lush with grass. And let caves cover them and the shadows of cliffs lie on them. Around the groves of Silarus and Alburnus flourishing with holm-oaks, there swarms an insect whose Roman name is *asilus*, but the Greeks in turn call it *oestrus*. It is fierce and makes a horrible sound, and all terrified by it the herds stampede through the woods. The sky and woods and banks of the dried-out Tanager go mad, struck by their bellowing. Once with this monster Juno exercised her dreadful wrath, devising disaster for the heifer daughter of Inachus. This too you will keep away from pregnant cattle and will (for in the midday heat it is more aggressive) pasture your herds just after sunrise or when stars bring on the night.

His initial debt is apparent: like Varro, he leads up to his discussion of the gadfly by prescribing pasture which is spacious, near the water, with lush grass and shade: *vacuis, flumina,* and *viridissima* correspond to Varro's *viridibus, aquosis, (non) angustius.* In artistic terms the passage from the *Georgics* is elevated through the etymological play resulting from Virgil's choice of the term *asilus,* through the polemic, lying beneath his mention of the Greek word *oestrus,* and through the generally allusive dimensions of the passage: Aeschylus, Callimachus, Apollonius, and probably Calvus are all subsumed into Virgil's lines.[26] But the lines have a thematic importance for the poem which transcends mere literary virtuosity. Varro's simple cattle fly, associated by Virgil with the excessive heat of southern Italy, becomes identified with the *pestis* which Juno set on Io, and which is both for Apollonius and Virgil a metaphor for the fury of *amor,* a passion which in *Georgics* 3 is soon to consume the herd. Its effect on the herd, moreover, is described at 150–1:

> furit mugitibus aether
> concussus silvaeque et sicci ripa Tanagri.

The parched riverbeds resound to the bellowing of the afflicted cattle. This is precisely the effect, in precisely the same setting, of the real *pestis,* the devastating plague which comes at the end of the book:

> balatu pecorum et crebris mugitibus amnes
> arentesque sonant ripae collesque supini.   (G. 3.554–5)

The streams and dried-out banks and sloping hills resound with the bleating of sheep and with frequent bellowing.

The gadfly in the *Georgics* serves as a metaphor for the effects of excessive heat, as the plague will be characterized by imbalance in both directions—excessive cold and excessive heat.[27] Virgil uses the insect, describing it as a *pestis,*[28] to suggest what will become explicit as the book proceeds: heat, passion, and plague are progressively intensified symptoms of nature's destructive power.

[26] See R. F. Thomas 1982*b*.
[27] Cf. 3.441–4, 458–9, 479, 500–1, 511–12, 566.
[28] The word is otherwise used three times in the poem—of the assailants of the threshing floor (1.181), of the plague itself (3.471), and of the ominous water snake which precedes and prefigures the plague (3.419, *pestis acerba boum*).

In the selective promotion of technical details Virgil clearly felt great freedom to distort, to transfer, and so on; this is not particularly surprising in that his poem was to be didactic only in appearance. Varro has a bizarre report at 2.7.9, which he relates as a θαῦμα: *tametsi incredibile, quod usu venit, memoriae mandandum* ('even though it is unbelievable, it should be committed to memory since it actually happened'). It seems that a stallion had been unwilling to mate, so the groom covered its head, and was thereby able to produce the desired result. Later, however, when its head was uncovered, it killed the groom, and in a particular way: *impetum fecit in eum ac mordicus interfecit*—it bit him to death ('it attacked him and killed him by biting'). At 3.266–8, in a passage dealing with the hazards of *amor* (in other words, in the section generally corresponding to Varro's passage), Virgil treats the notorious madness of mares:

> scilicet ante omnis furor est insignis equarum;
> et mentem Venus ipsa dedit, quo tempore Glauci
> Potniades malis membra absumpsere quadrigae.

Surely the madness of the mares is the most remarkable. Venus herself put it in their minds, at the time when the Potnian chariot-team tore off the limbs of Glaucus with their jaws.

Now there seem to be at least two distinct variants of the story of Glaucus, son of Sisyphus. One, reported by Probus and attributed to Asclepiades Tragilensis, has him feeding his mares on human flesh. When the supply runs out, and since they have acquired the taste, they turn on Glaucus. In the other variant, reported by Servius, Glaucus is a doublet of Hippolytus—his neglect of Aphrodite brings retribution through the instrument of the mares. Servius did not know of a precedent for Virgil's apparent suggestion that Glaucus' death was a result of his keeping his team, for obvious reasons, from mating, and it very much looks as if Virgil has first transformed the striking episode from Varro and then grafted it onto the mythical account of Glaucus. As occurred in the case of the gadfly, so here as well the episode is recapitulated later in the third book, when Virgil creates yet another connection between *amor* and the plague. He has the stricken horse inflict death on *itself* with its own teeth, a claim for which there is no technical precedent, and which would seem to be unlikely in reality:

>   discissos nudis laniabant dentibus artus.   (G. 3.514)

With bared teeth they tore apart their mangled limbs.

Varro's anecdote seems to provide the impulse for this strand of thought and for connecting *amor* and plague, but Virgil applies the anecdote to a different and original situation.

IV

Sometimes it is to Virgil's purpose not merely to expand or transform his technical sources, but quite simply to *falsify* them. There are other instances in the poem, but perhaps the clearest, and one to which we will return later, has to do with grafting and inoculation as a means of propagating trees. Varro, who is representative of the pre-Virgilian tradition, states that the prime prerequisites for successful graft unions have to do with the types of trees used, with the season, and with the method:

> videndum qua ex arbore in quam transferatur et quo tempore et quem ad modum obligetur. non enim pirum recipit quercus, neque enim si malus pirum. (*Rust.* 1.40.5)
> One must pay attention to from which tree there is transfer to which other, and at which time and in which manner the joining is done. For the oak does not receive the pear, not even if the apple receives the pear.

It is the first of these considerations (the nature of the tree) that is most important, as is clear from Varro's elaboration: *non enim pirum recipit quercus, neque enim si malus pirum.* Whatever the precise meaning of this sentence,[29] it seems at the very least to contain the dendrological truth that unions between families will not succeed: pears and apples are both Rosaceae and therefore potentially compatible (thus the *receptus* of Varro), while oaks are Fagaceae and will

---

[29] As it stands it seems to mean 'for an oak does not take on a pear, even if the apple does take on a pear.' But Ross 1980: 63–71 points up the difficulties in Varro's sentence and proposes to read *neque etiamsi* for *neque enim si*: 'nor, even if (it is) an apple, does it take the graft of a pear.' For Virgil's presentation of grafting see also Ross 1987: 104–9.

never take with pears. In fact, most successful grafts are not only within family, but within genus.[30]

What is Virgil's attitude? He mentions six graft unions early in book 2:

> et saepe alterius ramos impune videmus
> vertere in alterius, mutatamque insita mala
> ferre pirum et prunis lapidosa rubescere corna.   (G. 2.32–4)

And we often see how the one tree's branches turn into that of another, and how the pear, transformed, bears grafted apples, and how stony cornels grow red with plums.

> inseritur vero et fetu nucis arbutus horrida,
> et steriles platani malos gessere valentis,
> castaneas fagus; ornusque incanuit albo
> flore piri glandemque sues fregere sub ulmis.   (G. 2.69–72)

And the rugged arbutus is grafted with a walnut shoot, sterile planes bear healthy apples, and beeches chestnuts. The ash lights up with the white flower of the pear, and pigs munch on acorns under elms.

Of these six, two are theoretically possible: apple and pear at line 33, since both are Rosaceae, and chestnut and beech at 71–2, both Fagaceae. Both of these, however, are extremely improbable.[31] The remaining four involve cornel and plum (Cornaceae and Rosaceae), walnut and arbutus (Juglandaceae and Ericaceae), plane and apple (Platanaceae and Rosaceae), and pear and elm (Rosaceae and Ulmaceae)—in other words, these unions are simply impossible. Nor can there be any doubt that Virgil was aware of the fact, for not only did he have Varro's precepts, but in a list of *adynata* at *Ecl.* 8.52–3 he had included wolves fleeing from sheep, oaks producing golden apples (a double impossibility), and the alder producing the flower of the narcissus—that is, an interfamilial union, made doubly impossible

---

[30] On this subject see the very readable book of Garner 1958.

[31] There is reasonable success in the grafting of pears onto quince stocks, and it could be argued that Virgil's *mala* are quinces (*Malum cydoneum*), but the union of chestnuts and beeches (which in any case nobody in Virgil's day, let alone in ours, would attempt) is most unlikely. I am indebted here to discussion with Professor G. L. Good of the Department of Floriculture and Ornamental Horticulture at Cornell University.

by the fact that one is a woody plant, the other herbaceous.[32] I shall return to the question of Virgil's motive for creating such a distortion, but for now it is worth noting that even at a point in the poem where the theme appears to be purely technical and didactic he felt free to falsify scientific facts. One further observation is, however, of some interest. Before Virgil the attitude towards grafting in the technical literature was quite reasonable. Varro's views have been cited, and those of Theophrastus are equally sound: in book 2 of the *Historia Plantarum* he speaks only of grafts within the same genus. But after Virgil things seem to change. Columella, who often followed the poet in spite of his own superior scientific knowledge, 'begins his account (5.11.1) with the remarkable statement that any kind of scion can be grafted on any tree.'[33] The elder Pliny, although generally more skeptical than Columella and even at times vaguely hostile towards Virgil's science, is on the subject of grafting equally fanciful: 'his work abounds with absurd instances of incompatible grafting.'[34] It looks, then, as if the influence of Virgil, even when he blatantly falsified the information of his sources, may have created lasting distortions in the technical tradition.[35]

V

So far we have observed the various ways in which Virgil, through suppression, promotion, transference, or distortion, alters the original context and meaning of his prose models. Before we turn to a more wholesale type of transformation involving all of these categories, it will be useful to look at the transformations of the technical tradition which Virgil effects through *expansions* of the prose tradition—chiefly through the use of mythology, through the vivid vignette, and through simile. These features occur throughout the poem, for the most part in highly technical contexts, and therefore allow other, deeper levels of meaning to emerge precisely at those

---

[32] For more detailed discussion of the relationship of these *adynata* to grafting in the *Georgics* see Ross 1987: 107–8.
[33] White 1970: 257.   [34] Ibid.   [35] Cf. Ross 1980: 66–7.

points where Virgil, although following the technical tradition, intends to divert that tradition to his own new purpose.

The commentators constantly refer to Virgil's 'invigoration' or 'embellishment' of the didactic material through such means, and Wilkinson is not atypical when he says, for instance, that mythology was for Virgil an 'obvious source of colour and variety...which at times is apt to seem intrusive',[36] and, a little later (185), that 'mythology plays no great part in the *Georgics*, outside the Aristaeus epyllion, and such contribution as it does make may generally be classed as "ornament."' This view is symptomatic of the attitude toward the technical parts of the poem, which is where the mythological sequences generally appear—that they are in some way mere bridges between the purple passages, their intent instructional in the same manner as that of their models, and therefore in need of 'invigoration'.[37]

The present study will limit investigation of the mythological passages to those of the third book, where there is a single, consistent function to their appearance. In this book Virgil presents the animal world, particularly the worlds of horses and cattle, as analogous to human society. This in part anticipates the bee world of the fourth book, which is a complete paradigm for human society, but it is chiefly designed to suggest that the disasters which afflict livestock in the form of love and plague are our own disasters. The suggestion becomes open only in the final four lines of the book, when the plague, which so far has struck only at the animals, finally infects man himself:

> verum etiam invisos si quis temptarat amictus,
> ardentes papulae atque immundus olentia sudor
> membra sequebatur, nec longo deinde moranti
> tempore contactos artus sacer ignis edebat.   (*G.* 3.563–6)

And if anyone tried to don the loathsome clothing, then burning blisters and foul sweat would run along his smelling limbs, and he did not have to wait for long until the accursed fire would feed on his infected body.

---

[36] Wilkinson 1969: 183.

[37] The study of Frentz 1967 is an exception to this attitude. It appeared after the work of Otis, and seems not to have been available to Wilkinson; in general its arguments have not attracted sufficient attention.

At this point it is man's world, not just that of animals, which lies in ruins. Virgil pursues this suggestion throughout the third book, and in many ways. For instance, it explains the very close adaptation of the plague of Lucretius 6: we constantly identify Virgil's cattle plague with the human plague of Athens and inevitably see that cattle plague as having a human application. To the same end the terminology of Varro is consistently transformed. Varro speaks of male and female animals as *mas* and *femina*, but, for instance, never uses *femina* without either *mas* or a noun referring to the actual animal (e.g. *canis femina*). Virgil's practice is in complete contrast; he uses *mas* only once (64), uses *femina* with no qualification (216), and in general for such terms substitutes words which suggest a human dimension: *pater, mater, maritus, nati, iuvenes, pubes*, and so on. The boundaries are further diminished when at 3.105 *cum spes arrectae iuvenum* refers to the youths riding the horses, while a few lines later *iuvenem* (118) refers to the young horse itself.[38]

Mythology is used in the third book to underscore this theme of approximation. The myth of Glaucus has already been discussed in another context.[39] Of the other instances, all but one serve as clausulae to technical passages and therefore carry particular emphasis.[40] In each of these cases the story involved in some ways exemplifies the diminution of the boundary between man or divinity on the one hand and animals on the other. At 89–91, as a conclusion to the section, drawn from Varro *Rust.* 2.7.2–6 (on *dilectus equorum*), the ideal horse is compared to the obvious horses of mythology, first to Cyllarus, which was given by Juno to Pollux (somewhat odd, since it is Castor who is traditionally the horseman), then to the teams of Mars and of Achilles:

> talis Amyclaei domitus Pollucis habenis
> Cyllarus et, quorum Grai meminere poetae,
> Martis equi biiuges et magni currus Achilli.

Thus was Cyllarus, tamed by the reins of Pollux of Amyclae, and those of whom Greek poets make mention, the pair of Mars and the team of great Achilles.

---

[38] This anticipates an important play on the identity of *iuvenis* at 258; see below.
[39] Cf. above.
[40] The vignette is given the same structural emphasis; see below.

The next three lines, as much as is devoted to the better-known horses combined, refer to the story of Saturn and Philyra—a myth which is not particularly well known and which is among those considered intrusive by Wilkinson:

> talis et ipse iubam cervice effundit equina
> coniugis adventu pernix Saturnus, et altum
> Pelion hinnitu fugiens implevit acuto.   (G. 3.92–4)

Thus, swift at the arrival of his wife, Saturn himself flung his mane over his horse's neck and, fleeing, filled lofty Pelion with high-pitched whinnying.

The name of Philyra is suppressed, a stylistic feature which creates emphasis and often in Virgil suggests a Hellenistic source. In this instance the source is Ap. Rhod. *Argon.* 2.1231–41, an aetiological account of the island of Philyra, including the story of Cronos' affair with the Oceanid Philyra, of Rhea's discovery, and of Cronos' escape in the form of a horse. The somewhat illogical result was the birth of the Centaur Chiron. Far from being 'intrusive', the myth is central to Virgil's purpose: Saturn's duality as god and horse as well as the half-man, half-animal Centaur which results from the incident and which is the visual exemplum par excellence of the breaking down of the boundary between man and animal[41]—these are the reasons for Virgil's including it. Indeed this horse has no other reason to be present here; its associations are distinct from those mentioned at 89–91, and there is no suggestion in Apollonius or elsewhere that Cronos as horse was particularly outstanding or swift—Virgil's *pernix* is his own contribution.

Virgil's technical, if highly literary, treatment of the gadfly at 145–56,[42] part of the section on *cura matrum*, naturally contains mention of Io's metamorphosis and of the subsequent infliction imposed by Juno:

> hoc quondam monstro horribilis exercuit iras
> Inachiae Iuno pestem meditata iuvencae.   (G. 3.152–3)

---

[41] Chiron or the Centaurs will figure twice elsewhere in the book: obliquely, through mention of the Lapiths at 115–16, and later at 549–50, where the plague defeats the art of medicine, including that of Chiron, referred to by his matronymic *Phillyrides*.

[42] Cf. above.

The essence of the story is a sort of inverted doublet for that of Saturn and Philyra. In this case, of course, it is not the god but Io herself who through metamorphosis crosses the boundary, but the implications of the myth for Virgil's scheme in the third book are precisely the same. Then there is the account of Pan and Luna at 391–3, which concludes a brief passage on the selection and care of sheep:

> munere sic niveo lanae, si credere dignum est,
> Pan deus Arcadiae captam te, Luna, fefellit
> in nemora alta vocans; nec tu aspernata vocantem.

With such a gift of snow-white wool, if it is possible to believe, Pan, the god of Arcadia, tricked and deceived you, Luna, calling you into deep groves—and you did not refuse him as he called.

The myth, which looks like a variant of the story of Selene and Endymion, is extremely obscure.[43] Virgil seems to allude to a version in which Pan won Luna (Selene) with the gift of a fleece. But another form of the myth, to which Virgil also seems to refer—with the verb *fefellit*—has Pan either turning himself into a ram or disguising himself as a ram.[44]

There is a final myth in the book whose details are distinct from these, but which has a similar function. It is the story of Hero and Leander, a rare instance of a mythological episode which contains no proper name at all, either for the characters or the location. There is a reason for the omission. At 245–66 Virgil gives examples of the maxim *amor omnibus idem*. When afflicted by desire all animals are at their most savage and irrational: the lion, the bear, the boar, the stallions, the pig, lynxes, wolves, dogs, stags, and, above all, mares: *scilicet ante omnis furor est insignis equarum* (266). In the middle of this list come six lines:

> quid iuvenis, magnum cui versat in ossibus ignem
> durus amor? nempe abruptis turbata procellis
> nocte natat caeca serus freta, quem super ingens
> porta tonat caeli, et scopulis inlisa reclamant

---

[43] According to Macrobius (*Sat.* 5.22.9–10), who attributes it to Nicander, Valerius Probus, although a *vir perfectissimus*, confessed that he was unaware of its details or provenance.

[44] Cf. Serv. Auct. *ad* 391 *ut illi formosus videretur, niveis velleribus se circumdedit* ('to appear beautiful to her, he surrounded himself with a white fleece').

> aequora; nec miseri possunt revocare parentes,
> nec moritura super crudeli funere virgo. (G. 3.258–63)

What about the youth in whose bones harsh love kindles a great fire? Late in a dark night, he swims through waters disturbed by clashing storms, and above him the gate of heaven thunders, and the waves resound as they hit the rocks. His miserable parents cannot call him back, nor can the girl, about to die over his cruel death.

Given Virgil's prior application, intentionally confusing, of *iuvenis* to both man and animal, the reader does not at first clearly distinguish the exemplum, the only human one, from the animal ones which have preceded and which will follow, particularly since there is no mention of the names of Hero and Leander, of Sestos, or any other signpost, and since the next item on the list begins in precisely the same style: the rhetorical question at 264 (*quid lynces Bacchi?*) resumes and creates a close parallel with that at 258 (*quid iuvenis...?*). We recognize the myth and its human subject only as the details unfold, as the unnamed Leander swims across the straits for his love (259–60 *abruptis turbata procellis | nocte natat caeca serus freta*). But even that detail suggests a link with, rather than a distinction from, the animal examples, since Virgil immediately before and after the myth refers to the inability of natural barriers to separate animals when they are affected by *amor*:

> non scopuli rupesque cavae atque obiecta retardant
> flumina correptosque unda torquentia montis. (G. 3.253–4)

No cliffs or hollow rocks hold him [the stallion] back, nor opposing rivers bearing uprooted mountains in their waves.

> illas ducit amor trans Gargara transque sonantem
> Ascanium; superant montis et flumina tranant. (G. 3.269–70)

Love leads them [the mares] across Gargarus and the resounding Ascanius; they cross mountains and swim through rivers.

And earlier, in a more technical section, the need for such separation was primary:

> atque ideo tauros procul atque in sola relegant
> pascua post montem oppositum et trans flumina lata.
> (G. 3.212–13)

And therefore they remove the bulls to lonely pastures far away, behind an intervening mountain and across broad rivers.

The story of Hero and Leander serves to show that for man as for animals such precautions fail before the power of passion.

These, then, are the myths that Wilkinson refers to as 'apt to seem intrusive' and purely 'ornamental'; but they are only intrusive if the passages which they illuminate are viewed as simply didactic or technical, as simply restating the themes of the treatises on which they are based. If, on the other hand, those passages are seen as having a deeper function, then the myths are revealed for what they are, as restatements on a different level of the real and central concerns of the technical parts of the poem. In the case of the third book they serve to reinforce the suggestion that the world of animals is also the world of man, and that the afflictions suffered by those animals will also be shared by man.

Virgil employs the vignette in a similar way—to suggest meaning which expands the immediate technical context and suggests issues absent from the technical source. Sometimes the main function of the vignette is to provide color. At 2.177–224 Virgil treats the different types of soil and the suitability of each for different agricultural activities. It is an important subject, which had been handled by Theophrastus (*Caus. pl.* 2.4), Cato (*Agr.* 6), and Varro (*Rust.* 1.7.5–10; 1.9), but it is a subject potentially inimical to poetic treatment. One of the ways Virgil invigorates the passage is by mentioning areas of Italy possessing the type of soil under discussion; but he does more than simply mention them:

> et qualem infelix amisit Mantua campum
> pascentem niveos herboso flumine cycnos. (*G.* 2.198–9)

...land like that which unhappy Mantua lost, pasturing white swans with its grassy river...

> talem dives arat Capua et vicina Vesaevo
> ora iugo et vacuis Clanius non aequus Acerris. (*G.* 2.224–5)

Such soil rich Capua ploughs and the coast by the Vesuvian ridge and Clanius unkind to forlorn Acerrae.

In the first instance, as he mentions areas suitable for grazing, Virgil evokes the world of his youth, and of the *Eclogues*, with *infelix amisit* pointing to the land confiscations; and the whole couplet recalls *Ecl.* 9.27–9:

> 'Vare, tuum nomen, superet modo Mantua nobis,
> Mantua vae miserae nimium vicina Cremonae,
> cantantes sublime ferent ad sidera cycni.'

'Varus, if only Mantua is saved for us, Mantua, alas, too close to wretched Cremona, singing swans will bear your name up to the stars.'

If only for a moment, we are transported from the discussion of soil types to a world which we have seen before, in a very different way. The couplet at 224–5, which closes the whole passage, is less charged, although *vacuis* and *non aequus* are evocative; but it does provide an elegant finish, with the two place-names in the first line (*Capua/Vesaevo*) mirrored in position and shape by those of the second (*Clanius/Acerris*).

At 1.390–2 there is a vignette, also serving as a *clausula*, which does more than add color or heighten the poetic effect. The lines close a discussion of storm signs, adapted closely from Aratus' *Phaenomena*:[45]

> ne nocturna quidem carpentes pensa puellae
> nescivere hiemem, testa cum ardente viderent
> scintillare oleum et putris concrescere fungos.

Not even girls spinning their tasks at night are unaware of storms, since they see how the oil sputters in the burning lamp and mouldy fungus forms.

The information comes from *Phaen.* 976–81, lines which tell of the signs provided by the wick and light of the lamp. Absent from Aratus, however, is any reference to human involvement; Virgil's *carpentes pensa puellae*, therefore, is not merely a vivid touch, but a detail which implicates humans (along with the animals in the lines preceding) in his prognostic system. As throughout the poem, and as we saw in the case of mythological expansions, Virgil constantly suggests the unity and parallelism of his world.

The potential of the simile to expand the context to which it is attached is obvious; through it the poet is able to refer openly to a world that is only latent in his actual theme. There are many instances

---

[45] Admittedly not a 'prose' source, but straightforwardly technical nevertheless.

in the *Georgics*, and one may serve to exemplify Virgil's practice. Throughout book 2 he consistently presents viticulture as a sort of warfare against the natural tendencies of the plant. The suggestion becomes most explicit in the treatment of pruning:

> tum stringe comas, tum bracchia tonde
> (ante reformidant ferrum), tum denique dura
> exerce imperia et ramos compesce fluentis.   (G. 2.368–70)

Then trim their hair, then cut their arms (earlier they fear the knife), then finally establish harsh discipline and curb the flowing branches.

Somewhat earlier in the book, on the preparation of soil for the vineyard and the transplantation of cuttings (259–87), this theme is brought out in a vivid simile. Virgil has recommended the ordering of the vines into a *quincunx*, the pattern of juxtaposed and overlapping groups of five trees, one on each of the four corners, and one in the center. The arrangement prompts the simile:

> ut saepe ingenti bello cum longa cohortis
> explicuit legio et campo stetit agmen aperto,
> derectaeque acies ac late fluctuat omnis
> aere renidenti tellus, necdum horrida miscent
> proelia, sed dubius mediis Mars errat in armis.   (G. 2.279–83)

Just as often in a great war, when a legion has fanned out its cohorts in a long line and the army stands on the open field and the battle line is arranged and the land everywhere ripples with the reflecting bronze, they do not yet engage in fearsome battle, but Mars wanders undecided among the arms.

Through the simile the newly planted vine becomes a legion, waiting in formation for the battle which the *agricola* will wage with it.

VI

We may conclude by looking more broadly at Virgil's use of Theophrastus, specifically at the ways in which *Georgics* 2 develops and transforms the second book of the *Historia Plantarum*. In his use of Theophrastus Virgil employs in detail all of the features recorded so far: structural and stylistic improvement, suppression, promotion, distortion, expansion, and so on. But he also integrates the technical material in a more far-reaching manner and in important ways develops potential which is only implicit in Theophrastus. In fact it is this transformation, the poetic use to which Virgil puts Theophrastus, which ultimately explains the close and extensive use of the *Historia Plantarum*.

Theophrastus' second book begins with a list of the ways in which plants originate:

αἱ γενέσεις τῶν δένδρων καὶ ὅλως τῶν φυτῶν ἢ αὐτόμαται ἢ ἀπὸ σπέρματος ἢ ἀπὸ ῥίζης ἢ ἀπὸ παρασπάδος ἢ ἀπὸ ἀκρεμόνος ἢ ἀπὸ κλωνὸς ἢ ἀπ' αὐτοῦ τοῦ στελέχους εἰσίν, ἢ ἔτι τοῦ ξύλου κατακοπέντος εἰς μικρά· καὶ γὰρ οὕτως ἔνια φύεται. τούτων δὲ ἡ μὲν αὐτόματος πρώτη τις, αἱ δὲ ἀπὸ σπέρματος καὶ ῥίζης φυσικώταται δόξαιεν ἄν· ὥσπερ γὰρ αὐτόμαται καὶ αὐταί· δι' ὃ καὶ τοῖς ἀγρίοις ὑπάρχουσιν· αἱ δὲ ἄλλαι τέχνης ἢ δὴ προαιρέσεως. (Theophr. *Hist. pl.* 2.1.1)

The propagation of trees and of plants in general is either spontaneous or by seed or by root or by shoot or by branch or by twig or by the trunk itself or by wood cut into small pieces; for some grow even in this way. Of these, the spontaneous one takes the first rank, but the ones by seed and root also seem to occur quite naturally; thus, they too are spontaneous, and they happen also to wild trees. But the other ones take place through skill and choice.

That is, spontaneously, from seed, from root, from a piece torn off (i.e. suckering), from a branch or twig (i.e. rooting), from the trunk itself, or from small pieces of wood. He will later add to these the subcategories of grafting and inoculation, which are seen as combinations of the more simple methods, rather than as primary methods. Theophrastus then divides this overall group into two categories, the natural (φυσικώταται) which include spontaneous growth, growth from seed, and from root, all of which may be considered spontaneous (αὐτόμαται),[46] and the remaining methods of propagation, which are in contrast to the natural methods and depend on human skill or choice: αἱ δὲ ἄλλαι τέχνης ἢ δὴ προαιρέσεως.

---

[46] In fact, of course, of these only seed and root have any basis in reality; the notion of spontaneous generation goes back at least to Anaxagoras, who held that the seeds of plants are contained in the air and are germinated through contact with water or soil; cf. Theophr. *Hist. plant.* 3.1.4.

Tradition and Meaning in Virgil's Georgics

Virgil, at the beginning of his second book, in two corresponding sections of 26 lines each (9–34, 47–72) reproduces this division with great care, with reasonable fidelity to the original, but with an artistry not surprisingly absent from the model. It will be useful to cite the lines so as to bring out the careful arrangement:

διὰ φύσεως

principio arboribus varia est natura creandis.
namque aliae nullis hominum cogentibus ipsae   10
A   sponte sua veniunt camposque et flumina late
curva tenent, ut molle siler lentaeque genistae,
populus et glauca canentia fronde salicta;
B   pars autem posito surgunt de semine, ut altae
castaneae nemorumque Iovi quae maxima frondet   15
aesculus atque habitae Grais oracula quercus.
C   pullulat ab radice aliis densissima silva,
ut cerasis ulmisque; etiam Parnasia laurus
parva sub ingenti matris se subicit umbra.
hos natura modos primum dedit, his genus omne   20
silvarum fruticumque viret nemorumque sacrorum.

A   sponte sua quae se tollunt in luminis oras,
infecunda quidem, sed laeta et fortia surgunt;
quippe solo natura subest. tamen haec quoque, si quis
inserat aut scrobibus mandet mutata subactis,   50
exuerint silvestrem animum cultuque frequenti
in quascumque voles artis haud tarda sequentur.
C   nec non et sterilis, quae stirpibus exit ab imis,
hoc faciat, vacuos si sit digesta per agros;
nunc altae frondes et rami matris opacant   55
crescentique adimunt fetus uruntque ferentem.
B   iam quae seminibus iactis se sustulit arbos
tarda venit seris factura nepotibus umbram,
pomaque degenerant sucos oblita priores
et turpis avibus praedam fert uva racemos.   60

(*G*. 2.9–21, 47–60)

First, trees differ in their way of propagation. For some arise on their own, with no humans applying force, and far and wide occupy fields and curving rivers, such as the yielding osier and the pliant broom, the poplar and the willow white with gleaming leaves. But others spring from fallen seed, such as tall chestnuts, the lofty durmast that makes leafy Jupiter's groves, and the oaks, considered oracles by the Greeks. In the case of others, dense undergrowth sprouts from the root, as with cherries and elms; the laurel of Parnassus, too, arises, tiny, underneath its mother's mighty shade. These methods nature provided first, by them grow all woods and shrubs and sacred groves... Those which lift themselves up spontaneously onto the shores of light are infertile, but arise lush and strong, for natural power is present in their soil. But even these, if someone grafts them or transplants them into dug-out holes, will shed their woodland spirit and, with eager cultivation, will follow willingly to whichever artifice you want. Even the sucker, which rises barren from the root below, will do the same if planted well spread-out on open fields. Now the lofty leaves and branches keep it in the shadow, depriving it of offspring as it grows and burning it as it would bear. And the tree that rises from fallen seeds grows slowly and will give shade only later, to our grandchildren; and its fruit degenerates, forgetting its earlier taste, and the vine bears wretched grapes, a prey fit for birds.

	διὰ τέχνης	
	sunt alii, quos ipse via sibi repperit usus.	
A	hic plantas tenero abscindens de corpore matrum	
B	deposuit sulcis, hic stirpes obruit arvo	
	quadrifidasque sudes et acuto robore vallos;	25
C	silvarumque aliae pressos propaginis arcus	
	exspectant et viva sua plantaria terra;	
	nil radicis egent aliae summumque putator	
	haud dubitat terrae referens mandare cacumen.	
D	quin et caudicibus sectis (mirabile dictu)	30
	truditur e sicco radix oleagina ligno;	
	et saepe alterius ramos inpune videmus	
E	vertere in alterius, mutatamque insita mala	
	ferre pirum et prunis lapidosa rubescere corna.	
	scilicet omnibus est labor impendendus, et omnes	
	cogendae in sulcum ac multa mercede domandae.	
DC	sed truncis oleae melius, propagine vites	
B	respondent, solido Paphiae de robore myrtus,	
A	plantis edurae coryli nascuntur et ingens	65
	fraxinus Herculeaeque arbos umbrosa coronae,	
	Chaoniique patris glandes; etiam ardua palma	
	nascitur et casus abies visura marinos.	
E	inseritur vero et fetu nucis arbutus horrida,	
	et steriles platani malos gessere valentis,	70
	castaneas fagus; ornusque incanuit albo	
	flore piri glandemque sues fregere sub ulmis.	

(*G.* 2.22–34, 61–72)

There are other methods which experience in its course discovered for itself. One man cuts off suckers from the mothers' tender body and places them in furrows, another covers stems with earth, both shafts split crosswise at the end and stakes with pointed tip. Other trees are waiting for the arch of layering and for shoots alive in their own soil; others do not need a root, and the pruner does not hesitate to entrust their treetop to the earth. And even from the dry wood of a cut-up trunk, the root of an olive tree is coaxed (what a tale of wonder!). And we often see how the one tree's branches turn into that of another, and how the pear, transformed, bears grafted apples, and how stony cornels grow red with plums... Of course, toil must be spent on all of them, and all must be forced into trenches and tamed with much effort. But olive trees grow best from trunks, vines come from layering, and Paphian myrtles from solid stems. From suckers come hardy hazels, the tall ash, the shady tree of Hercules' crown, and the acorns of the Chaonian father. The lofty palm also grows from them and the fir that will see the hazards of the sea. And the rugged arbutus is grafted with a walnut shoot, sterile planes bear healthy apples, and beeches chestnuts. The ash lights up with the white flower of the pear, and pigs munch on acorns under elms.

Thirteen lines on the three natural methods (with *natura* representing $\phi \upsilon \sigma \iota \kappa \acute{\omega} \tau \alpha \tau \alpha \iota$), from 9–21, find responsion in 47–60, while thirteen on propagation by man (22–34) find their responsion in 61–72, and the four methods at 23–31 are given in reverse order at 63–8. Stylistic embellishment and expansion, with mythological references, convert the dryness of Theophrastus' list, but the details are all in place. Seldom is Virgil so faithful to a technical source or so careful to preserve and give added emphasis to technical categories. His concern in lavishing such care on these categories was to underscore as much as possible the separation of Theophrastus' two classes of propagation—the natural and the cultivated.

Virgil saw in Theophrastus' account terminology and concepts which could be extended to have implications throughout the second book and indeed throughout the poem. The central issue of the *Georgics* involves the ways in which man copes with the world of *labor*. In the age of Saturn, everything was produced freely and spontaneously:

> in medium quaerebant, ipsaque tellus
> omnia liberius nullo poscente ferebat. (G. 1.127–8)

They contributed to the common good, and the earth herself bore everything of her own accord, without anybody demanding it.

Jupiter ended this situation so that the arts of civilization might be hammered out:

> ut varias usus meditando extunderet artis
> paulatim.   (G. 1.133–4)

...so that experience might by meditation gradually hammer out the various arts

The result was a cessation of nature's spontaneity and beneficence:

> labor omnia vicit
> improbus et duris urgens in rebus egestas.   (G. 1.145–6)

Insatiable toil occupied all areas of existence, and pressing need in harsh circumstances.

These lines represent the cultural realities of the poem, which depicts, with infinite complexity, the successes and failures of man after the Fall. The failures are apparent in books 1 and 3: the storms of spring, civil strife, the destructive power of *amor*, and the desolation brought by plague, all of which set man's work to nought. As the plough-ox dies, Virgil asks *quid labor aut benefacta iuvant?*, 'what good his toil and his services?' It is a question posed by the ox itself, by Virgil, and by the reader who has followed the progress of the book. The issues of the second book are more complex than those of the third, but the terms are similar. Virgil detected and developed Theophrastus' contrast between natural and cultural propagation of trees, but in doing so invoked not just the technical categories of his model but more importantly, the terminology and themes familiar from the cultural history and theodicy of *Georgics* 1. The natural methods of Theophrastus are accommodated to the language of the age of Saturn. Consider 2.10–11, *namque aliae nullis hominum cogentibus ipsae | sponte sua veniunt*; or the corresponding line 47, *sponte sua quae se tollunt in luminis oras*. Theophrastus' αὐτόμαται is the technical impulse, but it is Virgil's own poetry which provides the real basis for the diction and, ultimately, for the thought—note again the description of the world in the age of Saturn (1.127–8): *ipsaque tellus | omnia liberius nullo poscente ferebat*. On the other hand there is line 22 of book 2, encapsulating the cultivated methods (*sunt alii, quos ipsa via sibi repperit usus*); and its corresponding line, 61 (*scilicet omnibus est labor impendendus*). Again the impulse is in Theophrastus (αἱ δὲ ἄλλαι τέχνης), but the terms are really from the same passage in *Georgics* 1, where it is practical experience which in the age of Jupiter will hammer out the arts of toil (133): *ut varias usus meditando extunderet artis*.

Theophrastus' divisions are converted into a virtual metaphor which is applied throughout *Georgics* 2—some trees belong to cultivation, or to the age of Jupiter, while others, which originate without cultivation, are representative of the age of Saturn. After establishing these terms by referring to the theodicy of *Georgics* 1, Virgil promotes, with distortion, an arboricultural method of relatively little importance in Theophrastus, namely grafting. As I noted earlier,[47] the method is absent from Theophrastus' opening paragraph, and where it occurs it only applies to trees of the same genus (*Caus. pl.* 2.5.3). For Virgil, however, grafting assumes great importance, unjustified by technical realities: at 32–4, 69–72, and 78–82—that is, at the ends of successive technical paragraphs[48]—Virgil presents a number of grafts, most, if not all, of which are impossible, and which are so phrased as to suggest that the process has transformed the natural world and made it unrecognizable. This is particularly the case at 80–2:

> nec longum tempus et ingens
> exiit ad caelum ramis felicibus arbos
> miratastque novas frondes et non sua poma.

Shortly thereafter an enormous tree rises to the sky with flourishing branches and marvels at its new leaves and at fruit that is not its own.

The closest parallel to this wording is not encouraging. In the pseudo-Virgilian *Ciris* Scylla, daughter of Nisus, reacts to her own metamorphosis (81–2): *heu quotiens mirata novos expalluit artus | ipsa suos* ('alas, how often did she herself pale in wonder at her new limbs'). Here, too, we find surprise at a transformation imposed on the subject. Virgil, then, promotes the subject of grafting so as to

---

[47] Cf. above.
[48] Always a place of prominence, as we saw in the use of mythological sequence; cf. above.

place it in a position out of proportion to its actual importance, and uses it as an example of the extremes to which arboriculture can extend and of the effects which it produces on the natural world.

As would be expected, the remainder of *Georgics* 2 focuses not so much on naturally propagated types, which are of less importance to man in the age of Jupiter, but precisely on those which are cultivated. After a general treatment of soils at 177–258, Virgil turns to the chief subject of the book, and the focus of such cultivation, namely the vine. For 160 lines he treats the application of the *artes* of *labor* to viticulture, treating the planting and care of the young vines, pruning, staking, and so on. In distinction to the movements of books 1 and 3, this labor seems to find success. The work is hard (*durus uterque labor*, 412), and the activity is depicted as a form of warfare.[49] In the end, however, the vine, unlike the crops and cattle of books 1 and 3, is standing and producing according to man's will. After 160 lines on the vine, Virgil turns to the representative of the spontaneous tree, the olive, which receives a bare six lines: *contra non ulla est oleis cultura* ('olive trees in turn do not require cultivation', 420). The olive yard needs no pruning, no heavy mattocks, none of the labor needed for the vine; just open up the earth around the olive, and it will produce in plenty: *hoc pinguem et placitam Paci nutritor oliuam* ('in this way tend to the fat olive, beloved of Peace', 425). Now Varro gives equal emphasis to vines and olives, and Cato (*Agr.* 10–11) states that an olive yard of 240 *iugera* needs a staff of 13 and lists 396 pieces of equipment, while for a vineyard of 100 iugera (the more space-intensive tree) he prescribes 16 workers and 382 pieces of equipment. Virgil's sharp distinction is motivated by symbolic, rather than agronomical, considerations. Against all the technical realities he sets the olive, specified as the tree of peace, outside the realm of cultivation, which is to say the realm of Jupiter, the age in which the agricultural struggle is conducted in the poem. After briefly treating various other spontaneous trees, all of which have their uses, Virgil returns to the cultivated tree whose care has preoccupied him throughout the book:

---

[49] Cf. above.

> quid memorandum aeque Baccheia dona tulerunt?
> Bacchus et ad culpam causas dedit; ille furentis
> Centauros leto domuit, Rhoetumque Pholumque
> et magno Hylaeum Lapithis cratere minantem.   (*G.* 2.454–7)

What have the gifts of Bacchus brought that would be equally worthy of praise? Bacchus has also given cause for crime; he laid the raving Centaurs low in death, Rhoetus and Pholus and Hylaeus, threatening the Lapiths with a great mixing-bowl.

At this point the technical material of the second book ends: that is, it ends with an attack on the vine, what Servius recognized as a formal piece of denunciation, a *vituperatio vitis*. The lines are an embarrassment to the critics, who generally see book 2 simply as extolling the virtues of toil: Servius claimed to know of some who read *et quae* for *aeque*; Peerlkamp and Forbiger (but nobody since) took the most convenient expedient of ejecting all four lines, Page ignores them, Conington thinks that Virgil lost control of the poem at this point, and R. D. Williams states that 'the final lines are playful';[50] Otis, for whom book 2 represents the 'happy cooperation, through *labor*, of man and nature', simply calls them a 'splendid conclusion',[51] while Wilkinson at least writes that the lines 'seem an odd and unsatisfactory conclusion to Book 2.'[52] On the contrary, the attack on the vine is completely satisfactory and is indeed a 'splendid conclusion', if seen as the climax of the opposition between nature and culture which informs the second book. The olive, the Saturnian tree of peace which grows without culture and produces in abundance, receives a mere six lines. Viticulture, on the other hand, receives the focus throughout. In viticulture lies the success which is possible in the age of Jupiter, provided the struggle is pursued with great toil, and is conducted as a kind of warfare against the resurgences of nature. Viticulture itself succeeds, but in the end the product of that success is morally vitiated. This amounts in itself to a spiritual failure which is hard to put into words—a failure which will be reflected in the actions of Aristaeus in the climax of the fourth

---

[50] R. D. Williams 1979: 173.
[51] Otis 1964: 168.   [52] Wilkinson 1969: 184.

book and which is ultimately more disturbing than the simple failures of books 1 and 3.[53]

As Varro did for the third book, so for the second Theophrastus provided Virgil with the terminology, with the technical categories, and with the basis of his vision, and to that extent the *Historia Plantarum*, like the *Res Rusticae* and the entire agronomical tradition, is a vital and indispensable component of the *Georgics*. But like all the diverse components of this poem, even when they appear in virtual translation, Theophrastus' prose treatise ultimately becomes unrecognizable as it is developed, transformed, and magnified to take its place in the complexity of Virgil's poetic world. It was Virgil's vision to see in the world of the farmer, in the soil, in weeds and in trees, in the balances and imbalances on which the farmer's survival depends, in the world of the ox and the world of the bee, a world of the spirit which exists not only on the farm or in Italy two millennia ago, but in general in the human endeavor, throughout all time and in every place.

[53] For a somewhat different approach to the vituperation of the vine see Ross 1987: 144–5.

4

Authorial Rhetoric in Virgil's *Georgics*

Richard Rutherford

I

The relation between the didactic poet and his addressee was an ambiguous one from the start. Already in Hesiod, the situation of Perses seems to shift according to the poet's tone and purpose.[1] Much that Lucretius says in his great poem seems more fittingly addressed to everyman, or at any rate a more ordinary man, than to the philistine consular Memmius. Even in shorter poetry with a didactic tendency (Horace's *Epistles* come to mind), it may be hard to define the exact point at which the writer moves from personal address to an individual patron or friend, to a more broadly didactic stance, where he seems to be speaking to all mankind. The distinction is related to the contrast between poet as individual and poet as *vates* or prophetic bard.

In the *Georgics* the situation is rather more complex, for an obvious reason. The poem is formally dedicated to Maecenas, who is named at the opening of each book, but it is also in a sense addressed to Caesar, the future Augustus, who is more prominent in the proem, and is referred to or invoked, often in the most

---

This paper was originally included in a volume of essays in honour of Professor D. A. Russell (Innes, Hine, and Pelling (eds.) 1995: 19–29), and began with an expression of some personal debts to that scholar. These initial remarks are omitted here. The piece appears otherwise largely unchanged from its original version; translations by the author have been added.

[1] M. L. West 1978: 33–40; Bowie 1993: 23.

grandiose terms, at important points thereafter. The bulk of the poem, however, is conceived as instructions to farmers, who are defined as the chosen audience in the proem and addressed at various stages later (1.101 *agricolae*, 210, 2.35–6, 3.288 *coloni*, 420 *pastor*). There is no need to waste space on the misconceived enquiry as to whether farmers would really read a poem like the *Georgics*, or whether Virgil really hoped to convince Caesar of the need for (say) a more traditional agricultural strategy: most scholars would answer both questions with an unhesitating negative. What concerns us here is the rhetorical and poetic consequences which follow from this split of addressees. Recent work on poetic 'voices' seems not to have considered this topic systematically. A simple model of the process by which a poem is communicated to its public postulates a direct relationship between poet and audience: the poet, as it were, reads aloud, speaking directly to that audience, as Virgil is said to have read the *Georgics* to Maecenas and Octavian until his voice gave out. In reality things are of course more complex: in poetry, as in oratory, we often find a number of addressees who may respond to or appreciate different aspects of the performance.[2] A subtler model might distinguish the actual author from the poet as seen or implied in the poem, and identify an implied addressee also distinguishable from 'real people' in contemporary society.[3] In what follows I offer some observations on a number of aspects of this relationship between 'poet' and 'addressee', which I hope will unite rhetorical analysis and interpretation.

The first general point is that, given this situation, Virgil's role as poet is inevitably an ambiguous one. On the one hand, he is a learned poet, writing for a sophisticated, wealthy, and highly literate audience; on the other, he is posing as an experienced countryman, practical and thorough, sometimes naïve or superstitious, giving advice to men of the soil, probably not men of great substance,

---

[2] Thus in Cicero's *Pro Caelio*, to take a simple case, the orator at various points addresses the prosecutors Atratinus and Herennius, and of course Clodia: he also plays the parts of Appius Claudius and Clodius in prosopopoiia; all of this is, in one way or another, intended to have an effect on the jury. A further aspect is opened up by the publication of speeches: once the case is over, the reader may be allowed to enjoy what the jurors missed (cf. Quint. 2.17.21 on the *Pro Cluentio*).

[3] Cf. de Jong 1987, etc.

advice which to Maecenas or Caesar would often seem trivial or sordid (brought out esp. at 1.79–81, 176–7; cf. 3.289–90, 4.3).[4] This is not to deny that Virgil is himself (at least in upbringing) a countryman, nor that distinguished figures might take pleasure in the activities of the country and even the down-to-earth practicalities of harvest-time or grape-picking.[5] But the contrast between Alexandrian-neoteric ingenuity and didactic detail and prosiness is a real one, and there is ample evidence in the poem to suggest that Virgil was aware of it, and indeed that he exploited it to achieve particular effects, for instance by humorous transitions from the grand to the low, from the sublime to the commonplace.

The poet's formal statements of his subject provide an illuminating starting-point. The opening lines summarize the topics of the four books: crops and seasons, vines, cattle and sheep, bees; they do not, however, give any indication of the moral, philosophic, and religious themes which give depth and breadth to these expositions. After the apocalyptic vision of war and despair at the end of Book 1, the poet opens Book 2 with a deliberately down-to-earth, even prosaic résumé: *hactenus arvorum cultus et sidera caeli* ('thus far the cultivation of the fields and heaven's stars'). The line sums up the first book once more in terms suited to the simple farming manual rather than the poem which has expanded its scope to include contemporary politics and the reflection of these events in cosmic terms. The concluding sphragis to Book 4 plays the same game: *haec super arvorum cultu pecorumque canebam | et super arboribus* ('thus did I sing of the care of fields and herds and of trees', 559–60)—no hint of Aristaeus and Orpheus, or even of the bees, only a minimal statement of the poem's subject-matter. Comparable are the many passages where the countryman yields place to the bard and vice versa, often involving a humorous anticlimax as we return to more down-to-earth advice or seemingly prosaic material (e.g. 2.288, 345, 3.286, 384).[6]

---

[4] Cf. Perkell 1989: 40.
[5] Cf. Cic. *Cato Maior* 51–60; rather differently, *De Or.* 2.22, echoed by Hor. *Serm.* 2.1.71–4. Later, note also Marcus Aurelius to Fronto, p. 62 van den Hout (1.180–2 Haines).
[6] See further 1.284 (incongruous juxtapositions in the 'Days' passage); 2.177 (from *laudes Italiae* to differing types of soil); 4.228 (after the sublimity of the bees' relation to the divine mind, back to the precise but earthbound detail of unsealing

The poet also presents himself as sharing in, observing, or affected by the country life which he praises and describes. This has obvious advantages for the exposition: rather than receiving impersonal admonitions, the reader is offered (so it appears) the fruits of experience. The poet's own recollection of pleasures and disappointments, his hopes and misgivings, raise the emotional temperature and vary the more obvious but potentially tedious sequences of imperatives. It is common sense (and sound rhetorical technique) for a speaker to emphasize what he has learned from the past.[7] Sometimes the authorial involvement goes further, as Virgil visualizes himself as part of a rural community: *ergo rite suum Baccho* dicemus *honorem* | *carminibus patriis lancesque et liba* feremus... ('and so *we shall give* Bacchus his proper praise, as the ritual requires, in songs passed down by our fathers, and *we shall bring* him platters and cakes', 2.393–4; cf. 192 ff.). Or he may celebrate a near-ecstatic self-surrender to the delights of country life (2.486–7, part of a larger context to which we shall return). Rapturous pleasure in his subject-matter is also important in the transitional passage half-way through Book 3, where the poet reminds himself that time is fleeting by, *singula dum capti circumvectamur amore* ('while we linger over every detail, captivated by love', 285). There is word-play here: on the one hand he means love of his subject, on the other 'by love'—which has been the subject, for the last 80 lines.[8] Realistic detail is mingled with mild self-mockery as he exclaims apotropaically at the dangers of sea-travel (1.456–7 *non illa quisquam me nocte per altum* | *ire... moneat*,

---

the hive—though even here *augustam* and *thesauris* preserve a certain grandeur). Cf. Wilkinson 1969: 71 ff.

[7] e.g. Hom. *Il.* 1.259 ff.; Thuc. 3.37.1; Arist. *Rhet.* 1393a23–b4, 1394a5–8.

[8] Rather similarly, perhaps, in *Ecl.* 6.10–11: *si quis tamen haec quoque, si quis* | *captus amore leget*... ('yet still, if anyone is prepared to read these words too, anyone to do so through love's compulsion...'). The passage in the *Georgics* is an example of a metaphorical usage common in classical literature, whereby the writer speaks of himself as doing, or as otherwise involved in, the actions he describes: cf. Macleod 1983: 205; Nisbet and Hubbard 1978 *ad* Hor. *Carm.* 2.1.18; Lieberg 1982 and 1985; and e.g. 'Longinus' 9.11, 14 (if πλάνος is right), 15.4; also Gibbon, *Decline and Fall of the Roman Empire*, Ch. 42: '*I shall lead* the Arabs to the conquest of Syria, Egypt, and Africa, the provinces of the Roman empire; nor *can I check* their victorious career till they have overthrown the monarchies of Persia and Spain' (my italics). In the *Georgics* cf. also 3.340: is *prosequar* there a pun on the poet pursuing the travelling nomads?

'let no one advise me to go forth on the deep on such a night'),[9] or dreads the attack of a snake while he basks in the sun (3.435–6 *ne mihi tum mollis sub divo carpere somnos | neu dorso nemoris libeat iacuisse per herbas*, 'never at that time of year may I be tempted to snatch soothing sleep under god's sky, nor to recline in the grass on a wooded hillside').[10] Elsewhere he adopts a didactic role in a more explicit way, issuing edicts and organizing herdsmen or beekeepers (3.295 *edico*, 300 *iubeo*, 329 *iubebo*, 4.264 *suadebo*). Yet this device can easily glide into more 'literary' poses: thus the superficially similar opening at 3.440 *morborum quoque te causas et signa docebo* ('I shall also instruct you in causes of diseases and their symptoms') carries more than a hint of the learned didacticism of Nicander (cf. *Ther.* 528).

More serious is an interesting series of claims to 'autopsy' running through Book 1: for the didactic writer, as for the historian, to have observed something personally adds to one's credibility and authority.[11] At 1.193 and 197 (*semina vidi...vidi lecta diu...*, 'I have seen the seeds...I have seen how, though chosen long in advance...'), an account of the tendency of grain to turn bad passes into memorable generalizations about natural decline: the prudent countryman becomes the sombre voice of wisdom. In 318 the scene that the poet claims to have witnessed is grander and wilder, as he describes violent winds clashing in combat, with the world in flood and the king of the gods hurling thunderbolts. At the climax of the book, the same technique is employed with a difference: the verb is in the plural, as the poet speaks for his generation: *quotiens Cyclopum effervere in agros | vidimus undantem ruptis fornacibus Aetnam* ('how often we beheld Etna's furnaces exploding, and the seething lava gushing forth over the Cyclopean fields', 471–2; cf. 502 *luimus*, 503 *nobis*). Here the scenes witnessed are of chaos and unnatural disorder on a cosmic scale. The concerns of both poet and poem are

---

[9] The misgivings are traditional in the genre: cf. Hes. *Op.* 618–94; Arat. *Phaen.* 110–11.
[10] Compare further 2.252–3, 3.513, and perhaps 1.448 *heu*.
[11] Cf. Nisbet and Hubbard 1970 *ad* Hor. *Carm.* 1.2.13 (where Horace is imitating Virgil); also Macleod 1983: 92 n. 14. For the historiographical background see Schepens 1980.

extended in a way quite unexpected as we read the earlier parts of the book.

The author's use of the first person does not exist in isolation: as suggested above, it must be discussed along with the relation of the author to his addressee. I exclude here the special case of apostrophe addressed to inanimate objects or places (e.g. the high-flown compliments paid to wines at 2.95–6, 102, rivers at 2.159–60, etc.).[12] Simple general address to *agricolae* and the like has already been mentioned. For variation, instruction can be conveyed not only in the second person singular or plural imperatives, but also by first plural indicatives (e.g. 1.257), or by jussive subjunctives, whether first person plural or third person singular (1.343) or plural. Most of these devices create a more vivid or dramatized scene; often, too, they stress the sympathetic collaboration of the poet, as in 2.393–4, already quoted. Similarly in Book 4, it is '*our* misfortunes' (251, *casus... nostros*) which are shared by the bees, also vulnerable to disease and death; and it is 'for us', including the poet, that some god has devised a remedy (315).

Variety of tone and pace can also be achieved by questions, which add a sense of urgency and challenge (1.56, 2.433, 3.103, 250 *nonne vides...?*), or by interjections (1.63 *ergo age*, 3.515 *ecce*). In one passage alarm and urgent calls for action are vividly dramatized as the poet affects to spy a threatening snake: *cape saxa manu, cape robora, pastor, | tollentemque minas et sibila colla tumentem | deice!* ('grab stones, shepherd, grab sticks, and strike him down as he rears threateningly, as his hissing throat swells!', 3.420 ff.) Sometimes the poet attributes a particular reaction or emotion to the addressee: wonder (4.197), misgiving (1.335 *hoc metuens*, 459, 4.239), and even fear (3.408 *horrebis*). He himself shares in their experiences and, despite his position of authority, admits his own dismay at alarming signs, and waxes eloquent on the transience of human success (3.66–8): in this last passage, *miseris mortalibus* (not, for instance, *agrestibus*) reminds us that the poem is concerned with more than just the farming community.

---

[12] In his commentary on 1.215 R. F. Thomas 1988 remarks that Virgil's apostrophes and personifications become more frequent in Books 2 and 3: he does not develop the observation, which might repay further study.

II

The poet's self-presentation involves further complexities which affect our interpretation of the poem's generic status, and perhaps also its meaning.

In the above discussion invocations were not considered, but since these bear on the overall tone of the work, they require some comment here. The elaborate proem to Book 1 juxtaposes the twelve gods of the countryside with the living yet near-divine Caesar, placing the rural and poetic alongside the political, however fantastically conceived. The end of the book obviously echoes this beginning, but in a darker mood, with more Roman concerns reflected in the sonorous invocation of *di patrii Indigetes*...—no Alexandrian cleverness here, but native tradition and patriotic anxiety, even national guilt (501–2). The fantasy of Caesar being translated among the constellations, which in the proem seemed extravagant and fanciful, in the manner of Callimachus' *Lock of Berenice*, is echoed in more sombre terms at lines 503 ff., in which the poet fears that Caesar, the potential saviour, may be taken from them before he has done his vital work. The invoking of Bacchus in Book 2 (2.388) and Pales in Book 3 (3.294) require no discussion: they are the appropriate deities for the subjects under discussion. In Book 4 the only figure directly addressed in the proem is Maecenas, but Apollo's blessing is hoped for. At 4.315 the new invocation to the Muses indicates a change to a more epic register, in preparation for the new phase of narrated mythology, the epyllion of Aristaeus. The Muses have not been involved in the composition of the *Georgics* so far, as 2.475 and 3.11 involve anticipation of future work. We are led to expect something grander in store, and our expectations are fulfilled by the imitations of Homeric epic, the introduction of speeches, the divine cast of characters, and the supernatural settings, beneath the sea and in the underworld. If the appeal to the Muses does indeed mark a shift in poetic style and ambition, it is perhaps appropriate that the narrative in the second half of the book should include as a central figure one of the great poets of myth.

Different issues arise with passages in which the poet's own role or status is defined or explored at greater length: esp. 1.1–5, 2.475–94,

3.1–48, 284–94, and 4.559–66.[13] In these passages we can find different conceptions of what a poet is or should be, what the worth and value of poet to community may be—questions which we know to have been aired in late Republican and Augustan Rome.[14] The main proem implies a view of the poet as a teacher, helping the ignorant countrymen with the support of a far greater helper, Caesar himself (1.41 *ignarosque viae mecum miseratus agrestis*, 'sharing my pity for the countryfolk who do not know the way'). Elsewhere this alignment of poet with ruler takes other forms. In the second book, at the climax of the *laudes Italiae*, Caesar and Virgil are both benefactors of Italy, the one defending her against foreign dangers, the other drawing upon fresh sources abroad to enrich her poetry (2.170–6).[15]

These concerns come together in a different way in the last part of Book 2 and the proem to Book 3.[16] Both passages set Virgil apart from the rural life he describes. In Book 2 this is because he shows himself to be aware of the real meaning and value of that life, which the ordinary countryman is not (458–9), and because he aspires to the higher themes of natural philosophy,[17] while accepting that he is unlikely to reach these austere heights of wisdom (475–86). In Book 3 a more positive note is struck, but again one which tends to separate the poet from his present subject-matter. Here Virgil seems eager to move on to a quite different, but again more ambitious project, a poem that will glorify Caesar, his victories and his ancestors. Here there is no hesitation or self-doubt, but exhilaration and ambition: in this, the most magniloquent of Virgil's self-characterizations, he himself is both encomiast of Caesar and triumphant victor in his

---

[13] On 4.116–48 see R. F. Thomas 1982*a*: 56–60.

[14] Cf. G. Williams 1968: 31–7, esp. on Cic. *Arch.* and Hor. *Epist.* 2.1; Newman 1967*a*: Ch. 4; Brink 1963: e.g. 199–209.

[15] Space forbids discussion of recent interpretations which detect negative and disturbing elements in the *laudes Italiae* (see R. F. Thomas 1982*a*: 36–51; the briefer account in his commentary seems to me much less satisfactory, esp. in his repeated use of the term 'lying'). While sympathetic to some of the points made, I feel that it is important not to underestimate the positive elements.

[16] The two passages are considered and compared from different points of view by Buchheit 1972: 45 ff. and P. R. Hardie 1986: 33–51.

[17] Innes 1979; P. R. Hardie 1986: Chs. 1–2, a book from which I have learned much.

own right.[18] It is almost with reluctance that he slackens his pace and returns to his present addressee (41) and his current project: the immediacy and anticipation of the encomiastic poem return in the last three lines of the proem (46 ff. esp. *mox... accingar*).

Again, the interpreter of poetry of this refined complexity must guard against too literal a reading. The two passages should not be read naïvely as the outpourings of an emotional poet prone to self-contradiction; nor should we assume that different dates of composition sufficiently explain the different attitudes presented in them.[19] The motives will include a desire to pay tribute to Lucretius, Virgil's greatest Latin model, and a wish to celebrate the successes of the victorious Caesar and (perhaps more important) what they meant for Italy. But within the poetic world of the *Georgics* we may also see that these passages perform other functions. Both enlarge the scope of the poem's concerns. The first makes explicit the concern with nature and with the need to understand her ways, of which we have so far had only hints;[20] a stronger note of moralistic approval for the country life also enters. The other passage, the proem to Book 3, recalls the military language used in the first book and horrifically deployed in its finale; developed in the praise of Italy, where Caesar was seen as defending the frontiers of the empire (2.170–2), this language is now used in a celebratory spirit, with wars won abroad and civil conflict forgotten. The *Georgics* is a poem much concerned with Italy, its fertility and beauty, its great potential for peace and prosperity.[21] In these passages, first the strength of Italy is described as resting on rural values associated with a primitive past, remote from and yet intertwined with intestinal violence; then, in Book 3,

---

[18] See further Buchheit 1972.

[19] Even a psychological reading as subtle as that of P. R. Hardie 1986: 44, 46–7 seems to me unsatisfactory unless complemented by an account of the function of these passages within the poem as it stands.

[20] Notably at 1.410–23 (the passage on the birds' premonitions), esp. 415 *haud equidem credo*; rather differently, 2.325–6, on the origins of the world and the union of Earth and Sky (Aether suggests a philosophic tone, cf. Eur. *Chrysipp.* fr. 898 N., Lucr. 1.250 ff., and other passages cited by Mynors 1990 *ad loc*). Much more ambitious claims for Virgil's philosophic content are advanced by Ross 1987.

[21] Doreen Innes suggests that the audience of the poem may be seen particularly as inhabitants of Italian townships, an area between city and country: thus Hesiodic song is being translated to Roman *oppida* (2.176), and Mantua is prominent in

patriotic pride supersedes learned mythology, now dismissed as a hackneyed tune (3.3–9). Whereas Virgil had faltered at the thought of tackling philosophy, he now warms to the project of panegyrical epic; yet the lofty strains of the proem do not entirely purge the reader's memories of the quietism and uneasy detachment from the political and military world which characterized the finale of Book 2. There are connections between the passages (both, for example, emphasize the poet's debt to Greece and Greek poetry), but the transition is startling, the means of reconciliation elusive.

By contrast, the conclusion of Book 4 opposes Caesar and Virgil, contrasting their careers and concerns. Caesar now seems remote and scarcely human, while Virgil's own efforts, summarized in banal terms (559–60), are seen as trivial, the product of inglorious ease in luxurious Naples. The passage, which associates his present work with the 'play' of the *Eclogues* (565), seems to represent a retreat, however ironic, from serious claims for his poetry.

III

As in the bucolic poems of his earlier years, Virgil repeatedly extends the scope of his formal subject and genre, both in his digressions and in the passages (such as the opening of Book 3) in which he points beyond what he has achieved to what could come later, or what he might achieve were his poetic gifts sufficient, or his powers fully mature. The literal or biographical sense of these passages (was he really engaged on a Trojan epic? would he really have turned to philosophy in his old age?) is less important than their effect in the overall context of the *Georgics*.[22] Self-praise needs to be balanced

---

3.12 ff. (reversing the sadder allusion at 2.198?). The ambiguities of Virgil's attitude to the country-city opposition may thus be related to the ambiguities of addressee; yet also, as a matter of historical fact, these townships would include persons of culture and devotion to the land, apt readers for such a poem (cf. Cic. *De Or.* 3.43, *nostri* [sc. Romans] *minus student litteris quam Latini*, 'our own folk are less devoted to literary pursuit than the Latin peoples').

[22] On such passages as a literary device see Ogilvie and Richmond 1967 *ad* Tac. *Agr.* 3.3; Woodman 1975: 287–8; and e.g. Dion. Hal. *Dem.* 58 fin.

by self-protection:[23] through such gestures Virgil draws attention, without excessive display of pride, to what he has in fact achieved (as in the passage which pays tribute to Lucretius in Book 2). While hugely extending the poem's range beyond its ostensible subject-matter, he regularly stresses that he must be selective (2.42, 3.284, 4.147), and also shows his awareness of the limited nature of his actual achievement; perhaps, in fact, his work is in the end play...but the reader will have to judge. The ambiguity of the poet's role, as teacher or entertainer, Lucretian instructor in cosmic truths or deft craftsman of Alexandrian artifice, committed supporter of Caesarian Italy or leisured versifier, reflects the complexity of poetry's relation to society in general. The story of Orpheus explores on a different, mythical plane the question of what poetry can and cannot achieve.[24]

The haunting inset story about Orpheus, which has called forth so many different readings, can only be treated selectively here.[25] It is natural, however, to associate Virgil with his fellow-poet (as ancient critics already saw Homer behind the bard Demodocus in *Odyssey* 8).[26] That identification need not be unqualified, and we may suspect, as with the song of Silenus in *Eclogue* 6, that the more plangent and self-indulgent aspects of his song represent only part of Virgil's own poetic range.[27] If, however, we see Aristaeus and Orpheus as opposed personalities, one passage in the most moving part of the epyllion leaps to our attention: the lines in which the singer is compared with a nightingale whose young have been stolen away by an *arator*:

> qualis populea maerens philomela sub umbra
> amissos queritur fetus, quos durus arator

---

[23] Cf. Plut. *On Inoffensive Self-Praise* (esp. 539b–d, 541e, 542ab, passages which concern literary figures). For the ethical background see Betz 1978: 373–7, and also Russell 1993.
[24] Cf. Rutherford 1989, a paper in which I tried to argue that the *Eclogues* similarly show a preoccupation with different paths of poetry and what they might offer a poet disturbed by the political turmoil of his time.
[25] For a brief satirical survey of recent views see J. Griffin 1985: 163–4.
[26] e.g. Σ EV on *Od.* 8. 63; cf. further P. R. Hardie 1986: 54–6.
[27] Somewhat similarly J. Griffin 1985: 173–6; cf. Rutherford 1989: 45, 47.

> observans nido implumis detraxit; at illa
> flet noctem, ramoque sedens miserabile carmen
> integrat, et maestis late loca questibus implet. (4.511–15)

...just as the nightingale mourns her lost brood, under the shade of a poplar, those nestlings whom a stern ploughman has spotted and snatched away unfledged from the nest; but the mother grieves all night long, and seated on a branch renews her song of sorrow, filling the region all around with her melancholy lament.

Here *durus*, formerly a term suggesting virtuous toughness and manliness, comes closer to 'callous, cruel', and the passage goes further than its model, Catullus 11, in that the farmer's act here is premeditated (unlike the random action of the plough in the lyric poem). Further, although we have seen the poet advocating ruthlessness and harsh action by the farmer in earlier passages (e.g. 3.95–6, 468–9, 4.106–7), those acts were normally justified by efficiency or the greater good; here, the cruelty of the *arator* seems unmotivated.[28] In short, the reader senses a gap opening up between farmer and poet, Aristaeus and Virgil; the poet of the *Georgics* appeals to a broader range of sympathies than those of farmers and realists.[29] Although it is over-schematic to assume equivalences between Aristaeus and Caesar, Orpheus and Virgil, it is perhaps not surprising that the subsequent sphragis sets the two Roman figures in contrast with one another: *bello* contrasts with *oti*, *Euphraten* with *Parthenope*, *dat iura* with *carmina lusi*. In a sense poetry is dependent on politics: Caesar needs to be victorious for Virgil to be able to enjoy his literary pursuits. Yet at the same time Caesar's conquests, like Aristaeus' miraculous recovery of his bees, are not the whole story.

These comments, which range from small-scale stylistic observations to overall lines of interpretation, are both sketchy and selective: they cannot hope to do justice to the richness of a long and highly sophisticated poem, still less serve as a substitute for a rereading. This essay can perhaps illuminate certain patterns and ideas in the poem,

---

[28] We should of course note that Proteus is actually speaking the lines in question; but we are given no particular reason to suppose that his words are to be viewed with any scepticism.

[29] For further comments on this passage see Perkell 1989: 48–9,184, and elsewhere.

without obscuring or doing justice to the far larger and subtler design of the artist. That criticism has a place, but one which must remain subordinate to the work of art, is one of the simple but vital truths which, with characteristic modesty and firmness, Donald Russell has regularly affirmed.[30]

[30] e.g. Russell 1973: 116; Russell 1981: 171–2.

5

Virgil's Metamorphoses: Myth and Allusion in the *Georgics*

Monica R. Gale

> felix qui potuit rerum cognoscere causas
> atque metus omnis et inexorabile fatum
> subiecit pedibus strepitumque Acherontis avari.
> fortunatus et ille deos qui novit agrestis
> Panaque Silvanumque senem Nymphasque sorores.
> (G. 2.490–4)

Happy is he who has been able to learn the causes of things, and has trampled underfoot every fear, and unyielding Fate, and the din of greedy Acheron. Fortunate, too, is he who knows the rustic gods, Pan and old Silvanus and the sister Nymphs.

In these famous words, Virgil expresses his ambivalent relationship with his great didactic model, Lucretius.[1] The double *makarismos* suggests a declaration of allegiance to two incompatible views of the world: the rationalist philosophy of Epicurus and a nostalgic longing for the simple rustic piety which the Romans of the late Republic and early Empire were so fond of attributing to the farmer and the

---

This article, originally published in 1995, was in the nature of a preliminary study for my book, *Virgil on the Nature of Things* (2000). Much of the above material is reworked in chapters 3 and 4 of the book: see esp. 123–42 for a fuller treatment of the mythological allusions discussed in §3. In this volume, the paper appears in its original 1995 version, with minor corrections and the addition of translations.

[1] Some critics have denied that the lines refer specifically to Lucretius (see e.g. Boyancé 1980, Novara 1982, R. F. Thomas 1988). The concentration of Lucretian language in 475–92, however, makes the reference certain. Cf. P. R. Hardie 1986: 33–51.

countryman. How are we to explain this strange contradiction, which lies at the very heart of Virgil's poem, in one of its most overtly programmatic passages?

The question is connected with two areas of debate which have dominated discussion of the poem over the last few decades. Is the *Georgics* an optimistic work, reflecting a belief in Providence and celebrating the end of the Civil Wars and the beginning of a new Golden Age; or is it a pessimistic work, painting a gloomy picture of a world dominated by conflict and failure and expressing a covert hostility towards the new regime?[2] And how are we to evaluate Virgil's relationship with his models? Is the *Georgics* really an *Ascraeum carmen*, a *De rerum natura*, or a work of Alexandrian *doctrina*, superficially concerned with agriculture, but really more interested in learned allusion, scholarly debate and ultimately in poetry itself?[3] Thomas, in particular, has argued that Hesiod and Lucretius are really far less important to Virgil than Callimachus and Homeric epic, which is transformed in characteristically Alexandrian fashion.

This multiplicity of views may be significant in itself. The optimism/pessimism debate seems to me somewhat sterile, but I suggest that it has arisen in part from the nature of the poem itself, and in particular from the complex network of intertextual relations which underlies it. The enormous discrepancy between the various readings of the poem may be attributed to its polyphonic character.[4] There is no single authorial voice guiding the reader through the text, but rather a multiplicity of voices which come to the fore one after another. Thus, one voice tells us that Jupiter is a benevolent father, another that he wilfully destroys the farmer's hard-won harvest. One

---

[2] The main representatives of the former view are Otis 1964, Wilkinson 1969 and (with some qualifications) Mynors 1990. The latter view has been more popular in recent years: see especially Putnam 1979, Miles 1980, Ross 1987, R. F. Thomas 1988. [Since the original publication of this article, the 'optimist' interpretation has enjoyed something of a revival: see now (2006) esp. Morgan 1999 and—less persuasively—Jenkyns 1998 and Cramer 1998; Cramer's reading, it should be said, relies on the wholesale excision of lines which would otherwise present problems for his interpretation. For 'political' readings of the poem which attempt to move beyond the 'Augustan'/'anti-Augustan' polarity, see also Cadili 2001 and Nappa 2005.]

[3] For Virgil and Hesiod, see especially Wilkinson 1969: 56–60; for Virgil and Lucretius, Farrington 1958 and 1963, Buchheit 1972 and Nethercut 1973; for Virgil, Callimachus and Homer, R. F. Thomas 1986 and 1988, and Farrell 1991.

[4] On the polyphonic character of the poem, cf. Perkell 1989 and Lyne 1993.

voice tells us that the farmer's life is one of unremitting toil, another that the Earth pours forth food for him of her own accord. The 'optimist' critic will say that the more positive voice predominates, while the 'pessimist' will say that it is undermined by the negative one. My own line of approach is rather different. It seems to me that Virgil is not concerned to give us a straightforward view of the world, either positive or negative. On the contrary, the contradictions express different possibilities, contributing to a picture of the world which is complex, uncertain and shifting: the same state of affairs can be explained in quite different ways, like the proverbial half-full (or half-empty) bottle.

The polyphonic character of the poem is intimately connected with Virgil's use of his models. Leaving aside Callimachus and Homer (whose importance cannot be fully discussed here), each of the main intertexts views the world in a different way. For Lucretius, there is no Providence, and death and decay are inevitable; on the other hand, happiness is easy to attain, simply by accepting the world as it really is. Hesiod's picture is grimmer: though worshipping the gods will bring its rewards, endless toil is inevitable, and success can be attained only through hard work. For Aratus, on the other hand, Zeus is a kindly father, akin to the Stoic *pronoia*,[5] and the universe is systematic and orderly. Virgil's text allows each of these models to predominate in turn (particularly in book 1, where Hesiod and Aratus are most prominent), orchestrating their different voices in such a way as to emphasize the differences between them, rather than to produce a homogenous, unified whole. In contrast with most recent critics, I believe that Lucretius is the major model throughout the poem. But Virgil is concerned neither simply to imitate his model, nor to react negatively against it. The effect of his Lucretian allusions could be described rather as subversion or problematization. Lucretius' tidy and basically optimistic world-view is challenged either by juxtaposition with the conflicting views of the other models, or by bringing together passages of the *De rerum natura* which can be made to seem contradictory, or by using Lucretian language to frame very un-Lucretian ideas. These different strategies can be traced in Virgil's treatment of myth and religion, which can be

[5] For Aratus and Stoicism, see Effe 1977: 40–56, with further bibliography. [See now also Kidd 1997: 10–12.]

seen in part as a response to Lucretius' complex and subtle use of mythological language and imagery.

I have argued elsewhere that Lucretius' use of myth is the product of an innovative and subtle theory of its nature and origins.[6] In two important passages, the accounts of the origins of religion in 5.1161–1240 and the phenomenon of echoes in 4.580–94, the poet hints at an explanation for the creation of myths. Early men (or ignorant rustics) observe the heavens or strange terrestrial phenomena which they are unable to explain. Either through fear or for the pleasure of tale-telling, they attribute these phenomena to the presence or influence of the gods: *ergo perfugium sibi habebant omnia divis | tradere* ('so they took refuge in handing everything over to the gods'), as Lucretius puts it in 5.1186–7. It is of course the duty of the Epicurean poet to rid mankind of superstitious fear by demythologizing these phenomena and banishing the gods once and for all to the *intermundia*. But Lucretius also sees myth as having an inherently attractive psychagogic power, which is of potentially immense value to him in his enterprise of converting the non-Epicurean reader to a philosophy which is superficially unattractive.[7] His solution to this problem is both to demythologize nature and, at the same time, to retain the use of mythological images. This is achieved in two ways: either by juxtaposing the mythological image with a blunt statement of its falsehood, and of the true, atomistic explanation; or by using mythological imagery without explicit reference to the myth, in the very process of providing the Epicurean account. So, for example, the myth of Phaethon is recounted to support the idea that the balance of the elements is precarious and will eventually bring about the destruction of the earth, but Lucretius immediately continues

> scilicet ut veteres Graium cecinere poetae.
> quod procul a vera nimis est ratione repulsum.
> ignis enim superare potest ubi materiai
> ex infinita sunt corpora plura coorta... (5.405–8)

---

[6] Gale 1994, esp. 129–55.

[7] Cf. 1.926–50 = 4.1–25. The 'bitterness' of the philosophy consists both in its demand for asceticism and rejection of the 'worldly goods' described in the proem to book 2, and in its abstract, impersonal view of the cosmos (cf. De Lacy 1957, Wardy 1988, Gale 1994: 144–5). On the psychagogic power of poetry and myth, see also Schrijvers 1970: 27–60.

... so, at least, the old Greek poets sang. But this is very far removed from true reason. For fire can prevail when more particles of its matter come together from infinite space...

In Lucretius' account of the origins of civilization at the end of book 5, there are numerous examples of implicit reference to myths. In explaining the discovery of fire, for example, he tells how a thunderbolt brought down the heavenly fire as a gift to mankind and distributed it amongst them. Later, the sun taught them the art of cooking. The choice of vocabulary here recalls the myths of divine benefactors, specifically Prometheus. The passage is almost an allegorical interpretation of the myth—but Lucretius never refers to it explicitly nor departs from the strictly rationalistic tone of his culture-history. This exploitation of mythological imagery allows Lucretius to have his cake and eat it. Myth is rationalized and thus disposed of as a serious account of natural phenomena, but mythological language is retained as an attractive and vivid way of speaking about the world. In addition, such passages implicitly suggest ways in which the myths might have originated: in attempts to account for droughts and floods, or to understand how cultural developments came about. The originality of Lucretius' theory lies above all in the suggestion that the myth-makers were the victims of error: other allegorists, such as the Stoics, were inclined to see myth as embodying some ultimate truth. For Lucretius, it is possible to explain myth via a scientific explanation of the natural world, but never vice versa.

A special case is the hymn to Venus in the proem. Here, we have to wait some time before the poet undermines the beautiful but ultimately misleading picture of the goddess's power over the natural world which inaugurates the poem.[8] Nevertheless, it *is* ultimately undermined, as the text carefully steers its reader away from a personal to an impersonal view of nature, and balances the images of nature's creative side with a grimmer view of *natura creatrix et*

---

[8] Exactly how long the reader will have to wait is determined in part by the textual problem at lines 44–9. Even if the lines are accepted as genuine, however, the process of enlightenment is still a gradual one. The reader is temporarily left either with a misleading image or with a blatant contradiction, which will be resolved only by a gradual process of substitution, as Venus' functions are taken over by Natura and Epicurus. For a more detailed account (and further bibliography) see Gale 1994: 208–23.

perfica ('nature the creator and the finisher'),[9] growth balanced by inevitable decay, culminating in the mass destruction of humanity in the Athenian plague at the end of book 6.

To return, then, to the *Georgics*. Virgil reacts to Lucretius' use of mythological imagery in three major ways, which may be termed conflation, remythologization and extension. Each of these has the effect of problematizing Lucretius' confident assurance that myth and the natural world can be explained simply. Virgil achieves this either by *conflating* Lucretian and non-Lucretian passages; or by *remythologizing* phenomena which Lucretius had demythologized; or by *extending* Lucretius' allegorizing method to myths which the earlier poet had treated in a rather different way. I now turn to some examples.

1. CONFLATION

In the first part of *Georgics* 1, the most obvious model is Hesiod. Lines 43–203 (where there is a strong break) correspond roughly to Hesiod's 'works', 204–351 to his 'days',[10] at which point Aratus takes over. On the other hand, although the framework is Hesiodic, the vocabulary and detail are highly reminiscent of Lucretius, especially in the opening lines which lead up to the first excursus, the 'aetiology of *labor*' (118–59). Virgil, like Lucretius and unlike Hesiod or the Roman agricultural writers, begins in spring, 'when the ice melts away from the white mountain-peaks and the crumbling clod is loosened by Zephyrus'. Similar imagery of loosening and opening occurs in Lucretius' proem, but Virgil's instructions for ploughing also recall the more negative pictures of the productive capacity of

---

[9] See especially 2.1105–74, where Lucretius describes how the earth was created and brought to completion by nature (*donec ad extremum crescendi perfica finem | omnia perduxit rerum natura creatrix*, 'until nature the creator of the world finished everything and brought it to the final limit of its growth', 1116–17), and is now on the way to inevitable collapse and destruction (*sic igitur magni quoque circum moenia mundi | expugnata dabunt labem putris<que>ruinas*, 'so too in the same way the walls which surround this great world will be stormed and fall in crumbling ruin', 1144–5).

[10] For a more detailed analysis, see Farrell 1991: 134–42.

the earth which Lucretius paints when arguing that the world is too imperfect to be the work of the gods.[11] Lucretius shows us different aspects of the natural world at different times, as it suits his argument: from one point of view the earth is fertile and productive, the source of all life; from another, it is worn out, like a woman past the age of child-bearing, since it can no longer produce crops and living beings spontaneously, as the first plants and animals were produced.[12] Already in the first four lines after his proem, Virgil is juxtaposing these two perspectives: Zephyrus helps the farmer by loosening the clods, but the bull must still 'groan' as it toils with the heavy plough.

Virgil then interrupts his instructions on ploughing, and advises the farmer first to find out what kind of crop his land is suitable for, since different areas and different regions of the world differ in their capacities. Once again, the language is highly Lucretian, recalling the theme of natural limits which runs through the *De rerum natura*.[13]

---

[11] Cf. Lucr. 1.10–11: *nam simul ac species patefactast verna diei | et reserata viget genetabilis aura favoni* ('for as soon as spring days show their face, and the fertile zephyr's breath blows free and strong'); 5.206–11: *quod superest arvi, tamen id natura sua vi | sentibus obducat, ni vis humana resistat | vitai causa valido consueta bidenti | ingemere et terram pressis proscindere aratris* [the metrical shape of this line is identical to G. 1.46]. | *si non fecundas vertentes vomere glebas | terraique solum subigentes cimus ad ortus...* ('As for the lands that remain, even these would be covered with brambles by the force of nature if human strength did not resist her, well used as we are to groaning over the sturdy mattock for our livelihood and furrowing the earth by pressure of the plough. If we did not encourage crops to grow by turning over the rich clods with the ploughshare and subduing the soil of the earth...'); 1.313–14: *uncus aratri | ferreus decrescit vomer in arvis* ('the hooked iron ploughshare is imperceptibly worn down in the fields'). The phrase *putris glaeba* ('crumbling clod') is also Lucretian (see Lucr. 5.142).

[12] Fertile earth: see especially 1.250–64, 2.991–8; worn-out earth: see 2.1150–74, 5.826–36.

[13] Note especially 53–4 ~ Lucr. 1.586–7 (*et quid quaeque queant per foedera naturae, | quid porro nequeant*, 'what each thing can do according to the pacts of nature, and what, moreover, they cannot do'), and cf. 1.75–6 = 1.595–6, 5.88–9 = 6.64–5, 5.545, 6.1106–9; 60–1 ~ Lucr. 5.923–4 (*quaeque suo ritu procedit et omnes | foedere naturae certo discrimina servant*, 'all [plants] grow according to their own kind, and all maintain their distinctions by a fixed pact of nature') and 5.58. The following are all favourite Lucretian words or phrases: *nonne vides?* ('don't you see?', 15 times), *continuo* ('forthwith', 15 times, 9 in this sedes), *foedera naturae* (*vel sim.*, 'pacts of nature', 7 times, *foedera/-e* 7 times in this sedes), *aeternus* ('everlasting', 29 times), *certus* ('fixed', 97 times), *loca/regio certa* ('a fixed place', 8 times).

But Virgil traces these limitations back to a mythological aetion, the repopulation of the world by Deucalion, after the flood. The myth is Hesiodic[14] (although it does not occur in the *Works and Days*); but, once again, the vocabulary is Lucretian. In his account of early man, Lucretius attributes his toughness to the fact that he was born of earth:

> at genus humanum fuit illud in arvis
> durius, ut decuit, tellus quod dura creasset.   (5.925–6)

But the human race living on the land was then much tougher, as was natural, since the hard earth had created it.

This amounts to a demythologized version of the Hesiodic and Pindaric pun on λαός ('race') and λᾶας ('stone').[15] But Virgil reverses the process of demythologization by echoing Lucretius' *durius/dura* ('tougher'/'hard'), while reintroducing the mythological figure Deucalion.[16] This remythologization is effected by conflating the Hesiodic and Lucretian accounts of the birth of men from the earth.

Virgil deals next with crop-rotation (including a pseudo-scientific/Lucretian account of the effects of stubble-burning[17]) and follows it

---

[14] See fr. 234 Merkelbach-West.
[15] Hesiod, *loc. cit.*, Pindar, *Ol.* 9.43–6.
[16] It is also worth noting that Lucretius demythologizes the flood in 5.411–15, and would of course reject the metamorphosis of stones into men as impossible. (See further below.)
[17] Lines 86–93 in general recall the Lucretian/Epicurean principle of citing a plurality of explanations where certainty is impossible (cf. Epicurus, *Ep. Pyth.* 86–8, Lucr. 6.703–11). It is notable, however, that Lucretius generally appeals to this principle only when discussing phenomena which are distant in time or space. Virgil's world is much more mysterious and uncertain. More specifically, note that Lucretius generally introduces these multiple explanations with the formulae *sive...sive* ('either...or', e.g. 5.509–33, 575–6 and esp. 1244–9, where the context is similar) or *aut quia...aut quia* ('either because...or because', e.g. 5.656–65, 680–704). The explanations themselves are full of Lucretian language: note especially *caeca* ('invisible', 89; very common in this sense in Lucretius, e.g. 1.277, 3.316, 3.247, 5.611, 6.1016), *excoquere / percoquere* ('to bake', 88; Lucr. 6.858 and 962), *spiramenta* ('pores', 90) ~ *spiracula mundi* ('the pores of the world', Lucr. 6.493), *penetra(bi)le frigus* (piercing cold', 93 ~ Lucr. 1.494). More generally, the second explanation recalls Lucretius' accounts of the discovery of metals (Lucr. 5.1252–7) and the 'sweating out' of the sea from the earth (5.487–8, and cf. *sudor...maris*, 'the sweat of the sea', 2.465 and *saxa...sudent umore*, 'rocks sweat with moisture', 6.943), the third recalls his explanation for hot and cold wells (6.830–78) and the fourth recalls numerous references to the drying power of the sun (e.g. 5.215, 252, 389; 6.616–22, 962).

up with another Hesiodic and very anti-Lucretian image, blonde Ceres looking down with favour from Olympus on the man who is assiduous in hoeing and cross-ploughing.[18] This then leads up, after a paragraph on irrigation, to the famous passage describing the end of the Golden Age and Jupiter's imposition of *labor* on mankind.

This is perhaps the most controversial section of the whole poem.[19] Critics have argued endlessly over the tone of the passage: is Virgil lamenting or celebrating the end of the Golden Age and the introduction of *labor*? Does the catalogue of discoveries in 136–45 constitute a celebration of human ingenuity and progress, or is it more ambivalent? And, perhaps most controversial of all, what is the precise significance of the phrase *labor improbus* (145–6)?

Once again, intertextuality and the conflation of models offer some valuable hints as to how we might go about answering these questions. The Golden Age is a very common theme in both Greek and Latin literature, but once again the main models here are Hesiod and Lucretius. Hesiod offers two explanations for the necessity to work: the 'degeneration' of humanity expressed in the Myth of Ages, and Zeus' punishment for Prometheus' theft of fire. Virgil combines the two: his account of the pre-Jovian age recalls Hesiod's Golden Age,[20] but the way the account is introduced (we might paraphrase, 'it is necessary to work hard because Jupiter brought the life of leisure to an end') corresponds to the beginning of the Prometheus story.[21] This is reinforced by the phrase *abstrusum... ignem* ('hidden fire') in 135, which recalls the hiding of fire by Hesiod's Zeus.[22] But there are two crucial differences from the Hesiodic account. For Hesiod,

---

[18] Cf. *Op.* 299–301. The recommendation to prayer in v. 100 reinforces the Hesiodic and anti-Lucretian tone.

[19] The bibliography on 1.118–59 is vast. In addition to the commentators, see especially Altevogt 1952, Taylor 1955, Wilkinson 1963, Stehle 1974, Putnam 1979: 32–6, Ross 1987: 79–92, Jenkyns 1993.

[20] Cf. especially *gravi veterno* ('heavy sloth [lit. age]', 124) and δειλὸν γῆρας ('terrible old age', *Op.* 113–14)—though the inversion in sense is important; *ipsaque tellus | omnia liberius nullo poscente ferebat* ('the earth itself brought forth all things freely and unprompted', 127–8) and καρπὸν δ' ἔφερε ζείδωρος ἄρουρα ('the bountiful earth brought forth fruit', *Op.* 117).

[21] *Op.* 42–6. Note especially ἄεργον ἐόντα ('without working', 44, cf. *gravi veterno*, 'heavy sloth', G. 1.124) and ἔργα βοῶν ('work of oxen', 46, cf. *boumque labores*, 'work of oxen', G. 1.118).

[22] Cf. esp. κρύψε δὲ πῦρ, 'he [Zeus] hid fire', *Op.* 50.

ἀεργίη ('idleness') is ultimately a desirable state, as we see from the introduction to the Prometheus myth and the description of the Golden Age. But in the Iron Age, work is vital and ἀεργίη is reprehensible, as Hesiod says explicitly in *Op.* 311: ἔργον δ' οὐδὲν ὄνειδος, ἀεργίη δέ τ' ὄνειδος ('work is no shame, but idleness is shameful'). Virgil collapses this distinction by having Jupiter end the Golden Age in order to bring an end to sloth, *gravis veternus*, rather than to punish mankind. We are, then, left in some doubt whether work is a good thing or not. On the one hand, the picture of the pre-Jovian age is based on Hesiod's nostalgic primitivism. On the other, Jupiter is now apparently acting rather like the Stoic Zeus, to benefit mankind—it seems particularly significant that he is referred to as *pater* ('father') in 121.[23]

Something rather similar seems to be going on in 145–6. Initially, the epigram *labor omnia vicit* ('work/toil overcame everything') sounds positive and hopeful—until we come up against the adjective *improbus* at the beginning of the next line. The enjambment makes the word both startling and emphatic, qualifying the sense of the previous line. But what precisely does *improbus* mean? Judging from other occurrences in Virgil, the nearest English equivalent would be something like 'insatiable': it is often used of predatory animals, with a shade of pity for the victim.[24] An obvious Greek equivalent would be σχέτλιη ('cruel', 'hateful'), which is of course used by Hesiod in distinguishing the two Erides in the opening lines of the *Works and Days*.[25] But Virgil has once again collapsed the Hesiodic opposition. There is no longer a good Eris which inspires competition and thus work, and a bad Eris which inspires hateful and unproductive strife. For Virgil, there is simply *labor*, with all the ambivalence the word entails. Agricultural work is *labor improbus*, carried on under the aegis of Ἔρις σχέτλιη, and the neat oppositions of Hesiod's world are no longer possible.

The passage is further complicated by a series of allusions to Lucretius. The main model is Lucretius' culture-history at the end

---

[23] For Stoic views on Providence and progress, see e.g. Chrysippus, *SVF* 2.1172, 1181, 1183; Posidonius *ap.* Sen. *Ep.* 90; Panaetius *ap.* Cic. *Off.* 1.11–13 and 2.15–17.
[24] e.g. crane (*G.* 1.388), snake (3.421), wolf (*Aen.* 9.62), lion (10.727), eagle (12.250). The *cornix improba* (*G.* 1.388) is discussed below (n. 89).
[25] *Op.* 11–26. Note especially the enjambment of σχέτλιη in 15.

of book 5, which itself alludes extensively to Hesiod. In describing the first phase of human prehistory, Lucretius alternately demythologizes and debunks the Hesiodic Golden Age: early man lived off the spontaneous fruits of the earth (acorns and arbutus), but enjoyed neither peace nor long life; there was no agriculture and no war, but people often starved to death or poisoned themselves through ignorance.[26] This stage was followed by the gradual development of civilization, a highly ambiguous process in Lucretius' eyes. Beneficial developments such as agriculture and language were inevitably accompanied by negative developments such as weapons and religion. Virgil echoes the gradual nature of the development (in highly Lucretian language[27]) and perhaps the ambiguity of some of the discoveries: *fallere* ('to trick') in 139 sounds a little dubious, and *ferri rigor* ('the rigidity of iron', 143) may hint at the rigours of the iron age.[28] But the real counterpoise to the hopeful tone of the catalogue is the Lucretian idea that some 'progress' is necessary just to maintain the *status quo*, because the earth itself is in decline. This idea is prominent at the end of book 2 and in the anti-teleological argument of book 5: in both places, Lucretius emphasizes the need for endless agricultural toil, and both passages are echoed by Virgil at the beginning and end of the 'aetiology of *labor*':

> nec tamen, haec cum sint hominumque boumque labores
> versando terram experti, nihil improbus anser
> Strymoniaeque grues et amaris intiba fibris
> officiunt aut umbra nocet.   (1.118–21)

---

[26] See further Gale 1994: 164–77.

[27] Cf. esp. *ut varias usus meditando extunderet artis | paulatim et sulcis frumenti quaereret herbam* ('so that, through experience and thought, man would gradually hammer out the various arts and seek from plough-land the blade of corn', 133–4) with *usus et impigrae simul experientia mentis | paulatim docuit pedetemptim progredientis. | sic unumquicquid paulatim protrahit aetas...artibus ad summum donec venere cacumen* ('Practice and the learning gained from experience by the quick mind taught them gradually as they advanced step by step. So time gradually brought each invention forth...until they advanced to the topmost pinnacle of the arts', Lucr. 5.1452–7). *paulatim* ('gradually') is a favourite word of Lucretius', occurring 23 times in the *De rerum natura* (only 9 times in the whole Virgilian corpus). Agriculture (5.1361–78), fire (1091–1104), sailing and astronomy (1435–42), hunting (1250–1) and tools (1266–8) are all discussed by Lucretius. The parenthesis in 144 is strongly reminiscent of Lucretius' style (cf. esp. 1250 ff.; and cf. 1283 ff., 1297–9, 1350–3).

[28] Cf. R. F. Thomas 1988 *ad loc.*

Yet even when the labours of men and oxen have tried all these things in ploughing the earth, the insatiable goose and Strymonian cranes and chicory with its bitter roots do damage, and shade is harmful.

> mox et frumentis labor additus, ut mala culmos
> esset robigo segnisque horreret in arvis
> carduus; intereunt segetes, subit aspera silva,
> lappaeque tribolique, interque nitentia culta
> infelix lolium et steriles dominantur avenae.   (1.150–4)[29]

Soon toil was imposed on the cultivation of grain too, so that evil mildew consumed the ears, and the idle thistle sprang up in the fields; the crops perish and a rough undergrowth of goose-grass and thorns grows up, and, amidst the shining plough-land, unfruitful darnel and sterile wild oats hold sway.

The Lucretian theory of natural decline thus frames the Hesiodic Golden Age and the Stoicizing reference to Jupiter's providential care, and we are presented with three possible views of the situation in a single passage. But it is, of course, important that Virgil attributes the whole sequence of development to the gods. Jupiter ends the Golden Age and inspires human beings to gradual development of the arts.[30] These developments also coexist with divine benefaction,

---

[29] The salient Lucretian passages are 2.1160–3 (*quae nunc vix nostro grandescunt aucta labore,* | *conterimusque boves et viris agricolarum,* | *conficimus ferrum vix arvis suppeditati:* | *usque adeo parcunt fetus augentque laborem*, 'crops are now grown with difficulty, in spite of our labours; we wear out our oxen and the strength of our farmers, we blunt our tools and scarcely harvest enough for our needs: the earth is so chary with her produce and demands so much more work') and 5.206–17 (partially quoted at n. 11 above); cf. also 1.208–14. Compare in particular 118 with Lucr. 2.1161 and 5.213; 119 with Lucr. 5.210 and the similar passage 1.211; 120–1 and, more generally, 150–4 with Lucr. 5.206–7 and 215–17; 125 with Lucr. 5.211 = 1.212; 128 with Lucr. 1.214 and 2.1158; 153 with Lucr. 2.1157. *labor* ('work', 'toil') is a key word in all three Lucretian passages. Cf. also *ipsaque tellus* | *omnia... ferebat* ('the earth itself brought forth all things', 127–8) and Lucr. 2.233–4: *quando omnibus omnia large* | *tellus ipsa parit* ('since the earth itself brought forth everything abundantly for all')—but it is only animals, not human beings who get food for nothing in Lucretius. It also seems significant that *labor* and *egestas* ('want') are paired in Lucr. 3.65 (a passage echoed by Virgil in *Aen.* 6.277) as things which are *generally thought of* as evils, and that one of the *harmful* discoveries, seafaring, is given the epithet *improba* in 5.1006.

[30] The terms of Jupiter's 'benefaction' in 122–3 recall Lucretius' Epicurus: compare *primusque per artem* | *movit agros* ('[Jupiter] first artfully stirred up the fields') with *quique per artem* | *fluctibus e tantis...* ('and by his art, from such great waves...', Lucr. 5.9–10; note also that Epicurus is *princeps*, 'first', in the previous line, *primus*, 'first', in

another very un-Lucretian touch. The whole of Lucretius' culture-history is an implicit denial of the rôle of divine *heuretai* in the growth of civilization. *Natura creatrix* ('nature the creator')[31] replaces Ceres as the motivating force behind the development of agriculture. But Virgil emphatically reinstates her: *prima Ceres ferro mortales vertere terram | instituit* ('Ceres first introduced to mortal men the art of turning the earth with iron'). The reversal is pointed with further Lucretian echoes.[32]

To recapitulate: the 'aetiology of *labor*' echoes the incompatible versions of Hesiod and Lucretius, adopting some elements from both accounts, and pointedly reversing others. The wonderful age of ease and leisure was ended by Zeus—but in order to benefit, not punish mankind. Work is a good thing (in view of *gravi veterno*, 'heavy sloth') and a bad thing (in view of *improbus*, 'insatiable'): the two Hesiodic *Erides* are one. The world is in decline—but that does not prove Lucretius' contention that the gods are not in control. The arts were gradually developed by human beings—but Jupiter and Ceres were behind the process. The gods both give and take away. Work is a necessary evil and a sign of the providential organization of the world. What are we to make of this tangle? Virgil is perhaps suggesting that the Hesiodic, Lucretian and Stoic interpretations of history and civilization are all possible ways of viewing the world, none of which finally excludes the others, although they cannot be fully harmonized.

A similarly ambivalent world-view is developed in two contrasting passages which span the end of the 'works' section of book 1 and the

---

1.67, 1.71 and 3.2 and *pater*, 'father', in 3.9). See further Farrell 1991: 181. Virgil has once again reversed Lucretius, who *replaces* the traditional divine *heuretai* with the saviour Epicurus (cf. Gale 1994: 196–9). But it is significant that Jupiter stirs up storms (130) where Epicurus rescues from (metaphorical) storms, and generally makes life harder where Epicurus makes it easy and pleasant.

[31] Lucr. 5.1361–78. Cf. Gale 1994: 178–9.

[32] Cf. esp. Lucr. 5.14–15: *Ceres fertur fruges... mortalibus instituisse* ('Ceres is said to have introduced crops to mortal men'; the distancing formula is important). Also 5.934, 1295 and references to *glandes* ('acorns') and *arbuta* ('arbutus') in 939–42 and 965 (acorns are of course traditional primitive fare—see e.g. Dicaearchus *ap.* Porph. *Abst.* 4.1.2, Paus. 8.1.6, Juv. 13.54–5, Macrob. *In Somn. Scip* 2.10.6—but the pairing with arbutus is less common and seems to point specifically to Lucretius). *Dodona negaret* ('Dodona refused') also seems a pointed reversal of Lucretius' claim that acorns simply went out of fashion (5.1416).

Myth and Allusion in the Georgics

beginning of the 'days' section.[33] The first (176–203) arises out of the poet's instructions for building a threshing-floor: once again, pests are a threat, and seeds must be hand-picked to counteract the tendency of everything in nature to go to the bad. The farmer is like an oarsman rowing against the current: it takes all the rowing he can do to stay in the same place. The train of thought here is familiar: Virgil is in fact following fairly closely the Lucretian argument that nature is in terminal decline, and once again, the allusion is 'flagged' with direct echoes of Lucretius' text.[34] But this pro-Lucretian stance (so to speak) is balanced by the second passage (231–56), in which Virgil describes the five celestial zones. This time, the Virgilian passage reverses Lucretius, by conflating his account of the zones with other models. The description of the zones itself is quite a close

---

[33] Cf. Farrell 1991: 172–80.

[34] Cf. especially *possum multa tibi veterum praecepta referre, | ni refugis tenuisque piget cognoscere curas* ('I can report to you many precepts of our ancestors, as long as you do not shrink back and think such slight concerns unworthy of your attention', 176–7) with *multaque praeterea tibi possum commemorando | argumenta fidem dictis corradere nostris...quod si pigraris paulumve recesseris ab re...* ('I can drum up support for my arguments by setting out for you many further proofs...but if you are slow and hang back a little from the matter in hand...', Lucr. 1.400–1 and 410; *cognoscere* is another of Lucretius' favourite words, occurring 20 times in this *sedes*—cf. esp. 3.1072; and the reluctant reader is a familiar figure throughout the *De rerum natura*); *vidi lecta diu et multo spectata labore | degenerare tamen ni vis humana quotannis | maxima quaeque manu legeret* ('I have seen seeds chosen carefully and watched over with great labour degenerate all the same unless human strength chooses the biggest ones by hand each year', 197–9) with *quod superest arvi, tamen id natura sua vi | sentibus obducat, ni vis humana resistat...et tamen interdum magno quaesita labore...aut nimiis torret fervoribus aetherius sol...* ('as for the lands that remain, even these would be covered with brambles by the force of nature if human strength did not resist her...and yet, even so, the crops tended with so much labour are sometimes either scorched with too much heat by the fiery sun...', Lucr. 5.206–7 and 213–15); and, more generally, 197–200 with Lucr. 5.306–17 and 2.1173–4. The latter passage may have suggested the image of the oarsman, if the MS reading *ad scopulum* ('onto the rocks') is retained (as I think it should be) in 1174: cf. Segura Ramos 1982 and Possanza 1990. Other examples of Lucretian vocabulary: *victa fatiscat* ('crumbles and cracks'; cf. *fessa fatisci*, 'grow old and crack', Lucr. 3.458 and 5.308—in both cases referring to degeneration and decay); *contemplator item* ('look, too'; cf. *contemplator enim*, 'so look', Lucr. 2.114 and 6.189), *magna cum magno* ('great...with great...'; cf. esp. Lucr. 4.902, 5.644; this kind of polyptoton is generally very common in Lucretius, but rare in Virgil, according to R. F. Thomas 1988 *ad loc.*), *vidi* ('I have seen'; cf. Lucr. 4.577 and 6.1044 and the frequent appeals to common experience throughout the *De rerum natura*).

imitation of a passage from Eratosthenes' *Hermes*,[35] but the Lucretian passage is bound to be in our minds, because Virgil has already referred to it several times: it is in fact part of the anti-teleological argument of *De rerum natura* 5.195 ff., and comes immediately before the lines in which Lucretius describes the problems caused by weeds and weather conditions, one of the major models for the 'aetiology of *labor*' and for the account of natural degeneration discussed above. In other words, our pair of passages, one 'pessimistic' and the other 'optimistic', both invoke the same Lucretian model. Virgil again points this allusion by dropping Lucretian phrases into his Eratosthenic framework. Most strikingly, the temperate zones are said to have been granted by the gods to *mortalibus aegris* ('wretched mortals'), where Eratosthenes simply says that they are inhabited by ἄνδρες ἀντίποδες ('antipodean men').[36] The same phrase is used by Lucretius in a context of 'divine' benefaction—the proem to book 6, where the godlike Epicurus is praised as the saviour of mankind. Once again, Virgil undoes Lucretius' displacement of the gods from their traditional rôle as benefactors.

The zones were also described by Aratus, who is echoed a few lines later in 243–6.[37] For Aratus, the celestial zones seem to constitute an example of Zeus' providential concern for mankind, since he emphasizes their 'usefulness' (462) and the perfection of their design (529–33).[38] In effect, Lucretius has appropriated the Stoic argument that the perfection of the world proves the existence of divine providence and stood it on its head, by using the zones as evidence against divine providence (*only* a fifth of the earth is habitable). Virgil turns this around again, emphasizing the gods' beneficence, to counterbalance

---

[35] Fr. 16 Powell. See R. F. Thomas 1988 *ad loc.* for details.

[36] Note also *dextra laevaque*, 'to the right and left' ~ Lucr. 4.276 for ἑκάτερθε ('on either side') and *via secta*, 'a path is cut' ~ Lucr. 5.272 = 6.638 (though in a different sense). It is perhaps also significant that Virgil omits to describe the εὐκρασία ('mildness') of the temperate zones (lines 15–19 in Eratosthenes), which are dealt with rather perfunctorily in 237–8 (cf. R. F. Thomas 1988 *ad loc.*). This brings his account more closely into line with Lucretius', where the emphasis is of course on the climatic *imbalance* in the polar and equatorial zones.

[37] Cf. *Phaen.* 45–8.

[38] *Phaen.* 462–544. For the zones as evidence of the providential design of the cosmos, cf. Heraclit. *Quaest. Hom.* 48–51, Philo *Quis Rer. Div. Her.* 147. The zones were also described by Chrysippus (*SVF* 2.649) and Posidonius (Strabo 2.2.1–2).

the Lucretian tone of the earlier passage. Once again, Virgil offers both Lucretian rationalism and Aratean providentialism side by side as plausible ways of viewing the world.

The passage continues with an almost explicit contradiction of Lucretius, as Virgil muses on the nature of the antipodes.[39] Whatever the precise meaning of 242–3, it is fairly clear that the Underworld is said to be somewhere beneath our feet. One of the reasons for the odd phrasing is surely that Virgil is echoing Lucretius, who, in the proem to book 3, describes the effects of Epicurus' philosophy in terms of a vision: he can see *beneath his feet* everything that is going on in the whole universe, but the Underworld (which does not exist) *is nowhere to be seen*.[40] Elsewhere, Lucretius ridicules the idea that anyone might live on the underside of the earth.[41] Virgil offers alternatives: either they live in perpetual darkness (like Homer's Cimmerians[42]), or they have daylight while we have night, and vice versa. This idea is developed into a picturesque pageant: Aurora leading the day, the rising Sun with his snorting chariot-team, Vesper lighting his lamp in the evening. We might be tempted to dismiss the lines as a slight elaboration on the standard epic dawn-formula; but the procession may be more than simply a decorative allusion to Homer and his successors. Once again, Virgil is repopulating the universe with the gods whom Lucretius had banished. The sun's chariot and Aurora both figure implicitly in a passage in book 5 (650–9), in which Lucretius discusses the causes of day and night:

> at nox obruit ingenti caligine terras,
> aut ubi de longo cursu sol ultima caeli
> impulit atque suos efflavit languidus ignis
> concussos itere et labefactos aere multo,
> aut quia sub terras cursum convertere cogit
> vis eadem, supra quae terras pertulit orbem.
> tempore item certo roseam Matuta per oras
> aetheris auroram differt et lumina pandit,
> aut quia sol idem, sub terras ille revertens,

---

[39] The language of 240–3 is somewhat obscure: Mynors 1990 *ad loc.* is more helpful than R. F. Thomas 1988.
[40] Lucr. 3.25–7. Cf. also 1.115 and 3.978.
[41] Lucr. 1.1052–82. The phrasing in 1065–7 is particularly close to *G.* 1.249–51.
[42] 248 ∼ *Od.* 11.19.

> anticipat caelum radiis accendere temptans,
> aut quia conveniunt ignes...

But night overwhelms the earth with its huge darkness, either when after his long course the sun has reached the end of the sky and wearily breathed out his fires, exhausted by their journey and weakened by their long voyage through the air; or because he is compelled to turn back his course beneath the earth by the same force which carried his orb above it. Likewise, Matuta spreads the rosy dawn through the etherial regions and shows her light at a fixed time either because the same sun, returning beneath the earth, first seizes the heavens with his rays and tries to set them aflame, or because fires come together...

This is an example of Lucretius' usual demythologizing technique, described above: mythological imagery is used in a context in which the true, Epicurean explanation for the phenomena is being given, and the juxtaposition both enlivens the atomistic account and helps to suggest how the myth might have grown up (the dawn is *like* a lamp, the sun travels across the sky *like* a charioteer). But the Virgilian context seems to suggest that taking the images more literally may be as satisfactory a way of accounting for the phenomena: the gods, or Providence, may be behind it all after all.[43]

2. REMYTHOLOGIZATION

The procession of day and night is thus an example of my second category of mythological allusion, remythologization. The problem with Lucretius' use of mythological imagery is that the process can easily be reversed. If the sun behaves like the mythological charioteer, might that not be because it is really controlled by the gods? Lucretius tries to avoid this problem by juxtaposing myth with reality and thus emphasizing the artificiality of his own images. But the effect of Virgil's remythologizing is once again to blur and problematize the clear and certain contours of the Epicurean universe.

---

[43] Cf. also Lucretius' procession of the seasons in 5.737–47. Virgil, like Lucretius (cf. Gale 1994: 81–3) may have artistic representations in mind: see for example the chariots of Helios and Nyx/Selene on the East pediment and the North metopes of the Parthenon.

Myth and Allusion in the Georgics 111

We have already seen some examples of this. The myths of Deucalion and of the Golden Age are reintroduced by Virgil in conjunction with Lucretian language and ideas, presenting us with a problematic account of human pre-history. I shall now turn to two further examples, the spring storm in 1.311–34 and the praise of spring in 2.323–45, which again form a contrasting pair.

In the first passage, Virgil describes how storms lay low the ripe corn and terrify man and beast. The language here is very reminiscent of Lucretius' atomistic accounts of bad weather in books 1 and 6 of the *De rerum natura*.[44] The battle of winds is a metaphor going back to Homer,[45] but the detailed working out in this passage seems specifically reminiscent of Lucretius.[46] But Virgil once again reverses the implications of the Lucretian passages. For Lucretius, the natural world is impersonal and indifferent to human life, and the violent forces of nature are often used to illustrate this indifference.[47] The thunderbolt, in particular, is not the weapon of Jupiter, as Lucretius argues at some length in book 6.[48] But Lucretius retains the image of the thunderbolt as a weapon, hinting that the mythological

---

[44] Cf. esp. 1.271–6, 6.96–101, 253–61 and 357–78.

[45] *Il.* 16.765; *Od.* 5.291–6. Cf. Enn. *Ann.* 432–4 Sk. (note especially the verb *concurrunt*, 'clash', which is echoed by both Lucretius and Virgil), Verg. *Aen.* 1.81–123, Ov. *Trist.* 1.2.17–32, Sen. *Agam.* 465–97, Luc. 5.597–677; but the later examples are clearly influenced by Lucretius and/or Virgil (cf. P. R. Hardie 1986: 237–9 on *Aen.* 1.81–123).

[46] Note esp. *ita* ('so', 320) ∼ *ita* ('so', Lucr. 6.275), *cum sonitu fervetque* ('noisily, and [the sea] surges', 327, with strong alliteration of f, c, s) ∼ *cum fremitu saevitque* ('with a roar, and [the wind] rages', Lucr. 6.276, same sedes, with strong alliteration of m, f, s), *concurrere proelia* ('clash in battle', 318) ∼ *concurrunt... nubes contra pugnantibu' ventis* ('clouds clash as the winds fight each other', Lucr. 6.97–8; cf. 2.116, 6.363 ff.), *nimborum in nocte corusca* ('flashing in the midst of the clouds' darkness', 328) ∼ *nimborum nocte coorta* ('in the darkness of gathered rain-clouds', Lucr. 6.253; cf. 4.168–73), *fulmina molitur* ('[Jupiter] hurls thunderbolts', 329) ∼ *commoliri tempestas fulmina* ('the storm [prepares] to hurl thunderbolts', Lucr. 6.255), *imbribus atris* ('pitch-black rain', 323) ∼ *niger... nimbus* ('black cloud', Lucr. 6.256), *gravidam... segetem* ('the pregnant crop', 319) ∼ *gravidam tempestatem* ('the pregnant storm', Lucr. 6.259). More generally, the destruction of crops in 319–21 recalls the destruction of trees in Lucr. 1.273–5 (based in turn on a Homeric simile, *Il.* 16.765–70) and 6.140–1, and the fleeing men and animals in 330–1 recall Lucr. 6.52–3 and 6.330–1 (again modelled on a Homeric passage, *Il.* 4.275–81). Cf. also 324 and Lucr. 6.291, 327 and Lucr. 6.428, 334 and Lucr. 6.115.

[47] See e.g. 5.195–234, which, as we have seen, is an important model throughout book 1.

[48] 6.379–422.

explanation contains an element of truth. Thunderbolts are 'forged' in the clouds (6.148–9, 278 and 365) and then 'hurled' down to earth (328–9); but the agencies involved are wind, moisture and fire, not gods.

Virgil complicates the picture in several ways. Firstly, he reinstates Jupiter, as the Lucretian image of the battle of winds merges into the traditional idea that the thunderbolt is wielded by Jupiter, rather than the impersonal *tempestas*:

> ipse pater media nimborum in nocte corusca
> fulmina molitur dextra, quo maxima motu
> terra tremit, fugere ferae et mortalia corda
> per gentis humilis stravit pavor; ille flagranti
> aut Atho aut Rhodopen aut alta Ceraunia telo
> deicit; ingeminant Austri et densissimus imber.   (1.328–33)

The father himself, in the midst of the clouds' darkness, wields thunderbolts in his flashing right hand. The great earth trembles at the impact; wild beasts flee and grovelling terror lays low men's hearts throughout the world: he, with his blazing weapon, casts down Athos or Rhodope or tall Ceraunia; the winds and pouring rain redouble...

By personalizing Lucretius' ambivalent view of nature, as both creative and destructive, Virgil leaves us with a deeply unsettling image of the workings of divine providence.[49] Virgil's *natura*, like Lucretius', is often indifferent to man, but Virgil does not draw the Lucretian conclusion, that the gods therefore have no concern with human beings. Instead, Jupiter is himself made responsible for the violent as well as the kindly aspect of the natural world. Furthermore, there is no suggestion that Jupiter is punishing mortal wrongdoing, as in the striking Homeric simile which forms a secondary model for the Virgilian storm.[50] Virgil's farmers are apparently innocent victims of Jupiter's caprice.[51]

---

[49] The epithet *pater* ('father', 328) is particularly startling in this context. It is also used of Jupiter in a much more benevolent rôle in 121 and 353. Cf. Härke 1936: 35–6.

[50] *Il.* 16.384–93. Cf. esp. 384 and G. 1.320 and 323; 385 and G. 311; 389–92 and G. 325–7. On the theodicy, see Janko 1992 *ad loc*. For Zeus thundering in autumn, cf. also *Op.* 415–16.

[51] The terror of men and animals in 330–1 is particularly important, because Lucretius' object is to *dispel* fear of thunderstorms, which he equates with superstitious

Myth and Allusion in the Georgics

Secondly, the literal storm anticipates the storm of civil war at the end of the book, where Roman battle lines 'run together' (*concurrere*) like the winds of 318. Thus, Virgil hints that natural violence and human violence are connected by a kind of cosmic sympathy, calling into question the Lucretian view that, while violent conflict is inherent in nature, conflict on the human level arises directly from ambition and fear, and can thus be 'cured' by Epicurus' *dicta*.[52] And thirdly, the Lucretian passage is immediately followed by the famous advice *in primis venerare deos* ('above all worship the gods'), and a description of the Cerealia, which contains several reminiscences of Hesiodic passages.[53] Thus, the Hesiodic view that hard work and piety will be rewarded is brought into conflict with the Lucretian view that the gods have no concern with human beings. Both views are problematized. Virgil accepts both the idea that the innocent suffer with the guilty *and* the idea that the gods demand and respond to worship, and thus leaves us with a complex and troubling picture of the gods' relationship with man and the natural world.

Jupiter's destructive rôle in the storm in book 1 is balanced by his rôle in the praise of spring, where he comes down in showers[54] to fertilize Mother Earth and nourish all living things. Again, the passage is a tissue of Lucretian echoes. The *hieros gamos* of Earth and Sky is evoked and demythologized in *De rerum natura* 1.250–1 and 2.991–7; the onset of spring is described in the Venus proem; and the spring-like conditions which prevailed at the time when animals and men were first born of earth are an important element in Lucretius' zoogony (5.780–820). All four passages are recalled

---

fear of the gods: see 5.1218–35 and 6.51–5. But in Virgil's version, fear is not confined to human beings (the shuddering beasts perhaps come from Hesiod's description of the month Lenaeon, *Op.* 516). For Virgil, both animals and human beings have good reason to be afraid of Zeus' wrath (which cannot be distinguished from the physical effects of the storm).

[52] See especially the proem to book 3.
[53] Cf. esp. *Op.* 327–37, 465–78 and 582–8.
[54] Cf. *fecundis imbribus Aether... descendit* ('the Sky comes down in fertile rain', 2.325–6) with *ruit imbriferum ver* ('rainy spring pours down', 1.313) and *imbribus atris... ruit arduus aether* ('the lofty sky pours down in pitch-black rain', 1.323–4). There is also a striking contrast between *diluit* ('washes away') in 1.326 and *alit* ('nourishes') in 2.327; *tremit* ('trembles') in 1.330 and *nec metuit* ('does not fear') in 2.333. Jupiter is *pater* ('father') in both places (in view of *omnipotens*, 'almighty', *pater Aether*, 'father Sky', in 2.325 must be identified with Jupiter).

here.[55] But once again, Virgil makes the mildness of spring a gift of the gods: *caeli indulgentia* ('the indulgence of heaven') in 345 seems deliberately ambiguous, and Aether, Tellus and Venus are not explicitly rationalized as they are by Lucretius.[56]

Further ambiguities persist: even the praise of spring is not a straightforward acknowledgement of the existence of a kindly Providence. Here, both intertextuality and self-allusion are important. I have already mentioned the pairing of the passage with the more troubling view of Jupiter in 1.311–34. The birth of animals and men also looks back to Deucalion's stones[57] and the 'aetiology of *labor*'. The zoogony here differs from the earlier passages in three important ways. Firstly, it seems more 'scientific', with its strong reminiscences of Lucretius' zoogony. Secondly, the new-born animals are no longer a *durum genus* ('tough race'), but *res tenerae* ('delicate things'), and could not survive without the kindly indulgence of heaven. And finally, the εὐκρασία('mildness') of spring here seems explicitly to contradict the statement in 1.311 that violent storms occur in autumn *and spring*. In addition, the positive view of animal sexuality here conflicts with the violent attack on *amor* in book 3.[58] Do these contradictions make the praise of spring a 'lie', as Ross and Thomas argue? Or do they invalidate the earlier passages? Once again, I prefer to see an example of polyphony or multiple points of view, particularly as precisely the same 'contradictions' occur in Lucretius. Spring is a mild and indulgent season in the proem and (less explicitly) in 1.803–11 and 5.737–40, but the time when thunderstorms are most prevalent in 6.357–78. Early man is tough, but enjoys a mild climate.[59] Animal sexuality is harmless and necessary in the proem, but

[55] Cf. esp. 325–7 with Lucr. 1.250–1 and 2.991–3; 328 with Lucr. 1.256; 329 with Lucr. 2.997; 330 with Lucr. 2.994; 328–35 with Lucr. 1.1–20; 331 and 334–5 with Lucr. 1.805–11; 331 with Lucr. 5.806; 332–3 with Lucr. 5.780–2; 336–42 with Lucr. 5.783–805 (cf. also 925–6 and 1427 for *terrea progenies*, 'the earthborn race'); 343–5 with Lucr. 5.818–20. There is a more detailed analysis in Klepl 1967: 11 ff.

[56] The personification (if such it is) is much stronger in 325–7 than in either of the Lucretian models; and Lucretius deliberately undermines the image by emphasizing in 2.652–4 and 5.110–45 that Tellus is not a goddess, or even alive. On the *hieros gamos* in Lucretius, see further Schiesaro 1990: 111–22, Gale 1994: 40–1.

[57] Note especially the brief evocation of spring in 1.43–4, and contrast *durum genus* ('tough race', 1.63) with *res tenerae* ('delicate things', 2.343).

[58] Note especially *vere magis* ('especially in spring') in 3.272.

[59] Lucr. 5.818–20.

human sexuality is dangerous and problematic in book 4.[60] Virgil simply draws attention to and exaggerates Lucretius' equivocation in order once again to problematize his model.[61]

A final example of this kind of remythologization occurs in the finale to book 1, where Virgil describes the horrific portents which followed the murder of Caesar and presaged the battle of Philippi. The whole catalogue can be seen to a certain extent as alluding to the sixth book of the *De rerum natura*, where Lucretius' main object is to demonstrate that frightening phenomena such as earthquakes, lightning, volcanoes and plagues are not manifestations of divine displeasure, but perfectly natural occurrences which are subject to a rational, mechanistic explanation.[62] The idea that thunder and lightning may be used for divination is explicitly ridiculed in 6.379–86. Most of the portents in Virgil's list are discussed by Lucretius,[63] but the most striking example is the eruption of Aetna in 471–3:

---

[60] Cf. Gale 1991: 419–21.

[61] It should perhaps be emphasized that this equivocation on Lucretius' part need not be seen as *inherently* problematic. Unlike Virgil, Lucretius represents the world as fully explicable on rational principles, despite its complex and multi-faceted nature. Creation and destruction are two sides of the same coin (as is made explicit on several occasions, e.g. 2.569–80); and though the poet may sometimes emphasize one aspect over the other, in accordance with the immediate demands of his argument, he will almost always provide a complementary passage which rights the balance. The most striking example is the overarching contrast between proem and finale, but there are many others. Similarly, the shifts in perspective just discussed are complementary rather than contradictory: early man was physically tough compared to modern man, but did not have the technological skills which would have enabled him to survive a modern climate. But Virgil's reading of Lucretius, like that of certain modern critics, insists on finding (or creating) contradictions. By playing up and exaggerating Lucretius' shifts in perspective, and combining his rationalist stance with other ways of understanding the world, Virgil abolishes the certainty and clarity of the Lucretian universe. It should be noted, furthermore, that many of the apparent contradictions in the *De rerum natura* contribute towards Lucretius' rhetorical strategy: the attractive images of the early books are gradually undermined or corrected as we progress through the poem and come nearer to an acceptance of the natural cycle of birth and death, growth and decay. Cf. Gale 1994: 204–5 and 211–15 for discussion of the similar 'discontinuity' in Lucretius' presentation of the sun and of Venus/Natura. For the natural cycle in Lucretius, see Minadeo 1965 and 1969.

[62] Cf. Lucr. 5.78–90 and 6.48–91. For the Epicurean, the study of physics is not an end in itself, but is only of value in so far as it is conducive to the attainment of *ataraxia*: see Epicurus, *KD* 11. On this aspect of *De rerum natura* 6, see further Jope 1989.

[63] Eclipses: 5.751–70; volcanic eruptions: 6.639–702; the clash of weapons: cf. the demythologization of the thunderbolt-as-weapon discussed above, and Lucretius' frequent references to the terrifying sound of thunder (e.g. 6.129, 155, 218, 288);

> quotiens Cyclopum effervere in agros
> vidimus undantem ruptis fornacibus Aetnam,
> flammarumque globos liquefactaque volvere saxa!

How many times we saw Aetna boil over and pour lava from cracked furnaces into the fields of the Cyclopes, hurling up balls of flame and molten rocks!

This recalls Lucretius' two descriptions of Aetna, in books 1 and 6,[64] both of which contain implicit references to the mythical inhabitants of the mountain. In book 1, rumbling noises which come from the mountain threaten that it is once again working up its anger, and will soon hurl its fires up at the heavens. The language recalls the myth of Typhoeus, the giant imprisoned by Zeus beneath the mountain, as described, for example, in the *Prometheus bound*:

> ἔνθεν ἐκραγήσονταί ποτε
> ποταμοὶ πυρὸς δάπτοντες ἀγρίαις γνάθοις
> τῆς καλλικάρπου Σικελίας λευροὺς γύας.
> τοιόνδε Τυφὼς ἐξαναζέσει χόλον
> θερμοῖς ἀπλάτου βέλεσι πυρπνόου ζάλης.   (PV 369–73)

Thence rivers of fire shall one day break out, devouring with savage jaws the level fields of fertile Sicily; so fiercely shall Typho's rage boil up, with hot darts of terrible, fiery rain.

This allusion ties in with a whole complex of imagery which is applied to the figure of Epicurus throughout the *De rerum natura*: he is represented as attacking heaven like the giants, with the purpose of overthrowing the gods of mythology.[65] Lucretius reverses the traditional moral which was drawn from the myth throughout antiquity: rather than representing *hybris*, disorder and barbarity, the 'giants'

---

earthquakes: 6.535–607; mysterious voices (traditionally attributed to Faunus, e.g. Varro, *Ling.* 7.36, Cic. *Div.* 1.101, *Nat. D.* 2.6): 4.580–94; ghosts: 4.35–45 and 759–67 (the phrase *simulacra modis pallentia miris*, 'phantoms, strangely pale', is a direct quotation from Lucr. 1.123, though Lucretius himself may be quoting Ennius. See Skutsch 1985: 155); floods: cf. 1.280–94; comets: cf. 2.203–9 and 5.1191; stones dripping blood and lightning from a clear sky are both *adynata* in Lucretius (1.884 and 6.247–8). The main model for 477–83 is, however, Apollonius (*Argon.* 4.1280–7). For other versions of the prodigy list, see Mynors 1990 *ad* 469 ff.

[64] 1.722–5; 6.680–93. Cf. also 3.294–8, where Lucretius is describing a 'fiery' character.

[65] See especially 1.62–79 and 5.113–21. On gigantomachy, see further Vian 1952 and P. R. Hardie 1986: 85–90 and 209–13.

have become heroic figures, challenging and overthrowing the tyranny of *religio*. The description of Aetna in book 1 is part of Lucretius' tribute to Empedocles, who is thus aligned with the Epicureans against religious tradition (though of course Lucretius goes on to emphasize that the whole basis of his physical theory was fundamentally flawed).[66]

In book 6, the reference is to another myth associated with Aetna, the home not only of Typhoeus but also of the Cyclopes, who labour there forging thunderbolts for Zeus.[67] The idea is latent in Lucretius' account of volcanic eruption, just as the figure of Jupiter the Thunderer is latent in his account of thunder and lightning. In 6.681, the poet speaks of 'the furnace of Aetna', and in fact the mountain turns out to behave rather like a forge or furnace, with the action of wind in underground caverns fanning its flames. In a word, the Cyclopes and their forge have been demythologized.

Virgil seems to combine these two passages in his version and also to refer back through Lucretius to the prophecy of Aeschylus' Prometheus. *Cyclopum agros* ('the fields of the Cyclopes') and *fornacibus* ('furnaces') recall the passage in *De rerum natura* 6, while the bursting of the mountain and hurling of rocks suggest that Typhoeus has escaped his prison, just as Prometheus prophesied. Virgil, then, has both remythologized Lucretius and restored the conventional moral value to the myth. Typhoeus no longer stands for the heroic philosopher, but is now a symbol of cosmic disorder, his escape presaging the terrible punishment of the *Laomedonteae periuria Troiae* ('perjury of Laomedon's Troy') which Virgil identifies as the ultimate cause of the Civil Wars in 502.

3. EXTENSION

The myths of Typhoeus and the Cyclopes, like most of those we have been considering so far, might be described as 'nature myths'.

---

[66] Note also the comparison with the Delphic oracle in 1.736–9, which is repeated, with reference to the *De rerum natura* itself, in 5.110–13. Here too Empedocles is allied with the enlightened Epicureans against conventional piety.

[67] The Cyclopes are denizens of Aetna in *G.* 4.173, and *Aetnaei* ('of Aetna') in *Aen.* 8. Cf. Cic. *Div.* 2.43.

Whatever their origins, they were by Virgil's day firmly associated with volcanic eruptions and thunderbolts, just as Ceres is associated with the growth of crops and Prometheus with the discovery of fire. Thus Lucretius is able to demythologize them by explaining the phenomena in a different, 'scientific', way. There are two further classes of myths, however, which he treats rather differently: myths of metamorphosis and composite monsters (centaurs, scyllas, the Chimaera). Like many of his contemporaries,[68] Lucretius is inclined simply to dismiss these stories as nonsensical. Throughout the *De rerum natura*, the species are regarded as fixed and unchanging, with their own distinct characteristics.[69] Although nature's laboratory must initially have produced some rejects, which died out because they were not fitted for survival (5.855–77), this does not amount to a process of natural selection in the Darwinian sense, in which the characteristics of species actually change to adapt to their environment. How, then, could a man and a horse possibly exist in the same body, when their physiological characteristics are so different (5.878–924)? Of course, such myths did not simply spring up out of nowhere, and Lucretius does offer in passing one or two suggestions as to their origins: explicitly in book 4.732–48, where he gives the usual Epicurean account of *simulacra* sticking together in flight, and implicitly earlier in the same book (129–40), where he describes how cloud pictures sometimes resemble giants and huge rocks blotting out the sun, and are transformed into one monstrous form after another. More often, though, giants, chimaerae and centaurs and myths of metamorphosis simply figure as *adynata*: if something could come of nothing, nature should be able to produce gigantic beings who could walk across the sea; if just any kind of atom could combine with any other, all kinds of portentous creatures and metamorphoses would be possible; if the atoms had colour as well as shape, every species should occur in every colour, and we would see white ravens and black swans.[70] 'All of which', remarks Lucretius drily (in 2.707), 'evidently does not happen.'

---

[68] e.g. Cic. *Tusc.* 1.11 and 1.48, *Nat. D.* 2.5; Sen. *Ep.* 24.18, 82.16; Ov. *Tr.* 4.7.11–18. The collections of rationalizing explanations of myths by Palaephatus and others (see Festa 1902) concentrate on myths of this type.

[69] See especially 1.188–90, 3.296–306.

[70] 1.199–203; 2.700–6; 2.817–25.

It seems significant, then, that references to these two kinds of myths—monstrous creatures and metamorphoses—are relatively common in the *Georgics*. No doubt this is due in part to the Alexandrian fascination with the bizarre and monstrous, manifested, for example, in Nicander's lost *Heteroiumena*. But the link with Lucretius also seems important, and Virgil himself points us in this direction by marking two of the relevant passages with clear verbal allusions.

Both passages occur in *Georgics* 3, which is the most Lucretian part of the poem. It revolves around the themes of *amor* and death, recalling the finales of the two central books of the *De rerum natura*, and the plague at the end of book 6. As numerous critics have noted,[71] it is also remarkable for the extreme anthropomorphism of Virgil's treatment of the animals. These two issues are, I think, related: Lucretius, too, repeatedly emphasizes the fundamental kinship between animals and human beings.[72] But where for Lucretius the relationship is physical—man and animals are similar in their make-up, and in their most basic drives and desires, indeed, before the dawn of civilization, early man behaves exactly like any other animal—for Virgil the relationship is more metaphorical. Man is akin to animals, in two slightly different senses. Firstly, he shares their vulnerability to age, disease, injury, death. From this point of view, Virgil's anthropomorphism evokes *sympathy* for the animals, even when their sufferings are the result of the advice which the poet himself is offering the farmer. But secondly, man is dangerously close to the beasts, in the sense that his civilization is merely a thin veneer, which easily cracks when subjected to the forces of passion or disease. In these circumstances, man *becomes* an animal—like the anonymous *iuvenis* ('youth') and *virgo* ('girl') amongst the list of animals driven to extreme and unnatural behaviour by the power of *amor*; or the Norici reduced to pulling their wagons and ploughs

---

[71] e.g. Liebeschuetz 1965; Wilkinson 1969: 121–32; Miles 1975; Putnam 1979: 191–201; R. F. Thomas 1988 *ad* 3.49–94 and *passim*; Gale 1991.

[72] Note especially the comparison of animal and human 'personality types' in 3.288–307. Cf. also the use of animal *exempla* in 2.263–5; 4.547–8, 638–41, 678–83, 710–21, 984–1010, 1194–1207; 6.738–829; and the repeated assertion (1.744, 808, 820–1; 2.1016 etc.) that crops, animals, trees, human beings and the earth itself are all made up of the same constituents.

because of the dire effects of the plague.[73] Lucretius' optimism is once again challenged: if passion and violence are part of the fundamental nature which is *common* to men and animals, how can human beings hope to attain happiness by the sheer force of reason?

This blurring of the boundary between man and animal is symbolically reinforced by the two references to myths of metamorphosis which I mentioned a moment ago. Virgil's description of the ideal horse culminates in a short list of exemplary mythological horses, the steeds of Pollux, Mars and Achilles, and the horse into which Saturn transformed himself to avoid Rhea's anger during his courtship of Philyra. There is a touch of humour in the picture of the god's swift flight from his angry wife, but the passage also anticipates the central 'diatribe' on the power of *amor*. Sexual passion (symbolically) transforms men and even gods into animals.[74] A little later, discussing the danger which gadflies represent to pregnant cows, Virgil introduces a second, rather similar myth, the transformation of Io and her persecution by Juno (152–3). Again, the metamorphosis is the result of sexual passion and sexual jealousy.[75] In both cases, Virgil introduces clear echoes of Lucretian passages. He describes the horses of Mars and Achilles with the phrase *quorum Grai meminere poetae*

---

[73] Cf. Putnam 1979: 132: 'Personification both distinguishes and equates man and his charges. Hierarchical distinction defends the actions of civilization. Equation arouses our sympathy for the resultant suffering.' Conte 1986: 168–72 also has some pertinent comments on the contrary effects of 'sympathy' and 'empathy'.

[74] Cf. R. F. Thomas 1988 *ad loc.*

[75] It must be admitted that Io was the victim, rather than the subject, of both (Jupiter's) passion and (Juno's) jealousy. On the other hand, it is noteworthy that, in the subsequent discussion of *amor*, sexual attraction is seen very much as something *inflicted* on both man and beast, as the gadfly is inflicted on Io: Venus with her *caeci stimuli amoris* ('the goads of blind love', 210) also victimizes animals and man, and breaks down the boundaries between them. Note too that both the gadfly and *amor* are associated with heat (cf. especially the parentheses in 154 and 272). Similar symbolism may be operating in the description of Turnus' shield (*Aen.* 7.371), which bears a picture of Io. Commentators generally explain this as a reference to Turnus' Argive ancestry, but it may also refer to his psychological condition and his 'transformation' by Juno's agent Allecto. Turnus is maddened by the fury as Io is by the gadfly, and transformed into an animal: as Pöschl 1962: 98–9 notes, he is very often compared to an animal in the later books. Cf. P. R. Hardie 1986: 118–19 and 1992; and Reckford 1961, who discusses other metamorphosis myths in book 7. It also seems appropriate that the individualistic Turnus' shield should refer to his own character and situation, while *pius* Aeneas' refers to his destiny and the destiny of his descendants.

('of whom Greek poets told', 90), which recalls the 'distancing formula', *Graium ut cecinere poetae* ('as Greek poets sang', 6.754; slightly varied in 2.600 and 5.405), used three times by Lucretius in *rejecting* the myths of Cybele, Phaethon and Minerva's hatred of the crow. The gadfly is described in the phrase *asper, acerba sonans* ('fierce and angry-sounding', 149), taken from Lucretius' ironic account of the labours of Hercules in the proem to *De rerum natura* 5, where the serpent of the Hesperides is *asper, acerba tuens* ('fierce and angry-looking', 5.33).[76] Virgil is taking up the myths dismissed by Lucretius, and by implication, applying to them the kind of 'allegorical' explanation Lucretius had applied to the nature myths. The 'inner meaning' of the stories of Saturn and Io is to be deduced from the context: passion erases the narrow boundary between men and animals. It may not be literally possible for a man to turn into a beast, but on the symbolic level, it is all too easy.

This interpretation can be reinforced by looking at two further examples from book 3. The catalogue of violent animal behaviour culminates in a mythological *exemplum*: the horses of Glaucus, which, maddened by Venus, devoured their owner (266–8).[77] Not precisely a metamorphosis, but certainly an extreme example of unnatural behaviour, the very opposite of the stereotypical and predictable behaviour of animals in Lucretius.[78] Again, the transformation of man into animal by the plague is pointed by mythological allusion. Echoing

---

[76] Note also that the gadfly is referred to as *pestis* ('a plague', 153) and *monstrum* ('a monster', 152). Both terms are used by Lucretius in anti-mythological contexts: the hydra is *Lernaea pestis* ('the plague of Lerna') in 5.26, and the fauns and satyrs of 4.580–94 are *monstra ac portenta* ('monsters and prodigies').

[77] The myth is somewhat obscure: different versions are recorded by Servius and Probus. See Mynors 1990 *ad loc.* for details.

[78] Contrast especially Lucr. 5.890–900, where Lucretius argues against the existence of centaurs and scyllas, on the grounds that each species has its own distinct characteristics—including *diet*—which could not be combined in a single body. The horse again behaves unnaturally as a result of the plague, this time tearing itself to pieces with its own teeth (3.512–14): this action, like the effects of *amor*, is attributed to *furiae* ('frenzy'; cf. 511 and 244, 266). The potentially monstrous behaviour of horses is perhaps hinted at already in 3.85, where the ideal horse *volvit sub naribus ignem* ('snorts fire from its nostrils'), echoing Lucr. 5.30, *Diomedis equi spirantes naribus ignem* ('the horses of Diomedes, breathing fire from their nostrils'). Again, Virgil hints that the monsters dismissed by Lucretius are in some sense real (and dangerous): the horse's fiery nature, cultivated by the farmer, is ready at any moment to break out into violence. (For reversal of the description of the healthy horse in 498–514, see R. F. Thomas 1988 *ad loc.*)

Lucretius' (and Thucydides') statement that the medical profession was helpless in the face of the epidemic, Virgil says that even the experts, *Phillyrides Chiron* and *Amythaonius Melampus* ('Chiron son of Philyra and Melampus son of Amythaon'), gave up hope.[79] Why these specific names? Of course both Chiron and Melampus were famous healers. But both are also connected with metamorphosis myths: Chiron was the offspring of Philyra and horse-Saturn, as Virgil reminds us with the resounding patronymic. Melampus cured the Proetides of the madness that made them believe that they were cows, alluded to by Virgil in *Eclogue* 6.[80] It is ironic that neither the man-horse nor the healer of the women-cows is able to cure the disease which reduces the Norici to the level of their animals. The failure of medicine in Lucretius is in its own way symbolic:[81] the benefits of civilization are fragile and partial, compared with the true healing conferred by Epicurus' philosophy. Virgil has shifted the emphasis and integrated the line into the symbolism of his own poem.

I have suggested that monsters and metamorphoses are most prominent in *Georgics* 3, because of its close engagement with Lucretius and its emphasis on the maddening, debasing effects of sex and disease. There are, however, several examples in the other three books. The significance of these references is not always as clear as in book 3, but they are generally associated with passion (especially sexual passion) and violence, and can thus be seen as building up towards the symbolic transformations of book 3. In any case, they serve to blur the boundary between man and the natural world, which is otherwise emphasized by the farmer's dominance and control over his crops and livestock.

The most explicit examples are references to Nisus and Scylla in book 1, Procne in book 4, the giants, again in book 1, and the centauromachy in book 2. The first two (1.404–9 and 4.15–7) are relatively straightforward: the birds are given their human names,[82]

---

[79] Thuc. 2.47.4.; Lucr. 6.1179; G. 3.550.

[80] See Apollod. 1.9.12; Vitr. 8.3.21.

[81] Note especially *timore* ('in fear', 1179). Lucretius lays greater emphasis on mental than physical suffering in his account of the plague: it is this kind of suffering which Epicurean philosophy can cure, as the poet claims in the proem to book 6.

[82] Indeed, it is unclear which species Scylla and Nisus are supposed to represent: see Mynors 1990 *ad loc*. Frentz 1969: 97 notes that Lucretius refers to the swallow by the normal Latin name *hirundo* (3.6).

and in each case there is a brief, allusive reference to the reason for the metamorphosis (Scylla's betrayal of her father, Procne's murder of her child). Once again, both stories connect metamorphosis with sexual passion and violence. The story of Procne and Philomela also has more extensive resonances: it is referred to again in the Aristaeus epyllion (4.511–18), where Orpheus' lamentations for Eurydice are compared to Philomela's lamentations. Here, however, Philomela is lamenting the loss of her nestlings, which have been taken from the nest by a *durus arator* ('cruel ploughman'). This in turn looks back to the vignette in 2.207–11 of the *iratus arator* ('furious ploughman'), who cuts down an old tree to clear plough land, thus depriving birds of their 'ancient homes', but putting the land to use which is attractive in itself. The three passages, taken together, hint at a cycle of violence in both nature and agriculture, which is cruel but necessary. Philomela (or Procne) murders her child to punish her husband. Transformed into a bird, she cruelly carries off bees to feed to her young (in expiation for her previous crime?), but in turn loses them at the hands of the farmer. The farmer deprives birds of their home— but the end result is 'shining' and useful plough land, which will ultimately 'learn'[83] to produce new life. This may remind us of the cycle of birth and death which dominates Lucretius' poem; but Virgil's delicate personification of animals and plants tends always to evoke sympathy for the victims rather than calm acceptance of the inevitable equilibrium of creation and destruction.

The centaurs are invoked at the end of book 2 (455–7) as an *exemplum* of the detrimental effects of wine. Again, they are associated with frenzy[84] and violence, and perhaps suggest the precariousness of civilization, since Virgil is here contrasting the virtues of uncultivated trees with the cultivated vine. If so, Virgil is using an un-Lucretian symbol to convey a very Lucretian idea: Lucretius is also keen to emphasize the possibility of social collapse, especially in the plague at the end of book 6.[85]

---

[83] *rudis* ('rough', 'untried', 211) hints at personification—cf. Mynors 1990 *ad loc.*
[84] *furentis* ('frenzied'), 455.
[85] Cf. Farrell 1991: 202–4, who links the references to the Lapiths in 3.113–17 and Chiron and Melampus in 3.549–50 with the rise and fall of civilization, specifically the rise and fall of Athens in Lucr. 6.1–6 and the plague. He also notes (203 n. 59) a contrast between the bestial centaurs in 2.455–7 and the 'civilized' Lapiths in book 3,

The gigantomachy has already been mentioned above, as implicit in Virgil's description of the eruption of Aetna at the end of book 1. The giants, it was suggested, stand for the forces of chaos and disorder, as they so frequently do in classical literature. This allusion, and the reversal of Lucretius' symbolism which it entails, links with two further references earlier in the book. The first is implicit: the pests which destroy the threshing-floor are 'earth-born monsters', *quae plurima terrae | monstra ferunt* (1.184–5). 'Earth-born monsters' would most naturally refer to the giants.[86] *Pace* Thomas, there is some humour in equating mice and ants with huge monsters; but again humour is combined with thematic significance. The earth is full of destructive forces which undo the order which the farmer tries to impose, as the poet emphasizes in the image of the rower fighting against the current. The giants are referred to again (with perhaps a touch of humour[87]) in Virgil's brief adaptation of Hesiod's *Days*, 1.276–86. Here, they are conspirators united in a desire to tear down the heavens.[88] Again they figure as opponents of civilization, born on an unlucky day, though this time they are defeated by Jupiter.

Examples could be multiplied. Many latent references to myth are assiduously hunted out by Servius, and Frentz, in his monograph *Mythologisches in Vergils Georgica*, discusses no fewer than twenty possible allusions to plant and animal metamorphoses and

and suggests that this is why Lapiths, rather than the more usual centaurs, are credited with the invention of riding. It is significant though, that *Bacchus*, not the Lapiths, is said to have 'subdued' the centaurs. This is no victory of civilization over brutality, but of the god's double-edged gift, which first makes the centaurs mad, and then destroys them. Like Jupiter in book 1, Bacchus is not unambiguously benevolent. (This is particularly troubling in view of Bacchus' association with poetic inspiration, both in the *Georgics* (see esp. 2.7–8 and 380–96, with R. F. Thomas 1988 *ad loc.*) and, implicitly, Lucretius (in the Dionysiac imagery of 1.922–5). Poetry is again associated with wild, uncontrolled frenzy in 3.284–94, where the poet's *amor* drags him over mountain heights, like the mares maddened by sexual passion in 269–70. Again, there are echoes of Lucretius: cf. esp. 291–3 and Lucr. 1.926–7).

[86] See e.g. [Hom.] *Batr.* 7; Aesch. *PV* 353; Hor. *Carm.* 3.4.73; Isid. *Etym.* 11.3.13; and cf. R. F. Thomas 1988 *ad* 184–5 and 278–9.

[87] Cf. Klingner 1967: 211.

[88] Cf. Lucr. 5.120: *caeli restinguere solem* ('to put out the sun in heaven'). Lucretius scornfully denies that the Epicurean 'giants' are committing any impiety by 'destroying' the sun (i.e. declaring it to be perishable and non-divine). Virgil again reverses Lucretius' unconventional use of the myth: in *Georgics* 1, the giants are once again represented as a threat to order and civilization.

catasterisms. Some of his examples are more convincing than others: when Virgil gives the spider the epithet *invisa Minervae* ('hateful to Minerva') in 4.246–7, it seems reasonable to detect a reference to the metamorphosis of Arachne, and halcyons are perhaps 'dear to Thetis' (1.399) for a similar reason.[89] But many will doubt that the simple phrase *Parnasia laurus* ('laurel of Parnasus', 2.18) can be expected to evoke the story of Daphne. The difficulty lies in deciding what is

[89] Cf. Frentz 1967: 72–107. Amongst the more convincing examples identified by Frentz (in addition to those discussed here) are the raven (1.388), halcyon (1.399; cf. 3.338, with Mynors 1990 *ad loc.*), hyacinth (4.137) and catasterisms in 1.222, 246 and 4.232–5. The raven is particularly significant because (as mentioned above) it is used as an *adynaton* by Lucretius. Virgil vividly describes the *cornix improba* ('shameless raven') stalking alone on the shore, calling for rain (1.388–9). Why *improba*? Presumably the epithet is chosen in part to reinforce the idea that the raven is actually *summoning* the unwelcome rain, rather than benevolently giving warning; but it seems also to recall the myth in which the bird is punished for talking too much. There may, in fact, be a specific reference to Callimachus, who describes the crow as λαίδρη ('impudent') in *Iamb.* 4 (fr. 194.82; cf. *garrula*, 'chattering', Ov. *Met.* 2.547), and in the *Hecale* (fr. 260) has the bird both describe its own punishment by Athene and prophesy the similar fate of the raven, which will be changed from white to black by Apollo. (The argument for seeing a Callimachean allusion here may be strengthened by the fact that Virgil is apparently conflating Aratus and Callimachus in the following lines, 390–2: cf. *Hec.* fr. 269, and see R. F. Thomas 1988 *ad loc.*) Virgil might have either or both elements of the story in mind: his *cornix* is apparently a raven, but both crows and ravens were regarded as weather-prophets, and the two species were often not fully distinguished (cf. Mynors 1990 *ad loc.*). Both parts of the story are dismissed by Lucretius: white ravens are an *adynaton* in 2.817–25, and the crow's avoidance of the Acropolis is explained 'scientifically' in 6.749–55 (with an allusion to the Callimachean account: cf. 753 and *Hec.* fr. 260.41). There are also echoes of Lucretius in the preceding lines: 383–5 recalls Lucr. 5.1078–82, where Lucretius is discussing bird cries. (Note especially the Lucretian formula *variae volucres*, 'many kinds of birds', in 383. Virgil also refers back through Lucretius to his Homeric model, *Il.* 2.459–63; cf. Mynors 1990 *ad loc.*) The idea that the raven is actually calling the rain is also Lucretian (Lucr. 5.1086; in the other examples cited by Mynors 1990 *ad loc.*, the crow/raven prophesies rain rather than summoning it), and the phrase *voce vocare* is used of the cock 'summoning' the dawn in Lucr. 4.711. The heavy alliteration in 389 also gives the line a Lucretian ring. Virgil thus brings together two quite separate passages of the *De rerum natura*, in one of which (2.817–25) Lucretius implicitly rejects the metamorphosis myth by treating the white raven as an *adynaton*, while in the other he describes the bird's behaviour without reference to the myth (5.1084–6). Virgil's *cornix*, like Scylla and Nisus, persists in the 'wicked' behaviour which was the cause of its metamorphosis. But the picture is further complicated by the statement a few lines later (415–23) that the birds' behaviour is not divinely inspired, but is the result of changes in air pressure. The language is again very Lucretian, particularly the catch-word *divinitus* ('by divine agency', 415), which occurs eight times in the *De rerum natura* and only here in Virgil.

mythological allusion and what is simply personification: phrases like 'the tears of Narcissus' (4.160) or 'the Bears that are afraid to dip themselves in Ocean' (1.246) could be regarded as either. In the long run, the distinction may be unimportant: the cumulative effect of *both* personification *and* references to metamorphosis myths is to emphasize the interconnectedness of the natural world, the resemblances between plants, animals and man. As I have suggested, this 'interconnectedness' is also an important principle for Lucretius, but Virgil has transformed its significance. Lucretius' readily explicable, mechanistic and materialistic world of atoms and void has become something much more mysterious and threatening, where the violent forces of nature and emotion can transform man into beast, and where the farmer's struggle to maintain order brings suffering, as well as benefit, to animals, plants and the land itself.

At the beginning of this paper, I raised three related problems: how should we interpret the apparent contradiction in the double *makarismos* at the end of book 2? Is Virgil's major model Hesiod, Lucretius or Callimachus and the Alexandrians? And is the work gloomy and anti-Augustan or celebratory and pro-Augustan? My discussion of Virgil's use of myth has, I hope, suggested that none of these questions has a simple answer. Although I see Lucretius as Virgil's main model, in the sense that the *De rerum natura* is the text with which Virgil engages most consistently throughout the poem, allusions to the other models are also woven into the *Georgics*, particularly in book 1, in such a way that their conflicting world-views are emphasized, rather than glossed over. Virgil offers us fragmentary glimpses of an ambiguous world, seen through the mirror of one model after another. Their conflicting points of view cannot be fully reconciled, but each of them proves equally adequate (or inadequate) as an explanation for the phenomena. It is possible to see the natural world as fruitful or barren, the gods as kindly or cruel, the farmer's life as an ideal or as hopelessly compromised by violence and failure, simply by a change in perspective. The complex, shifting world-view of the *Georgics* is intimately bound up with its place in the didactic tradition, a tradition in which a succession of poets had each offered their own model of the nature of reality, of man's relationship with the world, the gods and other men. Rather than presenting yet another new interpretation of the phenomena—or rather, as a means of doing so—Virgil's poem offers a commentary on the tradition, and on the conflicting values of the poets who shaped it. Some critics have denied that the *Georgics* is really 'about' agriculture at all. That is, I think, a mistake; but it is also concerned with the *rerum natura*, with man's place in the world, and with the didactic tradition itself.

6

Labor Improbus

Richard Jenkyns

The paragraph in the first book of the *Georgics*, running from lines 118–59, which describes the loss of the golden age and man's subsequent history, has been very diversely interpreted.[1] But one sentence, at 145–6, has been especially controversial:

> labor omnia vicit
> improbus et duris urgens in rebus egestas.

Three lines of interpretation seem worth consideration:

A. The words mean that toil and the pinch of need drove men on, with the result that they succeeded in defeating the obstacles before them. A laboured translation might be, 'Tiresome toil and the pressure of need amid hard circumstances conquered all.' On this account the sentence continues and sums up the account of progress in the preceding ten lines: man discovered agriculture, fire, astronomy, carpentry, metal working, then the various arts—in short, through effort, impelled by the goad of need, he got on top of his circumstances. This was the standard interpretation in earlier generations; among recent scholars, R. D. Williams, Huxley and Wilkinson

---

This paper was first published in 1993 (see also Jenkyns 1998: 337–40) and is reprinted here virtually unchanged.

[1] It is misleading to call the passage 'Virgil's Theodicy', not only because it implies a Christian concern to justify the ways of God to men which Virgil does not have, but also because the divine motivation plays only a small part in the passage, which is centred upon the consequences for humanity.

adopt it.[2] Let us call it the progressive interpretation. (It is better not to label it 'optimist', since it is compatible with a pretty dour view of man's lot).

B. The meaning is that trouble and neediness came to dominate man's life: to borrow Thomas's (partial) translation, 'Insatiable toil occupied all areas of existence.' On this account the sentence looks back to a point rather earlier in the paragraph, where Jupiter's destruction of the golden life of old is described. This is the interpretation adopted in Altevogt's monograph, and it is accepted by most recent commentators: Richter, Thomas and (probably) Mynors.[3] It is also followed by Putnam.[4] Possibly we should reckon it the orthodox view at the present time. Let us call it the pessimist interpretation.

C. In principle at least, we might consider some combination of A and B. Klingner's account could perhaps be put under this heading, though it seems better to regard it as a modified form of A.[5]

Let us now examine the arguments put forward in favour of B:

1. This is the argument on which Thomas relies. He maintains that A is wrong because '(*a*) in this poem (as in life) toil does *not* overcome all difficulties... (*b*) the realities of *labor* and its susceptibility to failure provide the major theme of the poem....'.

To this it can be answered (a) the *Georgics* contains plenty of statements which are not easily reconciled to a strict logic, and a few which, at least on the face of it, are flatly incompatible; and (b) the argument rests on a view of the poem as a whole which will seem to many misguided, or at least one-sided. As a rule, it is seldom satisfactory to try to solve the problems of a particular passage by reference to very general considerations. But the decisive answer to this argument is (c): that there is nothing in the progressive interpretation incompatible with the rest of the poem. The sentence (on this view) does not imply that hard work has removed every

---

[2] Commentators *ad loc.*; Wilkinson 1969: 141.
[3] Mynors's commentary (1990) is delphic; in his lectures he was plainly of the pessimist school.
[4] Putnam 1979: 32–6.   [5] Klingner 1967: 203–5.

awkwardness and made life comfortable: it refers back to the invention of arts and crafts in the distant past, and maintains that these gave man mastery over all his various areas of endeavour. Did he need food? He invented farming, trapping, hunting and fishing. Did he need to travel? He invented boats and the science of navigation. Did he need tools? He devised metal-working—and so on. There is nothing in this to deny that man may have to labour constantly and face painful setbacks and disasters, and thus nothing incompatible with the *Georgics* as a whole. We may conclude that there is no substance in this argument.

2. *labor omnia vicit* is to be compared with *omnia vincit amor; et nos cedamus amori* at *Ecl.* 10.69. Just as love has man in its power in the *Eclogue*, compelling his submission, so do *labor* and *egestas* in the *Georgics*.

At first sight this seems a strong argument; upon further reflection it looks less good. Let us presume that *vinco* can be translated 'conquer' or 'defeat'. 'Love conquers all' in the *Eclogue* presents no problem. In another context the meaning might be that lovers' wills are so strong that they can overcome every obstacle to their desires' fulfilment, but in this place the meaning is plain: no one can resist the power of love over himself. Now consider the context in the *Georgics*. We have ten lines describing one human discovery after another, culminating in the statement 'toil conquered all' or 'toil defeated all'. What would this mean to an English-speaker? Surely that toil overcame the difficulties in man's way. Could he understand 'toil conquered (*or* defeated) all' to mean 'toil ruined men's lives'? It is well-nigh impossible. We may notice that the pessimist school has to resort to paraphrase to convey what it supposes to be the significance of the words, whereas the translations given here and under A above, though stilted, stick close to the Latin. Now it is open to the pessimist interpreters to argue that the range of meaning covered by *vinco* is sufficiently different from English 'conquer' or 'defeat' for these translations to mislead, but the burden of proof is plainly on them, and it is pretty clear that such an argument could not be sustained. So the parallel does not work in the way that the pessimist interpreters believe; it may even be an argument in favour of A. Virgil may well have had the parallel consciously in mind, in which case it is between forces which dominate man's mental experience and determine his behaviour: in the *Eclogues* that force is, characteristically, love; in the *Georgics*, no less characteristically, the sterner *labor*-and-*egestas*. It might be noted, more subjectively, that the context in the *Eclogues* is by no means disagreeable: the surrender to all-powerful love has a voluptuousness about it. In other words, a reader of the *Georgics*, recalling the phrase in the *Eclogues*, is not going to say at once, 'Oh no, here's *another* ghastly thing coming along'; rather, 'Ah, here's another driving-force for mankind; I expect the mood will be tougher than in the *Eclogues*.'

3. (a) *egestas* is necessarily a pejorative word. (b) *labor* is not necessarily pejorative, but in association with *egestas* it becomes so: Egestas and Labos (an archaic variant of *labor*) are among the dread forms encountered in the underworld in the *Aeneid* (6.276–7).

(a) is certainly correct; Servius auctus comments that *egestas* is worse than *paupertas*, since *paupertas* can be honourable, whereas *egestas* is shameful.[6] (b) should perhaps be qualified, as we shall see, but it may at least be allowed that *egestas* (like *improbus*, which we shall consider shortly) reminds us of the unpleasant connotations of *labor*. It is also true that Virgil can use labor to mean something like 'woe';[7] this must be roughly the meaning at *Aen.* 6.277.[8] Not too much should be made of this passage, though: some of the personified abstractions in it, like Sleep, are made grim only by the context; Labos here seems sure to have a meaning somewhat different from that which it bears in our passage; and *labor* and *egestas* are not an obvious pair. It may be that a memory, conscious or unconscious, of the *Georgics* led Virgil once more to put the words in close proximity, and this in turn confirms what *improbus* has in any case made

---

[6] *peior est egestas, quam paupertas: paupertas enim honesta esse potest, egestas enim turpis est.*

[7] Compare English 'toil' in such usages as the 'toil and trouble' of Shakespeare's witches.

[8] This sense of *labor* may perhaps help us with one of the most perplexing passages in Virgil: Jupiter's speech at *Aen.* 10.104–13. *sua cuique exorsa laborem fortunamque ferent* (111–12) is commonly taken to mean 'let each man's efforts bring him his task and allotted outcome'. More probably *labor* and *fortuna* are in disjunction to each other: 'woe' and 'success'. One might translate, 'Let each man's efforts bring him ill fortune or good.' A consequence of this would be that *fortunam* in line 112 carries a meaning very different from that of *fata* in 113; some take them as near synonyms.

certain: that Virgil wants us to feel some disagreeable connotations to the idea of *labor*.

In sum, the advocates of B are right to find pejorative language in the sentence. But this is not necessarily an argument against A. *egestas* is not, after all, unqualified: *duris urgens in rebus egestas* is very much a single concept, conveying the idea of the pressure of need. The idea that something in itself unpleasant may have good consequences is not a difficult one (compare the English saw, 'Necessity is the mother of invention', though *egestas* is sharper than 'necessity' in modern usage), and though neediness in itself may be a bad thing, the driving force produced by neediness can be seen as good. So *egestas* cannot be used to refute A.

4. Altevogt has demonstrated that *improbus* must be a pejorative word: it cannot be translated (for example) 'unflinching' or 'unremitting', but must carry the idea of blame.[9] It might fairly be argued that the case here is different from that of *egestas* on two grounds. (a) *egestas* is basically a descriptive word. To make a comparison: 'hunger' and 'thirst' are pejorative words—they denote states of being which we know to be unpleasant—but they are descriptive none the less: it is not a matter of opinion that a man in the Sahara without water is thirsty. (They can also be said to have pleasant consequences: 'He enjoyed the drink immensely because of his great thirst.') *improbus*, by contrast, is purely evaluative, and without descriptive content: to say that something is *improbus* is precisely to find fault with it. And the word is emphatically placed. (b) It is common ground between A and B that the whole sentence refers back to the distant past. But B supposes the beginnings of a state of affairs that has persisted ever since: toil and misery overspread everything in consequence of Jupiter's acts, and mankind is toilsome and miserable to this day. The progressive interpretation, however, refers *egestas* to a situation that is over and done with. Virgil has been developing a version of the hard-primitivist myth: the life of early man was poor and needy, and that drove him to strive for the discovery of arts and crafts which would improve his lot. In other words, *egestas* was a

---

[9] Contrary to Servius, and to *ThLL*, Huxley 1963 translates 'unremitting drudgery'—fairly, since the blame is conveyed by the noun. But 'unremitting labour' or even 'unremitting toil' would not do.

pressure that led to discoveries that removed, or at least mitigated, *egestas*. But the same cannot be said of *labor*. Virgil has in fact coalesced two ideas in the preceding lines: the *labor* needed for the invention of crafts and the *labor* needed to practise them after they have been invented. So the *labor* which (according to A) overcame difficulties remains a permanent part of the human condition. In any case, since *labor* is such a central theme of the poem as a whole, we are bound to refer the word here to the world that we know. And it is this which is labelled, emphatically, as *improbus*.

All of this seems true, and indeed important, but not to counteract the case for A. Let us look closer at the interesting word *improbus*. First, a general consideration: a pejorative word may be used in a favourable sense, and for the very reason that it is pejorative. That may sound paradoxical, but it is in fact true to common experience. The word 'naughty' in 'naughty knickers' or 'naughty but nice' is a case in point: something is being recommended for the very reason that it is indecent or improper or self-indulgent. 'Tough' is used in the school playground in this way; compare the Glaswegian usage, 'hard man'. Anyone who supposed that the adjectives in these cases were synonyms for 'strong' or 'brave' would miss the point entirely; the pejorative flavour in the words is an essential part of the praise. Virgil's use of *durus* is a subtilization of this phenomenon—which is less a curiosity of language than a curiosity of human nature. Clearly, words that are very strongly pejorative—like 'vile' or 'detestable'—cannot be used in this way, except by a pervert; what we shall need to consider is whether *improbus* belongs to the milder range of adjectives which can be pejorative without conveying ultimate disapproval.

It seems that *improbus* can be used quite lightly, and in ordinary speech. Horace tells the story of Philippus, a gentleman who is so charmed by the sight of the humble auctioneer Vulteius Mena cleaning his nails outside a barber's shop that he sends his slave to invite him to dinner; the slave comes back saying *negat improbus*.[10] The tone of this must be 'the blasted man says no' or 'the ruddy man says no'; plainly *improbus* expresses light annoyance (maybe even humorous annoyance), not moral blame.

[10] *Epist.* 1.7.63.

Virgil was himself ready to exploit this side of the word: thus *cornix... improba*, the 'rascally crow', in a passage which is a masterpiece of smiling, affectionate observation.[11] A similar flavour must lurk in *improbus anser* ('the rascally goose', 'the wretched goose') at the beginning of the paragraph.[12] Thomas sternly denies the 'playfulness' that most have found in the phrase. Now it is right to insist that pests were a serious matter to the ancient farmer,[13] but serious matters can be handled with a light touch, and it is perverse to deny that Virgil derives some amusement from just this theme at 1.181 ff. Humour is almost too strong a word for Virgil's delicacy, but perhaps it can be used in default of a better. The ant anxious about her old age must have some humorous element, as must the uses of *populare*, 'ravage', (apparently here first applied to animals) to describe the activities of ant and weevil (this anticipates the affectionate quaintness with which the bees are treated in the fourth book). Then there is the *exiguus mus* of 181, with the stressed monosyllable at the end of the line producing a famous piquancy. 'Would commentators be so amused', Thomas asks, 'if we did not have the subsequent and famous line of Horace, *parturient montes, nascetur ridiculus mus, Ars P.* 139?' The answer is yes: Horace has picked up the touch of humour in Virgil but spoiled the best of the effect by destroying Virgil's understatement. The tone of *improbus anser* is similar. Virgil is serious about the nuisance of geese and weeds, but he can handle the matter with a certain wryness. To understand him fully here we shall need to think of the architecture of the paragraph as a whole:

---

[11] G. 1.388. Some nuances are lost to us. One might ask, tentatively, if a ghost of ordinary language does not survive even in such a passage of high emotion as *Aen.* 4.412, *improbe Amor*—is the tone of 'Love, you bastard' just hinted at?

[12] G. 1.119.

[13] Compare K. Thomas 1983: 274–5 (on early modern England): 'It is easy now to forget just how much human effort went into warring against species which competed with man for the earth's resources. Most parishes seem to have had at least one individual who made his living by catching snakes, moles, hedgehogs and rats... Every gardener destroyed smaller pests, and it was usual for the gardening-books to contain a calendar like the one drawn up by John Worlidge in 1668: "January: set traps to destroy vermin. February: pick up all the snails you can find, and destroy frogs and their spawn. March: the principal time of the year for the destruction of moles. April: gather up worms and snails. May: kill ivy. June: destroy ants. July: kill...wasps, flies." And so on throughout the year.'

when we come to examine this, we shall see that the passage both begins and ends with a kind of dour humour.

It is not an accident that the same adjective comes twice in so short a space of time. Virgil's texture is polyphonic: as part of it he wants one tone that will link the practicalities of the farmyard to the large thoughts about the human lot which grow out of it. Now the sentence about *labor improbus* comes, as we have seen, at the climax of twelve lines which have been devoted to human progress and invention; thus far the progressive interpretation seems irresistible, and the tone of *labor improbus* therefore needs to be something like 'bloody hard work' or 'hard work, dammit'—the adjective being pejorative but not without some dour pride. The fact that *labor* is forced upon mankind and the fact that it is disagreeable impose a certain austerity on the poet's vision here; but they do not require it to be pessimistic.

We must also consider the order of the words and the way that they are placed in the line: *labor omnia vicit* | *improbus*. The sentence seems complete at *vicit*, and the line-ending encourages the voice to make a pause. *improbus* is thus both unexpected and emphatic; its effect must be surprising, it must give the tone a new twist. The cheerful picture of the previous dozen lines is given a jolt; and *egestas* follows to reinforce the sterner note. Virgil's technique of construction also requires the word *improbus* to be interesting; a general expression of disapprobation will hardly be enough. The word needs something more to justify its prominence—the nuance of wryness, the tough grimace. Line 146 shifts the tone, but it cannot utterly change the meaning: if *labor omnia vicit* supports the progressive idea, as it must, *labor omnia vicit improbus* must do the same, if in more acid tone. The meaning of lines 133–45 requires the progressive interpretation, as does the construction of 145–6; for unless the mood is confident to begin with, there is nothing worth giving a twist to.

But we have yet to examine the bleakness in the lines which follow, where the pessimist case may perhaps seem strongest. After Ceres has taught men arable farming, they face more toil and trouble: mildew and weeds. Has the paragraph now turned firmly in a gloomy direction? Two considerations may deter us from a simple pessimism.

(a) Out of 147–59 one can extract these propositions. (i) Ceres taught men agriculture; (ii) they have to struggle against weeds and mildew; (iii) if you (the arable farmer) do not work hard, you will go hungry; (iv) meanwhile the good farmer piles up a big heap of grain. Put together, these propositions tell us that toil is necessary, but it brings success; in sum, they seem consistent with the rest of the paragraph and book.

(b) We might be tempted to think of lines 145–6 as a pivot: before, progress; after, pessimism. That is not exactly the case. At line 147 the account of progress continues to surge forward, with Ceres teaching man to plough: the picture of a god guiding men to new discoveries recalls the work's proem. This is the context in which the weeds and blight appear. The technique is again polyphonal. At line 146 the account of progress is given a twist of austerity; it presses on, but then is twisted again, and the gloomier note starts to predominate as the theme descends once more to the practical problems of farming. As Klingner observes, the sentence at 146–7 marks a boundary: before, the theme is man's invention, after, his exertion.[14] The second theme is naturally a tougher one, particularly since it is to lead us back to the topic of practical nuisances which began the paragraph. At its end the lazy farmer's troubles are more prominent than the good farmer's success, but the good farmer's success is none the less there for those who have ears to hear. The tone at the end is ironic and not to be taken too solemnly. The pictures of the lazy farmer gaping at the neighbour's heap and shaking acorns from the trees are quaint and bantering; the *heu* ('ah me') is humorously grave. If that *heu* were wholly serious, it would be a bad error of taste and proportion.[15]

In brief conclusion: the pessimist interpretation cannot stand. The progressive interpretation is broadly right, provided that it recognises the twist at 146–7 and does not try to draw the sting from 148 ff. It does not, of course, deny the sternness of Jupiter's purpose or the need for unremitting hard work.

For the purposes of argument in a controversial case, it has been necessary to treat the paragraph as a whole and lines 146–7 in particular as a problem to be tackled. That is a pity, because the

---

[14] Klingner 1967: 204.
[15] For a similar use of *heu*, compare Tibullus 2.3.2 and 49.

passage should not be intrinsically hard or puzzling and what we have been confronting as difficulty should rather be enjoyed as a brilliancy of poetic technique and complex, flexible rhetoric, various in tone. The paragraph describes a great parabola, beginning and ending with everyday nuisances: birds, weeds and the shadow of over growing trees.[16] The opening topic leads to a remark about Jupiter's severity, out of which grows a great picture of human progress which rises to a climax, twists, turns and descends again, back from god to man, from past to present, back too to that familiar tone of wry, dour irony which was never quite absent even when the declamation was at its height.

[16] It is a misjudgement to mark a new paragraph at line 147, as Geymonat 1973 and R. F. Thomas 1988 do, masking the poetic architecture.

7

Italian Virgil and the Idea of Rome

Michael C. J. Putnam

When Virgil proclaims near the beginning of his second book of *Georgics* that he is about to sing the praises of Italy, we may readily guess at his audience's expectations. They were no doubt prepared, as are we, for an uplifting, stirring hymn to her land and people. We anticipate any georgic, especially a Roman georgic, oriented toward the hardy, conservative ethics agriculture engenders, to manifest blunt pride in quality of earth, and bold patriotism when politics are at issue. In each category, whether his poetry focusses on country or city, on the nature of landscape or humankind, Virgil falls short either of the open eulogy we await or of the indirect criticism his provocative reading of Rome elsewhere elicits. The two texts which I will discuss, each confronting the relationship of Roman man and fruitful nature in contemporary Italy, do not exemplify a poet saying one thing and meaning its opposite. Rather they fall into that rich intervening area of intended friction where an author frets out ambivalent feelings, leaving his audience first puzzled, then enlightened from a dialectic elicited by imaginative virtuosity.

The reviewer of such climactic yet ambiguous verse must approach his task as a psychologist of irony, noting its stimulus on the poet's part as well as in the audience's reaction (they need not necessarily parallel or even complement each other). In the first of two segments from his second *Georgic* here under review, Virgil, briefly put, has taken a near golden-age setting (what we are prepared to hear) and

This paper was first published in 1975 and is reprinted here with minor modifications and the addition of translations of the Latin passages by the author.

Italian Virgil and the Idea of Rome 139

shown it first to have an unexpectedly intense natural potential and then to engender a race of warriors. These last are competitive even outside of Italy and typical therefore of an iron age of acquisitive, vehement activism. The topographical outline of productive Italy's poetic submission to Rome is coexistent with the interaction of quasi golden age in the land with blatant iron age in its ruling people. Responding to the elements in these 'praises' that are less than panegyric in tone, I will endeavor to plumb deeper levels of intent than have been recognized in Virgil. My treatment will attest, and rely on, a dialogue with the book's conclusion. This long disquisition on the good fortune of the farmer, in his separation from the extravagance, ambition, physicality and militarism of Rome, contemplates in a still sharper light many ironies Virgil has earlier suggested.[1] Finally, in pursuing the uses of power and the stylistics of its poetic exposure, I will turn for a moment to Virgil's epic masterpiece, the *Aeneid*, to watch many of the same imaginative impulses at work.

My first text is lines 136–76 of the second *Georgic*. Its common title, 'praises of Italy', is drawn from Virgil's own words (*laudibus Italiae, res antiquae laudis*).[2] It is an expansive climax after more earthbound topics: aspects of growth in plants and differences in various categories of botanical life or in their geographical distribution. It stands apart, too, from what immediately follows as Virgil turns back to practical subjects, to types of soil and the germination and rearing of vines and kindred trees. Here suddenly we are swept above the didactic world of terrestrial specifics into a hymnic litany of attributes

---

[1] My analysis runs counter to a trend in Virgilian scholarship exemplified by Friedrich Klingner, who characterizes Virgil's Italy as a land of mean and measure (1963: 77, 82, 85 ff.), of peace (77), a paradise, in fact (80–1, 85). The villain in his scenario, Virgil's *imbellem Indum* (2.172), is 'the threatening East' (82), 'die Ungeheuerlichkeit des Orients' (83, and cf. 84–5). His soothing view of the book as a whole makes no mention of lines 336–45, which endangers his thesis of Italy as an Eden in time, and sees Justitia still dwelling among farmers, those remnants of a golden age, though Virgil makes her withdrawal explicit (2.473 ff.).

For similar views see Otis 1964: ch. 5 *passim* (e.g., 164: 'Italy, in short, is the actual realization of that mean or measure within the exuberant variety of nature which corresponds to the primal paradise before the Fall'). L. P. Wilkinson, though he notes that the (positive) excesses of the piece may be attributed to the tradition of panegyric or encomium (1969: 52, 87, 245), entitles his most detailed analysis 'Italy the Ideal' (87).

[2] Lines 138, 174.

in land and people which lured the teacher-poet to write. I will follow the material division the poet makes in his final apostrophe:

> salve, magna parens frugum, Saturnia tellus,
> magna virum. (174–5)

Hail, land of Saturn, great mother of earth's fruits, great mother of men!

Let us leave aside for a moment the *viri* who create this world (and the paradox that it can be styled Saturnian) and look first at the *fruges* and their setting. They are 'heavy', pregnant (*gravidae*), and they, along with Bacchus' liquid, have filled the land (143–4). Possession is here of equal importance to gestation: olives and happy flocks hold her (144). And in this country of unceasing spring and summer heat during unwonted months, cattle, too, are twice heavy with young (*gravidae*), trees doubly fruitful (149–50). There are no tigers or lions, no aconite, not a scaly snake writhing his huge folds along the ground and winding himself with his great length into a coil (151–4). Yet the very explicitness of this serpentine parade suggests autopsy, inner fascination, or both.[3] Since there were snakes in Virgil's native soil (as he well knew) and aconite did exist (though of this Virgil may not have been aware), we need no excuse for seeing deliberate exaggeration in Virgil's glance at primaveral Italy, continually renewing itself.[4] And it is a simple matter to take a positive view of plants and animals![5]

---

[3] Circle and line intertwine in this two-verse summary of sinuous behavior. *Nec rapit*, which begins 2.153, receives its noun only with *anguis*, which ends 154. This line is bisected twice by verbal circles, one leading from the initial *rapit* to the nearly conclusive *colligit*, the other enclosing the second line in an adjective-noun frame (*squameus anguis*). On the presence of aconite in Italy see Wilkinson 1969: 246.

[4] There are elements in the rhetoric formulating these matters which leave Virgil's tone open to debate. Charles Witke has pointed out to me that the congeries of negatives surrounding *sed* at line 143 may tend to have a metamorphic influence over this positive particle, negating it and at the same time casting the preceding negative clauses in a more positive light. Objective negation becomes subjective asseveration: these things do symbolically exist and repeated denials only hide the poet's fears under the slim cover of rhetorical *variatio*. And ultimately *sed* is the source of the passage that begins at line 151 with *at* and leads forthwith to *nec...neque*. I am grateful to Professor Witke for sharing with me many valuable insights on the poetry covered by this paper.

[5] Even here, as we watch inanimate nature, references elsewhere in Virgil will not corroborate a totally optimistic interpretation. For instance the only other mention

Italian Virgil and the Idea of Rome

This almost hyperactive restlessness continues over into those aspects of the larger landscape that Virgil chooses to delineate. Rivers glide under ancient citadels (157), the Adriatic and Tyrrhenian seas bathe their shores (158)—both facile enough topics—but there are also grand lakes (even one that rises and roars like the sea, 160). The Lucrine harbor shrieks against its bonds (161–4), and earth's surface has displayed mines of silver and copper and flowed with gold (165–6).[6] The past tenses of the last item, important in themselves as we will see, only slightly mitigate the hyperbole that extends over from the initial description of nature's burgeoning. Here, however, the novelty is man's presence. On these sheer rocks above gliding streams are striking cities, towns and walls, the product of human effort, piled up by hand (155). The landscape's natural defensive postures are enhanced by the protective bastions that men rear to enclose their urban aggregates.[7]

These are strangely potent objects for a singer of *georgica* to magnify, yet Virgil singles out for attention the so-called Portus Iulius, made by Agrippa in 38 BC as a harbor for Octavian's fleet in its preparations against Sextus Pompeius. Here in particular the land's innate energy is regulated. The sea is named for—and therefore verbally tamed and possessed by—the Julian *gens*. The inherent power earth frames in the roaring lakes Larius and Benacus is in this case curbed by man, though the water may howl resonantly against its barriers. In this instance, as in the building of walls and cities, the

---

of Massic wine in the *Georgics* occurs at 3.526 ff. where the plague-stricken ox must die, though untainted by human corruption (*atqui non Massica Bacchi | munera, non illis epulae nocuere repostae*). Such recherché nourishment typifies humanity's foregoing of simplicity for a cancerous luxury.

[6] Virgil leaves *aequor* (2.162) ambiguous. Is he referring to the sea outside, roaring against man's new walls, or to the despairing rage of the newly entrapped Lucrine harbor? Weight is in favor of the latter interpretation, not least because the poet seems to make a distinction in the next line between the Julian wave he has just been describing and the sea water poured back from the barrier (*ponto refuso*). The word *indignor* is discussed below.

[7] It is curious, if we look at the nominally positive turn the rhetoric takes at line 155 (*adde...*), that in one sense the poet disclaims responsibility for what he is about to catalogue—you, the reader, may add these matters if you like! And the near *praeteritio* at 158 (*an memorem...*) helps us to see beyond the mere rhetorical question, to entertain firmer doubts about any positive thrust in the poet's continuing list: 'Ought I recall?' 'Should I remember?'

control of landscape is associated with the use of potential energy for hostile purposes. Men do not rear walls unless they have enemies to ward off nor do they, at least in this situation, expend the effort to curb the sea's turmoil save for their own militaristic projects.

Thus people have inhibited the land for many a day (they are, after all, *antiquos muros*, 157, visible justification for the poet's 'ancient praise', 174) down to the present campaigns of Octavian. What, then, of that other product of this *Saturnia tellus*, the men themselves, the *genus acre virum* (167)? The climactic order of their appearance is carefully chosen, leading first from Italian tribes—Marsi, Sabelli, Ligures, Volsci (167–9)—to Roman warriors in double numbers—Decii, Marii, Camilli, Scipiadae (169–70), plural, though our minds might dwell on an individual within each group. Finally we reach that unique hero, *maxime Caesar* (170).[8] All the warlike propensities of this 'sharp' race, the Ligur, accustomed to hardship, the javelined Volsci, the sons of Scipio hardened by battle, focus on Caesar, the greatest of all. This linguistic gathering up, however, reflects the historical process it adumbrates. A long line of martial instincts now converges toward one man. Just as the Italic tribes, not to speak of foreign territory, were gradually conquered and absorbed by Roman military genius during her Republican period, so these heroic Roman doublings now give place to empire and to the autocracy of the mightiest of all, who absorbs in himself the broad strength of Italy and of her past Roman overlords. Once more, but now from a strictly anthropocentric viewpoint, energy has been confined and concentrated, but not necessarily suppressed.

This martial instinct and its absorption is symbolized in the animals of Italy that Virgil chose to note: *bellator equus*, the fighter horse, and *maxima taurus victima*, the white bull of Clitumnus, choicest of sacrificial offerings (145–8). The horse is a reflection of the land and its people and must be tamed like them.[9] In the *Aeneid*, when Anchises views Italy for the first time, he analyzes an omen of four white horses:

---

[8] Is Caesar the human analogue of one of natural Italy's roaring lakes, *Lari maxime* (2.159)?

[9] Virgil is fond of symbolizing energy devoid of reason through the impulsiveness of the horse. See *G*. 1.512 ff.

> bellum, o terra hospita, portas:
> bello armantur equi, bellum haec armenta minantur.
> sed tamen idem olim curru succedere sueti
> quadripedes et frena iugo concordia ferre:
> spes et pacis ... (*Aen.* 3.539–43)

O harboring land, you bring war; men arm horses for war; these animals portend war. But nevertheless these same horses often become accustomed to pulling the chariot and to bearing peaceful bits under the yoke: there is hope for peace, too.

Our mind becomes adjusted to a series of conditions: Should these creatures become habituated to the reins, there remains a hope for peace. The possibility seems remote. The bull, on the other hand, more passive servant of the farmer, is an easier victim—an Umbrian beast subjugated to decorate repeated Roman triumphal pageants, their immolation before the gods.

With this rich animal potential—Italic might marshalled to Rome—serving as backdrop, it is more than a little curious how Virgil treats the final recipient of this prowess, Caesar: (you)

> qui nunc extremis Asiae iam victor in oris
> imbellem avertis Romanis arcibus Indum. (171–2)

... who, already victorious in Asia's farthest bounds, now drivest the craven Indian from our hills of Rome.

With everything nearer already under her sway, Rome must press her bellicose adventures to the farthest ends of the earth. The impetus of one-man rule, devolved upon Roman Caesar, is itself shifted to the farthest Indi. Yet, if they are that distant, what kind of threat could they pose to the *arces Romanae*, the citadels of Rome and her territory? Moreover, what need ought there be for walls and fortifications, if Rome's might is assured and the golden age has returned? Finally, Virgil reserves his severest irony for the word *imbellem.* Octavian, the mighty victor, warding off Rome's remote enemies from her heights, is expending his efforts on someone who is innately unwarlike. This, I suspect, is a clue to Virgil's own feelings—awe at the Italian might which Rome has harnessed, dismay at its use. This in turn suggests a psychic revolution on the poet's part, from the pronouncement that no other lands vie with the praises of Italy (135–9) to the final statement that he is embarking on the matter of her ancient praise (174–6). Ancient it may be, like her walls, but the poetic progress exposing Italy's chief attributes engenders increasing negativity. As Virgil sees it, this means a change from the hyperactivism of seasonal creativity, to the energy of nature controlled, to the dynamism of a martial populace restricted to the narrow purposes of Rome's greatest personage, which remain propulsive and hostile even against the remote and pusillanimous. It is as if, at least in Virgil's mind, warring were necessary even when war was not, as if Rome after subduing Italy and the world could not subdue her own bellicose instincts.

Something of this inner *volte-face* can be gleaned from reference to the tale of Jason and the hydra's teeth which opens the passage:

> haec loca non tauri spirantes naribus ignem
> invertere satis immanis dentibus hydri
> nec galeis densisque virum seges horruit hastis.   (140–2)

This land no bulls, with nostrils breathing flame, ever ploughed for the sowing of the monstrous dragon's teeth; no human crop ever bristled with helms and serried lances.

From all the possible Greek legends which Virgil might have drawn upon to illustrate what Italy was not like, it is initially perplexing why he chose the metamorphosis of a dragon's fangs into men armed with helmets and thick spears whom the hero must eliminate before reaching his goal. Virgil, I suggest, was already subconsciously fascinated by a myth whose very aptness for Italy only surfaces in the course of what follows. Fire-breathing bulls and hydras she does not possess, any more than ravenous tigers or lions, but her outstanding 'crop', the growth which is the poet's deepest concern, is in fact that *genus acre virum*, that brood of armed men the foremost of which, to some extent like competitive Jason, is now off making futile war in the farthest east. The war is futile not because he is endangered but because (now unlike Jason) there is no opposition to quell.

What would seem at first to be Virgil's negative attraction to apt myth is metamorphosed into a series of conscious ironies as the passage draws to a close. The phrase *Saturnia tellus* is a prime instance. At the outset we might expect in this land of rich harvests and double springs a renewal of Italy's once ideal past, when nature's bounty and the absence of greed and ambition urged on mankind a gentle community.[10] The advent of Jupiter's reign changed all this, bringing with it competition (the voyage of the *Argo* is a standard prototype) and war. At the end of the book, constructing in the past an idealized farmer's life that also, as we shall see, has its ironies, Virgil can openly state that

> ante etiam sceptrum Dictaei regis et ante
> impia quam caesis gens est epulata iuvencis,
> aureus hanc vitam in terris Saturnus agebat;
> necdum etiam audierant inflari classica, necdum
> impositos duris crepitare incudibus ensis.   (536–40)

Nay, before the Cretan king held sceptre, and before a godless race banqueted on slaughtered bullocks, such was the life golden Saturn lived on earth, while yet none had heard the clarion blare, none the swordblades ring, as they were laid on the stubborn anvil.

At the very conclusion of the whole poem we find Octavian in much the same posture as in *Georgic* 2, a *victor* still, now only *magnus* instead of *maximus*, placed more specifically by deep Euphrates than on Asia's distant shores. This time, however, he thunders (*fulminat*, *G*. 4.561). In *Georgic* 2 Virgil can make his point about the decay of the ages without the need to attach directly any Jovian attributes to Octavian. The universality of violence and battling among this nation of warriors supplies sufficient evidence of the downward change.

The same ambiguity inherent in the denotation of this energetic land as Saturnian also charges Virgil's heralding of his own song:

> Ascraeumque cano Romana per oppida carmen.   (176)

And through Roman towns I sing the song of Ascra.

We may characterize Hesiod as poet of the golden age, but such an attitude does as grave an injustice to his unrolling of the myth of the

---

[10] *Saturnia tellus* exerts its irony through the adjective's grammatical ambiguity. The land is not merely belonging to, akin to Saturn, that is, an appropriate setting for the aureate civilization over which he once presided. Linguistically it also implies a step beyond Saturn, in a chronological (and then ethical) sense. Thus we find the divine symbol of upsetting violence in the *Aeneid* regularly categorized as *Saturnia* Juno. The very phrase *Saturnia tellus*, in Evander's anthropological survey of Italy's decline, is used to define a post-Saturnian era given to rage for war and greed of possessions (*Aen.* 8.327 ff.).

ages in *Works and Days* as does ignorance of the way Virgil sets the phrase *Saturnia tellus* in a context devoted to self-aggrandizement and the play of power.[11] For Hesiod the era of gold has long since yielded to that of iron in which men now find themselves: 'Would that I were not among the men of the fifth generation, but either had died before or been born afterwards. For now truly is a race of iron, and men never rest from labor and sorrow by day, and from perishing by night.' This is the pessimistic spirit in which Hesiod concludes his tale. Nor is it sufficient to find a Hesiodic analogy for *Ascraeum carmen* in that message from Jupiter that permeates the *Georgics*—that man must forever labor by the sweat of his brow (ἔργον ἐπ' ἔργῳ ἐργάζεσθαι, *Op.* 382), that trouble and need are life's overlords.[12] Around the general context of brother's enmity with brother, Hesiod weaves a fabric of strife, decay, rampant evil, injustice and hatred. It is perhaps no accident for Virgil's purpose that on the only occasion in Hesiod's poetry where he mentions Ascra, the 'miserable hamlet' (*Op.* 639) near Mt. Helicon in which his father settled, he calls it 'bad in the winter, painful in the hot season, pleasant never' (*Op.* 640). This is the holy spring which it takes courage on Virgil's part to broach on the towns of Rome, those towns built above sheer cliffs, now no longer Italian but Roman.[13] And through the verb *recludere* Virgil carefully arrogates to himself

---

[11] I refer to the much discussed sentiment in which Virgil, earlier in the first book, summarizes the Jovian era (1.145–6): *labor omnia vicit | improbus et duris urgens in rebus egestas* ('relentless toil has conquered everything, and need, pressing hard on men through adversity'). The second phrase formally resolves the ambiguity of the first. It is possible to treat the opening colon by itself somewhat positively: effort, though importunate, has won its way over all obstacles. Yet counterpoised with 'oppressive need' *labor* loses any uplifting connotations of ethical uprightness through work and asks to be viewed more as toil or suffering. Suffering and need permeate Virgil's spiritual world, and it is no accident that their personifications, *Egestas* and *Labos*, cohabit near his gates of Hell as ready persecutors of mankind (*Aen.* 6.276–7).

[12] I owe much here to an enlightening conversation with Dr. Jenny Clay on the relationship of Virgil to Hesiod.

[13] *Romana per oppida* (2.176) glances back at Lucretius' Ennius, winning bright fame among Italian peoples (*per gentis Italas*, Lucr. 1.119). The possessive limitation which such an alteration of names imposes is the final Romanization of the land, in a metamorphic process that earlier altered *laudibus Italiae* into *Romanos triumphos* and *Romanis arcibus* (surely not the city of Rome's alone, but those others, *congesta manu praeruptis oppida saxis*, 2.154).

the notion of releasing pent-up impulses, in his case that of a poetic inspiration which complements the ambiguous efforts of the Roman landscape and populace.[14]

There are other means by which Virgil forces his readers to see beyond Hesiod as poet either of the golden age or of virtuous labor, and these help accomplish the transition to the book's finale. We can now see more clearly, for instance, the special importance of the perfect tense in Virgil's précis of Italy's mineral resources:

> haec eadem argenti rivos aerisque metalla
> ostendit venis atque auro plurima fluxit.   (165–6)

Yea, and this land has shown silver-streams and copper-mines in her veins, and has flowed rich with gold.

Even if Italy once flowed with streams of silver and gold (and the hyperbole itself tends to undercut any potential praise), grammar corroborates that this is a thing of the past.[15] How, then, are such metals used, or misused, in a more modern Italy? There is the wealthy Roman whose proud portals 'vomit' forth a flood of flatterers in the morning (461–2): the farmer need not 'gape' at such inlaid doorposts (463). The rich man boasts among his corrupting treasures Corinthian bronzes and garments 'mocked' by gold (*inlusas auro vestis*, 464). (Those streams of wealth are now frozen into a private hoard, and imported at that!) Or there is another example of the present, the miser who broods over gold that must now be dug up:

> condit opes alius defossoque incubat auro.   (507)

Another hoards up wealth and broods over buried gold.

Above all, as we would now expect, it is iron that characterizes this decadent age. There are those who use it in war:

---

[14] *Recludere* is of course cognate with *claustra*, those barriers of the Lucrine lake formed by Agrippa against the sea (2.161).

[15] The tense of *ostendit* is ambiguous: fitting enough link between *immittitur* and *fluxit... extulit*. A perfective action, however, claims a grander space in the book's ethical purview than a present. In an opulent past, when riches were only seen, metallic luster served only for symbolic value. The turn from sight to touch postulates questionable economic gain and certain moral decline. And what of Caesar who mediates between *extulit* and *avertis*? Where and how is he to be placed?

> sollicitant alii remis freta caeca, ruuntque
> in ferrum, penetrant aulas et limina regum.   (503–4)

Others vex with oars seas unknown, dash upon the sword, or press into the courts and portals of kings.

Virgil plays on the phrase *in ferrum*: by rushing to arms they kill themselves as well as others. In this non-golden, quite iron age it is the literal economic value put on the gleaming metal that drives acquisitive mankind into vicious use of its duller, harder, more deadly cousin. And among the several symbols of the central city that the fortunate farmer need not see are catalogued

> ... ferrea iura
> insanumque forum aut populi tabularia ...   (501–2)

... the iron laws, the Forum's madness, or the public archives.

It is sharp in itself that the core of Roman commercial and political life is branded *insanum*. The fact that the rights there promulgated (whose evidence was undoubtedly stored in the Tabularium which loomed over the western end of the Forum Romanum) are called *ferrea* contains a special linguistic jab. The Romans, relying on material endurance, ordinarily engraved their laws on bronze. It is therefore the metaphor in *ferrea* that is of primary importance. The iron laws of Rome, emanating from her maddened heart, enslave those bonded to her might.

I have turned to the end of *Georgic* 2 to illustrate the depth of Virgil's earlier musings. Whatever the idealistic intention he may have had in mind as eulogy for Italy and Rome, in his words we have watched gold turn to iron as the rule of Saturn succumbs to that of his son Jupiter. This last would find his terrestrial analogy in Octavian, *maxime Caesar*, on whom Virgil by grammar concentrates such power. We have seen the poet verbally subdue Italy to Rome, and Italians and earlier pairs of Romans to Octavian alone, who is now using this intense strength against peaceful Asia. Virgil need make no direct equation of Caesar and Jupiter; his point is reinforced by the constant iteration of the notion of Rome's present singular kingship, the earthly manifestation of the sceptre of the king raised at Dicte (*sceptrum Dictaei regis*, 536). We have seen it generalized in the desire of the greedily ambitious to penetrate the courtyards and thresholds of kings (*aulas et limina regum*, 504). Virgil makes pointed references to Rome in the first part of his list of the scenes of universal acquisitiveness and fraternal hatred that the blessed country dweller need not face:

> illum non populi fasces, non purpura regum
> flexit et infidos agitans discordia fratres
> aut coniurato descendens Dacus ab Histro,
> non res Romanae perituraque regna.   (495–8)

Him no honours the people give can move, no purple of kings, no strife rousing brother to break with brother, no Dacian swooping down from his leagued Danube, no power of Rome, no kingdoms doomed to fall.

The purple of kings and kingdoms about to fall are juxtaposed too nearly and neatly with *res Romanae* for us to disavow any intimacy between them. The presence of regality may threaten from the outside, its postures are equally a menace from within.

In fact the tension between Italian potential and its deepening misdirection by Rome is refocussed in these final lines into a specifically temporal differentiation between time present and time past, between an unpretentious life following the land's customary rhythms and rituals and the contemporary Roman immorality. But the one subtly shades into the other at a moment where once again we feel a deeper force in Virgil's words, challenging their superficial intent. He has just finished his portrait of a country life:

> hanc olim veteres vitam coluere Sabini,
> hanc Remus et frater; sic fortis Etruria crevit
> scilicet et rerum facta est pulcherrima Roma,
> septemque una sibi muro circumdedit arces.   (532–5)

Such a life the old Sabines once lived, such Remus and his brother. Thus, surely, Etruria waxed strong, thus Rome became of all things the fairest, and with a single city's wall enclosed her seven hills.

Though this is time past (a fact which both *olim* and *veteres* call to attention), it is still an un-Saturnian world where walls are necessary. We recall the generalized *muros* from the earlier overview of Italy (157), an easy anticipation of the *Romanis arcibus* from which Octavian wards off the Indi (172). Both subject matter and poetic irony pinpoint Rome as the source of this mutation for the worse. Rome became *rerum pulcherrima*, most beautiful of things. Exaggeration (and the potential irony of *scilicet*) aside, it is not long since Virgil has singled out *res Romanae* as a pernicious affair which the man who communes with rural gods can and must shun. Virgil may even mean to be specific about time as well as place. It was only for a brief moment that Remus and his brother could have led this visionary life together. The idyll came to an end when at the very instant of Rome's foundation Romulus killed his confrère: ambition (and one man's yearning for autocratic rule?) triumphing over any feelings of kinship.

The name Romulus is not mentioned, nor can Octavian now be brought directly into a context which hints at fratricide. But Virgil's contemporary readers would be fully aware that he was deliberately reaching toward that instant of violence which, to the Augustan poets, was the mythic source and prototype of the century of civil wars which ended only at the battle of Actium (though Virgil could not yet have been fully assured, as he wrote, that the ending had finally come). It is a stroke of particular genius that here Virgil shows the actual historical and intellectual framework in which this myth of civil strife collides with another archetypal schema which haunted the Roman imagination—the dream of a past heritage of peace, simplicity and bounty associated once upon a time on Italian soil. Time present and time past, imperfect Rome and ideal rusticity, reality and myth, merge centripetally in Virgil's mind at that moment when *Remus et frater* are conjoined.

Remus, the brother killed, is named. Romulus, the stronger, first king of Rome by an act of violence, is designated simply *frater*, but for a purpose. In emphasizing Romulus' role rather than his name Virgil turns our thoughts to one of the most explicit horrors of contemporary Rome—the continuing presence of Discord who pursues brothers treacherous to one another (*infidos agitans discordia fratres*, 496). In this upset world there are even those who gain pleasure from a drenching in a brother's blood (*gaudent perfusi sanguine fratrum*, 510). The model is one of ancient authority.

Yet even in his characterization of the farmer's life remote from Rome there are elements that suggest Virgil's continued awareness of Italy's potential energy that could be organized for negative as well as positive ends. The farmer's rigorous existence depends on a laborious, unceasing effort to control, tame, civilize nature to make her productive and ensure his livelihood. Unlike Rome—a bad *patria* which drives its offspring into exile—he keeps his children and grandchildren with him, his house is chaste, competition in his life is limited to fat kids battling with locked horns. It is watching his moments of ease that serves Virgil as transition back (or forward?) to the life of Romulus and Remus. The farmers keep festive days, first crowning the wine bowl and pouring libation to Lenaean Bacchus, then playing in rustic sport with javelins and wrestling. However, immediately before commencing his eulogy of the georgic way, Virgil had warned us of the ruinous power of Bacchus to set people (here Lapiths and Centaurs) against each other:

> Bacchus et ad culpam causas dedit; ille furentis
> Centauros leto domuit, Rhoecumque Pholumque
> et magno Hylaeum Lapithis cratere minantem.   (455–7)

Bacchus has even given reasons for blame. He tamed in death the raging Centaurs, Rhoecus and Pholus, and Hylaeus, threatening the Lapiths with a mighty bowl.

It is not difficult to match the sportive aim of javelin against elm with the life and death struggle which the age of Jupiter ushers in with trumpets and swords.

There are other ways in which Virgil detaches himself from the negative intensity of his contemporary Roman world. The first is the dream of a still more idealized rural life which, as Virgil begins his finale, contrasts with a 'civilization' that perverts nature-clothes 'deluded' by gold, wool 'stained' by poisonous dye, clear olive oil 'corrupted' by cheap cinnamon (464–6). Instead—and here is the dream—we have the earth pouring forth easy sustenance far from civil strife (*discordibus armis*, 469), we have careless peace, an existence incapable of deceit, a wealth of resources, leisure, grottoes, living lakes, cool vales, cattle lowing, soft sleep (467–71).

This may have been the fleeting aspect of Virgil (I am tempted to call it romantic) that appealed to English viewers of vistas in the eighteenth and nineteenth centuries. Yet the very context in which Virgil places such a fantasy offers proof of his awareness that he is dealing in make-believe, an inspirational Utopia. This easy sustenance, he states pointedly, is poured forth spontaneously by the most just earth (*iustissima tellus*, 460). The suspicions aroused by the hyperbole are soon confirmed when the poet states openly that it was among such folk that Justice trod her last steps before leaving the world entirely:

> extrema per illos
> Iustitia excedens terris vestigia fecit.   (473–4)[16]

Among them, as she quitted the earth, Justice planted her latest steps.

With her departure the glow of this georgic *locus amoenus* is darkened too. Not only does Virgil reveal how lacking in quiet, in fact how constantly filled with effort even the still partially idealized agricultural regimen of a sturdy, quasi-Saturnian past remains; more importunate is the presence of Roman *Discordia* whose effects on the landscape Virgil elsewhere evaluates with more realistic honesty.

Virgil's second mode of detachment, equally romantic but somewhat more tangible, is to rid himself entirely of the spectre of Italy and its gradations between remote and nearer to hand, ideal and real, Saturnian and Jovian, and fantasize on the image of Greece:

> rura mihi et rigui placeant in vallibus amnes,
> flumina amem silvasque inglorius. o ubi campi
> Spercheosque et virginibus bacchata Lacaenis
> Taygeta! o qui me gelidis convallibus Haemi
> sistat, et ingenti ramorum protegat umbra.   (485–9)

Let my delight be the country, and the running streams amid the dells—may I love the waters and the woods, though fame be lost. O for those plains, and Spercheus, and Taygetus, where Spartan girls hold Bacchic rites! O for one to set me in the cool glens of Haemus, and shield me under the branches' mighty shade!

Virgil had previously mentioned generalized 'chill vales' (*frigida tempe*, 469)[17] in his litany of beauties that grace the landscape's retreat. But the reader is scarcely prepared for this magical translation

---

[16] This view is a realistic reaction to Virgil's own suggestion in the fourth *Eclogue* that the virgin goddess of justice, Astraea, has returned along with Saturn's kingdom (*iam redit et virgo, redeunt Saturnia regna*, Ecl. 4.6). That passage in turn is a response to Aratus who originated the motif that she has already departed this world; for him, at the advent of the bronze age (*Phaen.* 133 ff.).

[17] The common noun, *tempe*, bespeaks familiarity as well as generalization.

into a more specific dream world of rivers, valleys and hillsides. Virgil calls himself *inglorius*, lacking the heroism to face the world around him or the poetic themes that evolve from duty, not desire.[18] Certainly there could scarcely be a more vividly succinct definition of a fantasy of escape. A style built around emotional, prayerful exclamation complements image after image of withdrawal—plains, virginal revels on Sparta's mountain, valleys in abundance (*vallibus, convallibus*), the mighty shade of protecting branches.

In its immediate setting this extended sigh of yearning for an Hellenic elsewhere follows on the poet's self-dedication to the 'sweet Muses,' who inspire, it would seem, a recoil from Lucretius' version of the nature of things. Lucretius and his predecessors among Greek physiologists analyzed powerful movements in the external aspects of nature. Virgil's negative, or at the very least ambivalent, reaction to such parts of nature can be sensed in the way he chooses to define the daily round of sun and moon (the 'collapses' of the sun, the 'struggles' of the moon, 478), the hasty falling of a winter's day, the lagging halt that besets the progress of the night (481–2). He would, given proper tutelage by the Muses, have told of earthquakes and tides:

> unde tremor terris, qua vi maria alta tumescant
> obicibus ruptis rursusque in se ipsa resident.   (479–80)

...whence come tremblings of the earth, the force to make deep seas swell and burst their barriers, then sink back upon themselves.

Virgil's imagination abjures these leviathan instincts in nature just as it does the more specific impulses in the seething continent of Italy. It is as hard to control the one by words as the other by the acts of man. Lucretius, verbal organizer of nature, Agrippa, tamer of waters, and mighty Caesar, conqueror of peoples, have a certain prowess in common. And Virgil shies away from all three.

Once more, as in the case of praises bestowed on Italy, beneath the surface of Virgil's obeisance to his great predecessor runs a deeper current of unease. Lucretius by analyzing the causes of things (*rerum causas*) rid the world—so his successor seems for a moment to

---

[18] The anti-heroic Virgil may therefore be gently siding with the *imbellis Indus*, warded off from Rome by Octavian.

claim—of fear and fate and Acheron's greed. Virgil, blessed by fortune like his farmers, believes more humbly in country gods.[19] That is, whereas Lucretius demythologizes nature by a scientific scrutiny extensive enough to limit even the domain of death, Virgil yields as we all must (and as I suspect Lucretius did also) to the numinous, mysterious or terrifying in nature, to the ceaseless claims of the ritual of birth and death. Virgil can escape from the potentially debilitating objectivity of Lucretius by appeal to religion, one of mankind's deepest psychological necessities.[20] Withdrawal from the pressures of Romanized Italy, however, takes a double road. The first is through topographical symbolism, by turning the mind's eye to Greece, imagination's source in a land of protective enclosure, not frenetic intensity. The second has recourse to time rather than space, to the myth of a golden past that shades into a purely rural (and therefore non-existent) present, a Rome once hardy but non-violent.

Most interpreters of the second *Georgic*, because they devote their attention only to the relieving aspects of each of these dichotomies, see the book as essentially positive, even spritely in its outlook. Apart from the better-known segments, it is in large measure a book about control, concerned with how man through his knowledge and efforts sets his sights on training, teaching and fructifying nature. Virgil intersperses stretches of relief from this struggle which I have not yet touched upon. There is the momentary instant of vernal calm, between winter's cold and the heat of summer, when Father Heaven

---

[19] Virgil defines his student of nature as *felix*, his devotee of country gods as *fortunatus*. One is 'well-omened', 'lucky', the other 'blessed by fortune'. The latter adjective the poet had already applied to his farmers: *o fortunatos nimium, sua si bona norint, | agricolas!* (2.458–9). It implies dependence on the whims of *Fortuna*, a more fickle, unstable position than *felix* suggests. If farmers were to 'know' of their blessings, to be aware of them intellectually, they would become too fortunate and therefore subject to change. The intimate of country gods is also *fortunatus*, participant in a world whose fearsome fluctuations the author of the *Georgics* sagely estimated. Again one suspects a subtle irony. The student of the causes of things seems to know his discipline better (*cognoscere*) than he who contemplates country gods (*novit*). But if fear and death are in fact permanent features of our lot and cannot be argued away, who is the more blessed, the 'lucky' scientist, who claims to manage nature's most sweeping forms, or the 'fortunate' believer in the ubiquitous presence of her divinity?

[20] Scientific objectivity, by regularly pursuing a utilitarian and didactic course, robs this strange world's matter of its subjective role as a vehicle for poetry, as a continuous source for metaphors raising the immediate to the symbolic.

joins with Mother Earth. (But this is myth and happened only when nature once chose to indulge her tender creations.) Furthermore the book begins and ends with festival. At the start Virgil invites Lenaean Bacchus (and us, implicitly) to celebrate the vintage harvest, and at the conclusion we see the farmer reserving festive days for drinking (once more calling on Lenaeus) and gaming. Like heaven's complaisant spring, ritual too relieves the daily round. Those times in between are necessary periods of refreshment both for farmers, dependent on their own efforts and on heaven's benison, and for poets who dream of Saturn (time when) and Greece (place where).

Yet this is not quite the end. There follows first the revelation we have already stressed, that such occasions are things of the past now that war and Jupiter hold sway. Then we return in the last two lines to the poet himself:

> sed nos immensum spatiis confecimus aequor,
> et iam tempus equum fumantia solvere colla.   (541–2)

But in our course we have traversed a mighty plain, and now it is time to unyoke the smoking necks of our horses.

And at the end of the first book, a much more unrelievedly pessimistic explication of man's works and days, Virgil compares our world—right and wrong reversed, laws broken, war ubiquitous—to horses heedless of their charioteer's dictates during the course of a race. And at the end of both books the forging of swords symbolizes the transformation and reversal of power from man civilizing nature to his own psyche disordering man. Virgil's boast that rounds off Book 2 is not that, having completed a stretch of poetry rivalling Ennian epic, he is now figuratively above the battle. Rather it is the claim that his words have kept rein over the extensive thematic track which the laps of the second book comprised. We have seen the many directions in which these intellectual energies pulled.

Virgil was drawn to these and similar problems throughout his writing career. It might be of value to conclude with a brief look at their evolution in the *Aeneid*. Throughout his epic Virgil is again fascinated by the tension of order and disorder, envisioned particularly in symbolism of violence, suppressed or rampant. We are ushered into a grandiose world sporting irate winds imprisoned in a cave and vengefully released, a wooden horse pregnant with armed men, a giant pinned beneath a volcano that belches forth its own innards. We find a rabid priestess who must be tamed before uttering ordered words, a reluctant bough that needs to be rent from its parent tree to serve as passport, a river whose turbid swelling must be calmed like the goddess' wrath it personifies.

There are moments, too, when Virgil allows himself the luxury of attending solely to past and future—the simple life on the site of Rome, the glorious expansion of empire through the impetus of heroism. Present reality, however, is a more difficult matter, more difficult than the matter of the *Georgics* if only because Virgil is dealing for the most part with the interactions of people and not with plants, animals and their relationship with humankind. The first six books of the *Aeneid* are psychologically simple enough. Aeneas must only face and withstand a series of emotional storms—Troy's fall, Ulyssean adventures, encounter with Dido, death of Palinurus—as he makes his fated way toward the promised land. Yet the merger of Italy and Rome is not an easy one, especially when overlordship of this hypothetical realm of future Rome must be secured by the pitting of native strength against native strength, one form of wildness against another, whose differentiation is more a question of degree than kind. The advent of Aeneas is as disturbing to this land as it is calming.

I would like to offer one specific illustration from his epic of Virgil's percipient view of the intimacy of Rome, Italy and empire. It is based on the word *indignor* and will take us for a moment back into the center of the second *Georgic*. We remember how Virgil views Agrippa's construction of the portus Iulius:

> an memorem portus Lucrinoque addita claustra
> atque indignatum magnis stridoribus aequor,
> Iulia qua ponto longe sonat unda refuso.   (161–3)

Shall I tell of our havens, and the barrier thrown across the Lucrine, and how Ocean roars aloud in wrath, where the Julian waters echo afar as the sea is flung back?

This is nature made unnatural, the sea confined within the land, man for his own uses taming the elements who react with displeasure at a strange imprisonment. At the start of the *Aeneid* we find the same reaction in the powerful winds whose wild nature is such (Virgil purposely treats them metaphorically as horses) that a mountain dungeon must be their lot:

> illi indignantes magno cum murmure montis
> circum claustra fremunt. (*Aen.* 1.55–6)

They in wrath roar reverberatingly around the barriers in the mountain.

This initiatory episode helps symbolize, as critics have long seen, interweaving patterns of violence suppressed and released which run through the epic.

Two other occasions where the poet uses the verb *indignor* in the second half of the poem stand out because of their climactic positioning. The first is in Book 8. As the final scene on the shield of Aeneas, one of Virgil's grandest ruses for surveying the future, we find Caesar Octavianus born in triple triumph after the battle of Actium. He receives before him in a long line images of conquered peoples and rivers. Among these, last in the row and the last object on the shield itself, is the river Araxes chafing at the bridge the Romans had built across it (*pontem indignatus Araxes*, *Aen.* 8.728). This is the final reluctant witness, the final acute emblem of Roman might swaying a varied world humbled before Caesar, doubly caught by Vulcan's sculpturing of metal and a poet's words. This moral pattern of future Rome is easy enough to contemplate and achieve, far distant temporally and geographically. Aeneas' own doings in the last books of the epic, however, are incapable of easy analysis, their very complexity caused largely by a change from figmented vision of a once and future Italy to the reality of establishing dominion over a land in which the hero was not nurtured.

And so we come to the final line of the epic. Turnus, focal leader of Italy but with his own private vendetta to press, has been beaten down by Aeneas in single combat. He prays his conqueror to spare him; Aeneas hesitates but glimpses on Turnus a belt once worn by Pallas, favored child of Evander from the locale of Rome and killed earlier by Turnus. The sight rouses Aeneas to a fury of rage and he buries his sword in the chest of his enemy. The epic ends, however, with our eyes on Turnus:

> ast illi solvuntur frigore membra
> vitaque cum gemitu fugit indignata sub umbras.
> (*Aen.* 12.951–2)

... but his limbs are undone with cold and his life with a groan flees resentful under the shades.

At last empire is stabilized, with the life of the most doughty opponent 'fleeing with a groan of dissent to the shades below'. Virgil had used this same line in the preceding book during the death agony of the Volscian warrior maiden Camilla. He thus verbally unites native heroine and hero, vicarious or immediate victims of Aeneas' advance. Each has lost his *dignitas* in a death which eliminates personal worth and authority. Like the *portus Iulius* or the bridged Araxes in the sphere of nature, Camilla and Turnus stand as examples of human energies reacting to subjugation by Rome's mythical ancestor and prototype. Wildness tamed by death is allowed only its fleeting moment of riposte.

But it would be simplistic of us to leave criticism there, thinking that the evil demon of opposing force has finally been exorcised, that the violence which impeded Aeneas' progress from the beginning of the epic until now has at last been stilled. Rechannelling of inimical dynamism to more positive goals is one thing, killing an antagonist turned suppliant is another.

Aeneas' actions in fact revive the same doubts about the morality of Rome's use of its inherent, natural power as those Virgil had suggested in his thoughtful survey of Italy in the second *Georgic*. For by his deed and by the way Virgil prepares him for it—he is seized by fierce passion (*saevus dolor, Aen.* 12.945), enflamed with madness and terrifying in his rage (*furiis accensus et ira | terribilis, Aen.* 12.946–7)—Aeneas becomes directly allied with another strand of violence which runs through the epic. It is usually seen in those who challenge Aeneas' fated march, personified in the chief opposer, Juno, queen of the gods, to whom we are introduced at the start of the epic: she also is *accensa* (*Aen.* 1.29), mulling wrathfully over the reasons for her anger (*causae irarum saevique dolores, Aen.* 1.25). We find it again in Dido, *subito accensa furore* (*Aen.* 4.697), maddened with ill-conceived love for a lingering hero whose victim she becomes. We meet the characteristic in Camilla, *furens acrique accensa dolore* (*Aen.* 11.709), stalking her last victim whom Virgil compares to a dove eviscerated by a hawk's talons.[21] *Dolor* and *ira*, to be sure,

[21] *Aen.* 11.723.

are the abstractions that arouse the Etruscans, Aeneas' future friends, against their former tyrant Mezentius. But in their case each word is given a morally positive designation, the first styled *iustus*, the second *merita* (*Aen.* 8.500–1). When at the end of the epic the qualities of unreason that had urged on Aeneas' opponents pass over to the titular hero himself, they are allowed by the poet to have no expressly redeeming features.

We may put this development in another way. The self-effacing hero in Book 2 is told by Hector to yield Troy because the situation is hopeless, yet still he fights blindly on (a natural enough reaction). The Aeneas who dallies in Carthage, once more forgetful, this time of his Latin mission, unwittingly causes Dido's suicide on his own sword. The end of the epic is different, however, for Aeneas is now fully master of his own behavior and destiny. It is he who now kills with his sword out of immediate passion, directly causing death. And he is once more disobedient, forgetting the words of his father Anchises (of whom Turnus has just reminded him), to leaven power with restraint.

I offer these summary thoughts not to pass a moral judgment on Aeneas' final deed (my own prejudice is apparent, but Virgil's words offer wide latitude for interpretation) but rather simply to illustrate how Virgil remained ever fascinated, throughout his career, by the stimulus of power and its effects on the minds and deeds of men. His version of Rome as a political entity complements a propensity for symbolism expressive of order and disorder, restraint and violence, or, as a combination, emotion controlled or exploited. Virgil may wish perfection on the land and inhabitants of Italy, and there is much to elicit his honest praise. It was for him a realm of physical and mental vitality, whose greatest gift to Western civilization still remains perhaps the very notion of patterning needed to frame this vitality, whether through roads or laws. But this is to deal in abstractions (of which sewers and aqueducts are only visible results) and forget the psyche of those who presided over the creation and management of this exemplar.

In the second *Georgic* Virgil allows us, first through gentle ambiguity, then by more vigorous statement, to ponder the reality of power's misuse and compare it to less troublous intellectual foci. In the *Aeneid* we chart the psychological process of a human being in the very act of responding to and working with its possession.

The *Aeneid* offers no final hope of an innocent Eden restored and revivified, nor at the opposite extreme does it glorify the realistic militarism which is one of its more prominent themes. For Virgil, the nature of man, like the nature of the land on which he lives, is rhythmic, now wintry, now flourishing, now sharply competitive, now claiming its moment of idealism. If the ending of the epic is illuminated more by iron's dull glow than gold's shimmer, it is because this is all we can honestly expect from a poem of force. And it is to the related aspects of the psyche, to the subjective modes of thinking toward which the possessors of power, the shapers of history, are drawn, that Virgil devotes his richest words.

8

Cosmology and National Epic in the *Georgics* (*Georgics* 2.458–3.48)

Philip Hardie

The most extended self-referential discussion of the poet's task in Virgil's œuvre occurs at the centre of the *Georgics*, at the end of the second and the beginning of the third books. In these two passages Virgil turns to consider poetic alternatives to his present rural themes, in the first place the poetry of *cosmos*, elevated philosophical didactic on cosmological themes, and in the second place the poetry of *imperium*, epic celebrating the power of Rome and its leader. An analysis of these passages, which were very possibly composed not long before the *Aeneid* was begun, is crucial for the understanding of Virgil's conception of the place of cosmological poetry in the epic. At first sight it would appear that the cosmological themes at the end of the second *Georgic* and the imperialist epic themes at the beginning of the third are quite unrelated; but it gradually becomes clear that Virgil is using the same complex set of terms to approach both areas of subject-matter. This indirect association makes it legitimate to ask what connection there might be between cosmology and historical epic in Virgil's mind at this point in his poetic development.

Vinzenz Buchheit has argued convincingly that these two adjacent passages are conceived as two halves of a grand structure straddling the central divide of the *Georgics*; here Virgil examines at length his

---

This paper first appeared as a chapter in P. R. Hardie 1986 (pp. 33–51) and is here reprinted virtually unchanged except for the addition of translations of the Latin quotations by the author.

own poetic goals, and at the same time develops the central themes of the whole poem.[1] In particular Buchheit indicates how the praises of Octavian at the beginning of the third book, so far from being a digression extraneous to the concerns of a poem about agriculture, may be understood as complementing the picture of the ideal country life at the end of the previous book. The climactic sequence of ideal Italian country life followed by the triumphs of the Italian poet and the Italian general repeats and expands the sequence of thought in the *laudes Italiae* earlier in the second *Georgic*. Buchheit's analysis of the Lucretian echoes in these passages is central to his argument; his conclusion is that Virgil effectively distances himself from his didactic predecessor and obliquely asserts his own absolute superiority over the claims of Lucretius to show mankind the way to salvation. This involves taking the passage at *Georgics* 2.475–94, in which Virgil intimates his inability to approach the themes of natural philosophy, as a concealed but decisive claim for the superiority of his own (anti-Lucretian) themes. This point is obviously of some importance for my concern with the interpenetration of natural-philosophical and epic themes and techniques in the *Aeneid*, and in particular for the argument, developed in P. R. Hardie 1986: Chapter 5, that in this respect the *De Rerum Natura* is a central model for the *Aeneid*; and I shall examine this passage carefully in order to test Buchheit's argument.

Lucretian echoes become dense at the beginning of the first section of the *laus vitae rusticae*, *Georgics* 2.458–74.[2] The key passage here imitated is the proem to the second book of the *De Rerum Natura*, which contrasts the false goods of the life of luxury in the city with the simple but sufficient pleasures of country life. Virgil's description of country life is introduced with a line pregnant with Epicurean overtones (467):

at secura quies et nescia fallere vita.[3]

Carefree calm and a life that cannot deceive.

---

[1] Buchheit 1972: 45 ff. The essential unity of these two passages also forms the basis of the rather different analysis in Wimmel 1960: 167–87.
[2] The parallels are assembled by Fenik 1962: 75 ff.
[3] *Quies, quietus, securus*, are all applied by Lucretius to the life of the gods or of the wise man; it is a little disconcerting that the combination *secura quies*, used by Lucretius twice, is applied both times to death (3.211, 939). *Nescia fallere vita* is a curious verbal echo, though not in sense, of the well-known Epicurean injunction λάθε βιώσας.

We may note in advance that the farmer's landscape, with its cool streams and shades, is a close approximation to the dream landscape for which the poet yearns in lines 485 ff. (to some extent, of course, this is explicable in terms of the common convention whereby the poet says that he is doing that which he writes about, as seen, for example, in Virgil's incorporation of his own poetic persona into the pastoral landscape of the *Eclogues*). But the rustic idyll ends in the most un-Lucretian *sacra deum* of line 473, followed by a glance at *mos maiorum* in the words *sanctique patres*, which is also alien to Epicurean concerns. As Buchheit says, we wait eagerly to hear how Virgil further defines his relationship to Lucretius.

Any idea that this might turn out to be, even indirectly, a confident assertion of superiority, based on the conviction that the Lucretian world-view is second best to the Virgilian, is deflected by the implications of lines 473–4:

> extrema per illos
> Iustitia excedens terris vestigia fecit.

As she departed from the earth Justice left her last footprints in their midst.

At line 460 we heard of the *iustissima tellus*; the later compliment to the countryside is not so straightforward, for, although superior in justice to the town by virtue of the fact that the goddess retired thence to the country, even the countryside has now been abandoned by *Iustitia*. To draw the logical conclusion, the only place to which corruption does not now extend is the sky.

With the departure of *Iustitia* from the earth (*excedens terris*) we are transported to the heavens and into a region of Aratean allusion;[4] these cosmological and literary coordinates also locate the immediately following lines, 475–7:

> me vero primum dulces ante omnia Musae,
> quarum sacra fero ingenti percussus amore,
> accipiant caelique vias et sidera monstrent.

As for me, my first wish is that the Muses, sweet above all things, and whose sacred objects I bear, smitten with a great love, should receive me and reveal to me the paths of the stars in the heavens.

---

[4] Δίκη: *Phaen.* 100 ff. The Aratean echoes in these lines are assembled by Buchheit 1972: 61 n. 252.

The address to the Muses is closely modelled on Aratus 16–18:

> χαίροιτε δὲ Μοῦσαι
> μειλίχιαι μάλα πᾶσαι· ἐμοί γε μὲν ἀστέρας εἰπεῖν
> ᾗ θέμις εὐχομένῳ τεκμήρατε πᾶσαν ἀοιδήν.

Hail Muses, most gentle every one of you: answer my prayer that I may rightly tell of the stars, and guide all my song.

Particularly close is the echo in *dulces ante omnia* of μειλίχιαι μάλα πᾶσαι.[5] Virgil, as we shall see, develops in his own way that extended use of religious language which in Aratus is determined by the fact that the conventional appeal or prayer to the Muses is incorporated in the structure of a hymn.

So far we are presented with a simple opposition between the themes of country life and the pure scientific themes of Aratus, an opposition engineered through the rather artificial intermediary of Aratean *Dikê*. But lines 475–7 also contain important Lucretian echoes. Before examining these it is convenient to ask why the sequence of thought in lines 458–74 should lead to the discussion of specifically *Lucretian* scientific themes. An answer is provided by the clear statement a few lines later of the intimate connection between Lucretius' natural-philosophical inquiry and his banishment of the bogies of the Underworld (which for the Epicurean is closely linked to the denial of divine intervention in the world). The vanity of the fear of the gods and of death is included in the argument of the proem to book two of the *De Rerum Natura* which, as we have seen, is the central model for lines 458–74 of the second *Georgic*. It is Virgil's awareness of the contradiction between Lucretius' further development of his diatribe topic and the point at which he himself has arrived with *sacra deum* at line 473 which brings up the whole question of the compatibility of the themes of Lucretian natural philosophy, on which the rejection of religion is based, and the values of the Roman countryside.

To return to lines 475 ff., the most obvious Lucretian echo is in line 476, *ingenti percussus amore*, which alludes to Lucretius' description of his own poetic inspiration at 1.922–5:

---

[5] Cf. also the *dulces Camenae* of *Catal.* 5.12; perhaps there is a suggestion that now Virgil sees the possibility of combining philosophy with the sweetness of the Muses that was then seen only as totally alien to the seriousness of the former.

> sed acri
> percussit thyrso laudis spes magna meum cor
> et simul *incussit* suavem mi in pectus *amorem*
> musarum.

But a great hope of praise has smitten my heart with the sharp thyrsus, and at the same time struck into my breast sweet love for the Muses.

The further extension of the list of natural-philosophical subjects after *caelique vias et sidera* of line 477 is also obviously Lucretian in content and language.[6] But even lines 475 and 477, which seem to be purely Aratean, conceal Lucretian allusion. The 'sweet' Muses correspond to Aratus' 'gentle Muses', but Lucretius also describes sweetness as the chief gift of the Muses in the central passage on his inspiration at 1.921 ff.; note especially line 947:

> et quasi *musaeo dulci* contingere melle.[7]

And as it were to touch [my theme] with the sweet honey of the Muses.

The astronomy of line 477 is also a central concern of Epicurean science, particularly as a way of subverting the Aristotelian appeal to the argument from design; celestial phenomena are one of the chief sources of false belief in the gods. The language of line 477 contains an ambiguity that points directly to Lucretian models:

> [Musae] accipiant caelique vias et sidera monstrent.

May [the Muses] receive me and reveal to me the paths of the stars in the heavens.

On the surface this is an appeal for the communication of information on matters astronomical, but, given the underlying tendency in this whole passage to identify the landscape of the poet with that of his subject-matter, it is easy to read this as a request for directions on literal 'paths to the sky' (rather than 'the paths of the heavenly

---

[6] Line 478: cf. Lucr. 5.751 *solis item quoque defectus lunaeque latebras* ('and likewise the eclipses of the sun and concealments of the moon'). 479–80: 6.535 *quae ratio terrai motibus exstet* ('what is the cause of earthquakes'), 6.577 *magni causa tremoris* ('the cause of a great quake'); 5.1002–3 *frustra mare saepe coortum | saevibat leviterque minas ponebat inanis* ('the sea often rose and raged in vain, and just as lightly put down its empty threats'). 482: 5.699–700 *propterea noctes hiberno tempore longae | cessant* ('therefore in winter-time the long nights linger').

[7] Cf. also *dulci*, 938; *suavem*, 924; *suaviloquenti*, 945.

bodies'). *Monstrare* frequently has the sense of 'point out' a path to be followed.[8] The image of following a path is commonly applied to the 'path' to philosophical enlightenment and salvation, and is especially prominent in Lucretius.[9] A close parallel in Greek for the image of a path to the skies in a context which combines the poetic and scientific in a religious setting, as in Virgil, is found in Heraclitus' *Homeric Questions* 76.1:

Homer, the great hierophant of heaven and the gods, who opened up the paths to heaven which till then were inaccessible and barred to human spirits.

In a Lucretian context, however, the immediate model for *caelique vias* is Epicurus' 'flight of the mind' in the proem of book one of the *De Rerum Natura*, a journey which ends in victory over the conventional inhabitants of the heavens. The chief difference between this passage and *Georgics* 2.475 ff. is that Epicurus' 'journey' is the result of his own unaided powers of mind, whereas Virgil must rely on the success of an appeal to the divine Muses.[10]

It is now time to examine in more detail the nature of the religious conception behind these lines. Buchheit[11] and others take line 476 to imply a confident identification of the poet as a *Musarum sacerdos*, and this encourages an extremely positive evaluation of the claims made by Virgil in the *recusatio*. J. K. Newman, in his discussion of the sources of the *vates*-concept, illustrates what he takes to be the image here from the Posidonian description of the Celtic *vates* as *hieropoioi* (priests) and *physiologoi* (inquirers into Nature);[12] Posidonius'

---

[8] *ThLL* 8.1440.82 'de monstrandis viis'. The figurative path to the sky that the astronomer follows is vividly described in Ov. *Fast.* 1.295 ff. (a passage heavily indebted to *G.* 2.475 ff.), summed up at 307 *sic petitur caelum*.

[9] e.g. Cic. *Fin.* 1.14.46 *sapientiamque esse solam, quae... omnis monstret vias, quae ad quietem et ad tranquillitatem ferant* ('[that] it is wisdom alone which reveals all the paths, which leads to peace and calm'); cf. Lucr. 6.27 *viam monstravit, tramite parvo | qua possemus ad id recto contendere cursu* ('revealed a path, by which on a narrow track we could reach that goal by a direct route'). Poetic and philosophical *viae* are closely linked in Lucretius, a significant fact for Virgil's use of the image.

[10] The image of a journey to the sky is developed at length by Manilius in announcing his astronomical theme (1.1 ff.); the whole passage is constructed out of Lucretian and Virgilian fragments.

[11] Buchheit 1972: 68–9, linking it to the *vates*-concept.

[12] Strabo 4.4.4; discussed in Newman 1967b: 16 ff.

Cosmology and National Epic in the Georgics 167

ethnographical account of the primitive poet, which is very possibly related to his historical reconstruction of the origins of music (discussed in P. R. Hardie 1986: 14–15), may well have been a part of the intellectual atmosphere out of which the Augustan *vates*-concept emerged, but the correspondence between it and Virgil's self-portrait here is not as exact as Newman claims.

The sense of lines 475–7 may be best elicited after discussion of the religious background of the rest of the passage, starting with line 483:

> sin has ne possim naturae accedere partis.

But if [I am prevented] from being able to approach these parts of nature.

Accedere here picks up the *poetic* initiation of Lucretius (1.927):

> iuvat integros *accedere* fontis.

I take pleasure in approaching untouched springs.

But for the poetic fountains of Helicon Virgil substitutes the topography of Lucretius' primary subject-matter, *rerum natura*. Conington compares Lucretius 3.29–30:

> quod sic *natura* tua vi
> tam manifesta patens ex omni *parte* retecta est.

Because by your power nature is thus revealed in all parts and laid so open to view.

The language of revelation here is heavily religious; Lucretius (with Epicurean precedents) is exploiting the Aristotelian (and common Hellenistic) idea of the contemplation of the universe as analogous to the shows of the mysteries.[13] The account of Epicurus' mental flight

---

[13] See Festugière 1944–54: 2.233 ff., 'Le monde temple de Dieu', drawing on Bywater 1877: 75 ff. For a later exploitation of this view of Nature see Sen. *Q Nat.* 1 prol. 3 *rerum naturae gratias ago, cum illam non ab hac parte video, qua publica est, sed cum secretiora eius intravi... nisi ad haec admitterer* ('I give thanks to the nature of things when I behold her not in the part open to the public, but when I have gained admission to her more secret parts... were I not granted admission to these secrets...'); also ibid. 7.30 (the secrets of Nature compared to the Eleusinian mysteries); Sen. *Ep.* 90.28–9; cf. Reinhardt 1953: 806; Nock 1972: 796–7 ('the metaphorical use of mystery terminology') (= Nock 1952: 184 ff.).

in the proem to book one of the *De Rerum Natura* may also echo the language of the mysteries.[14]

The language of religious initiation and revelation is picked up in the *makarismos* of lines 490 ff. The *makarismos* is a form that was originally particularly at home in the language of the mysteries, a congratulation on the benefits consequent on religious knowledge or experience.[15] It also became a common way of congratulating the wise man or philosopher on the fruits of his wisdom;[16] initially the blessings of philosophical insight were set up as a conscious alternative to the traditional insights of religion. In the case of Empedocles the religious and philosophical aspects are especially close (B 132):

ὄλβιος, ὃς θείων πραπίδων ἐκτήσατο πλοῦτον,
δειλὸς δ', ᾧ σκοτόεσσα θεῶν πέρι δόξα μέμηλεν.[17]

Happy the man who has acquired a wealth of divine understanding, but wretched he whose mind is filled with shadowy opinion about the gods.

The mixture of the religious and the philosophical is still present, or perhaps it would be better to say revived, in *Georgics* 2.490–2: the keyword *cognoscere* points to the claim of both the mysteries and of

---

[14] Cf. R. M. Jones 1926: 112–13, esp. 113 n. 2. Compare Apul. *Met.* 11.23 (the initiation of Lucius) *per omnia vectus elementa remeavi... deos inferos et deos superos accessi... ecce tibi rettuli, quae, quamvis audita, ignores tamen necesse est* ('after travelling through all the elements I returned... I approached the gods below and the gods above... see, I have told you things which must remain unknown to you, even if you hear them').

[15] See Dodds 1960 *ad* Eur. *Bacch.* 72–5.

[16] The following is based on Gladigow 1967.

[17] In thought and language this is close to Empedocles B 129, which is said to be in praise of Pythagoras, and whose terms are similar to those in which Lucretius praises the universal insight into the nature of things won by Epicurus, and hence also similar to the terms of the Virgilian *makarismos*. One wonders whether Virgil is deliberately exploiting an Empedoclean passage (we have already been alerted to the possibility of Empedoclean models in line 484) in a discussion of one of Empedocles' chief heirs, Lucretius, with an intention both complimentary (Virgil praises Lucretius in the language that Empedocles had used of *his* hero Pythagoras) and critical (Virgil implies that he has the correct δόξα about the gods that Empedocles desiderates). Boyancé 1927: 368 ff. uses the Empedoclean model to argue that Pythagoras is the immediate object of Virgil's *makarismos*. On the relationship of religion and philosophy in Empedocles B 132 see Gladigow 1967: 419: 'Die Aufnahme und Umformung des Makarismos des Epopten durch Empedocles manifestiert, dass der Erlösungsgedanke der Mysterien in die "Philosophie" übernommen worden ist. Von nun an tritt die Philosophie in Konkurrenz mit den Mysterien.'

Cosmology and National Epic in the Georgics 169

philosophy to beatify through *knowledge*;[18] Epicurean knowledge here serves the redemptive function of freeing mankind from the fear of death. This is particularly pointed since the *makarismos* of the Eleusinian mysteries seems traditionally to have dwelt on the benefits to be gained *in the next world* through initiation.[19] Virgil thus plays Lucretius' own game of using the vocabulary of religion to express an anti-religious point of view, before turning this vocabulary back into its proper channels at line 493:

> fortunatus et ille deos qui novit agrestis.
> Happy is also the man who knows the gods of the countryside.

Lines 490–2 are a tissue of Lucretian reminiscences.[20] It does not matter very much whether we take the primary subject of *felix* to be Lucretius or Epicurus, given that Lucretius consistently presents his own philosophical and poetic career as an imitation of the trailblazing expeditions of his master. The central Lucretian passages alluded to in these lines are, firstly, the proem to book three, a sustained attack on the fear of death, which, as we have seen, links up with the concerns of the proem to book two on which the initial praise of country life was based; and, secondly, the account of the 'flight' of Epicurus in the proem to book one: compare especially *Georgics* 2.492, *subiecit pedibus*, with Lucretius 1.78, *religio pedibus subiecta*. With this theme of vertical dominance we are thus brought back in a ring to the spatial implication (also Lucretian in origin) of *caelique vias* in line 477; and we are now in a position to evaluate those opening lines more fully, in the light of the language of initiation and revelation that dominates the rest of the passage.

The general religious setting of lines 475 ff. is, as we have seen, Aratean, but the specific colouring of *accipiant* and *monstrent* derive

---

[18] e.g. Eur. *Bacch.* 72 ff. ὦ | μάκαρ, ὅστις εὐδαίμων | τελετὰς θεῶν εἰδὼς | βιοτὰν ἁγιστεύει ('blessed he who knows the rites of the gods and lives a holy life'); Pindar fr. 137 Snell quoted in the next note.

[19] Cf. Pindar fr. 137 Snell ὄλβιος ὅστις ἰδὼν κεῖν' εἶσ' ὑπὸ χθόν'· | οἶδε μὲν βίου τελευτάν, | οἶδεν δὲ διόσδοτον ἀρχάν ('happy he who sees those things and goes under the earth; he knows the end of life, and he knows its god-given beginning'); Soph. fr. 837 Pearson.

[20] 490: Lucr. 3.1071–2, 5.7, 5.1185. 491: Lucr. 1.62 ff., 1.146, 2.14 ff., 3.91, 6.39. 492: Lucr. 1.78, 3.25 ff.

from the Lucretian framework of initiation and revelation. Virgil appears not as a priest, one who is already privy to the secrets of the gods, but as an initiate who demands admission and illumination.[21] In *monstrent* we have an allusion to the central action in mystery cults of *showing* the mystery-objects to the pious. 'The high priest of Eleusis is called the Hierophant because *he shows* the Hiera.'[22] *Accipiant* is less specific, but related words are commonly used of the reception of worshippers before a rite.[23] *Quarum sacra fero* is usually taken to refer to the sacrifice offered by the priest;[24] but if *sacra* means 'sacrificial offerings' one might expect a dative rather than the genitive after it. For the genitive one may compare Horace *Satires* 1.3.9–11:

> saepe velut qui
> currebat fugiens hostem, persaepe velut qui
> Iunonis sacra ferret.

Often like a man running to escape from the enemy, but very often like a man carrying the sacred objects of Juno.

The reference is here to a servitor rather than a priest.

A partial commentary on what is going on in the Virgilian lines is found in the first of Ovid's epistles *ex Ponto*. Ovid is discussing the possibility of his verses from exile finding acceptance in Rome, in the face of their likely exclusion. He uses the standard vocabulary of welcome and admission, *accedere* (*Pont.* 1.1.9), *accipere* (14), *admittere* (29), *patere* (35); it is a question of finding a path, *iter* (6, 35), for his poems. In support of his plea for admission Ovid states that his book contains praise of Caesar; the name of the emperor should act

[21] Poets and mysteries: cf. Dio Chrys. *Or.* 36.33 (poets, the θεράποντες Μουσῶν, like attendants of mysteries who stand outside the doors and who are not true initiates, but who may get an inkling of what is going on inside).

[22] Mylonas 1961: 298, with a list of passages referring to this act of *showing*. For help in elucidating the religious background to *G.* 2.476–7, I am indebted to Dr R. C. Parker.

[23] ὑποδέχομαι: *SIG* 1023.14; *IG* II² 1283.17. Cf. *LSJ* s.v. θεωροδόκος. Note also *Aen.* 1.289–90, *caelo... accipies*.

[24] Cf. *Aen.* 5.59–60, 9.86, 12.13; at 6.809 and 8.85 *sacra ferre* is used of non-sacrificial objects borne by a priest. In general, the carrying of sacred objects need imply nothing very exalted about the status of the bearer; cf. Pl. *Phd.* 69c8–9 ναρθηκοφόροι μὲν πολλοί, βάκχοι δέ τε παῦροι ('many are they who bear the fennel-wand, but few are the initiates of Bacchus').

Cosmology and National Epic in the Georgics

as an 'open sesame', as the olive branch opens the way to the ambassador, as the burden of Anchises opened a path through the flames for Aeneas, and as the several symbols of Isis, Cybele, and Diana open doors and purses to their devotees. At lines 45–8 Ovid applies these various analogies to his own case:

> en ego pro sistro Phrygiique foramine buxi
> gentis Iuleae nomina sancta fero.
> vaticinor moneoque. locum date *sacra ferenti.*
> non mihi, sed magno poscitur ille deo.

Instead of the sistrum or the stops of the Phrygian flute, see, I carry the sacred names of the Julian family. I utter the warnings of a seer. Make way for the bearer of sacred objects. I make the request not for myself, but for a great god.

The difference between the Ovidian and Virgilian conceptions is that in Ovid the bearer of *sacra* is already an accepted devotee of his chosen god, and uses the *sacra* to gain admission or money from outsiders, whereas Virgil bears the *sacra* of his goddesses in order to gain admission to the company and secrets of those same divinities. A closer analogy for the idea of admission to a place of religion or mysteries is provided by the sixth book of the *Aeneid*. At line 109 Aeneas asks the Sibyl to show him the way (*iter*) to his father's shade in the Underworld. The Sibyl tells Aeneas that this is only possible for one who carries the sacred object of the Golden Bough. Only after successfully delivering this to the gateway of Proserpina can Aeneas be received by his father (*accipio*, 693), who then proceeds to reveal (*ostendere*, 716) to Aeneas the future heroes of Rome.[25] Virgil's request for initiation may certainly be linked to the old idea of the poet as priest, but he does not himself achieve the status of priest until the beginning of book three of the *Georgics*, when he builds an earthly temple himself as a substitute for the celestial temples which he may not enter; in this temple the gifts that he bears (*dona feram*, 3.22) are sure of a welcome.

Both Ovid and the Sibyl regard the bearing of *sacra* as an automatically efficacious guarantee of admission, and it is in the nature of

---

[25] On possible allusions to the mysteries in the Descent to the Underworld in *Aen.* 6 see Luck 1973.

such rituals that while they may dramatize the anxieties that attend hazardous religious passages, they are normally regarded as inevitably operative if performed in the correct fashion. In Virgil's case there seems to be a conflict between his religious devotion and emotional attachment (*amore*, 476), which are not in doubt, and his intellectual capacity to understand, as expressed in the pre-Socratic physiological language of line 484. To describe his possible inadequacy to write scientific poetry Virgil uses the language of such poetry; more specifically he alludes to the theories of Empedocles, one of the most important models for Lucretius himself (484):

> frigidus obstiterit circum praecordia sanguis.[26]

The cold blood around my heart prevents me.

The language suggests the coldness of fear or of the failure of will, but the Empedoclean allusion indicates that what is really at issue is a failure of intellect, of *nous*. What should be stressed is that Virgil uses this physicalist explanation of cognition to suggest an affective reaction to what for Lucretius would be purely a matter of reason, *ratio*.

Virgil now turns to the alternative to the lofty secrets of Nature, the retreats of the countryside. Love for the Muses (*amore*, 476) is replaced by love for the rivers and woods (*amem*, 486); this love is to be without fame and honour (*inglorius*, 486). This is a disavowal of the Lucretian *laudis spes magna* (1.923), as Buchheit points out;[27] note further that Lucretius closely associates this ambition for glory with the love of the Muses (*simul*, 924). Virgil effects a disjunction between *laus* and *amor*, and also displaces the object of *amor*, from the Muses to the countryside.

The *recusatio* reaches its climactic and most clear-cut formulation in the double *makarismos* of lines 490–4 (*felix...fortunatus*). Buchheit sees here the definitive rejection of the Lucretian/Epicurean way to salvation in favour of an alternative of religious gnosis in the service of traditional Roman values. But line 490, *felix qui potuit rerum cognoscere causas* ('happy the man who was able to understand

---

[26] Although the doctrine implied here is not found in the extant fragments of Empedocles, the combined evidence of this line, Empedocles B 105, and Hor. *Ars P.* 465 makes an Empedoclean source more than likely: see Brink 1969.

[27] Buchheit 1972: 62. It may be relevant that the heart, *cor*, is the seat of Lucretius' ambition; it is in the regions round the heart, *praecordia*, that Virgil feels the chill.

the causes of things'), seems to contain no irony; it is an admission that such a man *has* found the truth about the universe,[28] and is thus qualitatively different from the usual rejected alternative in a *recusatio*, which is always a partial approach to reality. The parataxis of *felix... fortunatus* here refers to a truly unresolved dichotomy. In the first statement we are presented with an intellectualist explanation of the world and the gods, wrapped up (in Lucretian manner) in the non-intellectualist language of religion; in the second statement we are given a traditional religious form of confession, in which *novit* corresponds to a very different form of knowledge from the *cognoscere* of line 490. Virgil is confronted with an irreconcilable clash between Faith and Reason; he opts for Faith, but with a full awareness that this involves an abnegation of the (Lucretian) certainties of Reason.

Buchheit's argument rests largely on a comparative analysis of the *recusatio* in other poets. It is true that the *recusatio* frequently conceals a conviction of superiority beneath a display of mock-modesty (cf. *inglorius* here). But there is no real parallel to what Virgil does here. The normal *recusatio* justifies a decision not to write in a genre other than that chosen, and is provoked either by critical hostility to that other genre (Callimachus) or by the need to ease oneself of internal or external pressure to write in the other genre (the Roman elegiac and lyric *recusatio*). Virgil, however, is talking about different levels within the *same* genre. He certainly does represent himself as under the pressure of an internal urge to write the other kind of didactic, but this is quite different from the nagging guilt that reminds the elegists of their 'Roman' duties.[29] Buchheit produces as his trump-card Horace's account of his relationship to Lucilius, a poet writing within the same genre, but this is determined by the need to establish both a proper respect for and distance from a poet

---

[28] Buchheit talks of the demonstration by Virgil that Lucretius' is not 'die wahre Lehre' (1972: 76), but there is no demonstration of this in Lucretius' own intellectualist terms.

[29] The pressure on Virgil is well characterized by Wimmel 1960: 173, 'eine andere Bedrohung, eine gefährlichere, weil sie aus dem eigenen Willen kommt. Sie liegt im eingeborenen metaphysischen Streben nach dem umfassendsten Stoff, dem Vorwurf der ganzen Natur, dem Weltgedicht gleichsam.' Wimmel goes wrong, in my view, in failing to see that the pressure on Virgil is very specifically related to his predecessor Lucretius.

whom Horace has set up as the *inventor* of his genre. But there is, in formal terms, no such bond of necessity between Lucretius and Virgil, who rather holds up Hesiod as the great original of the *Georgics*.[30]

Buchheit takes the hypothetical *sin* of line 483 as a further indication that Virgil feels his superiority in the fact that he might well, anyway, be able to write scientific poetry.[31] This infringement of the convention of the *recusatio* whereby a decisive break is set between what the poet will (or can) and what he will not (or cannot) do is more reasonably interpreted as a sign of Virgil's real desire to write such poetry, as suggested by the language of line 476, *ingenti percussus amore*,[32] which is a world away from the polite sparring of Horace *Satires* 2.1.12–13 (adduced by Buchheit):

> *cupidum*, pater optime, vires
> deficiunt.

I am eager, good father, but my strength fails me.

There are two other curious features about Virgil's *recusatio*. Firstly, he has already shown elsewhere in the poem his interest in cosmological subject-matter, for example in the opening words of the great invocation at the beginning of the first book, where the gods are astronomical rather than mythological (5–6):

> vos, o clarissima mundi
> lumina, labentem caelo quae ducitis annum.

You, shining lights of the heavens, who guide the year in its course through the sky.

In the first book of the *Georgics* Virgil handles Eratosthenic and Aratean astronomical material in a quite unembarrassed way. Eclipses and violent floods figure prominently at the end of the first book, although in a context not natural-philosophical. The first line of the second book defines one of the two main subjects

---

[30] 2.176 *Ascraeumque cano Romana per oppida carmen* ('I sing an Ascraean song through Roman towns').
[31] Buchheit 1972: 66–7.
[32] It is *dulcis amor* that is the central and active driving-force of Virgil's poetry at *G*. 3.291 ff.; cf. P. R. Hardie 1986: 165–6.

of the previous book as *sidera caeli*. The *recusatio* at 2.475 ff. is thus not even strictly true to the nature of the poem as we have it.

Secondly, the terms in which the appeal to the Muses is framed make it appear that what is at stake is not merely their willingness to reveal the secrets of the heavens, but their willingness to receive Virgil *tout court*; this is the implication of *me...Musae...accipiant*. The failure to embark on scientific poetry appears also to entail the absolute failure to meet the Muses. It is perhaps significant that this (at almost the midpoint of the poem) is the first mention of the Muses in the *Georgics*. The rural alternative to scientific poetry seems deliberately to eschew the Muses; the Greek mountains of lines 487–8 are *not* the haunts of the Muses, and the final term of the whole passage is the recognition of the Nymphs, *Nymphasque sorores*, in line 494, who thus balance the appearance of those other sisters, the Muses, at the end of the first line of the passage, 475.

We can now suggest an answer to the question of why the Muses might not accept Virgil and initiate him into the mysteries of the universe. The passage starts from Aratean allusion, and is a patchwork of reminiscences of scientific didactic, including also allusions to Lucretius and Empedocles; we are given a composite picture of the whole range of cosmological poetry.[33] But, just as we have seen that underlying the superficial Aratean sequence of thought leading into lines 475 ff., a deeper concern with Lucretian themes connects the apparently disparate subjects of country life and natural philosophy, so it is Lucretius, lurking even when other models seem to be primary, who directs Virgil's reaction to this composite picture. The tensions and contradictions contained in the passage may be read as the product of the peculiarly involved mixture of attraction and repulsion that Virgil feels towards his Roman predecessor: attraction for the grandiose cosmic afflatus that pervades the *De Rerum*

---

[33] On the eclectic nature of this passage and also of the cosmogony in the Song of Silenus in *Eclogue* six see Stewart 1959: 185. The eclecticism of subject-matter is matched by the eclecticism in the religious framework of the passage, which combines Pindaric/Callimachean ideas of the poet as priest, with elements of a Hellenistic cosmic mysticism (partly mediated through Lucretius' peculiar exploitation of this current), and the more specifically Lucretian imagery of Bacchic inspiration (*bacchata*, 487); the Empedoclean allusions also suggest the pre-Socratic priest-philosopher image.

Natura, intellectual attraction to the resounding certainties of the Lucretian world-picture; but repulsion from the accompanying demand that the emotional ties to Rome and Italy, and perhaps to irrationality itself, must be cut once and for all. This is why Virgil chooses, to express his distancing from Lucretius, a peculiarly recondite piece of science, which allows him to state intellectual failure in almost affective terms.

Some such psychological explanation would appear to be necessary to explain the blockage which leads Virgil to misrepresent his own treatment of scientific matter within the *Georgics*, and may also help in the understanding of the emotional outburst of lines 486–9, in which Virgil longs for a Greek landscape which is conspicuously *not* that of the Italian farmer; this dream-landscape seems to function as an outlet for the tension which Virgil feels with regard to Lucretius. Obsession with Lucretius may also explain why Virgil here appears to be oblivious to the possibility of a non-Lucretian type of natural-philosophical didactic, possibly Stoic, Platonic, or Pythagorean in affiliation, which *could* accommodate Virgil's Roman and Italian attachments. Samples of such poetry could be found, for example, in Cleanthes, and (to some extent) in Aratus himself; and, once more, Virgil here ignores the fact that he gives a specimen of such philosophical didactic within the *Georgics* themselves, at 4.219 ff. (on the divine nature of the bees). The *recusatio* may often be a mere conventionality, but it would seem foolish to deny that in the elegists, for example, it sometimes acts as a vehicle for the expression and release of sincerely felt anxieties. Anxiety is certainly a word that comes to my mind in the context of Virgil's *recusatio* here.[34]

The choices at the end of the second *Georgic* are presented largely in topographical terms, and point us towards the conventions of poetic geography; the *recusatio* may be interpreted in terms of the opposition between high and low places of poetry, as found notably in the sixth *Eclogue*. The high place of poetry is defined initially in terms of the heavens as the present abode of *Iustitia*, which is to be contrasted with the ground-level of the countryside that she leaves

---

[34] The relationship of Virgil to Lucretius provides an interesting example of what Harold Bloom, using psychological models, has called 'the anxiety of influence'.

behind (*terris*, 474).³⁵ The sky (*caeli*, 477) then becomes the place to which Virgil aspires as scientific poet, following in the steps of Lucretius' Epicurus; the further Lucretian echoes demonstrate that the 'paths of the heavens' are also a transformation of Lucretius' *own* poetic high place, Helicon (Lucr. 1.921 ff.). With these celestial regions are contrasted the rivers and woods of the countryside.³⁶ As a place of poetry this last is reminiscent of the lower of the two places of Gallus' poetic activity in the sixth *Eclogue* (64–5):

> tum canit, errantem Permessi ad flumina Gallum
> Aonas in montis ut duxerit una sororum.

Then he sings of how Gallus, wandering by the streams of Permessus, was led up to the Aonian mount by one of the sisters.

Epicurus'/Lucretius' victory over the skies is alluded to again at line 492, *subiecit pedibus*. The rest of the epilogue to the second book plays itself out at the ground-level of the countryside.

Book three also begins with the woods and rivers (*silvae amnesque Lycaei*, 2), but the poet now prepares himself for another attempt to leave the earth (8–11):

> temptanda via est, qua me quoque possim³⁷
> tollere humo victorque virum volitare per ora.
> primus ego in patriam mecum, modo vita supersit,
> Aonio rediens deducam vertice Musas.

---

[35] Which in turn is contrasted with the negatively evaluated height of luxurious city-dwellings: 460–2 *fundit humo facilem victum iustissima tellus;* | *si non ingentem foribus domus alta superbis* | *mane salutantum… uomit… undam* ('the earth in her justice pours forth an easy living from her soil; if a lofty mansion does not pour forth a great wave of morning callers from its proud doors').

[36] It is true that Virgil goes on to talk about mountains in the countryside, as he had previously come down to earth and sea in the natural-philosophical questions of the previous lines; this may seem to weaken my argument. I would reply (i) that the vertical contrast is prominent in the *first* lines of each part of the opposition, and thus determines our response to the whole (*caelique vias et sidera*, 477; *rura… et rigui… in vallibus amnes*, 485); (ii) that this geography does not serve *solely* the function of finding a poetic level, but is also a vehicle for the concrete subject-matter of the poet. Natural science includes the inquiry into parts of the universe other than the sky; mountains are an inevitable presence in the Graeco-Roman rural world, and Virgil is not setting out to *climb* these mountains.

[37] Note the verbal echoes of the previous book: *caelique vias*, 2.477; *possim*, 2.483.

I must attempt a path on which I too can raise myself from the ground and fly victorious over the lips of men. If only I live long enough, I shall be the first to bring back the Muses with me to my fatherland, returning from the Aonian summit.

Buchheit analyses well the combination in line 9 of themes from the grave-epigram of Ennius and, in the word *victor*, from the triumphant flight of Epicurus through the universe at the beginning of the first book of Lucretius.[38] It may be added that the combination of Epicurus and Ennius is itself already given in Lucretius, who clearly treats the two as parallel sources of, respectively, philosophical and poetic inspiration. Epicurus and Ennius are also joint begetters of the next words in Virgil; in Lucretius each claims primacy in his sphere (*primum* of Epicurus, 1.66; *primus* of Ennius, 1.117; like both, Virgil too wishes to be *primus*, *G.* 3.10). The balanced *primum*...*primus* is also taken over by Virgil, for *primus* here picks up *primum* at *Georgics* 2.475. The notion of bringing down the Muses from Helicon is modelled in the first place on Lucretius 1.117–18:

> Ennius ut noster cecinit qui primus amoeno
> detulit ex Helicone perenni fronde coronam.

As our Ennius sung, who first brought down from lovely Helicon a garland of evergreen leaves.

But the substitution of *deducere* for *deferre* points to the triumphal vocabulary which Lucretius applies to Epicurus, and which now becomes the central area of imagery for Virgil.[39]

This flight from the earth/ascent to Helicon, executed in the language which Lucretius applies to the ascents of Epicurus, Ennius, and himself, is, as it were, Virgil's second attempt at take-off. It is also his second attempt to win the Muses (as it is the second mention of

---

[38] *Tollere* in line 9 may also glance at *tollere*, Lucr. 1.66 (Epicurus the first man to try to rise from mankind's oppression *in terris*, 63).

[39] On *deducere* see Nisbet and Hubbard 1970: 420. For the triumphal language in Virgil see Buchheit 1972: 102–3; note esp. *G.* 3.12 *referam*, modelled on Lucr. 1.75 *unde refert nobis victor quid possit oriri* ('whence victorious he brings back to us an account of what can come into being'). There is probably also an allusion to the statues of the Muses that Ennius' patron, M. Fulvius Nobilior, literally brought back in triumph from Aetolia. The construction of this temple in Rome was possibly described in the original conclusion to the *Annals*; if so, this episode will have been one of the models for Virgil's poetic temple. See Skutsch 1985: 18 ff.

the Muses in the *Georgics*), although here in the more violent form of leading them off in triumph rather than through the respectful approach of the religious initiate. Like the first attempt, this too is envisaged in the contingent form of the *recusatio*, although here processed in futures rather than subjunctives.[40] The Muses are still thought of as companions of the future; when Virgil returns to the themes of the countryside at line 40, it is to the company of Nymphs that he resorts, just as at 2.494. Buchheit is obviously correct in saying that the military and nationalistic themes are in some way a substitute for the Lucretian themes aired at the end of the previous book; particularly pointed is the almost audible din of Acheron at the end of the *ecphrasis* of the poetic temple (37 ff.). With regard to the restatement, at the very end of book two, of the evils that beset a mankind that has fallen from the innocence of a Golden Age, the remedy is found to lie in the historical appearance of a triumphing saviour rather than in the individual's intellectual conquest of Nature and hence of himself. It is also true, as Wimmel stresses, that the self-doubt of the end of *Georgics* book two is absent from the proem of book three. The future resolution of the problem of which poetic path to take seems assured: the Epicurean/natural-philosophical imagery of Lucretius merges into Lucretius' Ennian/poetic imagery, which now dominates and leads into an 'Ennian' subject-matter. The choice of nationalistic themes also appears to close the gap between the high and low places which had initially been opened up by the flight of the goddess *Iustitia* from earth; Virgil's poetic triumph will bring down (*deducere*) to the ground-level of the Italian countryside those other goddesses who dwell in high places, the Muses. The inhabitants of Helicon will be led to the banks of the river Mincius, certainly a low-lying place of poetry, in the same region as the rivers and woods of the end of the previous book. Furthermore, the failure to gain admission to sacred places in book two is now compensated for by the poet's officiating at the temple that he himself has built.[41] But, if my analysis of the nature of Virgil's desires and anxieties in the earlier *recusatio* is correct, we cannot simply see the Roman themes of

---

[40] I take the *via* of lines 8 ff. as closely connected with the 'epic' matter of the poetic temple. For a survey of the arguments on both sides of this notoriously vexed question see Wilkinson 1969: Appendix III.

[41] Compare G. 2.476 'sacra *fero*', with 3.22 'dona *feram*'.

book three as a confidently asserted replacement for the rejected and second-rate themes of natural philosophy. Rather, the end of book two and the beginning of book three are to be seen as complementary explorations of two alternative ways of taking flight in the grand manner. As here presented they seem to be mutually exclusive, and the description of the Underworld at *Georgics* 3.37–9 indicates the reason why. But one should note how evasive a counterblast to the Lucretian attack on religion this mythological picture of the Underworld is; Virgil takes that part of the traditional religious world-view which the educated Roman found most self-evidently fictitious, and further attenuates its reality by hinting that it is no more than an allegorical prison for a Pindaric or Callimachean *Phthonos*.

Within the *Georgics* themselves there are hints at how a synthesis of the two types of poetry, the cosmological and the nationalistic, might be achieved, even if it is a synthesis that sidesteps the central problems raised by Lucretius with regard to religion. The encomium of Octavian in the proem to book three deals entirely in historical, legendary, and mythical themes; signally absent is the cosmological aspect of ruler-panegyric as developed in an obtrusive manner in the opening invocation of book one, where Octavian's power is seen not in terms of historical victories or of the favour of the traditional gods, but in terms of his choice of dominion from the three great divisions of the *cosmos*, earth, sea, and sky. This itself is yet another transformation of Lucretian material: Octavian in effect replaces, as cosmic overlord, the Venus of the proem to book one of the *De Rerum Natura*, whose power is articulated with reference to these three major world-divisions. The integration of the ruler into the structure of the cosmos is powerfully restated at the opposite end of the *Georgics*, 4.560–2:

> Caesar dum magnus ad altum
> fulminat Euphraten bello victorque volentis
> per populos dat iura viamque adfectat Olympo.[42]

---

[42] These lines contain other significant Lucretian echoes: the juxtaposition of *victor* with the path to Olympus suggests the same reference to Epicurus' triumphal flight as *victor* at *G.* 3.9; in *per populos dat iura* we have a parallel to Lucretius' panegyric of the achievement of the *deus* Epicurus, 5.20–1 *ex quo nunc etiam per magnas didita gentis | dulcia permulcent animos solacia vitae* ('to this day he is the source of sweet comforts of life, spread through great nations, that soothe men's minds').

Cosmology and National Epic in the Georgics

While great Caesar thunders in war by deep Euphrates, and victorious gives laws to willing peoples, and sets out on a path to Olympus.

The mythological and cosmological are skillfully combined: *fulminat* refers to the god Jupiter, lord of *Olympus* (562), and suggests such myths as Gigantomachy, but it may also be understood of control over the *physical* processes of the weather, picking up 1.27, where the apotheosed Octavian is imagined as *tempestatumque potentem*. The path to Olympus alludes to future apotheosis, but it is also the final realization of the natural-philosophical/Lucretian aspiration to *caeli vias* (2.477), which Virgil himself was unable to fulfil in the *Georgics*.[43]

---

[43] P. R. Hardie 1986: Chapter 5 examines Virgil's synthesis of the cosmological and political in the *Aeneid*, through his imitation of Lucretius.

9

Pindar and the Proem to the Third *Georgic*

L. P. Wilkinson

The influence of Pindar on the proem to the third book of Virgil's *Georgics* seems to me to have been seminal and pervasive, but it has been little recognized by scholars so far. His name does not seem to occur in connection with the central passage, lines 10 to 39, in the commentaries from Heyne to Richter (1957).[1] A few critics have noted that the idea of speaking of a poem in terms of architecture is Pindaric,[2] but only Ulrich Fleischer, to my knowledge, has gone much further. I will quote what he says before trying to develop the argument.

Schon Pindar hatte, wie Büchner in Erinnerung bringt, ein Gedicht mit einem Tempel verglichen (Ol. 6, 1–5), und pindarische Motive sind mehrfach von hellenistischen Dichtern aufgegriffen worden. Selbst wenn wir keine unmittelbare Quelle angeben können, von der Vergil die Gleichung Tempel—Gedicht übernommen haben müßte, bestehen doch über die Bedeutung dieses pindarischen Motivs für das Proömium keine Zweifel. Den Tempel in unserem Proömium nur als poetischen Ausdruck für die persönliche Verehrung zu erklären, würde einen Verzicht auf die Deutung seines Symbolinhalts bedeuten. Olympische und Nemeische Spiele auf italienischem Boden und die Verpflanzung der Musen nach Italien sind Ausdruck der Synkrisis der Griechen mit den Römern, die Kampfspiele vielleicht Ausdruck des Strebens, den Griechen nicht nur nachzueifern, sondern sie zu übertreffen.[3]

This paper appears here as it was first published in 1970, with the addition of translations of the quotations from Greek, Latin, and German by Katharina Volk.

[1] Marsili 1965 does say on lines 19–20, 'Si pensa a Pindaro'.
[2] e.g. Highbarger 1935: 253 n. 147; Knight 1944: 65, 150; Büchner 1955–8: 1291.
[3] Fleischer 1960: 281–2.

As Büchner reminds us, already Pindar had compared a poem to a temple (*Ol.* 6.1–5), and Pindaric motifs were repeatedly picked up by Hellenistic poets. Even if we cannot point to an immediate source from which Virgil could have derived the equation temple—poem, there can be no doubt about the significance of this Pindaric motif for the proem. To explain the temple in our proem merely as a poetic expression of personal reverence would mean giving up on the interpretation of its symbolic significance. Olympic and Nemean games on Italian soil and the transfer of the Muses to Italy signify the *synkrisis* of Greeks and Romans, while the competitive games perhaps signify the wish not only to imitate the Greeks, but to surpass them.

I do not think there is any need to presume an intermediary source. Pindar must have been known to the Romans. Cicero in a letter to Atticus quotes from him. Admittedly the passage might have been familiar to him as an excerpt: it is known to us more fully from Maximus of Tyre, and had been quoted by Plato already with the formula κατὰ Πίνδαρον ἐκεῖνο τό...[4] But about the time of the Battle of Actium there is a marked burst of interest in Greek choral lyric on the part of Horace in which his friend could well have shared. In *Epode* 13 it has long been recognized that Chiron's speech to Achilles was probably inspired by some such poem, and Fraenkel's guess that Bacchylides might be the poet was confirmed by a papyrus find.[5] This is generally conceded to be one of the latest Epodes, Fraenkel thinks it may even have been later than *Odes* 1.15, which is undoubtedly one of the earliest *Odes* and also based, as Porphyrion says, on a poem of Bacchylides.[6] Pace Fraenkel, I believe that the *horrida tempestas* of the *Epode* is the impending storm that burst at Actium, and that the Ode was meant to be read with Antony and Cleopatra in mind.[7] Another early Ode, dating from this same period, is 1.2 (*iam satis*), and it has long been realised that this has close connections with the finale of *Georgics* 1.[8] Here there is possibly

---

[4] Cic. *Att.* 13.38.2 = 341 S.B.; Maximus 12.1 (145.13 Hob.) = fr. 213 Sn.; Pl. *Resp.* 365b.
[5] *P. Oxy.* 2364 (addendum); Fraenkel 1957: 191–2. Highbarger 1935: 227 had seen that choral lyric lay behind it, but went beyond the data when he said that it was 'very clearly based on Pythians III' and that 'it was the third Nemean that suggested the episode between Chiron and Achilles'.
[6] Fraenkel 1957: 188–91.
[7] Wilkinson 1956: 495–9 and 1945: 128, 73–4.
[8] Fraenkel 1957: 242–4.

a verbal reminiscence of Pindar: Δία φοινικοστερόπαν (*Ol.* 9.10) may have suggested *rubente dextera* as an attribute of Jupiter the thunderer. Another passage in the *Georgics* which may be late and therefore from this same period is the description of Aristaeus' visit to Cyrene beneath the waters of the Peneus, which may have been inspired by Bacchylides' description of Theseus' visit to his mother Amphitrite.[9] The extent to which Horace, in the years immediately following the appearance of the *Georgics*, was influenced by Pindar has been made clear by Fraenkel; and that such influence could sometimes be general rather than tangible has recently been urged by J. H. Waszink.[10]

It is thus reasonable to suppose that it was with a mind aware of Greek choral lyric that Virgil came to compose his proem to *Georgics* 3. This is certainly one of the latest portions of the work, since it was written in close anticipation, or even recollection, of Caesar's triple triumph of 13–15 August 29. Up till then his draft of this Book presumably began with line 49,

> seu quis Olympiacae miratus praemia palmae
> pascet equos...

Or if anyone breeds horses, marvelling at the prize of the Olympic palm...

One can see how his mind, full of Caesar's triumph, could conceive the idea of leading into his treatment of horses by a proem blending this theme with that of a chariot victory in the Olympic games and of himself as a Roman Pindar who would win for Rome a new domain of song, the epinician, leading the Muses in triumph[11] to Italy, as Ennius, whose proud epitaph he would recall at 3.9, was said by Lucretius to have done,

> qui primus amoeno
> detulit ex Helicone perenni fronde coronam,
> per gentis Italas hominum quae clara clueret.[12]

---

[9] 4.359 ff. Norden 1934: 638. Unless one believes, as I do not, that this passage was composed after the disgrace of Gallus in 27 as a substitute, the natural supposition is that it was composed at about the same time as the rest of Book 4.
[10] Waszink 1966: 113.
[11] For *deducere* meaning to 'lead in triumph' cf. Hor. *Carm.* 1.37.31.
[12] Lucr. 1.117–19.

… who first from pleasant Helicon brought down a crown of ever-lasting leaf, which would be renowned in fame among the Italian races of men.

He would bring the palms of victory to his native Mantua, and celebrate there the Olympian and Nemean games that Pindar had sung. The Mincius should be his Alpheus, and beside it, corresponding to the temple of Zeus at Olympia, he would build in imagination a poetic temple for Caesar, who was himself at that moment dedicating a real one to Diuus Julius,[13] adorning it with sculptures of symbolic import corresponding with those designated for the already rising shrine of Apollo on the Palatine.[14]

That Pindar was specifically in Virgil's mind is suggested in the first place by what seems a verbal reminiscence of him three lines before the main symbolic part of the proem begins, as many commentators have noted: *umeroque Pelops insignis eburno* ('Pelops, famed for his ivory shoulder', 7), cf. *Ol.* 1.27, ἐλέφαντι φαίδιμον ὦμον κεκασμένον ('distinguished by a shoulder shining with ivory').[15] Even the familiar metaphor of the 'way' of poetry—*temptanda uia est* (8)—is one chiefly associated with Pindar.[16] What other Pindaric traits can we detect in this proem?

In the first place, to conceive of a poem at all in terms of the visual arts is characteristically Pindaric. The architectural metaphor for the

---

[13] Dio 51.22.
[14] Dio 53.1. Drew 1924.
[15] This although the themes he is rejecting seem chosen, as we should expect, as being characteristically Hellenistic: De Saint-Denis 1957: 102.
[16] 'Zur Anwendung aufs Dichten S. bes. Pindar': Wimmel 1960: 103 n.1. The idea of a new way occurs at *Paean* 7b.11. Wimmel's excursus 'Die Symbolgruppen des Weges' (103–11) is a most valuable collection of passages; but intent as he is on tracing the influence of Callimachus in Roman poetry, he seems in this proem to diagnose as Callimachean what could have come directly from Pindar (177–87). The extent to which Callimachus himself may have been influenced by Pindar has not been sufficiently realised (but see Smiley 1919; Newman 1967a: 45 ff.). There is all the difference between *recusatio* of grand themes, where playing on the *Aitia* prologue was an obvious resource (as in *Ecl.* 6), and this 'Versprechen für später, ja für bald' (Wimmel 1960: 177). The Mincius seems to me to correspond here to the Alpheus, and to have no connection with the Callimachean symbolism of the 'grosse Fluss'. (*Ingens*, if it means 'vast', is in any case an odd epithet to apply to the Mincius. In an article on Virgil's use of the word, Mackail 1912 suggested that for him it seemed sometimes to have etymological connotations as if from the preposition *in* and the root *gen* ('natural' or 'native'). He cited 17 instances from the Georgics including this one. (Cf. *ingenuus*)

epic Virgil will compose for Caesar[17] recalls the opening of the sixth *Olympian*:

> χρυσέας ὑποστάσαντες εὐτειχεῖ προθύρῳ θαλάμου
> κίονας, ὡς ὅτε θαητὸν μέγαρον
> πάξομεν· ἀρχομένου δ' ἔργου πρόσωπον
> χρὴ θέμεν τηλαυγές.

Erecting golden columns to support the well-built vestibule of our abode, we will construct, as it were, a spectacular palace. One must create a far-shining front for the beginning of a work.

(πύλαι ὕμνων occur at line 27 of the same poem). In the sixth *Pythian* Pindar builds a treasure-house of song whose facade will proclaim a victory in the chariot-race (5–18). At *Pythian* 3.113 we hear of songs τέκτονες οἷα σοφοὶ ἅρμοσαν ('such as skilled builders constructed'), and at 4.81 Pindar erects a stele of song whiter than Parian marble. 'Foundations' are laid for the first *Nemean* (8). Sculpture too is used by Pindar, as by Virgil (26 ff.), to symbolise his poetry: at *Nemean* 7.70–9 his Muse creates a chryselephantine song,

> κολλᾷ χρυσὸν ἔν τε λευκὸν ἐλέφανθ' ἁμᾷ.

...(the Muse) fuses together gold and white ivory.

Illi uictor ego...(17): what astonishing assurance, that a shy poet from a small town only recently incorporated into Italy should juxtapose himself as *uictor* with Caesar in the very hour of his triple triumph! *Tyrio conspectus in ostro*: he has himself assumed the *toga picta* of the Roman *triumphator*, or at the very least the *praetexta* of an officiating magistrate. He will wear a wreath of olive,[18] and lead the procession to the shrines of the gods (21–3). This self-assurance, though it might owe something to Ennius, is strongly reminiscent of Pindar.[19] Pindar had spoken to rulers on an equal footing, praising, advising and warning; to Hiero, for instance, at *Ol.* 1.115–16, where,

---

[17] I take it that he was referring to this and not to the *Georgics*: see Klingner 1963: 136–40.

[18] As the Olympic victor did, *Ol.* 3.13. Pindar also (ibid. 6) had χαίταισι μὲν ζευχθέντες ἔπι στέφανοι ('crowns woven in his hair').

[19] 'Pindarische Selbstgewißheit muß den staunenden Vergil damals ergriffen haben', as Wimmel 1960: 181 rightly says.

Pindar and the Proem to the Third Georgic

as here, the supremacy of the poet is set beside the supremacy of the ruler:

> εἴη σέ τε τοῦτον ὑψοῦ χρόνον πατεῖν,
> ἐμέ τε τοσσάδε νικηφόροις
> ὁμιλεῖν, πρόφαντον σοφίᾳ καθ' Ἕλλανας ἐόντα παντᾷ.

May you walk on high for this time, and may I consort with victors whenever they win, outstanding in wisdom everywhere among the Hellenes.

> centum quadriiugos agitabo ad flumina currus.
> (Verg. G. 3.18)

I will drive a hundred four-horse chariots beside the river.

The chariots are, of course, his own hexameters in the epic to come. He has already prepared us for this idea at the end of the previous Book:

> sed nos immensum spatiis confecimus aequor,
> et iam tempus equum spumantia soluere colla.
> (Verg. G. 2.541–2)

But in my course I have covered a mighty plain, and it is time now to unyoke the sweaty necks of my horses.

A similar idea had occurred in the same poem as the architectural metaphor, the sixth *Olympian* (22):

> ὦ Φίντις, ἀλλὰ ζεῦξον ἤδη μοι σθένος ἡμιόνων...

Oh Phintis, yoke for me now the strength of the mules...

and in at least seven other places in Pindar.[20] Though it is important in the *Aitia* prologue, yet it is primarily Pindaric.[21]

Again, although Envy occurs prominently in the *Aitia* prologue (17: Βασκανίη) and twice elsewhere in Callimachus,[22] and is associated with his name because of the literary quarrel at Alexandria, it occurs eight times or more in Pindar (naturally enough, in a writer of epinicians), whether as θόνος or κόρος.[23] Sometimes it is personified—μὴ βαλέτω με λίθῳ τραχεῖ Φθόνος ('may Envy not cast a

---

[20] *Ol.* 9.81; *Pyth.* 10.65; *Nem.* 1.7; *Isthm.* 2.1, 5.38, 8.61; fr. 124.
[21] '... den Musenwagen (vor allem von Pindar ausgebildet)': Wimmel 1960: 105.
[22] *Hymn* 2.105; *Epigr.* 21.4.
[23] *Ol.* 2.95, 6.75, 8.55; *Pyth.* 1.85, 8.32 (cf. 72), 11.29 (cf. 54); *Nem.* 8.21–2, 10.20.

rough stone at me', *Ol.* 8.55); μὴ Κόρος ἐλθὼν κνίσῃ ('lest Insolence come and scratch us', *Pyth.* 8.32). So that the personified *Inuidia* of line 37 is at least as likely to have been suggested by Pindar as by Callimachus.

Once at least in the *Aeneid* Virgil was to recall Pindar, in his description of Etna at 3.570 ff. (cf. *Pyth.* 1.20 ff.); and it is possible that in his description of the tortures of the damned at 6.601–7 he had in mind *Ol.* 1.54–60.[24]

The silence of the commentators on the main part of the proem to *Georgics* 3 about Pindar may have been due to the fact that the similarities I have mentioned are not such as can severally be nailed down as certain results of influence; but I submit that the conjunction of such a number of probabilities makes it virtually certain that the inspiration of the whole is Pindaric.

[24] Nardi 1956.

10

Callimachus, the *Victoria Berenices*, and Roman Poetry

Richard F. Thomas

It is now five years since P. J. Parsons published the Lille Callimachus,[1] and the dust appears to have settled. The appearance of these fragments, which greatly increase our knowledge of the opening of the third book of the *Aetia*,[2] has been followed by no great critical reaction. Apart from the attractive suggestion of E. Livrea that the 'Mousetrap' (fr. 177 Pf.) may belong within the story of Heracles and Molorchus,[3] the episode has had somewhat limited impact.[4] This is against the usual trend of overreaction to the publication of new literary texts (witness the Cologne Archilochus and the new Gallus), and is in part a tribute to the thoroughness and clarity with which Parsons presented the fragments.

We might, however, have expected more of significance from the *Victoria Berenices*. Its placement, at the beginning of the third book of

---

Part of this paper was delivered in March 1980 at a conference on Alexandrianism held in Ann Arbor, Michigan. It was first published in 1983 and reprinted in R. F. Thomas 1999: 68–113, and it appears here virtually unchanged except for the addition of translations of the Greek and Latin passages by Katharina Volk.

[1] Parsons 1977: 1–50.
[2] See Parsons 1977: 46–8 for lucid arguments on the placement of the episode.
[3] Livrea 1979: 37–40.
[4] A number of scholars have in fact dealt with the fragments: Kassel 1977; Luppe 1978a and 1978b; Bornmann 1978; Livrea 1978; Barigazzi 1979 and 1980; Livrea *et al.* 1980. Most of these works, however, are concerned with technical matters relating to the text of the new fragments. None deals with the impact of the episode, which will be our chief concern.

the most important poem of the most influential Alexandrian poet, should lead us to delve deeper. Callimachus was clearly attuned to the possibilities in structural organization and, as Parsons has noted,[5] not only does the third book begin and end with epinician sequences (to Berenice and to Euthycles of Locri, fr. 84–5 Pf.), but the entire second half of the *Aetia* is framed by tributes to the poet's queen (*Victoria* and *Coma*, fr. 110 Pf.). *Prima facie* the opening lines of Book 3 will not have constituted a casual or incidental *aetion*.

What follows is an argument for the importance of Callimachus, specifically for the influence of the new episode, together with other Callimachean verse, on the poetry of Virgil, and to a lesser degree on that of Propertius and Statius. If such influence can be shown, then it may be possible to reverse the procedure and to increase our knowledge of the *Victoria Berenices*. While such an approach may appear in part based on circular argument, I believe that in most parts the combination of the demonstrable and the circumstantial will be persuasive. Much, however, is speculative, and I do not conceal that fact. Nevertheless, in the light of the importance of this subject, it will be worthwhile to pursue certain possibilities in spite of their tentative nature.

1. THE PROEM TO THE THIRD *GEORGIC*

The first 48 lines of the third *Georgic* constitute Virgil's most extensive statement of literary purpose. The poet, after a couplet addressing the theme of the third book, turns aside from the immediate project to treat his own poetic destiny. In seeking a new path to immortality (8–9), he first rejects certain themes as being well worn—*omnia iam vulgata* (3–8)—then turns to the alternative, the projection of his poetic future, metaphorically stated: victor in a pointedly Italian setting, Virgil will preside over games and construct a temple, complete with elaborate statuary, in commemoration of the exploits of Caesar Octavian (10–36). The perfection of

---

[5] Parsons 1977: 49–50.

this structure will quell the voice of *Invidia* (37–9). Meanwhile the present task must be completed (40–8). All in all, then, an elaborate *recusatio*.

At what specific tradition, or to what poet, are these lines, particularly the opening ones, directed? The critics have been at odds. W. Wimmel claimed to find reminiscences and adaptations of Callimachean programmatic poetry.[6] On the other hand, U. Fleischer,[7] L. P. Wilkinson,[8] and S. Lundström[9] have argued against this and in favour of the importance of Pindar, Wilkinson in particular concluding: 'the influence of the whole is Pindaric.' As will emerge, I believe that each of these views contains a half-truth: the former is correct in the choice of poet (Callimachus), but incorrect on the type of poetry (programmatic purple passages); the latter proposes the right type of poetry (epinician), but the wrong poet (Pindar). New assessment of these lines is warranted, both as a result of the publication of the Lille papyri, and on more general grounds.

The third *Georgic* opens with an address to Pales, Apollo Nomius, and the woods and streams of Mt Lycaeus—normal enough at the beginning of a book on the care and raising of animals. However, the manner of reference to Apollo is noteworthy: *pastor ab Amphryso* (2). This constitutes a gloss on Callim. *Hymn* 2.47–9:

> Φοῖβον καὶ Νόμιον κικλήσκομεν ἐξέτι κείνου,
> ἐξότ᾽ ἐπ᾽ Ἀμφρυσσῷ ζευγίτιδας ἔτρεφεν ἵππους
> ἠιθέου ὑπ᾽ ἔρωτι κεκαυμένος Ἀδμήτοιο.

We call him Phoebus Nomius ever since by the Amphrysus he pastured the yoked mares, burning with love for young Admetus.

Virgil's wording is surely intended as a direct reference. As Servius noticed, *pastor* is a gloss on Νόμιος: ἀπὸ τῆς νομῆς, *id est a pascuis* (*ad loc.*). More important is the supporting phrase *ab Amphryso*. Richter rightly identified the manner as Alexandrian,[10] but it is so in a special way: in connection with Apollo and his service to

---

[6] Wimmel 1960: 177–87, *passim*.
[7] Fleischer 1960. [8] Wilkinson 1970.
[9] S. Lundström 1976. Lundström was unaware of Wilkinson's article.
[10] W. Richter 1957 *ad loc.* Cf. such expressions as *incola Itoni* (= Athena) at Catull. 64.228.

Admetus this river appears in Greek only at *Hymn* 2.48.[11] The connection may be presumed to be original with Callimachus, and Virgil's periphrasis for Apollo Nomius must be an acknowledgement of the fact.

In justification of the change of direction that his poetic career is to take, Virgil proceeds to enumerate the topics which, through prior treatment, are no longer valid:

> quis aut Eurysthea durum
> aut inlaudati nescit Busiridis aras?
> cui non dictus Hylas puer et Latonia Delos
> Hippodameque umeroque Pelops insignis eburno,
> acer equis?   (*G.* 3.4–8)

Who does not know of harsh Eurystheus or the altars of notorious Busiris? Who has not sung of the boy Hylas and of Latona's Delos, of Hippodamia and of Pelops, famed for his ivory shoulder, a daring horseman?

Three references to Hercules (or to characters associated with him), one to Delos, and one to Hippodamia and Pelops. To begin with the last, it has long been noticed that line 7 recalls Pindar *Ol.* 1.27: ἐλέφαντι φαίδιμον ὦμον κεκαδμένον ('distinguished by a shoulder shining with ivory').[12] This, however, does not require that Virgil's concerns throughout the proem are Pindaric, and we should keep in mind that the ornamental reference to Pelops functions mainly as a transition to the theme of games (*acer equis*, 8—an emphasis absent from the Pindaric context).[13]

The other references in Virgil's lines argue for an Alexandrian influence, predominantly that of Callimachus. First, *Latonia Delos* (6) as the subject of a poem recalls exclusively the fourth *Hymn*. And then there are the three allusions to Hercules (through Eurysthems,

---

[11] Indeed, before Virgil, apart from the Callimachean instance, the only appearance of the river is at Ap. Rhod. *Argon.* 1.54, where there is no connection with Apollo. Quite possibly Callimachus drew it from obscurity and dealt with it in his treatise on the world's rivers (*Frag. Gram.* 457–9 Pf.).

[12] See Conington and Nettleship 1898 *ad G.* 3.7.

[13] As we shall argue below, Pindaric elements may in fact have undergone a Callimachean transformation which is now lost to us. In this connection it should be noted that the first *Olympian* elsewhere influenced Callimachus (cf. Pfeiffer, *Index Rerum Notabilium*, s.v. Pind.).

Busiris, and Hylas, 4–6)—in fact, the skeleton of a *Heracleis*.[14] As Pfeiffer has noted, even in its fragmentary state the *Aetia* can be seen to have dealt considerably more with this figure than with any other: 'Herculis fabulae in omnibus Aetiorum libris' (*ad* fr. 698).[15] Although Eurystheus does not appear in the extant fragments, he is implicitly present throughout the labors. Hylas, prominent for both Theocritus and Apollonius, although probably not the subject of Callimachus fr. 596 (see Pfeiffer *ad loc.*), perhaps figured at least in passing in the *Aetia*,[16] and the encounter with Busiris survives towards the end of the second book of that poem (fr. 44–7—with Phalaris). More generally, all of Virgil's examples are Alexandrian, or Callimachean, in nature, in that they all betray an interest in aetiological concerns, and this even applies for the reference to Pelops.[17]

While this is not necessarily conclusive, it at least provides a basis for the suggestion that at the outset Virgil's proem in some way responds to Alexandrian and Callimachean poetry. It remains to be seen whether such a view is required and, if so, to determine the purpose of the proem. With this in mind we turn to the *Victoria Berenices*.

The episode is, as its title suggests, an epinician. Callimachus announces that he has just received the news of the victory of Berenice II, consort of Ptolemy III Euergetes, in the chariot race at Nemea. Pure epinician leads (although the transition is missing) to the bulk of the poem, an *aition* on the founding of the Nemean Games—in effect an epyllion in the style of the *Hecale* leading to

---

[14] See W. Richter 1957 *ad* 3.3 ff.

[15] This, of course, is hardly surprising since, through his ubiquitousness, he was involved with numerous areas which came to be the subjects of aetiological studies.

[16] Certainly the encounter between Heracles and the youth's father, Theiodamas, figured (*Aet.* 1 fr. 24–5), and it is unlikely that Hylas, in the light of the appeal he held for the Alexandrians, did not also appear.

[17] Servius' commentary at this point is of interest; he seems to give weight to the aetiological associations of the myth: *qui* (sc. Myrtalus) *factis cereis axibus cum, victore Pelope, a puella promissum posceret praemium, ab eius marito praecipitatus in mare est, cui nomen imposuit: nam ab eo Myrtoum dicitur pelagus* ('after Myrtalus had fabricated the axles of wax and Pelops had won the race, when he asked the girl for the arranged payment, he was thrown by her husband into the sea, to which he gave its name: for because of him it is called the Myrtoan Sea').

Heracles' killing of the Nemean lion. This panel, perceptively described by Parsons as a 'rococo exercise in rustic chic', focused mainly on the hero's stay with the impoverished Molorchus, a figure possibly invented by Callimachus, and at least lifted by him from total obscurity. A characteristic of the genre, the lion was doubtless dispatched in summary manner, and there can be little doubt, as Parsons has suggested, that after mentioning Heracles' founding of the games (and possibly the second foundation by Adrastus) Callimachus returned to the celebration of Berenice's victory: 'epinician embraces epyllion.'[18]

We begin with a simple, but unstated, observation. Parsons noted that the only witness connecting Callimachus with the story of Molorchus is Probus on Verg. *G.* 3.19 (*lucosque Molorchi*), the first post-Callimachean reference to Heracles' host. It is plausible to suggest that the placement of Virgil's allusion, at the outset of the third book, may not be gratuitous—that is where he found it in the four-book poem of his Alexandrian predecessor.[19] That the proem to the third *Georgic* is a modified epinician needs no argument.[20] This, however, should not necessarily lead, as it has done, to the conclusion that Pindar was Virgil's model. Two points: first, with the exception of Horace, Roman poets seem to show little interest in (or possibly little understanding of) Pindaric poetry.[21] An even more important argument can be made against the

[18] Parsons 1977: 39.

[19] Since we are discussing structural similarities between the *Aetia* and the *Georgics*, I put forward the following observation, suggested by the anonymous referee of this article. *Aetia* 3 began (*Victoria Berenices*) and *Aetia* 4 ended (*Coma Berenices*) with encomiastic pieces. The opening of the third *Georgic* follows that of *Aetia* 3. What of the end of the fourth *Georgic*? Servius' comment is notorious: (*Gallus*) *fuit autem amicus Vergilii adeo, ut quartus georgicorum a medio usque ad finem eius laudes teneret* ('Gallus was such a good friend of Virgil's that the fourth book of the *Georgics* contained his praises from the middle to the end', *ad Ecl.* 10.1; cf. also *ad G.* 4.1). If there is any truth in this (and neither the reader nor I believes that there is), then the structural parallel that emerges between the proem to the third *Georgic* and the *Victoria Berenices*, together with the placing of the *Coma Berenices*, provides the first concrete support for Servius' claim.

[20] At lines 22–33 the theme of military triumph is conflated with the epinician material.

[21] Fraenkel 1957: 276–85, 291–3, 426, 435–40, has best demonstrated Horace's interest in Pindar, but that interest is for Horace, the most eclectic of the Roman poets, a late one. A glance at Gerber 1969 is instructive: 19 entries for Horace, seven for all other Latin authors.

presence of Pindar in this proem: 'epinician' and 'Pindaric' are not interchangeable terms. And, as Parsons has noted of the new fragments: 'In [them] Callimachus visibly borrows from Pindar and Bacchylides.'[22] Given Virgil's preference among this group, it is fair to note that Pindaric elements in his poetry may be only apparently so.[23]

The Lille papyri not only restore the framing epinicians to Callimachus' third book; they also add more generally to our awareness of that poet's interest in this type of poetry.[24] Of the actual epinician, addressed to Berenice, only ten lines survive, in reasonably good condition, with interlinear scholia. However, the common elements between the openings of the third books of Callimachus and Virgil (epinician to queen or *princeps*, reference to Molorchus, and apparent dictional connection), together with clear reference to other Callimachean contexts at the beginning of the third *Georgic*, validate the attempt to define the nature of Virgil's entire proem, specifically by investigating the possibility of a more pervasive Callimachean influence.

The most extended portion of Virgil's proem, and the most striking, is his description of the temple and statuary he will create (12–36), a metaphorical allusion, as most would now agree,[25] to a future poetic project. Again, the 'model' has been found in Pindar:[26]

χρυσέας ὑποστάσαντες εὐτειχεῖ προθύρῳ θαλάμου
κίονας, ὡς ὅτε θαητὸν μέγαρον
πάξομεν.   (*Ol*. 6.1–3)

---

[22] Parsons 1977: 45–6; also Livrea *et al.* 1980: 238–45.

[23] On this point it may be worth noting that the Pindaric reference in the proem to the third *Georgic* (*umeroque Pelops insignis eburno*, 7) may even have had a Callimachean intermediary particularly since the ultimate source is *Olympian* 1, a poem which Callimachus surely knew and to which he appears to refer (fr. 194.58 and Pfeiffer *ad loc.*).

[24] Clearly the genre interested Callimachus both in the *Aetia* and elsewhere: fr. 84–5, Euthycles of Locri; fr. 98, Euthymus; fr. 384, Sosibius; fr. 666, Astylus of Croton; fr. 758, Milon of Croton. See Pfeiffer *ad* fr. 85 for other possible instances; also, dealing with the founding of games, fr. 76–7, 'Eleorum Ritus', again from the third book of the *Aetia*.

[25] Whether or not the reference is specifically to the *Aeneid* is another matter. I personally have little difficulty reconciling that poem with the details in the proem to the third *Georgic*, particularly with the final two lines: *Caesaris et nomen fama tot ferre per annos, | Tithoni prima quot abest ab origine Caesar* ('and to carry Caesar's name and fame through so many years as Caesar is removed from Tithonus' birth long ago'), G. 3.47–8.

[26] Wilkinson 1970: 287–8.

Erecting golden columns to support the well-built vestibule of our abode, we will construct, as it were, a spectacular palace.

While it is not out of the question that these lines, if Virgil knew them, could have been the ultimate impulse for his elaborately developed metaphor, it will be useful for now to confine the discussion to *Callimachean* epinician. The evidence is somewhat fragmentary, but it is sufficient: to an extent unparalleled in Pindar,[27] Callimachus, in his treatment of athletic victories, appears to have dealt with statues erected or adorned on the return of the victor. This is definitely the case with Euthycles of Locri (fr. 84–5), Sosibius (fr. 384), and Astylus of Croton (fr. 666).[28] Moreover, in the last two of these, it is stated that statues were placed in temples in commemoration of the successes. So Virgil:

> in medio mihi Caesar erit templumque tenebit. (G. 3.16)

I will have Caesar in the middle, and he will dominate the temple.

> stabunt et Parii lapides, spirantia signa,
> Assaraci proles demissaeque ab Iove gentis
> nomina, Trosque parens et Troiae Cynthius auctor. (G. 3.34–6)

There will stand also Parian marbles, lifelike statues: the progeny of Assaracus and famous names of a family descended from Jove, father Tros and Cynthian Apollo, the builder of Troy.

This feature of Callimachean epinician reflects, I think, a heightened interest on the part of this poet, and of the Alexandrians in general, in the plastic and visual arts.[29] Most important for our purposes is the statue of Delian Apollo (*Aet.* inc. lib. fr. 114), which conducts a conversation with the poet. Virgil was to place a statue of this same

---

[27] Pindar, incidentally, specifically dissociates himself in one passage from the static art of the sculptor: οὐκ ἀνδριαντοποιός εἰμ' ('I am no sculptor', *Nem.* 5.1).

[28] This is doubtless related to Callimachus' general aetiological interests; statues are visible attestations of, and ensure the continuance of, cult practice.

[29] Such interest is best exemplified by the *Greek Anthology*, which abounds in epigrams describing, conversing with, or in some other way treating statuary. In most the poetic motivation is in the realism of the work of art. So the poems on Myron's *Cow*, to take an obvious example (*Anth. Pal.* 9.713–42)—thirty epigrams making much the same point: the realism is such that the observer (herdsman, calf, etc.) is deceived. They are not all Hellenistic, but the impulse is quintessentially Hellenistic. This feature of the Hellenistic mentality will be important when we come to consider the ecphrasis.

god in his temple, referring to him with an epithet which is not only unmistakably Callimachean (*Troiae Cynthius*[30] *auctor*, 3.36), but which Callimachus actually employed in his address to the statue (Κύνθιε, fr. 114.8). Virgil used the word at the beginning of the second half of the *Eclogues* (6.3) and of the *Georgics* (3.36)—both are influenced by Callimachus and stand as centrally placed acknowledgements of him. Also in the *Aetia* were two statues of Samian Hera (fr. 100, 101), and one of Diana Leucadia (*Dieg.* fr. 31 b-e [Addend. II Pf.]). Outside this poem, *Iambus* 6 (fr. 196) described in some detail the dimensions of Pheidias' chryselephantine statue of Olympian Zeus, and in its sequel, *Iambus* 7 (fr. 197), a wooden representation of Hermes Perpheraeus gives a description of himself in the manner of a sepulchral epigram.[31] Again, in *Iambus* 9 (fr. 199), we find an ἐραστής and an ithyphallic Hermes discussing the latter's condition. Finally, in the epigrams, there appear statues of a hero (*Epigr.* 24) and of Berenice herself (*Epigr.* 51), the latter included in effigy with the three Graces—just as Octavian mingles with other representations in Virgil's temple (3.16).

And what of temples themselves? It is true that Pindar's sixth *Olympian* begins with an architectural simile, but it is extremely brief, and in spirit has little to do with Virgil's extended metaphor.[32] The differences in the proem to the third *Georgic* are considerable, the context distinct. He treats a temple which is appropriate as a repository of statuary commemorating Octavian's victory and as a metaphor for his future poem. For impulses we should rather seek real temples in epinician settings, and here again the Callimachean instances are illuminating. Both Sosibius (fr. 384) and Astylus (fr. 666) have statues placed in temples of Hera in commemoration of their victories. It would, I think, be a strange lapse if the victory of Berenice were not attended by some sort of celebration involving statues

---

[30] See Clausen 1976 for the demonstration that the formation of this epithet is Callimachean.

[31] Statues which come to life in this manner are in fact artistically the equivalent of the tombstone which delivers an epitaph, either on behalf of the person buried beneath it, or *in propria persona*.

[32] Apart from its brevity and the fact that it is not strictly a metaphor (ὡς ὅτε), Pindar's treatment is distinct in that it refers very generally to a μέγαρον. Virgil's *templum*, and the elaborate details which accompany it, are qualitatively distinct.

and/or a temple.³³ It would be even more peculiar if Callimachus (in the light of his usual practice) made no reference to such an event. But Virgil's temple is also metaphorical. This was probably his own contribution, and yet, even here, there may have been a Callimachean impulse. Fr. 118 of the *Aetia* is an unplaced scrap, preserved in poor condition:

>   ].φ.ρ ε ι ς οἵ τε μάλι σ[τα
>   ]ν [λ]ειαίνουσι· τὸ δ' ἱερ[ὸν
>   ἐξ αὐ]τ ο σ χε δίης κεῖνο τ ε κ.[
>   ]..ύ..ι σταφύλῃ. [.]ρ.[
>   ].......... ν λειαμε.[5
>   ].......ιησι μελιχρ οτ [
>   ]ἄκρι βὲς καὶ τότε Λητο[ῒδ
>   ]..τόδε μέλλεν ἔσ[εσθαι
>   ]..ἀμφιπερικ[
>   ]ωη.αν..ε.[10
>   ].[

Difficult to construe, but a sense, and certainly an emphasis, of sorts, emerges. Callimachus is dealing with temples (τὸ δ' ἱερ[ὸν, 2), probably two of them, built with contrasting levels of workmanship.³⁴ The first is a polished, well-finished product ([λ]ειαίνουσι, 2), while the other is of a hastily constructed nature (ἐξ αὐ]τοσχεδίης, 3). The contrast is suggestive, and the diction, or what remains of it, evocative. The verb λειαίνω can, at least from Dionysius of Halicarnassus,³⁵ be used in application to perfection of literary style—compare English 'polish'.³⁶ The contrasting term, ἐξ αὐτοσχεδίης, is likewise potentially

---

³³ A curious coincidence: in *Epigram* 51 Callimachus included Berenice in a statue of the Graces, while in the *Victoria Sosibii* statues of the Graces are adorned in commemoration of the victory (*Ep. et Eleg. Min.* fr. 384.44–5); on this, see below.
³⁴ So Pfeiffer *ad loc.*
³⁵ *Comp.* 16; doubtless the formulation is earlier, almost certainly Hellenistic.
³⁶ Cairns 1969: 155, treating this metaphor in Catullus (*pumice expolitum*, 1.2) and Propertius (*exactus tenui pumice versus eat*, 3.1.8), remarks: 'The context of this sudden metaphor strongly suggests that it is part of the traditional material upon which Propertius is drawing in 3.1 and therefore that Catullus in his own Alexandrian prologue was drawing on similar sources' (we should keep in mind that the chief influence in Prop. 3.1 is Callimachean). Now Catullus dealt with a polished *libellus*, or rather the polished ends (*frontes*) of the scroll, as seems clear from Ovid *Trist.* 1.1.11 (cf. Luck 1967–77 *ad loc.*), but the poetic metaphor originates, I believe, in the polishing of marble or stone. *Polire* (λειαίνειν) and *limare* (ῥινεῖν), 'to polish' and

Callimachus, the Victoria Berenices, and Roman Poetry

significant, referring as it does to improvised (and therefore undesirable) construction.[37] In line 6 we find μελιχροτ[, presumably the remnants of the comparative or superlative of μελιχρός, which appears twice elsewhere in the fragments of Callimachus, both times in programmatic references to the 'correct' type of poetry: ἀ̣[ηδονίδες] δ' ὧδε μελιχρ[ό]τεραι ('but nightingales are sweeter', Aet. 1 fr. 1.16); ἀλλ' ὀκνέω μὴ τὸ μελιχρότατον | τῶν ἐπέων ὁ Σολεὺς ἀπεμάξατο· χαίρετε λεπταί | ῥήσιες... ('but I am not in doubt that the man of Soloi has swept off the sweetest part of (Hesiod's) words; greetings, slender discourses...', Epigr. 27.2–4).[38] Finally, in line 7, there is the likely reading ἀκριβές.[39] If this is correct (and it is supported by the interlinear gloss above line 4: διηκρίβωσαν [sc. οἱ τέκτονες] τὸ ὕ̣[ψ]ο̣ς),[40] it is worth referring to Iambus 12 (fr. 202, Addend. II Pf.), where we find the only other form of ἀκριβ- in Callimachus:

ὑπτίῳ παίσαντες ἄνθρωποι ποδί
χρυσὸν αἰνήσουσι τίμιον κ....[.
τὴν Ἀθηναίης δὲ καὶ ἑτέρων δόσιν,
καίπερ εὖ σμίλῃσιν ἠ̣κ̣ριβωμένην,
ὁ πρόσω φοιτέων ἀμαυρώσει χρ[ό]νος·
ἡ δ' ἐμὴ τῇ παιδὶ καλλίστη δόσις...   (63–8)

...pushing away with the soles of their feet..., men will praise the honoured gold...but the gift of Aphrodite and the others, though well wrought with chisels, passing time will efface. But my gift to the child is the most beautiful...

'to file down', are used together of polishing stone (Plin. HN 36.53–4) and of polishing literary style (Cic. Or. 20; especially Quint. Inst. 10.4.4, ut opus poliat lima, non exterat ('let the file polish the work, not wear it down'); also Cic. De or. 3.185, Brut. 294, Fam. 7.33.2; Hor. Sat. 1.10.65, Ars P. 291; Quint. Inst. 2.4.7, 2.8.4, 2.12.8, 11.1.3, 12.10.17, 50). So too τορεύειν, 'to work on a relief', can be used in a lapidary sense (Anth. Pal. 7.274), as well as metaphorically (Dion. Hal. Thuc. 24). I have no doubt that the entire construct is Alexandrian.

[37] It is applied to poetry as early as Aristotle (Poetics 1448b23; also Dion. Hal. Ant. Rom. 2.34), and acquires a pejorative force early: so Xen. Lac. 13.5, αὐτοσχεδιαστής (contrasted with τεχνίτης) = 'bungler'.

[38] On this second instance see Reitzenstein 1931: 44–7. For other occurrences of the word in the same context cf. Pfeiffer ad Aet. 1 fr. 1.16.

[39] Although Pfeiffer (ad loc.) is tentative: ']ακρι dispicere sibi visus est L(obel).' The rest of the word is clear.

[40] For this compound as a term used for artistic precision, cf. Philostr. Imag. 10; Phld. De mus. 90 K (Pfeiffer ad fr. 202.66, Addend. 2); also Gow 1952 ad Id. 15.81.

Again the context is programmatic. Callimachus has written a poem in celebration of the newborn child of his friend Leon. He compares this event, and his participation in it, with the vying of the gods in their donations at the birth of Hebe: 'Apollo scorning to draw upon the treasures of his Delphic sanctuary (47 ff.) outdid them all with his glorious song—evidently the divine prototype of Callimachus' own gift for the child of his friend.'[41] The gifts of the other gods, although finely carved (καίπερ εὖ σμίλησιν ἠκριβωμένην, 66), will be surpassed by the song of Apollo.[42] Diction apart, we again find in these lines of *Iambus* 12 a poetic work presented in close proximity to, and in favourable contrast to, a sculpted object.

Ultimately the remains are not sufficient to support speculation that *Aetia* fr. 118 contains an architectural metaphor—that the poet made some connection between his own art and that of the architect or sculptor. Nevertheless, even without such intent on the part of Callimachus, even if fr. 118 is merely a contrasting depiction of actual temples, there can be little doubt that Virgil, familiar as he was with the programmatic diction of Callimachus, could have seen in these lines the potential for creating the metaphor that appears in the proem of the third *Georgic*.

In summary, it seems extremely probable that a temple and perhaps some statuary appeared in the *Victoria Berenices*. These are hallmarks of Callimachean epinician, and it is hardly conceivable that they would not have figured in this celebration of the victory of the poet's own queen. At the same time, somewhere in the *Aetia*, Callimachus wrote of the construction of temples in language which elsewhere he reserved for the polemical definition of literary style. Virgil, at the beginning of the third *Georgic*, presented a temple which is both real and metaphorical. It is appropriate to the epinician setting, and as a metaphor for poetry it and the sculpture it is to contain are marked by their lifelike perfection. At the conclusion of this section, Virgil referred to these statues: *stabunt et Parii lapides,*

---

[41] Bonner 1951: 135.
[42] So, in lines 56–7 of the same poem, even the craft of Hephaestus is to fall short in comparison to the art of the new Alexandrian god of poetry: χρεὼ σοφῆς ὢ Φοῖβε πε[ιρ]ᾶσθαι τέχνης, | ἥτις Ἡφαίστεια νικήσει καλά ('it is necessary, o Phoebus, to make use of wise art, which will surpass the beauties of Hephaestus').

spirantia signa (3.34). This is a thoroughly Alexandrian claim for the supremacy of the work of art and, through it, for the excellence of the poem in which the objects appear.

In demonstrating that Virgil's epithet *Cynthius* (*G.* 3.36) is a Callimachean coinage, Clausen pointed to the next line of the *Georgics*, which begins with *Invidia*, 'a near relative of [Callimachus'] Βασκανίη'.[43] This personified Envy will cower in submission, rendered powerless by the greatness of Virgil's theme and, presumably, that of the poetry itself:

> Invidia infelix Furias amnemque severum
> Cocyti metuet tortosque Ixionis anguis
> immanemque rotam et non exsuperabile saxum. (*G.* 3.37–9)

Wretched Envy will fear the Furies and the merciless stream of Cocytus, the twisted snakes and enormous wheel of Ixion, and the unmasterable rock.

Again the critics are divided about the source of this curiously worded claim. Wilkinson, favouring Pindaric influence, points to the eight or so instances of φθόνος in that poet, noting that it is a natural enough ingredient of epinician verse.[44] None, however, is in the Virgilian sense, for they all enjoin caution against excessive praise in the face of the destructive power of φθόνος.[45] What we need is triumph *over* Envy. Wimmel[46] mentions programmatic references to Βασκανίη in the *Aetia* preface (*Aet.* 1 fr. 1.17) and in the epigrams (*Epigr.* 21.4), and to Φθόνος at *Hymn* 2.105, all contexts with which Virgil was thoroughly familiar.

Support for the influence of Callimachus emerges if we examine the actual manner of Virgil's reference: *Invidia* will be subject to fear of and, it is implied, domination by the Underworld—in other words, that is to be the destiny of *Invidia*. Now while Wimmel refers generally to Apollo's supremacy over Φθόνος at the end of *Hymn* 2, the reference needs more precision. Consider Apollo's final words:

---

[43] Clausen 1976: 245 n. 2.
[44] Wilkinson 1970: 289–90; he concludes: 'it [*Invidia*] is at least as likely to have been suggested by Pindar as by Callimachus.'
[45] The instance at *Pythian* 1.85 is fairly close in sense to the Virgilian reference, but even there, in keeping with the archaic mentality, there is a caution which is wholly lacking from Virgil's attitude.
[46] Wimmel 1960: 183–4.

χαῖρε, ἄναξ· ὁ δὲ Μῶμος, ἵν' ὁ Φθόνος, ἔνθα νέοιτο ('greetings, lord: as for Blame, let him go to the same place as Envy!',113). In general, then, an ἀποπομπή,[47] but one whose implications are clear: ἐς κόρακας—that is, to Hell.

As has been the case with other features of Virgil's proem, the critics, in seeking possible sources for the attitude towards *Invidia*, have neglected one crucial area—Callimachean epinician. The most extensively surviving epinician of this poet is the *Victoria Sosibii* (fr. 384). Just as the fragment breaks off, and at a point where praise of the victor is becoming excessive, Callimachus arrests himself:

οὔτε τὸν αἰνήσω τόσον ἄξ[ι]ος οὔτε λάθωμαι
–δείδια γὰρ δήμου γλῶσσαν ἐπ' ἀμφοτέροις— (fr. 384.57–8)

I will not praise him as much as he deserves nor neglect him—for in both cases, I fear the people's tongue.

Although the word does not appear (and hence the passage has escaped notice), this is φθόνος pure and simple.[48] What follows these lines is unsure, but it seems very likely that the term actually occurred and was not merely implicit.[49]

Here then, in Callimachean epinician, is a traditional reference to epinician Envy, and for Virgil we are again dealing with the correct poet (Callimachus) as well as the correct genre. But while Callimachus,

---

[47] F. J. Williams 1978 *ad loc.* has a useful discussion of this motif. On the final lines, see also Köhnken 1981: 411–22. A. Henrichs alerts me to Timocreon 5, *PMG* 731.

[48] Sallust's reticence with regard to the writing of history is curiously close to this: *in primis arduum videtur res gestas scribere: primum quod facta dictis exequenda sunt; dein quia plerique quae delicta reprehenderis malevolentia et* invidia *dicta putant, ubi de magna virtute atque gloria bonorum memores, quae sibi quisque facilia factu putant, aequo animo accipit, supra ea veluti ficta pro falsis ducit* ('writing history appears to be especially difficult: first because your words must be appropriate to the deeds (that you describe); and second because most people think that it is out of malevolence and envy that you criticize faults; however, when you speak of the great excellence and reputation of good men, everybody accepts readily what he thinks he himself might do easily, but considers as invention and falsehood what goes beyond this', *Cat.* 3.2).

[49] See Pfeiffer *ad* fr. 384.59–60 for possible supplements. μ[εμφ]ομένῳ (59) would be appropriate (cf. Sallust's *reprehenderis* above), as presumably would οὐδέπ[οτ' ἐ]σθλὸν ἔρεξεν (vel ἔλεξεν); cf. Sallust's *ubi de magna virtute atque gloria memores*. So, ἀ]ψ[ε]υδῆς is tantalizing (cf. *ficta pro falsis ducit*). Hunt's supplement for the whole line, rejected by Pfeiffer (but in sense what we need), is extremely close to Sallust: μ[ὴ τ]ὸ μέν (sc. ἐὰν αἰνήσω) ὦδ' [εἴ]πῃσιν [ὅ] δ' οὐδέπ[οτ' ἐ]σθλὸν ἔλεξεν (vel ἔρεξεν).

as befits the traditional encomiast, will temper his praises through fear of Envy (δήμου γλῶσσαν), Virgil has no such fear: his song and the greatness of Octavian will render such moderation unnecessary. Sallust again provides a parallel; Micipsa, in praising his king, Jugurtha: *postremo, quod difficillimum inter mortalis est, gloria invidiam vicisti* ('finally, you have conquered envy with your fame, which among mortals is the most difficult thing', *Iug.* 10.2).[50] Nor was Callimachus elsewhere so humble; in his own epitaph, he claimed:

> ὁ δ' ἤεισεν κρέσσονα βασκανίης. (*Epigr.* 21.4)

He sang what was stronger than Envy.

This, then, constitutes a part of the Virgilian claim, that the poet has performed beyond the reach of Envy.

Now for a final hypothesis. It seems reasonable, on the basis of the Callimachean, as well as the general epinician, evidence, to suggest that in the *Victoria Berenices* φθόνος received some treatment.[51] If so, the attitude will have been clear: both the poetry of Callimachus (as in *Epigr.* 21) and the subject of the epinician (unlike Sosibius in fr. 384.57–8) would have been presented as immune to Envy. There is, then, a strong case for suggesting that, against normal practice, in the case of Berenice's victory, Callimachus claimed that both her praises and his participation in them were unimpeachable, just as Virgil was to do in the case of Octavian and his own poetry.

It has been suggested, I believe correctly, that the third *Georgic* was originally intended to begin at line 49:[52]

> seu quis Olympiacae miratus praemia palmae
> pascit equos...

Or if anyone breeds horses, marveling at the prize of the Olympic palm...

---

[50] We find the same sentiment at 6.1: *cursu cum aequalibus certare et, quom omnis gloria anteiret, omnibus tamen carus esse* ('he competed with his agemates in running, and even though he surpassed them all in glory, he was nevertheless dear to all of them').

[51] Presumably at the end, when Callimachus turned back from Heracles and Molorchus to his praises of Berenice.

[52] Wilkinson 1970: 287; although presumably the opening three lines, recalling, as they do, the opening of the second book, always stood there.

Later, the work virtually completed, and with his mind 'full of Caesar's triumph' (Wilkinson), he composed the proem as it now stands, blending an epinician to Octavian with a program for his own poetry, possibly with the temple he was to build standing as a glimpse forward to the epic to which he would devote the remainder of his life.[53]

If this proem is seen as having as its primary reference Callimachean poetry—epinician as well as purely programmatic—then Virgil's intent becomes clearer. By the twenties the Callimachean program, as it is best stated by Virgil himself in the opening lines of the sixth *Eclogue*, had (at any rate for this poet) served its purpose. With the aid of Callimachus and the Alexandrian poets in general, and through the filter of the Roman neoterics, Roman poetry had matured. In its attention to detail, its refusal to emulate classical genres, and its focus on exclusiveness, it had achieved artistic perfection. Without Virgil the story might have ended here, with the creed one of ever-increasing concern for detail, poetic metaphor, and recondite reference.

It was Virgil, and Virgil alone, who saw from within the ultimate barrenness of such an art, and it is the tension created by this vision that finds expression in the proem to the third *Georgic*. *Cui non dictus Hylas*—the rejection of Alexandrian, and particularly of Callimachean themes—is a heartfelt plea of justification for the apparent change which the *Aeneid* was to represent.[54] That this transition was presented (as has been our claim) through reminiscence of the

---

[53] We may, of course, see the proem to the third *Georgic* as a pure *recusatio*, no more implying that an actual epic will follow than does Propertius 3.1. The details and extent of Virgil's lines, however, seem to resist such a reading (as does the existence of the *Aeneid*).

[54] This change is reflected at the opening of the second half not only of the *Georgics*, but also of Virgil's other two poems. The progression seems deliberate: *cum canerem reges et proelia, Cynthius aurem | vellit et admonuit:...| nunc ego...| agrestem tenui meditabor harundine Musam* ('when I was singing of kings and battles, Cynthian Apollo plucked my ear and admonished me:... now I... will practice the woodland muse with slender reed', *Ecl.* 6.3–8); *dicam horrida bella, | dicam acies actosque animis in funera reges |... maius opus moveo* ('I will sing of terrible wars, I will sing of battle lines and kings driven to death by fury... I begin a greater work', *Aen.* 7.41–4). Between the refusal to sing of kings and battles (a result of attenuated stylistic concerns) and the preface to such themes (with the exhortation for a loftier strain) comes the proem to the third *Georgic*, the exact middle point of Virgil's career, looking both ways. This is not the place for a

opening of the third book of the *Aetia* makes it all the more pointed. So we return to the lines with which we began:

> cuncta mihi Alpheum linquens lucosque Molorchi
> cursibus et crudo decernet Graecia caestu.
> ipse caput tonsae foliis ornatus olivae
> dona feram. (G. 3.19–22)

Leaving Alpheus and the groves of Molorchus for my sake, all of Greece will compete in running and with the rough boxing glove. I myself will bear gifts, my head crowned with the leaves of the shorn olive tree.

The new Italian setting, with the Italian Virgil himself supreme, argues for the supremacy of the poem he is to create and for the freedom that a now matured Roman poetry may enjoy. His periphrasis for Nemea, and possibly even the reference to Olympia,[55] in part specifies Callimachus as the ultimate addressee of the lines. Callimachean themes were no longer valid as, in the face of a new classicism, the poetry of rejection, its function fulfilled, was itself rejected.

2. PROPERTIUS 3.1

> Callimachi Manes et Coi sacra Philitae,
>   in vestrum, quaeso, me sinite ire nemus.
> primus ego ingredior puro de fonte sacerdos
>   Itala per Graios orgia ferre choros. (Prop. 3.1.1–4)

Shades of Callimachus and sacred rites of Coan Philitas, let me enter, I beg you, into your grove. As the first I attempt, priest from a pure fountain, to carry out Italian rituals in Greek choruses.

---

defence of the phrase, 'apparent change', but few, I trust, would deny that the *Aeneid*, or much of it, continues to be Callimachean in spirit, if not in the letter.

[55] In the same third book of the *Aetia* (*Eleorum Ritus Nuptialis*, fr. 76–7a Pf.) there seems to have been treatment of Heracles' founding of the Olympic games (see Pfeiffer, Dieg. i, fr. 77). In this book, then, we have Heracles involved in both the Nemean and Olympic foundings.

The first poem of the third book[56] of Propertius begins and ends with Callimachus,[57] just as the *Monobiblos* did with Cynthia (*Cynthia prima...*). The polemical nature of this poem has long been acknowledged. Abundant in references to the poetry of Lucretius, Virgil, and Horace,[58] it proclaims the superiority of the poet's Callimachean verse in the typical style of the *recusatio*. For our purposes, the specifically Virgilian references (which, incidentally, are more numerous than any others in Propertius' poem) are clearly of primary importance. The allusions are all to the proem of the third *Georgic* and, in that they occur within the framework of Propertius' declaration of allegiance to Callimachus, they may be seen as the elegiac poet's assertion of the importance of Callimachus and as his acknowledgement of the Callimachean impulse behind the opening of the third *Georgic*.

Wimmel has conveniently indicated most of the relevant connections, and we need only list them here:[59]

Verg. G. 3	Prop. 3. 1
primus ego...deducam (10–11)	primus ego ingredior...(3)
temptanda via est, qua me quoque possim | tollere humo (8–9)	quo me Fama levat terra sublimis (9)
Aonio...deducam vertice Musas (11)	opus hoc de monte sororum | detulit intacta pagina nostra via (17–18)
virum volitare per ora (9)	maius ab exsequiis nomen in ora venit (24)

---

[56] I follow Lachmann in the view that book 2 of Propertius is in fact a conflation of two books and agree with Birt 1882: 422–6 that at least in terms of publication the *Monobiblos* is to be separated from the rest of the collection. If so, and few now have any doubts, then 3.1 is still to be considered the opening poem of the third book. Skutsch 1975: 229–33 has in fact removed any doubts on the matter, but for those who do not believe in a *Monobiblos* and in the fact that the second book is a conflation, 3.1 will still be 3.1.

[57] *Lycio...deo* (38), as has been recognized, is intensely Callimachean (*Aet*. 1 fr. 1.22, *Hymn* 4.304): 'only the self-styled Roman Callimachus dared use it' (Clausen 1976: 246). It is, I think, in part a restoration of the Callimachean Λύκιος, following Virgil's substitution of Cynthius at *Ecl*. 6.3 (for Λύκιος at *Aet*. 1 fr. 1.22).

[58] Generally, see Nethercut 1970; his concern is mainly with Horace.

[59] Wimmel 1960: 216–18; I shall include only the undeniable references, although Wimmel has more possible ones.

Callimachus, the Victoria Berenices, and Roman Poetry

illi victor ego et Tyrio conspectus in ostro | centum quadriiugos agitabo ad flumina currus (17–18) Invidia infelix Furias... metuet ...(37–9)	a me | nata coronatis Musa triumphat equis, | et mecum in curru parvi vectantur Amores... (9–11) at mihi quod vivo detraxerit invida turba | post obitum duplici faenore reddet Honos (20–1)

Beyond these reminiscences in Propertius' first poem, there is also the opening of the second:

> carminis interea nostri redeamus in orbem,
>   gaudeat in solito tacta puella sono.   (3.2.1–2)

Meanwhile let us return to the accustomed sphere of my song; may my girl be touched and rejoice in the well-known sound.

Interea has caused some commentators trouble, in that Propertius never left off the writing of elegy.[60] But such a reading of these lines ignores the fiction of *recusatio*. And, moreover, the difficulties vanish if we recognize Propertius' source:[61]

>   interea Dryadum silvas saltusque sequamur.   (*G.* 3.40)

Meanwhile let us pursue the woods and glades of the Dryads.

With *interea*, Virgil made the transition from discussion of his future poetic plans to the subject at hand,[62] and Propertius followed suit. A final indication: a few lines later both Virgil (*G.* 3.43) and Propertius (3.2.5) have references to *Cithaeron*, a word which appears only once elsewhere in the poetry of each.

Propertius, then, at the beginning of his third book, deliberately recalled the proem to the third *Georgic* in order to validate his own

---

[60] Camps 1966 *ad loc.* has a long note on the word, and Richardson 1977 *ad loc.* gives it the meaning 'from time to time' (based on Sil. 7.395). His refusal to allow a close connection between 3.1 and 3.2 exposes a modern prejudice in the attitude towards divisions of poems. Clearly within a book of poetry (and particularly within a connected group of poems such as Propertius 3.1–3) there can be reference to a context outside the immediate poem. One thinks perhaps of the *Roman Odes* where the second poem begins (*pauperiem*) with a reference to the end of the first (*divitias*), as does the third (*iustum*) to the end of the second (*scelestum*).

[61] Wimmel 1960: 217 briefly noted the connection.

[62] Precisely the same pattern is found in the tenth *Eclogue*, where Gallus' future poetic project (*ibo et Chalcidico quae sunt mihi condita versu...*, 50–1; cf. *G.* 3.10, *primus ego in patriam mecum...* \| *deducam... Musas*) is interrupted by his present task (*interea mixtis lustrabo Maenala Nymphis, Ecl.* 10.55).

poetic fame and to argue for the supremacy of elegiac verse. At the same time, certain features of his poem (the poet as victor, the reference to *Invidia* and its ultimate subjugation) are those which we have suggested were possibly elements of the *Victoria Berenices*. Propertius, moreover, presented all of this within the framework of a poem that begins, ends, and is imbued with Callimachean poetic theory.[63] It seems reasonable to regard Propertius' conflation of Callimachean and Virgilian verse as further evidence for the presence of the Alexandrian poet in the proem to the third *Georgic*.

3. STATIUS *SILVAE* 3.1

With the exception of a passing reference in the *Panegyric to Messalla* (*Alcides*... | *laeta Molorcheis posuit vestigia tectis*, 'Hercules happily set foot into the house of Molorchus', 12–13), Hercules' lowly host is not found after Virgil until Statius, who has three references—more than any other author. Here Parsons' observation should be kept in mind: 'In principle, then, all later mentions (of Molorchus) look back to Callimachus.'[64] Statius is unusual, possibly even unique, in standing with the Augustans in his appreciation of Callimachus. At *Silvae* 1.2.253 he sets his poetry in a tradition that includes Philitas, Callimachus, and the Roman elegists. Indeed, if we are to believe him, this interest is a legacy from his father, a *grammaticus* and poet to whom Statius ascribes an early training in the allusive art of Callimachean and other poetry:

> tu pandere docti
> carmina Battiadae latebrasque Lycophronis arti
> Sophronaque implicitum tenuisque arcana Corinnae.
> (Stat. *Silv.* 5.3.156–8)

You explained the songs of the learned son of Battus, the obscurities of twisted Lycophron, complicated Sophron, and the riddles of subtle Corinna.

---

[63] See Wimmel 1960: 215–16 for references in Prop. 3.1 to the *Aetia* prologue and the second *Hymn*.

[64] Parsons 1977: 43.

Statius was clearly familiar with the details of the story, which is to say that he was presumably familiar with Callimachus' version of it:

> dat Nemea comites, et quas in proelia viris
> sacra Cleonaei cogunt vineta Molorchi.
> gloria nota casae, foribus simulata salignis
> hospitis arma dei, parvoque ostenditur arvo,
> robur ubi et laxos qua reclinaverit arcus
> ilice, qua cubiti sedeant vestigia terra. (*Theb.* 4.159–64)

Nemea gives them comrades, and all the forces which the sacred vineyards of Cleonaean Molorchus raise for battle. The fame of the hut is well-known, on the doors the arms of the visiting god are depicted, and on the small property one is shown where he put down his club and against which holm-oak he rested his weary limbs, where on the earth the traces of his elbow still remain.

The passage is far from ornamental. *Cleonaei . . . Molorchi* is original in Latin,[65] the adjective is Callimachean (Κλεωναῖοι χάρωνος, fr. 339 Pf.),[66] and so, no doubt, is its use with Molorchus.[67] Apart from this, the reference to the fame of the hut (*gloria nota casae*, 161), together with the details which follow, implies an acquaintance on the poet's part with the emphasis and details of Callimachus' treatment.[68]

---

[65] Elsewhere we find the epithet applied to Hercules and to the lion (*ThLL, Onomast.* 2.490.31–2).

[66] It is used in Pindar as an epithet for the Nemean games (*Nem.* 4.17) and for the local inhabitants (*Nem.* 10.42), but the extension of its application seems to be Callimachean.

[67] A passage in Nonnus makes this certain; he is dealing with Brongus' hospitality towards Dionysus, and is reminded of a parallel situation:

> τεύχων δεῖπνον ἄδειπνον ἀδαιτρεύτοιο τραπέζης
> οἷα Κλεωναίοιο φατίζεται ἀμφὶ Μολόρχου,
> κεῖνα, τά περ σπεύδοντι λεοντοφόνους ἐς ἀγῶνας
> ὥπλισεν Ἡρακλῆι. (*Dion.* 17.51–4)

'Preparing a meager meal of vegetarian fare, such as the story goes about Cleonaean Molorchus and the meal which he furnished for Heracles, who was eager to rush into his lion-killing fight.' Noun and epithet appear in the same position as at Stat. *Theb.* 4.158, that is, at caesura and line-end. The last word of Callim. fr. 177 (the 'Mousetrap'), which may be from the *Victoria Berenices*, is κλεων[. On this, see Livrea *et al.* 1980: 234.

[68] See Parsons 1977: 43–4 and Bornmann in Livrea *et al.* 1980: 247–51 for the tradition in which the *Victoria Berenices* belongs: gods or heroes entertained by humble hosts, with careful description of the details of the host's surroundings.

Of the other two appearances of Molorchus in Statius, one (*Silv.* 4.6.51) comes in an ecphrasis on a statue of Hercules owned by Novius Vindex.[69] The statue is praised for its artistry, its dimensions are given, and in many ways the poem has its source in the Callimachean interest in the plastic arts.

Potentially, then, reference in Statius to Molorchus is not merely casual. We can now turn to the final instance, which once again is found in the opening poem of a third book—*Silvae* 3.1. Here the context is even more suggestive. The poem concerns construction of a temple of Hercules built by the wealthy Pollius Felix. Henceforth the hero will have no need of his former, dangerous haunts:

> non te Lerna nocens nec pauperis arva Molorchi
> nec formidatus Nemees ager antraque poscunt
> Thracia nec Pharii polluta altaria regis.   (*Silv.* 3.1.29–31)

Harmful Lerna and the fields of poor Molorchus do not call for you, nor the feared realm of Nemea, the Thracian caves, or the polluted altars of the Pharian king.

Again, mere mention of Molorchus, together with allusive reference to Busiris (*Pharii...regis*), is sufficient to suggest Callimachus.[70] Other details are suggestive. The temple is contrasted with the lowly hut, once the seat of Hercules, which it is to replace:

> stabat dicta sacri tenuis casa nomine templi
> et magnum Alciden humili lare parva premebat.   (82–3)

There stood a lowly hut bearing the name of a sacred temple and, though tiny, it confined great Hercules in its humble house.

Callimachus' own *Hecale*, Nonnus' Brongus, and Ovid's Baucis and Philemon are the best examples. Parsons 1977: 44 urges some caution, in that Nonnus' reference to Molorchus (*Dion.* 17.52) is immediately followed by a quotation from the *Hecale* (17.55; Callim. fr. 248). Conversely, however, this may serve as additional evidence that Nonnus saw the two Callimachean episodes as parallel examples of the same tradition.

[69] The same statue (purportedly by Lysippus) appears in Martial (9.43) where, once again, Molorchus also figures as one of two references in this poet.

[70] Busiris, we will recall, figured at the end of the second book of the *Aetia* (fr. 44–7), shortly before the *Victoria Berenices*.

One thinks of better-known *casae*, that of Molorchus (*gloria nota casae*, *Theb.* 4.161), or, just as relevant, the one which Baucis and Philemon exchanged for a temple:[71]

> illa vetus dominis etiam *casa parva* duobus
> vertitur in *templum*.   (Ovid, *Met.* 8.699–700)

That old house, small even for two inhabitants, is turned into a temple.

Hercules' temple is finely crafted, as befits the subject of an ecphrasis; indeed, it represents a θαῦμα (*stupet ipse labores | annus, et angusti bis seno limite menses | longaevum mirantur opus*, 'the year itself marvels at the labors, and the months, confined in their twelve boundaries, admire the timeless work', 17–19; *artifices mirantur opus*, 'the craftsmen admire the work', 135).[72] The structure, moreover, is treated in lofty, aetiological style, which perhaps recalls Virgil's metaphorical temple in the proem of the third *Georgic*:

> sed quaenam subiti, veneranda, exordia templi
> dic age, Calliope.   (*Silv.* 3.1.49–50)

But come, venerable Calliope, tell which were the beginnings of this sudden temple.

Finally, again close in sense to Virgil's actual reference to Molorchus, the games held in the Italian arena around Hercules' temple will surpass their traditional Greek counterparts:

> hos nec Pisaeus honores
> Iuppiter aut Cirrhae pater aspernetur opacae.
> nil his triste locis; cedat lacrimabilis Isthmos,
> cedat atrox Nemee.   (*Silv.* 3.1.140–3)

Pisaean Jupiter or the lord of leafy Cyrrha would not spurn these honors. There is no sadness in this place: let tearful Isthmos and harsh Nemea give way.

We are back in the realm of epinician, and it is difficult to avoid recalling the Virgilian lines with which we began:

---

[71] The ultimate source is Eumaeus' κλισία, which he offers to Odysseus (*Od.* 14.404, 408). Typically, Callimachus in the *Hecale* uses the word in the sense of 'cot' (fr. 256), while clearly borrowing from the Homeric context. There can be no doubt that Molorchus' hut received extensive and literary treatment.

[72] See below for this as a feature of ecphrasis.

> cuncta mihi Alpheum linquens lucosque Molorchi
> cursibus et crudo decernet Graecia caestu.   (G. 3.19–20)

Leaving Alpheus and the groves of Molorchus for my sake, all of Greece will compete in running and with the rough boxing glove.

Synthesis is called for. Three Roman poets—Virgil, Propertius, and Statius—each at the outset of a third book provide reference to Molorchus (Virgil and Statius), are influenced by epinician (Virgil, Propertius, and Statius), allude to or mention Callimachus (Virgil[73] and Propertius), treat *Invidia* and its failure to detract from the poet's art (Virgil and Propertius), or refer to an elaborately constructed *templum*, real or metaphorical, in a manner evocative of the Callimachean attitude towards the plastic arts (Virgil and Statius). In addition, in spite of the numerous points of contact between the passages of Virgil and Statius, there is no suggestion of any direct Virgilian influence on *Silvae* 3.1. In short, an archetype seems to be indicated, and the one which potentially or in fact meets all the requirements is the *Victoria Berenices*.

4. THE *VICTORIA BERENICES*

On the basis of Callimachean poetry, particularly of his epinician, and taking into account the influence of this poet on subsequent poets, we have suggested that certain elements will almost surely have figured in the entire episode. Doubtless the notion of φθόνος occupied some place in Callimachus' celebration of the victory, and it seems likely that Berenice's success was marked by some commemoration, possibly involving a dedication made in a temple, or possibly involving statuary. Here it may be relevant that the *Coma Berenices*, an episode which Callimachus intended to stand out as structurally parallel with the *Victoria*, contains a dedication, that of the lock itself: τὸν Βερενίκης | βόστρυχον ὃν κείνη πᾶσιν ἔθηκε θεοῖς ('the lock of Berenice, which she dedicated to all the gods', *Aet.* 4 fr. 110.7–8). We are told, rightly or otherwise, that Berenice dedicated

---

[73] See above for the implicit presence of Callimachus in the proem to the third *Georgic*.

Callimachus, the Victoria Berenices, and Roman Poetry 213

the lock in the temple of Arsinoe-Aphrodite at Zephyrium.[74] There are attested a number of offerings, both to and on behalf of Berenice, usually in the company of Euergetes, and sometimes with Isis, Sarapis, and others.[75] At the same time, epigrams by Callimachus, Hedylus, and Posidippus record dedications, real or fictional, to Berenice's dynastic mother, again in her capacity as Arsinoe-Aphrodite.[76] Such dedications, then, in connection with the Ptolemies, abound in literature as in fact, and it would be extraordinary if no such honor attended the queen's victory, more so if it were not treated by Callimachus in his epinician to her.

The proposition that there was indeed such a dedication leads to consideration of a difficult part of the *Victoria Berenices*, the opening fragment, which, although its context was not fixed, existed before the discovery of the Lille papyri. As *Ep. et Eleg. Min.* fr. 383 Pf. (= fr. 254 *SH*) breaks off, the following text is preserved:[77]

ἠμὲν δή πο [
καὶ πάρος Ἀργεί[
καιρωτοὺς τε[
Κολχίδες ἢ Νείλω[ι
λεπταλέους ἔξυσαν.[
εἰδυῖαι φαλιὸν ταῦρον ἰηλεμίσαι
....]υκων ὁτε[
.....].ν κομα[
........] ... [.]..[

(fr. 383.11–19 Pf. = fr. 254.25–32 *SH*)

This immediately follows the opening ten lines of the third book, lines in which the poet hails the actual victory of Berenice. The next point, either after an interval of one column or, more likely, straightaway,[78] places us *in medias res* with Heracles and Molorchus (col. B(i)). Parsons 1977: 7 notes on the above lines: 'Argos and Egypt in problematic context'; and later: '25 ff. Argos; Colchian and Egyptian

---

[74] *Aet.* 4 fr. 110.54–8; Catull. 66.54–8; Hyg. *Astr.* 2.24; cf. Pfeiffer *ad* Dieg. 5.40.
[75] For these see Fraser 1972: 2.194, 234, 263, 272.
[76] Callimachus *Epigr.* 5 Pf.; Hedylus *Epigr.* 4 (Page, OCT, *ap.* Athen. 2.497d); Posidippus *Epigr.* 12, 13 (Page, OCT). On these, see Gow and Page 1965: 2.168, 491.
[77] The line numbers are those of Pfeiffer (i.e. excluding the interlinear scholia of the Lille papyrus).
[78] On this question, see Parsons 1977: 39.

weavers. Callimachus may intend a simple parallel: formerly an Egyptian king (Danaus) ruled in Argos; now an Egyptian queen triumphs in the Argive games.'[79] While this is possible, it does not entirely account for what remains of the diction of these lines nor, if the epyllion followed immediately, does it help in recovering the means of transition from epinician to epyllion. What follows is a suggestion which, I trust, may fulfill both of these requirements.

Let us begin with the intuition of Pfeiffer: 'Call. de textilibus linteis antiquissimis Argivorum, ut de bugonia Nemeaea, ex libris Περὶ Ἀργολικῶν?'[80] The diction of these lines, fragmentary though they be, supports this suggestion, and it requires further examination. Καιρωτούς, a hapax legomenon, appears to mean 'well woven'.[81] Pfeiffer suggested as a supplement τε[λαμῶνας;[82] some form based on τεχν- (or even τευχ-) cannot be ruled out.[83] If so, the implications will have been that the weaving involved a high level of artistry. The same may be implied in line 14, Κολχίδες ἢ Νείλω[ι. As Pfeiffer has shown, the only known attribute shared by Colchian and Egyptian women is their ability and method in the working of yarn: λίνον... ἐργάζονται κατὰ ταὐτά, Hdt. 2.105. And again, at line 15 of the fragment, we find the phrase λεπταλέους ἔξυσαν. For Callimachus the adjective (or its simple form, λεπτός) can have only one reference—to a highly finished object, in this case, presumably, to a finely spun piece of weaving.[84]

---

[79] Parsons 1977: 10; he also suggests the possibility of a reference 'to Egyptian women or to formerly Egyptian (now Argive) women, who celebrate Berenice's victory' (11).
[80] Pfeiffer ad fr. 383.16—although we now know that the fragment is from the Aetia.
[81] Pfeiffer ad loc. The word occurs only here, although it is clearly related to an instance at Od. 7.107 (καιροσέων δ' ὀθονέων ἀπολείβεται ὑγρὸν ἔλαιον)—καιροσέων also being unique. The Homeric lines will be dealt with shortly.
[82] He compares adesp. Anth. Pal. 11.25.3: ἀπ' ἐνταφίων τελαμῶνας. Thus the reference would be to Apis' shroud. Now that we have a context for fr. 383, it is difficult to imagine how such a reference would operate.
[83] Cf. in the same Odyssean passage containing καιροσέων: ὡς δὲ γυναῖκες/ἱστῶν τεχνῆσσαι, 7.109–10.
[84] In general, on the word, see Reitzenstein 1931: 25–40. It is perhaps of note that in the description of Achilles' shield (itself a well-crafted object) the adjective is twice used in reference to details presented by the poet: λεπταλέῃ φωνῇ, Il. 18.571; λεπτὰς ὀθόνας, 595.

Callimachus, the Victoria Berenices, and Roman Poetry 215

Now the implications of these three lines should be clear.[85] Callimachus can hardly have been making a passing reference to weavers; what was obviously prominent, for it is what remains, was an emphasis on the excellence of the *product* of their industry. Support comes from Homer. At *Od.* 7.86–111 the activities of Alcinous' serving women are described. Athena has given them supremacy in their art, weaving. Pfeiffer has suggested, correctly, that Callimachus had line 107 of this passage in mind when he wrote καιρωτούς.[86] But there appear to be further links with the entire passage:

> ἔνθ᾽ ἐνὶ πέπλοι
> λεπτοὶ ἐΰννητοι βεβλήατο, ἔργα γυναικῶν.
>
> αἱ δ᾽ ἱστοὺς ὑφόωσι καὶ ἠλάκατα στρωφῶσιν
> ἥμεναι, οἷά τε φύλλα μακεδνῆς αἰγείροιο·
> καιροσέων δ᾽ <u>ὀθονέων</u>[87] ἀπολείβεται ὑγρὸν ἔλαιον.
> ὅσσον Φαίηκες περὶ πάντων ἴδριες ἀνδρῶν
> νῆα θοὴν ἐνὶ πόντῳ ἐλαυνέμεν, ὣς δὲ γυναῖκες
> <u>ἱστῶν</u> τεχνῆσσαι· περὶ γάρ σφισι δῶκεν Ἀθήνη
> ἔργα τ᾽ ἐπίστασθαι περικαλλέα καὶ φρένας ἐσθλάς.
>   (Hom. *Od.* 7.96–7, 105–11)

Over them were spread light, well-sewn blankets, the works of women... They weave at looms or twist their spindles, sitting, like the leaves of a tall poplar tree, and liquid olive oil drips from their well-woven linens. As much as the Phaeacians are knowledgeable beyond all other men in steering a swift ship on the sea, so are their women skilled in weaving. For Athena put in their minds understanding of beautiful works and noble intelligence.

Both here, then, and in Callimachus, we find women, their activity (weaving), and diction (the first pair *hapax legomena*) suggesting the excellence of their art: καιροσέων/καιρωτούς; λεπτοί/λεπταλέους.

If, as I have argued, we are led to expect a dedication for Berenice's victory, then it seems plausible to suggest that it may have been the object whose vestiges appear at the end of Parsons' Text A, specifically

---

[85] The remaining lines, 12, 16, and 17, will be dealt with below.
[86] Cf. above, n. 81.
[87] Cf. also the garments on the shield: τῶν δ᾽ αἱ μὲν λεπτὰς ὀθόνας ἔχον ('some of them were wearing light linen garments', Hom. *Il.* 18.595).

that Callimachus in these lines referred to a *peplos* or tapestry of some kind offered in commemoration of the victory. Elaborately woven objects seem to have held a particular fascination for this poet. He clearly treated the most famous *peplos* of the ancient world, that of Athena, the center of attention at the Panathenaic Festival.[88] Fragment 66, which also comes from the third book of the *Aetia*, deals with the prefatory rites to be performed by the young women who weave the robe of Hera at the Argive Heraeum.[89] In three other fragments (547, 640, 672) weaving appears in unclear contexts. This interest is doubtless connected with Callimachus' awareness of the metaphorical potential implied by this activity: elaborate weaving may stand for highly artistic poetic production.[90] Finally, there are preserved in the fragments two separate instances of robings of statues of the Graces.[91] In the first the emphasis is on the beauty, and presumably the artistry, of these adornments: ἐν δὲ Πάρῳ κάλλη τε καὶ αἰόλα βεύδε' ἔχουσαι ('in Paros, having beautiful and shining robes', *Aet.* 1 fr. 7.11 Pf.). The second instance is striking; it appears in Callimachus' only other extensively surviving epinician, the *Victoria Sosibii*:

ἀμφοτέρων ὁ ξεῖνος ἐπήβολος· οὐκέτι γυμνάς
παῖδας ἐν Ἡραίῳ στήσομεν Εὐρυνόμης.
(*Ep. et Eleg. Min.* fr. 384.44–5)

In both contests the stranger has been successful. No longer will we put up naked daughters of Eurynome in the Heraeum.

Like Berenice, Sosibius has been successful in the chariot race; he, however at both the Isthmian and Nemean games. In commemoration of this, an unidentified speaker states that statues of the Graces in the Heraeum at Argos will receive robes or, more likely, that new statues, fitted out with robes, will be dedicated. Elsewhere in

---

[88] Fr. inc. sed. 520 and Pfeiffer *ad loc*.

[89] Indeed, this may even have been the context of line 12 of the *Victoria Berenices*: καὶ πάρος Ἀργει[('and before at Argos [the young women wove a robe for Hera]'?). On this, see below.

[90] Cf. fr. 532: τῷ ἰκελὸν τὸ γράμμα τὸ Κώιον. On this question, see Reitzenstein 1931, *passim*; Lyne 1978: 109–10.

[91] And elsewhere (*Epigr.* 51), in fact, Callimachus includes Berenice as the fourth Grace.

Callimachean epinician, then, we find *peploi*, possibly with statuary, dedicated in commemoration of the victor's achievement.[92]

The suggestion is, then, that the woven object discernible at *Victoria Berenices* A 25–31 may have been a *peplos*, or other woven object, offered either on her behalf, or by the queen herself, in acknowledgement of her victory.[93]

The obvious question remains: what has all of this to do with the epyllion on Heracles and Molorchus? In other words, particularly if that portion of the poem followed immediately after Text A, how did Callimachus make the transition from epinician to epyllion? It is of course possible that he merely turned from the present to the mythical past, offering an *aetion* on the founding of the games. Yet other possibilities emerge which would, I think, account for the surviving fragments, particularly for the one with which we have been dealing. Could it be that the epyllion on Heracles and Molorchus was an artistic ecphrasis, an account in the manner of Catullus 64 of scenes woven into the fabric which was the subject of A 26–31? With our present state of knowledge this can only be a matter of hypothesis, and as we shall see there are serious objections, but since the 'source' ('impulse' is perhaps a more appropriate term) for Catullus 64 has been sought for two centuries, it is clearly a hypothesis worth pursuing.

As one critic has noted in a different and more general context, the style of ecphrasis is often close to that of epyllion,[94] and in the case of Catullus 64 the two actually merge. This is true of our poem. The studied, artificial tone of the inner panel of the *Victoria Berenices*, what Parsons referred to as a 'rococo exercise', and familiar from Theocritus' description of the cup or, again, Catullus' of the tapestry, may suggest an artificial setting. Callimachus' account of the devastated countryside, his description of Molorchus' hut, his aetiological

---

[92] Pausanias reports that at the festival of Hera in Elis the women who weave the *peplos* hold a race and that the winning girls are entitled to dedicate statues of themselves: καὶ δὴ ἀναθεῖναί σφισιν ἔστι γραψαμέναις εἰκόνας, 5.16.3.

[93] Incidentally, Callixenus of Rhodes (*FGH* 627 fr. 2 = Athen. 196a–206c) recorded evidence of the Ptolemaic interest in elaborate tapestries, embroidered cloaks, and the like. See Fraser 1972: 1.138.

[94] Lyne 1978: 110.

treatment of the lion's affliction of Argos—all of these are consistent with poetic exegesis of a work of art.

So too with the structure of the *Victoria Berenices*. Under Parsons' reconstruction, the entire episode was shaped thus: (*a*) outer story (Berenice's victory); (*b*) inner and prominent story (Heracles and Molorchus); (*c*) outer story (return to Berenice).[95] This pattern, where the inner section is presented as a digression, but in fact receives the focus and is intended to be predominant, is familiar from all other examples of extended ecphrasis,[96] and can best be demonstrated from the most elaborate instance—again, Catullus 64. The description of the tapestry is framed by the wedding of Peleus and Thetis, which is for Catullus the present narrative setting, with strictly responding diction supporting the structure, and bridging past and present: *haec vestis priscis hominum variata figuris* ('this tapestry, decorated with images of the men of old', 50) (immediately before the ecphrasis); *talibus amplifice vestis decorata figuris,* ('the tapestry, beautifully adorned with such images', 265) (immediately after).[97] It is precisely these features, or the traces of them, that appear in the *Victoria Berenices*: between (*a*) (Berenice) and (*b*) (Heracles and Molorchus) we find reference to an object woven with great artistry.

Elsewhere Callimachus seems to have realized the proximity of epyllion to ecphrasis. In the *Hecale*, which of course shares more than a little with the account of Heracles and Molorchus, at one point the old woman appears to be relating to Theseus events from her past:

> μέμνημαι καλὴν μὲν ᾳ [
> ἄλλικα χρυσείῃσιν ἐεργομένην ἐνετῇσιν,
> ἔργον ἀραχνάων...];..[(*Hec.* fr. 253.10–12 Pf.)

I remember a beautiful...cloak, held up by golden pins, the work of spiders...

---

[95] This sequence does not survive, but will certainly have figured (see Parsons 1977: 42).

[96] We need only mention the shields of Achilles and Aeneas.

[97] The responsion does not stop here: at both ends there is admiration at the excellence of the artistry (*mira...arte,* 51; *spectando Thessala pubes | expleta est,* 267–8), together with parallel treatment of the arrival (31–44) and departure (267–77) of the mortal guests at the wedding.

Callimachus, the Victoria Berenices, and Roman Poetry 219

Not just any cloak, it seems. As Pfeiffer noted on ἔργον ἀραχνάων: 'chlamys ita appellari posse videtur si est vestis "picturata" ut opera Arachnae Ov. *met.* VI 5 sqq., vel Verg. *A.* IV 137. V 250.'[98] As one critic has noted: 'It seems... likely that what followed our fragment was an *ekphrasis*, put in the mouth of Hekale, of the scenes on this garment.'[99]

The poetic ecphrasis,[100] from Homer to Statius, and particularly from the Hellenistic period on, required two related features: first the claim, almost as a piece of advertisement, that the object in question is of outstanding artistry,[101] and then the subsequent awe or amazement it evokes from those who are involved with it in the narrative. In each case, the object thus functions as a θαῦμα, and it is usually specified as such. Here are some selective examples:

Artistry

πᾶν μὲν γάρ κύκλῳ τιτάνῳ λευκῷ
τ' ἐλέφαντι | ἠλέκτρῳ ν' ὑπολαμπὲς
ἔην χρυσῷ τε φαεινῷ
(Hes. [*Sc.*] 141–2)
τι θεῶν δαίδαλμα (Theoc. *Id.*
1.32)[102]
ἐν δ' ἄρ' ἑκάστῳ | τέρματι δαίδαλα
πολλὰ διακριδὸν εὖ ἐπέπαστο
(Ap. Rhod. *Argon.* 1.728–9)
ἕω τῷ δαίδαλα πολλὰ τετεύχατο
μαρμαίροντα (Mosch. *Eur.* 43)
tincta tegit rosco conchyli

Marvel

θαῦμα ἰδέσθαι (140)

αἰπολικὸν θάημα· τέρας κέ τυ θυμὸν
ἀτύξαι (56)
τῆς μὲν ῥηίτερόν κεν ἐς ἠέλιον
ἀνιόντα | ὄσσε βάλοις ἢ κεῖνο
μεταβλέψειας ἔρευθος (725–6)
τάλαρον...μέγα θαῦμα (37–8)

haec vestis... *mira* arte (50–1)

---

[98] Pfeiffer *ad loc.*
[99] Shapiro 1980: 270; he also points to Callimachus' reminiscence of the description of Odysseus' brooch at *Od.* 19.226 ff.—itself a small-scale ecphrasis.
[100] Still the best general treatment of this motif (and the only comprehensive one) is Friedländer 1912: 1–103.
[101] For most of the Greek examples of this feature see Bühler 1960: 85–6, 92–3.
[102] In fact Theocritus here refers to the artistry of a single feature of the cup. Note too his variation of the *topos* at 15.78–86 where the element of wonder (at the excellence of the tapestries) is contained within the general dramatic setting of the poem: τὰ ποικίλα πρᾶτον ἄθρησον, | λεπτὰ καὶ ὡς χαρίεντα· θεῶν περονάματα φασεῖς ('look first at the embroideries, so delicate and pleasing; you might think them clothes fit for gods', 78–9).

| purpura fuco (Catull. 64.49) | postquam cupide *spectando* Thessala pubes \| *expleta est* (267–8) |
| clipei non enarrabile textum[103] (Verg. *Aen.* 8.612–13) | *expleri* nequit atque oculos per singula volvit, \| *miraturque* (618–19) talia ... *miratur*[104] (730) |

Returning to the *Victoria Berenices* with this tradition in mind, we find at the end of Text A (which is where the transition to ecphrasis would appear) traces of the first of these categories, that is the diction of artistic excellence: καιρωτούς (A 27); λεπταλέους (A 29).[105] What of the element of awe or wonder? The last intelligible line of Text A is independently preserved:

εἰδυῖαι φαλιὸν ταῦρον ἰηλεμίσαι (A 30)

'Women who know how to wail for the bull (Apis)', or, stated without the Alexandrian periphrasis, 'Egyptian women'. This is merely a subject clause; it tells us nothing of the women's present activity. We may get some help from Tibullus, whose reference to this line has long been realized:

te [sc. Nile] canit atque suum pubes miratur Osirim
   barbara, *Memphiten plangere docta bovem.*   (Tib. 1.7.28–9)

The barbarian girls sing of you and marvel at their Osiris, knowing how to bewail the bull of Memphis.

The Roman poet has taken Callimachus' ornamental periphrasis and grafted it on to a new setting;[106] the Tibullan context, an aretalogy to Osiris, can hardly have been a part of the *Victoria Berenices*.[107] But there is a point of interest beyond Tibullus' mere adaptation of the periphrasis: one of the activities of the women in his poem is their

---

[103] Virgil, perhaps as we would expect, is terse here, in fact applying the diction of artistic excellence not to the shield (which will speak for itself), but to Aeneas' greaves: *tum levis ocreas electro auroque recocto* (624)—a borrowing of the language Hesiod used of his shield ([*Scut.*] 142).

[104] In his use of *expleri*, and in framing the ecphrasis with a form of *miror*, Virgil is clearly acknowledging Catullus' ecphrasis. So too of Dido's temple murals: *miratur* (*Aen.* 1.456); *miranda* (494)—both in framing positions.

[105] See above, nn. 81, 84.

[106] Tibullus' reference is particularly learned in that only by recognizing the Callimachean source do we realize that *pubes* refers to a group of young *women*.

[107] On Tibullus' poem, and particularly on the Egyptian elements in it, see Koenen 1976: 128–59.

Callimachus, the Victoria Berenices, and Roman Poetry 221

awe or admiration: *pubes miratur*... | *barbara*. If Tibullus took from Callimachus not only the periphrastic subject (Egyptian women) but also their activity (wonder), then the case for ecphrasis is strengthened, for in the vicinity of Callimachus' women there appears to be a finely woven object. Again we think of those observing the tapestry in Catullus 64: *quae postquam cupide spectando Thessala pubes* | *expleta est* (267–8).

External arguments may be adduced for the possibility that Callimachus' epyllion was an ecphrasis.[108] In the case of Catullus 64, the fact that the story of Theseus and Ariadne was a popular theme in vase-painting doubtless helped the poet to conceive of a visual poem—that is, an ecphrasis. The same can obviously be said of the encounter of Heracles with the Nemean lion.[109] Indeed, although Molorchus does not figure,[110] an epigram ascribed to Damagetus (*Anth. Plan.* 95) is itself a miniature ecphrasis on the struggle between the hero and the lion. Moreover, Callimachus seems to have had Athena watching over the fight (*Victoria Berenices* fr. 57.4 Pf.); as Parsons has noted,[111] vase-paintings often include the goddess as a witness.

---

[108] It is again worth referring to the account of Callixenus of Rhodes (above, n. 93), dealing with a procession arranged by Ptolemy Philadelphus. His description of the details of the royal pavilion demonstrates that in actual life *vestes picturatae* abounded:... καὶ χιτῶνες χρυσουφεῖς ἐφαπτίδες τε κάλλισται, τινὲς μὲν εἰκόνας ἔχουσαι τῶν βασιλέων ἐνυφασμένας, αἱ δὲ μυθικὰς διαθέσεις ('and tunics of gold-cloth and most beautiful military cloaks, some with interwoven pictures of the kings, others with mythical subjects', Athen. 196f). And the couch coverlets: καὶ περιστρώματα ποικίλα διαπρεπῆ ταῖς τέχναις ἐπῆν ('and colored coverlets outstanding in their workmanship were spread over', 197b). Finally the carpets: ψιλαὶ δὲ Περσικαὶ τὴν ἀνὰ μέσον τῶν ποδῶν χώραν ἐκάλυπτον, ἀκριβῆ τὴν εὐγραμμίαν τῶν ἐνυφασμένων ἔχουσαι ζῳδίων ('smooth Persian carpets covered the space for the feet in the middle, with an excellent design of images woven in', 197b). With this as background, it is not difficult to imagine Callimachus setting the epyllion on Heracles and Molorchus in terms of an elaboration of a real or imaginary garment associated with the victory celebration of Berenice, dynastic daughter of Philadelphus. Gow 1952 *ad Id.* 15.78 deals with the increase in elaboration of weaving at Alexandria, citing (*inter al.*) Plin. *HN* 8.196: *plurimis vero liciis texere quae polymita appellant Alexandria instituit* ('Alexandria invented the weaving with multiple threads, which they call *polymita*').

[109] Luce 1916: 460–73; Parsons 1977: 41.

[110] It is, of course, the obscurity of the variant including Molorchus that appealed to Callimachus.

[111] Parsons 1977: 41.

As a coda I give a possible paraphrase of A 25–32 as the lines may have stood. Obviously the subjective element is increased, but I think respect is paid to the existing fragments: 'Just as before at Argos [the young women] fashioned well-woven [peploi, sacred gifts for Hera,[112] and more skillfully than] Colchian or Egyptian women [who with great art] worked the slender [threads,[113] so] the women who know how to bewail the bull [will marvel at your tapestry,[114] Berenice,] when [the labour of the] silkworms (?)[115] [is placed in commemoration of your victory].'

We noted that there are serious problems with this proposal. The first is that the body of the epyllion on Heracles and Molorchus is more in the nature of narrative than description, which militates against the possibility of its having been an ecphrasis. However, in the light of the audacity of the central panel of Catullus 64 (see below), it is not inconceivable that Callimachus could have departed radically from the traditional tone of ecphrastic description. As the reader for this journal has pointed out, we must also be able to conceive of a notional tableau accounting for the action of the epyllion. That, I think, is less serious. Heracles, Molorchus, the lion, and possibly Athena would have to appear, as would the actual hut, and it is easy enough to imagine their having done so on a static picture. The rest would be up to the imagination of the poet.

---

[112] Cf. above, n. 89, for this as a possible restoration (of sense at least). This possibility is perhaps strengthened by the fact that these women, or the prefatory rites they must perform, are the subject of an episode later in the same book of the *Aetia* (fr. 65–6).

[113] See above for this as a skill shared by Colchian and Egyptian women.

[114] If we have in this line Egyptian women admiring a tapestry, which is on display in commemoration of Berenice's victory, then the situation has a fairly close parallel to the visit to the art-gallery in *Idyll* 15.

[115] I mention, with no real confidence, that line A 31 (...]υκων ὀτε[) could possibly have referred, through periphrasis, to the material on which the scene appeared (βομβ]ύκων...ἔργον). In the *Hecale*, the material on which an ecphrasis may have occurred is so evoked: ἔργον ἀραχνάων (fr. 253.12 Pf.). On the question of the working of silk (certainly under way by the Ptolemaic period), see G. M. A. Richter 1929. The βόμβυξ occurs as early as Aristotle (*Hist an.* 5.19); there is a full discussion of the creature and its product at Plin. *HN* 11.75–7. Servius *ad* Verg. *G.* 2.121 is of interest: *vermes et bombyces... qui in aranearum morem tenuissima* (= λεπταλέος, Parsons 1977: A 29) *fila deducunt, unde est sericum* ('worms and silk-moths...who in the manner of spiders produce extremely thin threads, which is where silk comes from').

Ultimately, however, the first of these objections may be overwhelming. And yet we are still left with the fabric of A 25–32. A final possibility: the poet may have mentioned the woven object offered for Berenice's victory, noting briefly that it contained the encounter of Heracles with the lion. This would then have provided a natural transition from epinician to epyllion ('For once upon a time...' [καὶ γάρ ποτε...])—elaboration of the subject matter of a work of art, if not an actual ecphrasis.

5. CATULLUS 64

Catullus 64 is a unique and curious poem. The events and scenes on the tapestry, which occupy more than 250 lines and constitute the central panel of the epyllion, are without precedent. In no other ecphrasis is the description of such proportions, nor do the figures involved in any other such work come to life and speak, acting as they do for Catullus like characters in a narrative poem. While the notion that Poem 64 is a 'translation' of a lost Hellenistic work has on the whole been laid to rest, stylistically a Hellenistic model does seem to be indicated. In short, the tone and attitude of the poem are Hellenistic, or rather, Alexandrian. As Friedländer noted: 'Es bedarf kaum eines Wortes, dass Catull diesen Stil nicht erfunden haben kann.'[116] T. B. L. Webster, who thought Catullus 64 a translation, was otherwise perceptive in claiming: 'The source should therefore be sought in a poem which is certainly later than Apollonios and probably later than the *Hekale*.'[117] Such a poem is the *Victoria Berenices*. It is from Callimachus that we would expect such influence on Catullus (the translator, after all, of the *Coma Berenices*, companion-piece of the *Victoria*), and it is from him that we would expect such extreme experimentation.[118] The poet who presented himself in conversation with statues and composed an *agon* between the olive and the laurel, will have felt at ease in allowing a work of art to come so fully to life. C. H. Whitman noted of the shield in *Iliad* 18 that

[116] Friedländer 1912: 16.   [117] Webster 1964: 309.
[118] On the late dating of the *Victoria Berenices*, see Parsons 1977: 50; Livrea *et al.* 1980: 245.

the poet 'seems to stand a little bewildered between the realism of the finished panels, and the limitations of the material.'[119] It is a mark of Alexandrian, and certainly of Callimachean, poetry that such bewilderment or discomfort has no place in the attitude towards art in poetry.

Ultimately the experiment failed to take hold. Whatever the source, this type of epyllion was a typical product of Alexandrianism—a thorough literary convention pushed to its extreme and thereby distinguished from earlier examples of the genre. Catullus attempted it as an experiment and, if my suggestion is possible, as a profession of his Callimachean allegiance. In this, as in other ways, he can be seen as transferring unaltered to Rome the essence of Alexandria.

Virgil, in spite of his deep admiration for Catullus' epyllion, drew only from its content, not from its stylistic peculiarities. Examples of the ecphrasis in his poetry, the murals in Dido's temple, Daedalus' doors, the shields of Turnus and Aeneas—and, indeed, the temple of the third *Georgic*[120]—these, for all their claims for artistic perfection, represent a return to the more restrained convention. The Virgilian practice stands as an acknowledgement that the ecphrastic epyllion of Catullus (and Callimachus?) was an experiment, an attempt to break from and surpass the inherited tradition, an attempt appropriate to Alexandrianism as to Roman neotericism, but one which was ultimately rejected by Roman classicism.

[119] Whitman 1958: 205.

[120] Indeed, among the objects in Virgil's temple, there is even a curtain into which human figures are woven: *vel scaena ut versis discedat frontibus utque | purpurea intexti tollant aulaea Britanni* ('or how the scene changes with the set being turned and how the Britons raise the purple curtain into which they are woven', 24–5). It is worth noting that Statius *Silv.* 3.1, for which we also claimed influence by the *Victoria Berenices*, is another ecphrasis.

11

The Fourth *Georgic,* Virgil and Rome

Jasper Griffin

> So work the honey-bees,
> Creatures that by a rule in nature teach
> The act of order to a peopled kingdom.
> (Shakespeare)

'The last word has not yet been spoken on the relation of the second half to the first half, and to the *Georgics* as a whole', said the sage Friedrich Klingner.[1] Never were more prophetic words penned. Many and various have been the interpretations put forth since then, and some of them have been very strange indeed. The reader who has duly confronted Coleman, Otis, Segal, Bradley, Wender, Wilkinson, Wankenne, Coleiro, Hardie, Joudoux, Wormell, Otis again, Parry, Putnam, Cova, Chomarat, Stehle, Crabbe, and Nadeau,[2] feels dismay; perhaps despair. For some, the point of the Aristaeus and Orpheus episodes is political propaganda (so Coleiro: Gallus could have survived had he humbled himself like Aristaeus, the moral being the duty of subordination to the Princeps; so rather differently, Joudoux: the poem is propaganda for the supremacy of Octavian, in terms of the threefold Indo-European structure of Dumézil). For others, it is moral (so, for instance, Wender: Orpheus turned away from the hard and morally

---

This paper was first published in 1979 and reprinted, with revisions, in J. Griffin 1985: 163–82. The version presented here is that of 1985, virtually unchanged.

[1] Klingner 1963: 161 = 1967: 298.

[2] Coleman 1962; Otis 1964; Segal 1966; Bradley 1969; Wender 1969; Wilkinson 1969; Wankenne 1970; Coleiro 1971; C. G. Hardie 1971; Joudoux 1971; Wormell 1971; Otis 1972; Parry 1972; Putnam 1972; Cova 1973; Chomarat 1974; Stehle 1974; Crabbe 1977; Nadeau 1984.

ambiguous farmer's life, as lived by Aristaeus; Aristaeus gets bugonia as his reward, while Orpheus is dismembered and scattered in order to fertilize the earth); or religious (so Chomarat: the experience of Aristaeus is presented under the schema of initiation into a mystery religion);[3] or political and moral (so Wormell and Otis: Aristaeus 'stands for the sinful self-destruction, atonement and revival of the Roman people'; life emerges from death, 'in political terms, the Augustan restoration from the anarchy of civil war'; 'Aristaeus, it is to be presumed [sic], was induced to heed the lesson').

Some find very general solutions indeed: perhaps Virgil 'posits existence as made up of this strange mixture of tragic and comic, human and divine, of death and birth... serving as complements and inextricably intertwined' (Putnam); Castiglioni[4] and Klingner give accounts not dissimilar. For others, the answer is more specific, one might almost say more specifically modern. Thus for Bradley, 'the myth of Orpheus provides an alternative view of culture'; while Aristaeus stands for 'the work culture',[5] the control of Orpheus is exerted through play, not work, 'not productivity but creativity', and so the work culture inevitably destroys Orpheus because his existence is an intolerable affront to it; he is doomed 'at the hands of a repressive civilisation'—represented, rather to our surprise, by the Maenads of Thrace. Others have taken the episode as being primarily concerned with poetry. The eloquent paper of Adam Parry shows us Orpheus' grief for Eurydice becoming eternal song, and 'the song in turn becomes the condition for the recreation of life': the cruel and dark sides of nature, revealed in the rest of the *Georgics*, can be faced and comprehended only in song, in art. In a more specific way, Hardie sees the poem as about Virgil's own quest for the inspiration and poetic power to write epic. Having killed Orpheus within himself, Virgil as Aristaeus goes down to consult his own *anima*, makes the sacrifice of his excess of ambition, and regains the honey of poetic inspiration. Nor, finally, are those lacking who argue that the episode may be virtually, or entirely, unconnected with the rest of

[3] See already Scazzoso 1956: 25–8.
[4] Castiglioni 1947: 185.
[5] So for Bovie 1956: 355, Aristaeus is 'a silhouette of the Roman practical man'—whose characteristic utterance, it seems, is in the plangent tones of 321 ff.: '*mater, Cyrene mater...*'.

the *Georgics*,[6] added either as a lament for Gallus (Coleman), or simply following the fashion for epyllia (Richter). The last word of this whirlwind doxography[7] shall be the magisterial *non liquet* of Wilkinson:

> To sum up, I believe that Virgil would have thought an *aition* for 'Bugonia' a suitable ending for a book on bees, Aristaeus a suitable hero for this *aition*, and epyllion a suitable form for it. He would have looked for a contrasting story to insert in his epyllion. Why he chose Orpheus for this is more a matter of speculation, and also to what extent either the Orpheus passage or (more plausibly) the Aristaeus epyllion has a symbolic meaning for the interpretation of the *Georgics* as a whole.[8]

We have been warned: *parcite, oves, nimium procedere; non bene ripae | creditur*, 'Do not go too far, my flocks: the bank is not to be trusted' (Virgil, *Eclogue* 3.94). And yet the attempt is worth making. After all, this is one of the most beautiful things in ancient poetry, and here as strongly as anywhere in Virgil's work we must feel that more is meant than meets the ear. He will not lightly have put at the end of a long poem a strikingly melodious and pathetic conclusion, whose connection with what precedes, and whose position in his work as a whole, he has made merely mysterious. We are entitled to expect that the poet would not end his poem with so complex and unexpected an episode, and one whose interpretation has proved so difficult, if he had not had something complex to say; but also something to which he attached importance. *Itur*, therefore, *in antiquam silvam*.

---

[6] This old view still has its supporters. Sellar 1965: 251: 'It must be difficult for anyone who is penetrated by the prevailing sentiment of the *Georgics* to reach this point in the poem (sc. 4.315) without a strong feeling of regret that the jealousy of Augustus had interfered with its original conclusion.' Conway 1928: 31: 'Yet no one who approaches the Fourth Book of the *Georgics* with an open mind, after reading the others, can possibly doubt that there must be some reason for the startling break in the middle of the Book.' Schmidt 1930: 173–7 found the Aristaeus-epyllion a 'disturbing and tasteless intrusion'. Not many scholars now would actually deplore the insertion of this uniquely beautiful piece of poetry; but Coleiro 1971 (see note 1) apologises for its feebleness with the argument that Virgil naturally found it distasteful to have to suppress his *laudes Galli* and replace them with an apologia for his disgrace and death.
[7] A fuller one: Cova 1973: 290 ff.
[8] Wilkinson 1969: 120.

Virgil treats his bees, in the fourth *Georgic*, as if they formed a sort of human society.[9] They have *domus, lar, sedes, statio, tectum; fores, limina, portae; aula, oppidum, patria, penates, sedes augusta, urbs.* They have divine reason and practise high-minded communism. Their patriotism is absolute. They will work themselves to death (204) or give their lives in battle (218). Their devotion to their ruler is incomparable (210). They are thrifty (156, 177), orderly (158), indefatigable (185); they all move and rest as one (184, *omnibus una quies operum, labor omnibus unus*). At 201 Virgil calls them Romans, *Quirites*, and scholars have pointed out that the characteristic Roman virtues of *labor* and *fortitudo* ('Those are Roman virtues *par excellence*', Dahlmann 1954: 11), and also *concordia*, are their leading qualities.[10] There are clear resemblances with the praise of the Italian countryman and his virtuous life at the end of the second *Georgic* (work, justice, concord, and defence of home, children, and *penates*). All this is clear enough, but disagreement begins when we come to interpret these facts.

At one extreme, especially in Germany, some have felt confident that Virgil means his bees to represent an absolute model for human society. Dahlmann goes so far as to say that this separates Virgil from other ancient writers: 'We are dealing with a framework which is simply and absolutely paradigmatic, which corresponds to the absolutely valid, rational, and right.'[11] Schadewaldt speaks of 'a charming model of a charmingly ordered natural ideal state'.[12] In English, Wormell implies a similar view, ending his account of the bees' nature by saying that 'this description constitutes a challenge to contemporary human standards and attitudes'.[13] Reservations of

---

[9] See Dahlmann 1954: 6 (but Klingner was right to reject Dahlmann's idea that the bees are expounded in the regular form of an ethnographical *ecphrasis*: 1967: 310 n. l); Maguinness 1962: 443; Servius *ad G.* 4.219; Olck 1897: 446.19 ff. The general point is an obvious one, and I have not laboured it. *Haec ut hominum civitates, quod hic est et rex et imperium et societas*, Varro, *Rust.* 3.16.5.

[10] See Oppermann 1938: 28 = Oppermann (ed.)1963: 123: 'In the society of the bees is reflected the Roman *res publica*.'

[11] 'Es handelt sich um ein Gefüge schlechthinniger, absoluter Vorbildlichkeit, das dem absolut Gültigen, Vernünftigen, Richtigen entspricht' (Dahlmann 1954: 13).

[12] '... Das zierliche Musterbild eines zierlich geordneten natürlichen Idealstaats', Schadewaldt 1970: 1.716.

[13] Wormell 1971: 429.

several sorts arise, if we try to imagine Virgil recommending to his contemporaries as an absolute model a society like this: impersonal, collective, Stakhanovite, without art. Did the author of the sixth *Eclogue* and the fourth *Aeneid* really think that is what the ideal society would be like—a place with no comprehension or sympathy for Corydon, for Nisus and Euryalus, for Virgil himself?[14]

Fortunately we are not left with no other counter-argument than this general one. Virgil deals with his bees in a tone which does not exclude irony. The epic battle of bees (*ingentes animos angusto in pectore versant*, 'Mighty passions rage in their tiny breasts') ends with these two lines:

> hi motus animorum atque haec certamina tanta
> pulveris exigui iactu compressa quiescent.   (86–7)

These mighty passions and these great battles will lie still, put down by casting a little dust.

With consummate skill, Virgil combines a grave humour (the warriors are after all only tiny insects), with a deep and poignant undertone: human battles, too, end with a handful of dust.[15] Such a phrase as that he uses of the aftermath—*melior vacua sine regnet in aula* (90)—has a similar irony, 'Let the better rule in a palace without a rival'; so has, for instance, 106–7,

> nec magnus prohibere labor; tu regibus alas
> eripe...

It is not hard to prevent them: pluck out the wings of the kings.

Nor can the choice of Cyclopes (170 ff.) as a comparison for bees be without its humour.[16] One could labour the point; but it is clear that Virgil presents the bees and their community in a way which combines admiration (*ingentes animos*) with a cool sense of proportion

---

[14] 'Aspiration towards a society of rules and of work under a beloved chief, that is Virgil's conclusion after ten years of toil', Bayet 1930a: 247 = 1967: 241.

[15] The technical writers know of this dust as only one of a number of ways of settling bees: Varro, *Rust.* 3.16.30, Pliny, *NH* 11.58. Virgil's phrasing is designedly pregnant; compare Lucan on the impromptu burial of Pompey, 8.867: <u>pulveris exigui sparget non longa vetustas</u> | <u>congeriem, bustumque cadet</u>..., 'A short space of time will disperse that little pile of dust; the tomb will disappear...'.

[16] Klingner 1967: 314.

(*angusto in pectore*). Adam Parry was right to pick out this complexity,[17] which surely rules out any straightforward paradigmatic purpose on Virgil's part. From another point of view, it seems to me incredible that the poet could have expected, or even hoped, that his audience (in 29 BC!) would accept as their own ideal future a society in which the king is treated with more than Oriental devotion:

> praeterea regem non sic Aegyptus et ingens
> Lydia nec populi Parthorum aut Medus Hydaspes
> observant... (210–12)

They honour their king yet more than the Egyptians, Lydians, Parthians, or Medes.

What, then, did he mean by his treatment of the bees? A clue is given by a remarkable omission. Bees and honey in antiquity were constantly associated with poetry and poets. The connection is indeed so familiar that I relegate to a footnote[18] an anthology of evidence, stressing merely that even Varro, a source of Virgil and by no means an excessively poetical writer, in his treatment of apiculture, says of the bees: 'Rightly are they called the winged creatures of the Muses' (*Rust.* 3.16.7). But Virgil does not make any such connection, and by choosing to suppress it he makes us realise that the society represented by the bees is one from which the arts are consciously excluded. Instead of singing, his bees make mere noise—*fit sonitus, mussantque oras et limina circum* (188), or in time of war they 'imitate the trumpet' (72).[19] Their honey is never brought by Virgil

---

[17] Parry 1972: 43. See also Otis 1972: 58: 'The co-operative state is of course one aspect of reality—Roman and human as well as animal and natural reality—but it is not the whole.'

[18] *Musaeo melle*, Lucr. 4.22; *ego apis Matinae more modoque...*, Hor. *Carm.* 4.2.27; *poetica mella*, Hor. *Epist.* 1.19.44; Pl. *Ion* 534b; Olck 1897: 447.40; poets, orators and philosophers were brought into connection with bees; Cook 1895: 7 and 1914: 443; Artemidorus, *Oneir.* 5.83; Theocr. 1.146, and Gow 1952 *ad loc.*; Usener 1902: 177 ff. = 1912–13: 4.398 ff., esp. 400–1.

[19] Contrast the beautiful line, admired by G. K. Chesterton, in the description of bees in *King Henry V* 1.2:

> Others like soldiers, armed in their stings,
> Make boot upon the summer's velvet buds;
> Which pillage they with merry march bring home
> To the tent-royal of their emperor;
> Who, busied in his majesty, surveys
> *The singing masons building roofs of gold...*

into connection with poetry or the Muses, although it is *aërii mellis caelestia dona*, 'the divine gift of aerial honey' (1), and although in the second half of the poem he will be dealing with the song of Orpheus, son of a Muse. When is it permitted to argue from silence? This silence, it seems to me, is striking enough for us to feel that it has a significance. I venture on to speculative ground in trying to say what it signified.

Virgil did not want to connect his bees, inspired though they are, with poetry or song. They exhibit many great virtues, but they are not poetical, and they are free from the bitter-sweet pains and pleasures of love (*Ecl.* 3.110; *G.* 4.198 ff.). In both they contrast clearly with Orpheus, the fabulous singer who dies for love (and who in this poem is never shown as doing any work or having any other function than song).[20] The virtues they exhibit are indeed the virtues of the old Roman people; but so are their deficiencies. Rome, great in *mores antiqui*, was not a home of the arts, in the view of the Augustans, until

> Graecia capta ferum victorem cepit et artes
> intulit agresti Latio.[21]

Captive Greece led her rude conqueror captive and brought the arts to uncouth Latium.

At *Ars Poetica* 323 ff., in a famous passage, Horace laments that the traditional Roman education unfitted the Roman for the arts. It is from this point of view that we must, I think, handle the problem. When Virgil was still at work on the *Georgics* he had already in mind the Roman epic which he hoped to be able to produce. The prologue to the third *Georgic* shows him grappling with it, and already keenly aware of the difficulties which such a poem would offer. At that time he apparently was thinking, or wished to give the impression that he was thinking, in terms of a poem on Octavian, with glances back to Troy—the reverse of the *Aeneid* (a poem on Aeneas with glances forward to Augustus).[22] Difficulties of style (was Octavian to be

---

[20] Those who, like Wankenne 1970: 25–6, talk of Aristaeus and Orpheus as 'two shepherds', are on the wrong track.
[21] This view is already implicit in Porcius Licinus, fr. 1 Morel, *Poenico bello secundo*... Cf. now Funke 1977: 168.
[22] See Norden 1966: 400 ff., and e.g. Fleischer 1960: 327, Wilkinson 1969: 172.

handled like a Homeric hero? What of the gods?), difficulties of material (Horace, *Odes* 2.1 warns Pollio of the risks involved in writing of recent history), the immense difficulty of making recent politics in any way poetic: all these, and others, must have been weighing on Virgil's mind. But not least of his problems, I think, was the nature of imperialism itself, and of Virgil's attitude to Rome.

It is not my intention to depict Virgil as 'anti-Augustan';[23] the term is a crudity. But justified revulsion against its excesses must not conceal the central fact about the *Aeneid*; that it is a poem of loss, defeat, and pathos, as much as it is of triumphant destiny.[24] Aeneas loses his country, his wife, Dido, Pallas; he must kill Lausus and meet among the dead the mistress who killed herself when he left her. To console him he has the vast impersonal gifts of destiny. But not only Aeneas must sacrifice all the wishes of his heart in the service of his fate; the imperial people, too, must pay a high price for its imperial calling. Nowhere does that emerge more poignantly than in the famous passage, *Aen.* 6.847–53:

> excudent alii spirantia mollius aera
> (credo equidem), vivos ducent de marmore vultus,
> orabunt causas melius, caelique meatus
> describent radio et surgentia sidera dicent:
> tu regere imperio populos, Romane, memento
> (hae tibi erunt artes), pacique imponere morem,[25]
> parcere subiectis et debellare superbos.
>
> Let others better mould the running mass
> Of metals, and inform the breathing brass,
> And soften into flesh a marble face;
> Plead better at the bar; describe the skies,
> And when the stars descend, and when they rise.
> But Rome! 'tis thine alone with awful sway

---

[23] Some salubrious reservations on this word are expressed by Galinsky 1975: 210–17. Also Clarke 1976/7: 322: 'One of the most amazing trends in recent literary criticism of ancient literature—the attempt to describe Vergil and Ovid as anti-Augustan, anti-establishment radicals, ideologically opposed to a proto-fascist dictator... there is virtually no hard evidence to support it...'.

[24] See the masterly article by Clausen 1964, reprinted in Commager (ed.) 1966. Suggestive but more vulnerable is Parry 1963, reprinted in the same volume; see also, in the same book, Brooks 1953.

[25] The discussion of the passage by Otis 1964: 313 ff. is flawed by his adoption of the bad reading *pacisque*, 'the habit of peace'. See Fraenkel 1962: 133 = 1964: 2.143.

To rule mankind and make the world obey:
To tame the proud, the fettered slave to free,
These are imperial arts, and worthy thee.
(Transl. Dryden)

This unrivalled speech is at once a boast and a lament, a proud claim by a conqueror and a sigh of regret for the cost. Virgil, poet, philosopher, and aesthete, in the middle of his great poem, in which the Latin language and the Roman destiny alike were carried to a beauty which must have seemed impossible, yet must surrender to the Greeks (*alii*—he cannot bring himself to name them) the arts and the sciences. The traditional claim of the Roman patriot, that native morals outshone Greek accomplishments (*ut virtutis a nostris sic doctrinae ab illis* [sc. *Graecis*] *exempla petenda sunt,* Cic. *De or.* 3.137, 'Examples of good practice are to be drawn from us: of good theory from the Greeks'), is given a pregnancy and a pathos which transform it. *Hae tibi erunt artes*: these are your arts, man of Rome—not the seductive beauties of Greece, which meant so much to Virgil as a man, and without which his poems could not have come into existence, but the hard and self-denying 'arts' of conquest and dominion. It is the price of empire that the Roman must abandon for this imperial destiny, splendid and yet bitter, so many forms of beauty.

Virgil embodies this cruel cost again in an episode of his own invention, much criticized in antiquity, from Probus onwards:[26] the shooting of the stag of Silvia in the seventh book. The beautiful tame creature (*forma praestanti,* 483) is shot by Ascanius, without malicious intention on his part. 'Ascanius does not mean any harm: he yields to a young man's keenness to excel in sport, *eximiae laudis succensus amore* and thus, by wounding poor Silvia's pet, becomes a

---

[26] Macrob. *Sat.* 5.17.1–2: 'How much Virgil owed to Homer is very clear from the fact that when he is obliged to describe the way a war began, which Homer did not include... he found the gestation of this new subject difficult. He has made the chance wounding of a deer the cause of the fighting; but seeing that this was lightweight and all too childish, he worked up the indignation of the country people...'. Probus as the likely source: Norden 1915: 4 ff. With Macrobius' *cervum fortuito saucium,* compare Denniston and Page 1957: xxv on the portent at Aulis: 'The poet tells us in plain language [sic] that Artemis was enraged *because eagles, sent by Zeus to be an encouraging portent, happened* [sic] *to devour a hare together with its unborn young...*'. The ways of poets do not change. Nor do those of commentators...

tool in the hands of Allecto.'[27] The Italian rustics flock up with improvised weapons, 506–8:

> improvisi adsunt, hic torre armatus obusto,
> stipitis hic gravidi nodis; quod cuique repertum
> rimanti telum ira facit.

Hastily they come up, one armed with a fire-sharpened stick, one with a heavy knotted club—anger makes a weapon of what each one finds.

Then the Trojans come rushing from their stronghold (521), and the fighting becomes a regular battle in full armour (523 ff.).

Such a beginning to the great war, the *maius opus* of the second half of the *Aeneid*, has not unnaturally distressed or perplexed some scholarly readers.[28] As a *casus belli*, says Macrobius, all this is 'slight and all too childish'. Why did Virgil put such an unexpected scene in so important a position? R. Heinze suggested that he was concerned to make the responsibility of the Trojans for the war as venial and as slight as possible; a mere accident while hunting.[29] Klingner drew the distressingly flat moral[30] that 'if one looks more closely, it is not the death of the tame stag which creates the danger, but the presence of a population of shepherds, half civilized and easily aroused by a triviality'—almost as if he were making an official report to King Latinus on a regrettable incident in a country district. Wimmel sees here a device for making the war 'pastoral' and 'unheroic', one of Virgil's many 'anti-epic procedures'.[31] None of these suggestions seems to do justice to the emotional weight and force of the passage. The stag is tame and beautiful: shot by the incomers, it flees home to its loving mistress, like a human creature:

[27] Fraenkel 1945 = 1964: 2.153.
[28] Klingner 1967: 511. Heyne was gravely dissatisfied with Virgil here (*Nolo defendere poetam*), as were many earlier scholars. Conington gives a strikingly tepid defence: 'Some have objected to the incident of the stag as too trivial, as if there were anything unnatural in a small spark causing a large train to explode, or as if the contrast itself were not an element of greatness.' The first point—a mere naturalistic defence of plausibility—is flat; the second, I confess, I can make nothing of.
[29] Heinze 1903: 186. Heinze was sufficiently in the grip of the hostile tradition about the episode to say that Silvia's distress over the death of her stag can only be understood in the light of an hypothetical Hellenistic poem about Cuparissus—surely a severe criticism of Virgil. But his main point, that nobody is to blame, is, of course, an important one.
[30] Klinger 1967: 513.
[31] Wimmel 1973: 48 and 118 ff.: 'a bucolic outbreak of war'.

> successitque gemens stabulis, questuque cruentus
> atque imploranti similis tectum omne replebat.   (7.501–2)

Moaning it returned home, bleeding and plaintive; it filled the house with cries that seemed to beg for help.

One surely need invoke no hypothetical lost poem to explain the grief it causes. It remains true that Ascanius did not know what he was doing; he meant no harm—but the harm is done. Aeneas has no wish to fight the Italians, and he does all he can to avoid war, but he must fight and kill his future allies. He tries hard to avoid killing Lausus (10.809 ff.), but he must kill him. He does not even want to kill Turnus (12.938)... Above all, he had no desire to cause the death of Dido, and yet she, who would have been 'all too happy, if only the Trojan ships had never touched my shores' (4.657), who was so splendid, attractive, and noble when they arrived, is driven to disgrace and suicide when the destiny of Aeneas takes him to Carthage. And Dido, in the first frenzy of her love, is compared to a deer, shot by a shepherd, who does not even know that he has hit her:

> uritur infelix Dido totaque vagatur
> urbe furens, qualis coniecta cerva sagitta,
> quam procul incautam nemora inter Cresia fixit
> pastor agens telis liquitque volatile ferrum
> nescius: illa fuga silvas saltusque peragrat
> Dictaeos; haeret lateri letalis harundo.   (4.68–73)

Poor Dido burns and roams in madness through the town, like a doe shot with an arrow, whom from afar a herdsman has shot and left the steel in her side, unawares. The doe flees through the woods, the deadly dart sticking in her side.

The recurrence of the image deserves more attention than it receives.[32] The climax of the three stages in which Juno and Allecto stir up the war is given a form that recalls the suffering of Dido; she too was beautiful, destroyed by the Trojans not by their will (*liquitque volatile ferrum nescius—invitus, regina, tuo de litore cessi*, 'He left the

---

[32] 'Some personal experience must lie behind both this passage and 7.483 ff.' is Austin's not very helpful comment. Viktor Pöschl surprisingly does not mention the stag of Silvia in his treatment of 4.68 ff. (Pöschl 1950: 131 ff. = 1962: 80 ff.). The discussion in Raabe 1974: 56 ignores this question.

steel in her side, unawares'—'It was against my will, o queen, that I left your country'). Like the archer in the simile, Aeneas does not know what he has done: *nec credere quivi | hunc tantum tibi me discessu ferre dolorem*, 'I could not believe my going would cause you such distress' (6.463). But that is the effect of the Trojan destiny; to cause suffering without willing it, to cause the destruction of so many beautiful things, from Silvia's stag to the singer Cretheus, slain by Turnus:

> ... et Clytium Aeoliden et amicum Crethea Musis,
> Crethea Musarum comitem, cui carmina semper
> et citharae cordi numerosque intendere nervis,
> semper equos atque arma virum pugnasque canebat. (9.774–7)

And Clytius he slew, and Cretheus dear to the Muses, Cretheus the Muses' friend, who loved to sing and play the lyre...

...the singer Cretheus, to whom Virgil gives so moving a farewell. And with the poet go the lovers—Dido, and Nisus and Euryalus, and Cydon, lover of boys:

> tu quoque, flaventem prima lanugine malas
> dum sequeris Clytium infelix, nova gaudia, Cydon,
> Dardania stratus dextra, securus amorum
> qui iuvenum tibi semper erant... (10.324–7)

You too, luckless Cydon, as you followed Clytius, your latest darling, whose cheeks were golden with his first down, you were laid low: you forgot your constant love for boys...

At the end of the *Aeneid* Aeneas is left only a bride he has never met.

In the *Aeneid* Virgil has succeeded in devising ways of bringing out this complex of ideas, central to his vision of Rome and of history: of Roman destiny as an austere and self-denying one, restraining *furor* and *superbia*, and imposing peace and civilisation on the world; at the cost of turning away, with tears but with unshakable resolution, from the life of pleasure, of art, and of love. *Mens immota manet, lacrimae volvuntur inanes*, 'The will is fixed; in vain the idle tears.' In the *Georgics* he was already confronting the same problem,[33] and not

---

[33] It is a commonplace of Virgilian criticism to say that he was working his way towards the solutions eventually found in his epic. See e.g. Dahlmann 1954: 13, C. G.

finding it easy.³⁴ The bees presented him with a powerful image for the traditional Roman state, in its impersonal and collective character. To avoid cluttering the argument, and to enable those who need no evidence for this description of Roman society to proceed more lightly, I have put some support for it into Appendix 1.

No wider contrast can be imagined than that between the exquisite and sensuous beauty of the evocation of Pasiphae in the sixth *Eclogue*, or the self-indulgent and lyrical passion of Gallus in the tenth, or the love-lorn singer Orpheus, living and dying entirely for art and love, and, on the other side, the old Roman, *non sibi sed patriae natus*, 'Born not for himself but for his country', whose subordination of his own emotions to the state goes so far that for patriotic reasons he will put his own sons to death.³⁵ Virgil does show us how, in his own style and ethos, he can deal with this traditional Roman figure; Anchises points out to Aeneas the unborn shade of L. Brutus, first consul, who killed his sons for conspiring with the Tarquins:

> vis et Tarquinios reges animamque superbam
> ultoris Bruti, fascisque videre receptos?
> consulis imperium hic primus saevasque securis
> accipiet, natosque pater nova bella moventis
> ad poenam pulchra pro libertate vocabit,
> infelix, utcumque ferent ea facta minores:
> vincet amor patriae laudumque immensa cupido. (6.817–23)

Would you see the Tarquin kings and the proud soul of Brutus the avenger, with the fasces he restored? He shall be the first to hold the office of consul and the cruel axes: he shall summon his own sons to execution, to defend liberty against their treason. Unhappy man! however posterity will judge his deed; love of country will prevail, and boundless desire for glory.

Hardie 1971: 27 ff., Segal 1966: 321: 'In the Fourth *Georgic* Virgil is already dealing with some of the issues of the Aeneid.' The end of Segal's article (I am unable to agree with most of it) seems to me to be nearer the truth than most recent work which I have read.

³⁴ The well-known problem of the apparently contradictory attitudes expressed at the end of the second *Georgic* towards the greatness of Rome and rustic life (contrast the philosophical *ataraxia* of 490–9 with the patriotism of 532–5), is surely connected with this uncertainty. See most recently Clay 1976: 232 ff.

³⁵ Polybius was impressed by this extremely Roman habit, 6.65.5: he accepts this as part of the 'zeal for the constitution' of the Roman citizen; no hint of moral ambiguity.

I cannot do better than repeat the judgment of Eduard Norden (1957 ad 6.822): 'The lines are a noble monument for the poet who succeeded in combining without disharmony his tender sensibility with his admiration for the rigid grandeur of the old *fortia facta*.'[36] In such passages of his epic Virgil has succeeded in bringing together two attitudes and doing full justice to them both. The axes of Republican authority are cruel, and Brutus must be an unhappy man; and yet political liberty is a thing of beauty, and his motive was glorious. Unhappy, he is also proud, with all the moral complexity of that word and that quality, and of the very ambiguous 'boundless desire for glory'. Anchises, legendary founder, both extols and grieves for the work of his people. His history of Rome begins as a glorification (756). It ends with the pathetic lament for Marcellus: *o nate, ingentem luctum ne quaere tuorum... heu miserande puer...,* 'My son, ask not the dread sorrow of your people... Alas, unhappy boy...'. Not only in detail but also as a whole, the utterance of Anchises juxtaposes the two aspects and leaves them unresolved. In the *Georgics* Virgil has not yet mastered this tremendous technique of compression. The bees and Orpheus do not approach each other in so small a compass, and Virgil indulges himself with a long episode in the plangent and exquisite style which he has learned and improved from Catullus and the Neoterics. It is a style which in most of his writing he denied himself.

The bees, then, with their collective virtues and their lack of individuality and art, serve as a counterpart to the old Roman character. Their patriotism and self-denial (and devotion to their 'king' is only devotion to the state and to authority, not an encouragement to emperor-worship) are admirable. If Rome had only retained more of such qualities, then the tragedies and disasters of the Civil Wars, and of the end of the first *Georgic*, would never have occurred. Hence a real, not a feigned or insincere, admiration and nostalgia for them—and for their human form, the old Italian way of life:

> hanc olim veteres vitam coluere Sabini,
> hanc Remus et frater. (*G*. 2.532–3)

---

[36] 'So verstanden sind die Verse ein schönes Monument für den Dichter, der sein weiches Empfinden mit der Bewunderung für die starre Grossartigkeit der alten "fortia facta" harmonisch zu vereinigen wusste.'

This was the life lived by the Sabines of old, this was the life of Romulus and Remus.

In the *Aeneid* this strand of thought and feeling will be fully represented: the austere life of Euander (especially 8.364–5), the speech of Numanus Remulus (9.598 ff.), the tempering of Trojan luxury with Italian toughness (*sit Romana potens Itala virtute propago*, 12.827).[37]

But as the *Aeneid* does justice also to the sacrifice demanded of the Imperial people, so too in the *Georgics* we see the human incompleteness of such a collective state.

In the first *Georgic* Virgil depicted with passion the disasters which lack of order has brought on the word: *fas versum atque nefas, tot bella per orbem, | tam multae scelerum facies*. Only Caesar can rescue a world turned upside down, and Virgil prays desperately for his success. The reconstruction longed for in the first *Georgic* is, we may feel, under way by the fourth; order is being restored, and the poet becomes aware of the cost—a society efficient and admirable, but impersonal and dispassionate.

The deficiency hinted at in the actual account of the bees emerges with great emotional force when they are juxtaposed with Orpheus and Eurydice. The bee-master Aristaeus has inadvertently caused the death of the beautiful Eurydice—we are reminded of the archer in the simile in *Aeneid* 4, and of Ascanius in *Aeneid* 7. Like Aeneas, he does not even know what he has done. Like Aeneas, too, he has a divine mother who helps and advises; like him, he is a founder. He has bequeathed us an art (*artem*, G. 4.315), but the practical one of regaining lost *parvos Quirites*, not the art of song.[38] It is, in fact, an *ars* like that promised to the Roman by Anchises—*hae tibi erunt artes*. And it is a harsh one, whose cruel side is not glossed over: *huic*

---

[37] In the *Aeneid*, bees appear as the subject-matter of two similes. At 1.430–6 Aeneas sees the Carthaginians hard at work on the construction of their new city, like bees busy with the care of their home and their young—a poignant contrast with the homeless Trojans and their enforced idleness. At 6.707–9 he sees the unborn souls of all nations, 'like bees in a flowery meadow on a fine summer day, busy with their pursuits and humming cheerfully' (Austin 1977 *ad loc.*); he marvels that they can wish to be born into the human world of pain—*quae lucis miseris tam dira cupido*? In both passages Virgil finds it natural to compare bees with men, and his picture of them as industrious, and also as oblivious of the sorrows of human life, certainly does not conflict with my interpretation of them in the fourth *Georgic*.

[38] Cf. Buchheit 1963: 151 ff., Galinsky 1969: 98 n.4.

geminae nares et spiritus oris | multa reluctanti obstruitur (300–1): *sacrum iugulis demitte cruorem* (542), 'Block up the nose and mouth of the ox, for all its struggles', and 'Let the consecrated blood flow from the throat.'

The bees, patriotic, rational, and impersonal, are brought back from death by the device of bugonia. In the fullest sense, *genus immortale manet* (*G.* 4.208–9):

> ... multosque per annos
> stat fortuna domus, et avi numerantur avorum.

The race survives eternal, the house stands through long years, and generation follows generation.

So too will Rome stand for ever: *his ego nec metas rerum nec tempora pono*, says Jupiter (*Aen.* 1.278). As Rome is upheld by his will, the bees too derive their nature from him (*G.* 4.149). But what of the singer and his love? And how is the poem as a whole to be understood?[39]

The sweet singer Orpheus, robbed of his love through Aristaeus' fault, is shown in poignant endless lamentation. The emotional style and the verbal beauty of Proteus' account of his suffering and song make it a unity, and it is here that the emotional emphasis surely falls, not on the episode of Aristaeus:

> te, dulcis coniunx, te solo in litore secum,
> te veniente die, te decedente canebat...
>
> On thee, dear wife, in deserts all alone
> He called, sighed, sung: his griefs with day begun,
> Nor were they finished with the setting sun.
> (Transl. Dryden)

The narrative is given a 'neoteric' structure; the scene in which the gods of the dead give back Eurydice and impose the prohibition on looking at her is compressed to nothing (487, a mere parenthesis—*namque hanc dederat Proserpina legem*, 'for Proserpina had given this commandment'), as in the *Ciris* the decisive actions of the wicked

---

[39] Adam Parry was therefore misleading to say that 'the song becomes the condition for the recreation of life' (1972: 52). Not Orpheus but Aristaeus recreates the bees; song does not set free the half-regained Eurydice. This central fact seems to me to rule out his interpretation of the poem, seductive and powerful as it is.

heroine, her crime, her appeal to Minos, and her rejection, are compressed into five lines (386–90). But what was a mannerism in such a poem, or even in Catullus 64, is here put to emotional use: after Orpheus' long lament (464 ff.) and the pathetic description of the dead (471 ff.), no explicit passage of hope and optimism is allowed to break the mood; already at 488, *subita incautum dementia cepit amantem*, 'sudden madness seized the careless lover'. The whole is plangent, mellifluous, pathetic.[40] No work of art, no human love, can prevail over the power of death; Eurydice is gone for ever, and Orpheus, still singing, has been sent by the cruel maenads to join her.

The account of the first bugonia, 528–58, forms in style a remarkable contrast. A dry and matter-of-fact tone succeeds to the languorous beauty of Orpheus and Eurydice, emphasised by the exact repetitions of lines (538, 540, 544, with 550–62, as if to say: This is what he was told to do, and this is what he did). The bees are reborn. Some readers are content to regard this as a happy ending: 'Catastrophe reigns over the conclusion of the Third Book, confident elevation is restored at the end of the Fourth';[41] 'Books 1 and 3 are gloomy or pessimistic; 2 and 4 are cheerful and optimistic.'[42] For my part I cannot feel that the restoration of bees outweighs the suffering and death of Orpheus and Eurydice, especially in view of the way Virgil has handled the story. An exquisite ambivalence surely prevails. Life goes on, and the virtuous bees will for ever practise their virtuous collectivity; but the artist and his love must die, leaving nothing but the song. For love and art go hand in hand with *furor* and *dementia*, with subordinating reason and interest to emotion. We think of Corydon, who accuses himself of *dementia*, and neglects his work to sing (*Ecl.* 2.69–72), of the erotic myths of which Silenus sang all day (*Ecl.* 6), of the ingenuous Meliboeus, who neglects his work to listen to singing, and confesses, *posthabui tamen illorum mea seria ludo* (*Ecl.* 7.17), 'I put their play ahead of my serious work', of the suicidal passion of Nysa's lover (*Ecl.* 8), of Gallus abandoning himself to love and song and idleness (*Ecl.* 10), of the ravages of passion in the third *Georgic*. And yet the song outlasts the singer: still in death Orpheus' voice proclaims his love, and his song fills the air—

---

[40] Cf. Norden 1966: 509.   [41] Bovie 1956: 347.   [42] Otis 1972: 45.

> Eurydicen toto referebant flumine ripae.

'Eurydice!' resounded all along the shore.

It would be an optimistic writer who should hope for universal assent, at this time of day, to an unprovable account of the fourth *Georgic*. The theory here proposed, that this poem bears upon Rome and poetry, upon imperialism and individual sensibility, perhaps finds some support in the poem's very last words:

> haec super arvorum cultu pecorumque canebam
> et super arboribus, Caesar dum magnus ad altum
> fulminat Euphraten bello victorque volentis
> per populos dat iura viamque adfectat Olympo.
> illo Vergilium me tempore dulcis alebat
> Parthenope studiis florentem ignobilis oti,
> carmina qui lusi pastorum audaxque iuventa,
> Tityre, te patulae cecini sub tegmine fagi. (559–66)

This ends my song on the care of fields and crops and trees, composed as mighty Caesar thunders on the Euphrates in war, gives law in triumph to willing peoples, and forges a path to godhead. Meanwhile I Virgil have been living in sweet Parthenope, flourishing in the pursuits of ignoble ease: I who played with the shepherds' songs and in my presumptuous youth sang of Tityrus lying under the spreading beech.

These eight lines divide naturally into two juxtaposed halves; while Caesar is thundering on the Euphrates, civilising a welcoming world, and winning immortality, Virgil for his part, the frivolous (*lusi*) author of the *Eclogues*, has been writing the *Georgics* at Naples, flourishing in the studies of inglorious ease. The urbanity of this exquisite signature, a Virgilian combination of pride and humility, is easily missed.[43] The *Eclogues* were not serious and the *Georgics* are not glorious, he says; he has been taking it easy in a cultured resort with a Greek name. Caesar, on the other hand, has been working wonders... And yet of course we remember that the poem is 'your hard command, Maecenas', and that *in tenui labor, at tenuis non gloria*, 'the theme is humble but not so the glory'. These two memorable lines alone, casting as they do so ironical a light on *otium* and *ignobile*, suffice to indicate the complexity of the tone. By good old

---

[43] I think it is much underestimated by Buchheit 1972.

Roman standards, Caesar's actions are glorious, Virgil's are not; Virgil bows gravely to those standards. But the shape of the period puts the poet, not the ruler, in the climactic position, and Virgil overshadows Octavian. Here too Virgil is concerned with the relationship of poetry and the traditional Roman values, as, on the view here put forward, he has been all through the poem. Is poetry less glorious than imperialism? In the *sphragis* to the *Georgics* Virgil has found a way of agreeing that it is, which at the same time, with equal force, implies that it is not. To generalise that *tour de force* through a whole epic—an impossible task! And yet the story of the bees and of Orpheus showed, perhaps, a way in which it might be done.

In this poem, then, the poet is saying something which will be said on a greater scale and with greater mastery in the *Aeneid*. Here the link between the suffering of Orpheus and Eurydice, and the rebirth of the civically virtuous bees, is not as convincing as Virgil makes the link between the triumph of Roman *fata* and the suffering of Dido, of Pallas, and of Aeneas himself. In the *Aeneid* the establishment of empire, which will be the justification and the lasting meaning of history, inevitably involves defeat and sacrifice. In the *Georgic* the role of Aristaeus has something of the arbitrariness of purely Hellenistic mythological combination, the same man appearing both as inventor of an art, and as seducer, a combination by no means inevitable. In the same way, the balance which Virgil keeps so beautifully in his epic is here less certain; the separate elements have not been fused as completely as they might have been, and the pathos of Orpheus is in grave danger of running away completely from the rest. The 'neoteric' use of mythology reminds us of links like those in Callimachus' *Hecale*, or in Catullus 64; the fullness of passionate lamentation and pathos recalls Catullus' Ariadne or Attis, or the Zmyrna of Cinna. In the *Aeneid* Virgil has out-grown and mastered for his own style these youthful models; the fourth *Georgic*, in addition to its own beauties, shows us a vital stage in that development.

APPENDIX I

Rome as a collective state

The *locus classicus* on the collective nature of early Rome is the sixth book of Polybius, who at 2.41.9 contrasts the concord of Romans with the 'quarrelsome and ill-conditioned' politics of Greeks. The refusal of Cato to name individual Roman generals in the last four books of his *Origines*, because he regarded their achievements as *populi Romani gesta* (fr. 1 Peter), appeals to the same sentiment; cf. Kienast 1954: 109–10. Cicero cites him (*Rep.* 2.2.3) as saying that the Roman constitution was better than any Greek one because it was not the work of a single legislator but created *multorum ingenio*, by many minds.

Concordia is the positive name for this quality: see Skard 1967: 177 ff. In the old days there was *concordia maxima* among Romans, says Sallust, *Cat.* 9; his meaning is illuminated by *Cat.* 52.23, the opposite: 'When each of you takes thought individually for himself...'

Ancient Roman society may perhaps fitly be compared to life in one of the monastic orders in the middle ages. Both systems display the same methodical combination of example and precept, of mutual vigilance and unremitting discipline. Both show us a community in which the individual is entirely at the mercy of the feelings and opinions of his fellows, and where it is impossible for him to become emancipated from the tyranny of the group. (Ferrero 1907–9: 1.5)

As far back as we can trace the beginnings of Roman life into the darkness of the remote past, we find the citizen no individualist. He is already living in a well-organised community, in which the exercise of personal rights is rigorously subordinated to public opinion and to public jurisdiction... (Merrill 1907: 374)

[In early Rome] an unusually high level of uniformity in thought and action is taken for granted—in direct contrast with, say, Athens... (Heinze 1921: 9 =1960: 12)

Rome was never to emancipate herself entirely from the collective ideal whereby the individual is completely in the hands of the state... The fundamental idea of the old Roman education was respect for the old customs—*mos maiorum;* the principal task of the teacher was to explain them to the young, and to get them respected as an idea beyond discussion, as the standard to judge every action and thought... (Marrou 1965: 229, 342)

The Fourth Georgic

Until the third century no one even had a memorial tombstone. Cumulative pride in the family and in the community were the rewards of life. And even down to the beginning of the second century the Romans are of interest to us for what they were collectively, indeed for the degree to which they succeeded in repressing individuality. (Wilkinson 1975: 26)

Nicolet 1976: 521 summarises Polybius 6:

Rome is altogether saturated in a discipline which is collective but also freely accepted, which strongly reinforces social cohesion. This discipline is not merely repressive; it has a happy combination of encouragement and prevention, rewards and punishments. Hence the normal patriotism of the Romans.

Cf. also pp. 27 (on *consensus*), 514–16.

The expression *non sibi sed patriae natus*, which of course has just this meaning, is a favourite one of Cicero's (*pro Murena* 83, *pro Sestio* 138, *Philipp.* 14.32, *de Fin.* 2.45).

I have not found anything on Rome as penetrating as the essay by Hermann Strasburger, 'Der Einzelne und die Gesellschaft im Denken der Griechen' (Strasburger 1954). By contrast, it sheds much light on Rome.

APPENDIX II

The alleged change to the end of the fourth *Georgic*

One of the most celebrated statements of Servius (*ad Ecl.* 10.1, and *ad G.* 4.1) is to the effect that originally the fourth Book of the *Georgics*, 'from the middle right down to the end', contained the praises of Cornelius Gallus, 'which afterwards at the bidding of Augustus he changed to the story of Aristaeus'. Wilkinson deals judiciously with the story in his excellent book on the *Georgics* (1969: 108 ff.), concluding, with Norden[44] and W. B. Anderson,[45] that it is untrue, deriving originally perhaps from a confusion between 'the end of the *Bucolics*' and 'the end of the *Georgics*'.

I am sure that this verdict is correct, and my purpose is to add another argument to those pressed by others, of artistic coherence[46] and of personal tact (how would Octavian have enjoyed a long recital in praise of a subordinate?).[47] Chronological grounds, it seems to me, rule out the story. Virgil at the end of the fourth *Georgic* says he wrote the poem 'while mighty Caesar was thundering on the Euphrates' (560), which doubtless means before Octavian's return to Rome from the East in August 29 BC. In a circumstantial story which there is no reason to doubt,[48] coming to us from Suetonius through Donatus, we are told that 'when Augustus was on his way home after his victory at Actium and was staying at Atella to get over a relaxed throat, Virgil read the *Georgics* to him for four days on end, Maecenas taking over whenever his voice failed and he had to stop'. Now, Gallus came to grief in Egypt and felt himself driven to suicide either in 27 BC (Jerome) or 26 BC (Dio).[49] For at least two years, then, a version of the *Georgics* must have been

---

[44] Norden 1934 = 1966: 468–532.
[45] W. B. Anderson 1933.
[46] Otis 1964: 408 ff.
[47] 'The over-riding objection', according to Anderson and Wilkinson. The story of Orpheus 'undoubtedly' replaces a panegyric of Gallus, according to Gagé 1982: 612.
[48] Wilkinson 1969: 69.
[49] Syme 1939: 309 n. 2.

in circulation containing a different ending, which was then replaced 'at the bidding of Augustus'; and replaced so effectively that not a word of it was preserved.

Now this sequence of events is, surely, inconceivable. Rome in the early twenties was not like Stalin's Russia, with an efficient and ubiquitous police which could have enforced such a decree throughout the private houses of readers of poetry, even if Augustus had wanted to do so. Even under the grimmer and more frankly autocratic rule of his successors, attempts to suppress books were a failure. We need only recall Tacitus' comment on the affair of Cremutius Cordus, under Tiberius (*Annals* 4.35):

> His books, so the Senate decreed, were to be burnt by the aediles; but they remained in existence, concealed and afterwards published. And so one is all the more inclined to laugh at the stupidity of men who suppose that the despotism of the present can actually efface the remembrances of the next generation. On the contrary, the persecution of talented writers fosters their influence...

We know that soon after Virgil's death there was a hunger for more Virgilian poetry, which was fed with so mediocre a composition as the *Culex*;[50] in such an atmosphere, could somebody have failed to unearth a copy of such a gem as a suppressed version of a great poem?

I have no doubt that we can name one man, at least, who would have kept a copy—Asinius Pollio, a patron of poets, including Virgil at the time of the *Eclogues*, a friend of Gallus,[51] and a man who under the Principate 'defended his ideals in the only fashion he could, by freedom of speech. Too eminent to be muzzled without scandal, too recalcitrant to be won by flattery, Pollio had acquired for himself a privileged position.'[52] An episode with Timagenes, about which we happen to be informed, gives the flavour of his relationship with Augustus.[53]

The waspish historian Timagenes, who had won the friendship of Augustus, could not refrain from offensive jokes at the expense of the Princeps and his family; in the end, Augustus forbade him the palace.

> After this, Timagenes lived to old age in the house of Asinius Pollio and was lionised by the whole city. Although the Emperor had banned him from the palace, no other door was closed to him. He gave public readings of the histories which he had written after the incident, and he burnt the books dealing with the achievements of Augustus Caesar. He conducted a feud with the Emperor, and nobody was afraid to be his

---

[50] Fraenkel 1952: 7 = 1964: 2.193.
[51] Pollio to Cicero (*Fam.* 10.32.5): *Gallum Cornelium, familiarem meum*...
[52] Quoted from Syme 1939: 482; cf. 320, 'Pollio...was preserved as a kind of privileged nuisance'.
[53] Seneca, *De ira* 3.23.4–8 = 88 *FGH* T3. On Timagenes: Sordi 1982.

friend... The Emperor made no complaint to the man who was maintaining his enemy. All he said to Asinius Pollio was, 'Are you keeping a zoo?' Then, when Pollio began to excuse himself, he cut him short, saying 'Make the most of him, Pollio, make the most of him!' 'If you tell me to, Caesar, I shall bar my house to him at once', said Pollio. The Emperor replied, 'Do you think I would? Why, it was I who made you friends again.' The fact was that Pollio had at one time been at enmity with Timagenes, and his only reason for ceasing was that the Emperor had begun...

This story is highly instructive. We see how urbanely, how moderately, Augustus saw fit to treat a writer who personally angered him; and we see how provocative was the attitude of Pollio. Augustus, we are told, publicly lamented the death of Gallus.[54] It is hard to reconcile all this with the Princeps ordering the universal suppression of a poem praising him; it is perhaps even harder to imagine Pollio failing to seize the opportunity to keep a copy of a poem by a former protégé of his own, praising one of his friends, and suppressed in circumstances discreditable to Augustus. The compromise favoured by some scholars,[55] of supposing that Virgil wrote and suppressed not half the poem but a few lines only, seems to me to founder on the same considerations.

[54] Suet. *Aug.* 66.2.
[55] Otis 1964: 412–13; Wilkinson 1969: 111–12.

Bibliography

Adler, E. (1983). 'The Invocation to the *Georgics*'. *Interpretation* 11: 25–41.
Altevogt, H. (1952). *Labor improbus: Eine Vergilstudie*. Münster: Aschendorff.
Anderson, W. B. (1933). 'Gallus and the Fourth *Georgic*'. *CQ* 27: 36–45.
Anderson, W. S. (1982). 'The Orpheus of Virgil and Ovid: *flebile nescio quid*'. In J. Warden (ed.), *Orpheus: The Metamorphoses of a Myth*. Toronto: University of Toronto Press, 25–50.
Austin, R. G. (1977). *P. Vergili Maronis Aeneidos Liber Sextus*. Oxford: Clarendon Press.
Balot, R. K. (1998). 'Pindar, Virgil, and the Proem to *Georgic 3*'. *Phoenix* 52: 83–94.
Barchiesi, A. (1981). 'Letture e trasformazioni di un mito arateo (Cic. Arat. XVII Tr.; Verg. georg. 2,473 sg.)'. *MD* 6: 181–7.
—— (1982). 'Lettura del secondo libro delle Georgiche'. In Gigante (ed.), 41–86.
Bardons, H. and Verdière, R. (eds.) (1971). *Vergiliana: Recherches sur Virgile*. Leiden: Brill.
Barigazzi, A. (1979). 'Callimaco e i cavalli di Berenice (Pap. Lille 82)'. *Prometheus* 5: 267–71.
—— (1980). 'Per la ricostruzione del Callimaco di Lilla'. *Prometheus* 6: 1–20.
Batstone, W. W. (1988). 'On the Surface of the *Georgics*'. *Arethusa* 21: 227–45.
—— (1997). 'Virgilian Didaxis: Value and Meaning in the *Georgics*'. In Martindale (ed.), 125–44.
Bayet, J. (1930). 'Les premières "Géorgiques" de Virgile (39–37 avant J.-Chr.)'. *RPh* 4: 128–50, 227–47.
—— (1967). *Mélanges de littérature latine*. Rome: Edizioni di Storia e Letteratura.
Betensky, A. (1979). 'The Farmer's Battles'. *Ramus* 8: 108–19.
Bettini, M. (1981). 'La follia di Aristeo: Morfologia e struttura della vicenda virgiliana al quarto libro delle Georgiche'. *MD* 6: 71–90 (= id. (1986), *Antropologia e cultura romana: Parentela, tempo, immagini dell'anima*. Rome: La Nuova Italia Scientifica, 236–55).
Betz, H. D. (1978). 'De laude ipsius (Moralia 539A–547F)'. In id. (ed.), *Plutarch's Ethical Writings and Early Christian Literature*. Leiden: Brill, 367–93.

Birt, T. (1882). *Das antike Buchwesen in seinem Verhältnis zur Litteratur.* Berlin: Hertz.
Bonner, C. (1951). 'A New Fragment of Callimachus (*Iamb.* XII, 57–70)'. *Aegyptus* 31: 134–7.
Bornmann, F. (1978). 'Zum Siegeslied des Kallimachos auf Berenike, P. Lille 79 c III 6'. *ZPE* 31: 35.
Bovie, S. P. (1956). 'The Imagery of Ascent–Descent in Vergil's *Georgics*'. *AJPh* 77: 337–58.
Bowie, E. L. (1993). 'Lies, Fiction, and Slander in Early Greek Poetry'. In C. Gill and T. P. Wiseman (eds.), *Lies and Fiction in the Ancient World.* Exeter: University of Exeter Press, 1–37.
Boyancé, P. (1927). 'Sur quelques vers de Virgile (Géorgiques II v. 490–492)'. *RA* 25: 361–79.
—— (1980). 'La réligion des "Géorgiques" à la lumière des travaux récents'. *ANRW* 2.31.1: 549–73.
Boyle, A. J. (1986). *The Chaonian Dove: Studies in the Eclogues, Georgics and Aeneid of Virgil.* Leiden: Brill.
Bradley, A. (1969). 'Augustan Culture and a Radical Alternative: Vergil's *Georgics*'. *Arion* 8: 347–58.
Briggs, W. W., Jr. (1980). *Narrative and Simile from the Georgics in the Aeneid.* Leiden: Brill.
Brink, C. O. (1963). *Horace on Poetry: Prolegomena to the Literary Epistles.* Cambridge: Cambridge University Press.
—— (1969). 'Horace and Empedocles' Temperature: A Rejected Fragment of Empedocles'. *Phoenix* 23: 138–42.
—— (1982). *Horace on Poetry: Epistles Book II. The Letters to Augustus and Florus.* Cambridge: Cambridge University Press.
Brooks, R. A. (1953). '*Discolor aura*: Reflections on the Golden Bough'. *AJPh* 74: 260–80 (=Commager (ed.) 1966: 143–63).
Brunt, P. A. (1971). *Italian Manpower 225 B.C. – A.D. 14.* Oxford: Clarendon Press.
Buchheit, V. (1963). *Vergil über die Sendung Roms: Untersuchungen zum Bellum Poenicum und zur Aeneis.* Heidelberg: Winter.
—— (1972). *Der Anspruch des Dichters in Vergils Georgika: Dichtertum und Heilsweg.* Darmstadt: Wissenschaftliche Buchgesellschaft.
Büchner, K. (1955–8). 'P. Vergilius Maro'. *Pauly-Wissowa* 8: 1021–1486.
Bühler, W. (1960). *Die Europa des Moschos.* Wiesbaden: Steiner.
Bywater, I. (1877). 'Aristotle's Dialogue "On Philosophy"'. *JPh* 7: 64–87.
Cadili, L. (2001). *Viamque adfectat Olympo: Memoria ellenistica nelle 'Georgiche' di Virgilio.* Milan: LED.

Cairns, F. (1969). 'Catullus 1'. *Mnemosyne* 22: 153–8.
Camps, W. A. (1966). *Propertius:* Elegies, *Book III*. Cambridge: Cambridge University Press.
Carilli, M. (1986). 'Aspetti lessicali dell'umanizzazione di elementi naturali nelle Georgiche: La terminologia del *labor* e del *bellum*'. *CCC* 7: 171–84.
Castiglioni, L. (1947). *Lezioni intorno alle Georgiche di Virgilio*. Milan: Marzorati.
Chomarat, J. (1974). 'L'initiation d'Aristée'. *REL* 52: 185–207.
Christmann, E. (1982). 'Zur antiken Georgica-Rezeption'. *WJA* 8: 57–67.
Clare, R. J. (1995). 'Chiron, Melampus and Tisiphone: Myth and Meaning in Virgil's Plague of Noricum'. *Hermathena* 158: 95–108.
Clarke, W. M. (1976/7). 'Ovid: A Review Article'. *CJ* 72: 317–26.
Clausen, W. V. (1964). 'An Interpretation of the Aeneid'. *HSPh* 68: 139–47 (= Commager (ed.) 1966: 75–88 = P. R. Hardie (ed.) 1999: 3.65–73).
—— (1976). '*Cynthius*'. *AJPh* 97: 245–7 (= P. R. Hardie (ed.) 1999: 1.385–7).
Clay, J. S. (1976). 'The Argument of the End of Vergil's Second Georgic'. *Philologus* 120: 232–45.
—— (1981). 'The Old Man in the Garden: *Georgic* 4.116–148'. *Arethusa* 14: 57–65.
Coleiro, E. (1971). 'Allegory in the IVth Georgic'. In Bardons and Verdière (eds.), 113–23.
Coleman, R. (1962). 'Gallus, the Bucolics, and the Ending of the Fourth *Georgic*'. *AJPh* 83: 55–71 (= P. R. Hardie (ed.) 1999: 2.289–300).
Commager, S. (ed.) (1966). *Virgil: A Collection of Critical Essays*. Englewood Cliffs, New Jersey: Prentice-Hall.
Comparetti, D. (1997). *Vergil in the Middle Ages*. Transl. by E. F. M. Benecke. Princeton: Princeton University Press.
Conington, J. and Nettleship, H. (1898). *P. Vergili Maronis Opera*, Vol. 1, 5th edn. London: Bell.
Conte, G. B. (1986). *The Rhetoric of Imitation: Genre and Poetic Memory in Virgil and Other Latin Poets*. Transl. by C. Segal. Ithaca: Cornell University Press.
—— (1998). 'Aristeo, Orfeo e le *Georgiche*: Una seconda volta'. *SCO* 46: 103–28 (= id. (2002), *Virgilio: L'epica del sentimento*. Turin: Einaudi, 65–89. English version in id. (2007), *The Poetry of Pathos: Studies in Virgilian Epic*. Ed. by S. J. Harrison. Oxford: Oxford University Press, 123–49).
Conway, R. S. (1928). 'Poetry and Government'. *PCA* 25: 19–38.
Cook, A. B. (1895). 'The Bee in Greek Mythology'. *JHS* 15: 1–24.
—— (1914). *Zeus: A Study in Ancient Religion*, Vol. 1. New York: Biblo and Tannen.

Cova, P. V. (1973). 'Arte allusiva in Georg., IV, 471–484'. *BStudLat* 3: 281–303.
Crabbe, A. M. (1977). *'Ignoscenda quidem...*: Catullus 64 and the Fourth Georgic'. *CQ* 27: 342–51.
Cramer, R. (1998). *Vergils Weltsicht: Optimismus und Pessimismus in Vergils Georgica*. Berlin: De Gruyter.
Dahlmann, H. (1954). 'Der Bienenstaat in Vergils Georgica'. *Akademie der Wissenschaften und Literatur Mainz, Abhandlungen* 1954.10.
Dalzell, A. (1996). *The Criticism of Didactic Poetry: Essays on Lucretius, Virgil, and Ovid*. Toronto: University of Toronto Press.
De Jong, I. J. F. (1987). *Narrators and Focalizers: The Presentation of the Story in the Iliad*. Amsterdam: Grüner.
De Lacy, P. (1957). 'Process and Value: An Epicurean Dilemma'. *TAPhA* 88: 114–26.
De Saint-Denis, E. (1957). *Géorgiques*, 2nd edn. Paris: Les Belles Lettres.
Denniston, J. D. and Page, D. (1957). *Aeschylus:* Agamemnon. Oxford: Clarendon Press.
Dewar, M. (1988). 'Octavian and Orestes in the Finale of the First Georgic'. *CQ* 38: 563–5.
—— (1990). 'Octavian and Orestes Again'. *CQ* 40: 580–2.
Dodds, E. R. (1960). *Euripides:* Bacchae, 2nd edn. Oxford: Clarendon Press.
Domenicucci, P. (1985). 'L'elegia di Orfeo nel IV libro delle *Georgiche*'. *GIF* 37: 239–48.
Drew, D. L. (1924). 'Virgil's Marble Temple: *Georgics* III. 10–39'. *CQ* 18: 195–202 (= P. R. Hardie (ed.) 1999: 2.211–22).
Effe, B. (1977). *Dichtung und Lehre: Untersuchungen zur Typologie des antiken Lehrgedichts*. Munich: Beck.
Erren, M. (1985–2003). *P. Vergilius Maro: Georgica*, 2 vols. Heidelberg: Winter.
Farrell, J. (1991). *Vergil's* Georgics *and the Traditions of Ancient Epic: The Art of Allusion in Literary History*. New York: Oxford University Press.
Farrington, B. (1958). 'Vergil and Lucretius'. *AClass* 1: 45–50.
—— (1963). 'Polemical Allusions to the *De Rerum Natura* of Lucretius in the Works of Vergil'. In L. Varcl and R. F. Willetts (eds.), *Geras: Studies Presented to George Thomson on the Occasion of his 60th Birthday*. Prague: Charles University, 87–94 (= P. R. Hardie (ed.) 1999: 1.18–26).
Fenik, B. (1962). 'Horace's First and Sixth Roman Odes and the Second Georgic'. *Hermes* 90: 72–96.
Ferrero, G. (1907–9). *The Greatness and Decline of Rome*, 5 vols. Transl. by A. E. Zimmern (Vols. 1 and 2) and H. J. Chaytor (Vols. 3–5). New York: Putnam.

Festa, N. (1902). *Mythographi Graeci*, Vol. 3.2. Leipzig: Teubner.
Festugière, A.-J. (1944–54). *La Révélation d'Hermès Trismégiste*, 4 vols. Paris: Lecoffre.
Fleischer, U. (1960). 'Musentempel und Octavianehrung des Vergil im Proömium zum dritten Buche der Georgica'. *Hermes* 88: 280–331.
Food and Agriculture Organization of the United Nations (1973). *Modern Olive Growing*. Rome: United Nations Development Programme.
Fraenkel, E. (1945). 'Some Aspects of the Structure of Aeneid VII'. *JRS* 35: 1–14.
—— (1952). 'The Culex'. *JRS* 42: 1–9.
—— (1957). *Horace*. Oxford: Clarendon Press.
—— (1962). 'Zum Text von Aeneis 6, 852'. *MH* 19: 133–4.
—— (1964). *Kleine Beiträge zur klassischen Philologie*, 2 vols. Rome: Edizioni di Storia e Letteratura.
Fraser, P. M. (1972). *Ptolemaic Alexandria*, 3 vols. Oxford: Clarendon Press.
Frayn, J. M. (1979). *Subsistence Farming in Roman Italy*. London: Centaur Press.
Frederiksen, M. W. (1970/1). 'The Contribution of Archaeology to the Agrarian Problem in the Gracchan Period'. *DArch* 4–5: 330–57.
Frentz, W. (1967). *Mythologisches in Vergils Georgica*. Meisenheim am Glan: Hain.
Friedländer, P. (1912). *Johannes von Gaza und Paulus Silentarius: Kunstbeschreibungen justinianischer Zeit*. Leipzig: Teubner.
Funke, H. (1977). 'Porcius Licinus fr. I Morel'. *RhM* 120: 168–72.
Gagé, J. (1982). 'Auguste écrivain'. *ANRW* 2.30.1: 611–23.
Gagliardi, P. (2003). *Gravis cantantibus umbra: Studi su Virgilio e Cornelio Gallo*. Bologna: Pàtron.
Gale, M. R. (1991). 'Man and Beast in Lucretius and the *Georgics*'. *CQ* 41: 414–26 (= P. R. Hardie (ed.) 1999: 2.41–57).
—— (1994). *Myth and Poetry in Lucretius*. Cambridge: Cambridge University Press.
—— (1995). 'Virgil's Metamorphoses: Myth and Allusion in the *Georgics*'. *PCPhS* 41: 36–61.
—— (2000). *Virgil on the Nature of Things: The* Georgics, *Lucretius and the Didactic Tradition*. Cambridge: Cambridge University Press.
—— (ed.) (2004). *Latin Epic and Didactic Poetry: Genre, Tradition and Individuality*. Swansea: Classical Press of Wales.
Galinsky, G. K. (1969). *Aeneas, Sicily, and Rome*. Princeton: Princeton University Press.
—— (1975). *Ovid's* Metamorphoses: *An Introduction to the Basic Aspects*. Berkeley: University of California Press.

Garner, R. J. (1958). *The Grafter's Handbook*, 2nd edn. London: Faber & Faber.

Gerber, D. E. (1969). *A Bibliography of Pindar, 1513–1966*. Cleveland: Case Western Reserve University Press.

Geymonat, M. (1973). *P. Vergili Maronis Opera*. Turin: Paravia.

Gibson, R. K. (1997). 'Didactic Poetry as "Popular" Form: A Study of Imperatival Expressions in Latin Didactic Verse and Prose'. In C. Atherton (ed.), *Form and Content in Didactic Poetry*. Bari: Levante, 67–98.

Gigante, M. (ed.) (1982). *Lecturae Vergilianae II: Le Georgiche*. Naples: Giannini.

Gladigow, B. (1967). 'Zum Makarismos des Weisen'. *Hermes* 95: 404–33.

Glei, R. F. (1991). *Der Vater der Dinge: Interpretationen zur politischen, literarischen und kulturellen Dimension des Krieges bei Vergil*. Trier: Wissenschaftlicher Verlag Trier.

Gow, A. S. F. (1952). *Theocritus*, 2 vols, 2nd edn. Cambridge: Cambridge University Press.

—— and Page, D. L. (1965). *The Greek Anthology: Hellenistic Epigrams*, 2 vols. Cambridge: Cambridge University Press.

Gransden, K. W. (1982). Rev. of A. J. Boyle, *Ancient Pastoral: Ramus Essays on Greek and Roman Pastoral Poetry*, T. Oksala, *Studien zum Verständis der Einheit und der Bedeutung von Vergils Georgica*, R. D. Williams, *Virgil: The Eclogues and Georgics*, M. C. J. Putnam, *Virgil's Poem of the Earth: Studies in the Georgics*, W. W. Briggs, *Narrative and Simile from the Georgics in the Aeneid*, and P. A. Johnston, *Vergil's Agricultural Golden Age: A Study of the Georgics*. *JRS* 72: 206–9.

Griffin, J. (1979). 'The Fourth *Georgic*, Virgil, and Rome'. *G&R* 26: 61–80 (= McAuslan and Walcot (eds.) 1990: 94–111 = P. R. Hardie (ed.) 1999: 2.268–88).

—— (1981). 'Haec Super Arvorum Cultu'. *CR* 31: 23–37.

—— (1985). *Latin Poets and Roman Life*. London: Duckworth.

Griffin, M. T. (1976). *Seneca: A Philosopher in Politics*. Oxford: Clarendon Press.

Gummerus, H. (1906). *Der römische Gutsbetrieb als wirtschaftlicher Organismus nach den Werken des Cato, Varro und Columella*. Leipzig: Dieterich.

Habinek, T. N. (1990). 'Sacrifice, Society and Vergil's Ox-Born Bees'. In M. Griffin and D. J. Mastronarde (eds.), *Cabinet of the Muses: Essays on Classical and Comparative Literature in Honor of Thomas G. Rosenmeyer*. Atlanta: Scholars Press, 209–23 (= P. R. Hardie (ed.) 1999: 2.328–43).

Hardie, A. (2002/3). 'The *Georgics*, the Mysteries and the Muses at Rome'. *PCPhS* 48: 175–208.

Hardie, C. G. (1970). 'Virgil'. *OCD*, 2nd edn., 1123–8.

—— (1971). *The* Georgics: *A Transitional Poem*. Abingdon-on-Thames: Abbey Press.
Hardie, P. R. (1986). *Virgil's* Aeneid: *Cosmos and* Imperium. Oxford: Clarendon Press.
—— (1992). 'Augustan Poets and the Mutability of Rome'. In A. Powell (ed.), *Roman Poetry and Propaganda in the Age of Augustus*. London: Bristol Classical Press, 59–82.
—— (1998). *Virgil*. Oxford: Oxford University Press.
—— (ed.) (1999). *Virgil: Critical Assessments of Classsical Authors*, 4 vols. London: Routledge.
—— (2004). 'Political Education in Virgil's *Georgics*'. *SIFC* 97: 83–111.
Härke, G. (1936). 'Studien zur Exkurstechnik im römischen Lehrgedicht (Lukrez und Vergil)'. Diss. Freiburg im Br.
Harrison, E. L. (1979). 'The Noric Plague in Virgil's Third *Georgic*'. *Papers of the Liverpool Latin Seminar* 2: 1–65.
Harrison, S. J. (1990). 'Some Views of the *Aeneid* in the Twentieth Century'. In Harrison (ed.), 1–20.
—— (ed.) (1990). *Oxford Readings in Vergil's* Aeneid. Oxford: Oxford University Press.
—— (2004). 'Virgil's *Corycius Senex* and Nicander's *Georgica*: *Georgics* 4.116–48. In Gale (ed.), 109–23.
Heckel, H. (1998). *Das Widerspenstige zähmen: Die Funktion der militärischen und politischen Sprache in Vergils Georgica*. Trier: Wissenschaftlicher Verlag Trier.
Heinze, R. (1903). *Virgils epische Technik*. Leipzig: Teubner.
—— (1921). *Von den Ursachen der Grösse Roms*. Leipzig: Edelmann.
—— (1960). *Vom Geist des Römertums: Ausgewählte Aufsätze*, 3rd edn. Ed. by E. Burck. Stuttgart: Teubner.
Hermes, J. (1980). 'C. Cornelius Gallus und Vergil: Das Problem der Umarbeitung des vierten Georgica-Buches'. Diss. Münster.
Heurgon, J. (1978). *Varron: Economie Rurale*, Vol. 1. Paris: Les Belles Lettres.
Highbarger, E. L. (1935). 'The Pindaric Style of Horace'. *TAPhA* 66: 222–55.
Hollis, A. J. (1996). 'Octavian in the Fourth Georgic'. *CQ* 46: 305–8.
Holzberg, N. (2006). *Vergil: Der Dichter und sein Werk*. Munich: Beck.
Horsfall, N. (1995). 'Cato, Cicero and the *Georgics*: A Note'. *Vergilius* 41: 55–6.
—— (ed.) (1995). *A Companion to the Study of Virgil*. Leiden: Brill.
Huxley, H. H. (1963). *Virgil: Georgics I and IV*. London: Methuen.
Innes, D. C. (1979). 'Gigantomachy and Natural Philosophy'. *CQ* 29: 165–71.
——— Hine, H., and Pelling, C. (eds.) (1995). *Ethics and Rhetoric: Classical Essays for Donald Russell on his Seventy-Fifth Birthday*. Oxford: Oxford University Press.

Jacobson, H. (1984). 'Aristaeus, Orpheus, and the *laudes Galli*'. *AJPh* 105: 271–300 (= P. R. Hardie (ed.) 1999: 2.301–27).

Jahn, P. (1903). 'Eine Prosaquelle Vergils und ihre Umsetzung in Poesie durch den Dichter'. *Hermes* 38: 244–64.

Janko, R. (1992). *The* Iliad*: A Commentary. Vol. IV: Books 13–16*. Cambridge: Cambridge University Press.

Jenkyns, R. (1993). '*Labor improbus*'. *CQ* 43: 243–8 (= P. R. Hardie (ed.) 1999: 2.154–61).

—— (1998). *Virgil's Experience: Nature and History, Times, Names, and Places*. Oxford: Clarendon Press.

Jermyn, L. A. S. (1949). 'Virgil's Agricultural Lore'. *G&R* 18: 49–69.

—— (1951). 'Weather-Signs in Virgil'. *G&R* 20: 26–37, 49–59.

—— (1954). *The Ostrakon*. Sunderstead: Virgil Society.

Jocelyn, H. D. (1984). 'Servius and the "Second Edition" of the *Georgics*'. In (no ed.), *Atti del convegno mondiale scientifico di studi su Virgilio*, Vol. 1. Milan: Mondadori, 431–48.

Johnson, W. R. (2004). 'A Secret Garden: *Georgics* 4.116–148'. In D. Armstrong *et al.* (eds.), *Vergil, Philodemus, and the Augustans*. Austin: University of Texas Press, 75–83.

Johnston, P. A. (1980). *Vergil's Agricultural Golden Age: A Study of the Georgics*. Leiden: Brill.

Jones, A. H. M. (1970). *Augustus*. London: Chatto & Windus.

Jones, R. M. (1926). 'Posidonius and the Flight of the Mind through the Universe'. *CPh* 21: 97–113.

Jope, J. (1989). 'The Didactic Unity and Emotional Import of Book 6 of *De rerum natura*'. *Phoenix* 43: 16–34.

Joudoux, R. (1971). 'La philosophie politique des "Géorgiques" d'après le livre IV (v. 149 à 169)'. *BAGB*: 67–82.

Kassel, R. (1977). 'Nachtrag zum neuen Kallimachos'. *ZPE* 25: 51.

Kaster, R. A. (2002). '*Invidia* and the End of *Georgics* 1'. *Phoenix* 56: 275–95.

Kenney, E. J. (1971). *Lucretius:* De Rerum Natura *Book III*. Cambridge: Cambridge University Press.

Keppie, L. (1983). *Colonisation and Veteran Settlement in Italy 47–14 B.C.* London: British School at Rome.

Kidd, D. A. (1997). *Aratus:* Phaenomena. Cambridge: Cambridge University Press.

Kienast, D. (1954). *Cato der Zensor: Seine Persönlichkeit und seine Zeit*. Heidelberg: Quelle & Meyer.

Klepl, H. (1967). *Lukrez und Virgil in ihren Lehrgedichten: Vergleichende Interpretationen*. Darmstadt: Wissenschaftliche Buchgesellschaft.

Klingner, F. (1963). *Virgils Georgica*. Zurich: Artemis (= Klingner 1967: 175–363).
—— (1967). *Virgil: Bucolica, Georgica, Aeneis*. Zurich: Artemis.
Knight, W. F. J. (1944). *Roman Vergil*. London: Faber & Faber.
Knoche, A. (1877). 'Vergilius quae Graeca exempla secutus sit in Georgicis'. Diss. Leipzig.
Knox, P. E. (1992). 'Love and Horses in Virgil's *Georgics*'. *Eranos* 90: 43–53.
Koenen, L. (1976). 'Egyptian Influence in Tibullus'. *ICS* 1: 127–59.
Köhnken, A. (1981). 'Apollo's Retort to Envy's Criticism (Two Questions of Relevance in Callimachus, Hymn 2, 105ff.)'. *AJPh* 102: 411–22.
Kraggerud, E. (1998). 'Vergil Announcing the *Aeneid*: On *Georgics* 3.1–48'. In H.-P. Stahl (ed.), *Vergil's Aeneid: Augustan Epic and Political Context*. London: Duckworth, 1–20.
Kramer, G. (1979).'The Didactic Tradition in Vergil's Georgics'. *Ramus* 8: 7–21.
Kronenberg, L. J. (2000). 'The Poet's Fiction: Virgil's Praise of the Farmer, Philosopher, and Poet at the End of *Georgics* 2'. *HSPh* 100: 341–60.
La Penna, A. (2005). *L'impossibile giustificazione della storia: Un'interpretazione di Virgilio*. Bari: Laterza.
Lee, M. O. (1989). *Death and Rebirth in Virgil's Arcadia*. Albany: State University of New York Press.
Lefèvre, E. (1986). 'Die *laudes Galli* in Vergils Georgica'. *WS* 99: 183–92.
Leigh, M. (1994). 'Servius on Vergil's Senex Corycius: New Evidence'. *MD* 33: 181–95.
Lieberg, G. (1982). *Poeta Creator: Studien zu einer Figur der antiken Dichtung*. Amsterdam: Gieben.
—— (1985). '*Poeta Creator*: Some "Religious" Aspects'. *Papers of the Liverpool Latin Seminar* 5: 23–32.
Liebeschuetz, W. (1965). 'Beast and Man in the Third Book of Virgil's Georgics'. *G&R* 12: 63–77.
Lipking, L. (1981). *The Life of the Poet: Beginning and Ending Poetic Careers*. Chicago: Chicago University Press.
Livrea, E. (1978). 'Nota al nuovo Callimaco di Lille'. *ZPE* 32: 7–10.
—— (1979). 'Der Liller Kallimachos und die Mausefallen'. *ZPE* 34: 37–42.
—— *et al.* (1980). 'Il nuovo Callimaco di Lille'. *Maia* 32: 225–53.
Luce, S. B., Jr. (1916). 'The Origin of the Shape of the "Nolan" Amphora'. *AJA* 20: 438–74.
Luck, G. (1967–77). *P. Ovidius Naso*: Tristia, 2 vols. Heidelberg: Winter.
—— (1973). 'Virgil and the Mystery Religions'. *AJPh* 94: 147–66.
Lundström, S. (1976). 'Der Eingang des Proömiums zum dritten Buche der Georgica'. *Hermes* 104: 163–91.

Lundström, V. (1897). 'Magostudien'. *Eranos* 2: 60–67.
Luppe, W. (1978*a*). 'Zum Anfang des Liller Kallimachos'. *ZPE* 29: 36.
—— (1978*b*). 'οὐδεὶς εἶδεν ἁματροχιάς (Kallimachos Fr. 383,10 Pf.)'. *ZPE* 31: 43–44.
Lyne, R. O. A. M. (1974). '*Scilicet et tempus veniet*...: Virgil, *Georgics* I. 463–514'. In A. J. Woodman and D. West (eds.), *Quality and Pleasure in Latin Poetry*. Cambridge: Cambridge University Press, 47–66 (= P. R. Hardie (ed.) 1999: 2.162–83).
—— (1978). *Ciris, A Poem Attributed to Vergil*. Cambridge: Cambridge University Press.
—— (1993). Rev. of Mynors 1990. *JRS* 83: 203–6.
McAuslan, I. and Walcot, P. (eds.) (1990). *Virgil*. Oxford: Oxford University Press.
Mackail, J. W. (1912). 'Virgil's Use of the Word *Ingens*'. *CR* 26: 251–5.
Macleod, C. (1983). *Collected Essays*. Oxford: Clarendon Press.
Maguinness, W. S. (1962). 'Les *Géorgiques* de Virgile'. *BAGB*: 441–51.
Mahaffy, J. P. (1890). 'The Work of Mago on Agriculture'. *Hermathena* 7: 29–35.
Marasco, G. (1990). '*Corycius senex* (Verg. *Georg*. 4, 127)'. *RFIC* 118: 402–7.
Marrou, H.-I. (1965). *Histoire de l'éducation dans l'antiquité*, 6th ed. Paris: Éditions du Seuil.
Marsili, A. (1965). *Georgiche III*. Pisa: Studi e Testi.
Martindale, C. (1997). 'Introduction: "The Classic of All Europe"'. In Martindale (ed.), 1–18.
—— (ed.) (1997). *The Cambridge Companion to Virgil*. Cambridge: Cambridge University Press.
Merrill, E. T. (1907). 'On Certain Roman Characteristics'. *CJ* 2: 369–86.
Miles, G. B. (1975). '*Georgics* 3.209–294: *Amor* and Civilization'. *CSCA* 8: 177–97.
—— (1980). *Virgil's Georgics: A New Interpretation*. Berkeley: University of California Press.
Millet, P. (1984). 'Hesiod and his World'. *PCPhS* 30: 84–115.
Minadeo, R. (1965). 'The Formal Design of *De Rerum Natura*'. *Arion* 4: 444–61.
—— (1969). *The Lyre of Science: Form and Meaning in Lucretius'* De Rerum Natura. Detroit: Wayne State University Press.
Mitsdörffer, W. (1938/9). 'Vergils Georgica und Theophrast'. *Philologus* 93: 449–75.
Morgan, L. (1999). *Patterns of Redemption in Virgil's Georgics*. Cambridge: Cambridge University Press.

Bibliography

Morsch, H. (1878). 'De Graecis auctoribus in Georgicis a Vergilio expressis'. Diss. Halle.

Mylonas, G. E. (1961). *Eleusis and the Eleusinian Mysteries*. Princeton: Princeton University Press.

Mynors, R. A. B. (1990). *Virgil: Georgics*. Oxford: Clarendon Press.

Nadeau, Y. (1984). 'The Lover and the Statesman: A Study in Apiculture (Virgil, *Georgics* 4.281–558)'. In T. Woodman and D. West (eds.), *Poetry and Politics in the Age of Augustus*. Cambridge: Cambridge University Press, 59–82.

Nappa, C. (2005). *Reading after Actium: Vergil's Georgics, Octavian, and Rome*. Ann Arbor: University of Michigan Press.

Nardi, C. (1956). 'Reminiscenze pindariche in Virgilio'. In (no ed.), *ΑΝΤΙΔΩΡΟΝ Hugoni Henrico Paoli oblatum: Miscellanea philologica*. Genoa: Istituto di Filologia Classica, 242–9.

Nelis, D. (2004). 'From Didactic to Epic: *Georgics* 2.458–3.48'. In Gale (ed.), 73–107.

Nelson, S. A. (1998). *God and the Land: The Metaphysics of Farming in Hesiod and Vergil*. New York: Oxford University Press.

Nethercut, W. R. (1970). 'The Ironic Priest'. *AJPh* 91: 385–407.

—— (1973). 'Vergil's De Rerum Natura'. *Ramus* 2: 41–52.

Neumeister, C. (1982). 'Aristaeus und Orpheus im 4. Buch der Georgica'. *WJA* 8: 47–56.

Newman, J. K. (1967a). *Augustus and the New Poetry*. Brussels: Latomus.

—— (1967b). *The Concept of Vates in Augustan Poetry*. Brussels: Latomus.

Nicolet, C. (1976). *Le Métier de citoyen dans la Rome républicaine*. Paris: Gallimard.

Nisbet, R. G. M. and Hubbard, M. (1970). *A Commentary on Horace: Odes, Book I*. Oxford: Clarendon Press.

—— and —— (1978). *A Commentary on Horace: Odes, Book II*. Oxford: Clarendon Press.

Nock, A. D. (1952). 'Hellenistic Mysteries and Christian Sacraments'. *Mnemosyne* 5: 177–213.

—— (1972). *Essays on Religion and the Ancient World*, 2 vols. Ed. by Z. Stewart. Oxford: Clarendon Press.

Norden, E. (1915). *Ennius und Vergilius: Kriegsbilder aus Roms grosser Zeit*. Leipzig: Teubner.

—— (1934). 'Orpheus und Eurydice: Ein nachträgliches Gedenkblatt für Vergil'. *Preussische Akademie der Wissenschaften Berlin, Phil.-Hist. Kl., Sitzungsberichte*, 626–83.

—— (1957). *P. Vergilius Maro: Aeneis Buch VI*, 4th edn. Stuttgart: Teubner.

Norden, E. (1966). *Kleine Schriften zum klassischen Altertum*. Ed. by B. Kytzler. Berlin: De Gruyter.
Novara, A. (1982). 'La *physica philosophia* et le bonheur d'après Virgile, *Géorg.*, II, v. 490–492'. *REL* 60: 234–47.
Ogilvie, R. M. and Richmond, I. A. (1967). *Cornelii Taciti De vita Agricolae*. Oxford: Clarendon Press.
Olck, F. (1897). 'Biene'. *Pauly-Wissowa* 3.1: 431–50.
Oppermann, H. (1938). *Vergil*. Frankfurt: Diesterweg (= Oppermann (ed.) 1963: 93–176).
—— (ed.) (1963). *Wege zu Vergil: Drei Jahrzehnte Begegnungen in Dichtung und Wissenschaft*. Darmstadt: Wissenschaftliche Buchgesellschaft.
Otis, B. (1964). *Virgil: A Study in Civilized Poetry*. Oxford: Clarendon Press.
—— (1972). 'A New Study of the Georgics'. *Phoenix* 26: 40–62 (= P. R. Hardie (ed.) 1999: 2.119–42).
Page, T. E. (1974). *P. Vergili Maronis Bucolica et Georgica*. London: Macmillan.
Parain, C. (1966). 'The Evolution of Agricultural Technique'. In M. M. Postan (ed.), *The Cambridge Economic History of Europe*, Vol. 1, 2nd edn. Cambridge: Cambridge University Press, 125–79.
Parry, A. (1963). 'The Two Voices of Virgil's *Aeneid*'. *Arion* 2.4: 66–80 (= Commager (ed.) 1966: 107–23 = Parry 1989: 78–96 = P. R. Hardie (ed.) 1999: 3.49–64).
—— (1972). 'The Idea of Art in Virgil's Georgics'. *Arethusa* 5: 35–52 (= Parry 1989: 265–85).
—— (1989). *The Language of Achilles and Other Papers*. Oxford: Oxford University Press.
Parsons, P. J. (1977). 'Callimachus: Victoria Berenicis'. *ZPE* 25: 1–50.
Perkell, C. G. (1986). 'Vergil's Theodicy Reconsidered'. In J. D. Bernard (ed.), *Vergil at 2000: Commemorative Essays on the Poet and his Influence*. New York: AMS Press, 67–83.
—— (1989). *The Poet's Truth: A Study of the Poet in Virgil's* Georgics. Berkeley: University of California Press.
—— (1990). 'Vergilian Scholarship in the Nineties: Eclogues'. *Vergilius* 36: 43–55.
—— (2002). 'The Golden Age and Its Contradictions in the Poetry of Vergil'. *Vergilius* 48: 3–39.
Perutelli, A. (1980). 'L'episodio di Aristeo nelle Georgiche: Struttura e tecnica narrativa'. *MD* 4: 59–76.
Pfeiffer, R. (1949–53). *Callimachus*, 2 vols. Oxford: Clarendon Press.
Pöschl, V. (1950). *Die Dichtkunst Virgils: Bild und Symbol in der Äneis*. Wiesbaden: Rohrer.

—— (1962). *The Art of Vergil: Image and Symbol in the* Aeneid. Transl. by G. Seligson. Ann Arbor: University of Michigan Press.
Possanza, M. (1990). 'The Text of Lucretius 2.1174'. *CQ* 40: 459–64.
Putnam, M. C. J. (1965). *The Poetry of the Aeneid: Four Studies in Imaginative Unity and Design.* Cambridge, Mass.: Harvard University Press.
—— (1970). *Virgil's Pastoral Art: Studies in the* Eclogues. Princeton: Princeton University Press.
—— (1972). 'The Virgilian Achievement'. *Arethusa* 5: 53–70.
—— (1975). 'Italian Virgil and the Idea of Rome'. In L. L. Orlin (ed.), *Janus: Essays in Ancient and Modern Studies.* Ann Arbor: University of Michigan Press, 171–99.
—— (1979). *Virgil's Poem of the Earth: Studies in the* Georgics. Princeton: Princeton University Press.
Quinn, K. (1979). *Texts and Contexts: The Roman Writers and Their Audience.* London: Routledge & Kegan Paul.
Raabe, H. (1974). *Plurima mortis imago: Vergleichende Interpretationen zur Bildersprache Vergils.* Munich: Beck.
Rawson, E. (1978). 'The Introduction of Logical Organisation in Roman Prose Literature'. *PBSR* 46: 12–34.
Reckford, K. J. (1961). 'Latent Tragedy in *Aeneid* VII, 1–285'. *AJPh* 82: 252–69.
Reinhardt, K. (1953). 'Poseidonios'. *Pauly-Wissowa* 22.1: 558–826.
Reitzenstein, E. (1931). 'Zur Stiltheorie des Kallimachos'. In (no ed.), *Festschrift Richard Reitzenstein.* Leipzig: Teubner, 23–69.
Richardson, L., Jr. (1977). *Propertius: Elegies I–IV.* Norman: University of Oklahoma Press.
Richter, G. M. A. (1929). 'Silk in Greece'. *AJA* 33: 27–33.
Richter, W. (1957). *Vergil: Georgica.* Munich: Hueber.
Ross, D. O., Jr. (1980). 'Non sua poma: Varro, Virgil, and Grafting'. *ICS* 5: 63–71.
—— (1987). *Virgil's Elements: Physics and Poetry in the* Georgics. Princeton: Princeton University Press.
Rostagno, E. (1888). *Vergilius quae Romana exempla secutus sit in Georgicis.* Florence: Barbèra.
Royds, T. F. (1918). *The Beasts, Birds, and Bees of Virgil: A Naturalist's Handbook to the Georgics.* Oxford: Blackwell.
Russell, D. A. (1973). '*Ars Poetica*'. In C. D. N. Costa (ed.), *Horace.* London: Routledge & Kegan Paul, 113–34.
—— (1981). *Criticism in Antiquity.* London: Duckworth.
—— (1993). 'Self-Disclosure in Plutarch and in Horace'. In G. W. Most, H. Petersman, and A. M. Ritter (eds.), *Philanthropia kai Eusebia: Festschrift*

für Albrecht Dihle zum 70. Geburtstag. Göttingen: Vandenhoeck & Ruprecht, 426–37.

Rutherford, R. B. (1989). 'Virgil's Poetic Ambitions in *Eclogue* 6'. *G&R* 36: 42–50.

—— (1995). 'Authorial Rhetoric in Virgil's *Georgics*'. In Innes, Hine, and Pelling (eds.), 19–29.

Scazzoso, P. (1956) 'Riflessi misterici nelle Georgiche di Virgilio'. *Paideia* 11: 5–28.

Schadewaldt, W. (1970). *Hellas und Hesperien: Gesammelte Schriften zur Antike und zur neueren Literatur*, 2 vols., 2nd edn. Zurich: Artemis.

Schäfer, S. (1996). *Das Weltbild der Vergilischen* Georgika *in seinem Verhältnis zu* De rerum natura *des Lukrez*. Frankfurt: Lang.

Schepens, G. (1980). *L'*autopsie*' dans la méthode des historiens grec du V*[e] *siècle avant J.-C.* Brussels: Paleis der Academiën.

Schiesaro, A. (1990). *Simulacrum et imago: Gli argomenti analogici nel* De rerum natura. Pisa: Giardini.

—— (1993). 'Il destinatario discreto: Funzioni didascaliche e progetto culturale nelle Georgiche'. In A. Schiesaro, P. Mitsis, and J. S. Clay (eds.), *Mega Nepios: Il destinatario nell'epos didscalico / The Addressee in Didactic Epic* (= *MD* 31). Pisa: Giardini, 129–47.

—— (1997). 'The Boundaries of Knowledge in Virgil's *Georgics*'. In T. Habinek and A. Schiesaro (eds.), *The Roman Cultural Revolution*. Cambridge: Cambridge University Press, 63–89.

Schindler, C. (2000). *Untersuchungen zu den Gleichnissen im römischen Lehrgedicht (Lucrez, Vergil, Manilius)*. Göttingen: Vandenhoeck & Ruprecht.

Schmidt, M. (1930). *Die Komposition von Vergils Georgica*. Paderborn: Schöningh.

Schrijvers, P. H. (1970). *Horror ac divina voluptas: Études sur la poétique et la poésie de Lucrèce*. Amsterdam: Hakkert.

Segal, C. P. (1966). 'Orpheus and the Fourth *Georgic*: Vergil on Nature and Civilization'. *AJPh* 87: 307–25 (= Segal 1989: 36–53).

—— (1989). *Orpheus: The Myth of the Poet*. Baltimore: Johns Hopkins University Press.

Segura Ramos, B. (1982). 'Ad Lucr. d.r.n. II,1173–4'. *Faventia* 4: 97–9.

Sellar, W. Y. (1965). *The Roman Poets of the Augustan Age: Virgil*, 3rd edn. New York: Biblo and Tannen.

Serpa, F. (1987). *Il punto su Virgilio*. Bari: Laterza.

Shapiro, H. A. (1980). 'Jason's Cloak'. *TAPhA* 110: 263–86.

Skard, E. (1967). 'Concordia'. In H. Oppermann (ed.), *Römische Wertbegriffe*. Darmstadt: Wissenschaftliche Buchgesellschaft, 173–208.

Skutsch, O. (1975). 'The Second Book of Propertius'. *HSPh* 79: 229–33.
—— (1985). *The Annals of Q. Ennius*. Oxford: Clarendon Press.
Skydsgaard, J. E. (1968). *Varro the Scholar: Studies in the First Book of Varro's De re rustica*. Copenhagen: Munksgaard.
Smiley, M. T. (1919). 'Callimachus' Debt to Pindar and Others'. *Hermathena* 18: 46–72.
Sordi, M. (1982). 'Timagene di Alessandria: Uno storico ellenocentrico e filobarbaro'. *ANRW* 2.30.1: 775–97.
Speranza, F. (1974). *Scriptorum Romanorum de re rustica reliquiae*, Vol. 1, 2nd edn. Messina: Università degli Studi.
Spurr, M. S. (1983). 'The Cultivation of Millet in Roman Italy'. *PBSR* 51: 1–15.
—— (1986). 'Agriculture and the *Georgics*'. *G&R* 33: 164–87 (= McAuslan and Walcot (eds.) 1990: 69–93 = P. R. Hardie (ed.) 1999: 2.1–24).
Stehle, E. M. (1974). 'Virgil's *Georgics*: The Threat of Sloth'. *TAPhA* 104: 347–69.
Stewart, Z. (1959). 'The Song of Silenus'. *HSPh* 64: 179–205.
Strasburger, H. (1954). 'Der Einzelne und die Gemeinschaft im Denken der Griechen'. *HZ* 177: 227–48.
Suerbaum, W. (1980). 'Spezialbibliographie zu Vergils Georgica'. *ANRW* 2.31.1: 395–499.
Syme, R. (1939). *The Roman Revolution*. Oxford: Clarendon Press.
Taylor, M. E. (1955). 'Primitivism in Virgil'. *AJPh* 76: 261–78.
Theodorakopoulos, E. (1997). 'Closure: The Book of Virgil'. In Martindale (ed.), 155–65.
Thibodeau, P. (2001). 'The Old Man and his Garden (Verg. Georg. 4, 116–148)'. *MD* 47: 175–95.
Thomas, K. (1983). *Man and the Natural World: A History of the Modern Sensibility*. New York: Pantheon Books.
Thomas, R. F. (1982*a*). *Lands and People in Roman Poetry: The Ethnographical Tradition* (= Cambridge Philological Society Suppl. 7). Cambridge: Cambridge Philological Society.
—— (1982*b*). 'Gadflies (Virg. Geo. 3.146–148)'. *HSPh* 86: 81–5 (= R. F. Thomas 1999: 305–10).
—— (1983). 'Callimachus, the *Victoria Berenices*, and Roman Poetry'. *CQ* 33: 92–113 (= R. F. Thomas 1999: 68–100 = P. R. Hardie (ed.) 1999: 2.223–52).
—— (1985). 'From *recusatio* to Commitment: The Evolution of the Vergilian Programme'. *Proceedings of the Liverpool Latin Seminar* 5: 61–73 (= R. F. Thomas 1999: 101–13).
—— (1986). 'Virgil's *Georgics* and the Art of Reference'. *HSPh* 90: 171–98 (= R. F. Thomas 1999: 114–41 = P. R. Hardie (ed.) 1999: 2.58–82).

Thomas, R. F. (1987). 'Prose into Poetry: Tradition and Meaning in Virgil's *Georgics*'. *HSPh* 91: 229–60 (= R. F. Thomas 1999: 142–72).
—— (1988). *Virgil: Georgics*, 2 vols. Cambridge: Cambridge University Press.
—— (1990). 'Vergilian Scholarship in the Nineties: Ideology, Influence, and Future Studies in the *Georgics*'. *Vergilius* 36: 64–70.
—— (1991). 'The "Sacrifice" at the End of the *Georgics*, Aristaeus, and Vergilian Closure'. *CPh* 86: 211–18 (= P. R. Hardie (ed.) 1999: 2.344–53).
—— (1992). 'The Old Man Revisited: Memory, Reference, and Genre in Virg., Georg. 4, 116–48'. *MD* 29: 35–70 (= R. F. Thomas 1999: 173–205).
—— (1993). 'Callimachus Back in Rome'. In M. A. Harder, R. F. Regtuit, and G. C. Wakker (eds.), *Callimachus*. Groningen: Forsten, 197–215 (= R. F. Thomas 1999: 206–28).
—— (1998). 'Virgil's Pindar?'. In P. Knox and C. Foss (eds.), *Style and Tradition: Studies in Honor of Wendell Clausen*. Stuttgart: Teubner, 99–120 (= R. F. Thomas 1999: 267–87).
—— (1999). *Reading Virgil and His Texts: Studies in Intertextuality*. Ann Arbor: University of Michigan Press.
Toynbee, A. J. (1965). *Hannibal's Legacy: The Hannibalic War's Effect on Roman Life*, 2 vols. London: Oxford University Press.
Toynbee, J. M. C. (1961). 'The "Ara Pacis Augustae"'. *JRS* 51: 153–6.
Usener, H. (1902). 'Milch und Honig'. *RhM* 57: 177–95.
—— (1912–13). *Kleine Schriften*, 4 vols. Leipzig: Teubner.
Van Wageningen, J. (1888). 'De Vergili Georgicis'. Diss. Utrecht.
Vian, F. (1952). 'La guerre des géants devant les penseurs de l'antiquité'. *REG* 65: 1–39.
Volk, K. (2002). *Die Poetics of Latin Didactic: Lucretius, Vergil, Ovid, Manilius*. Oxford: Oxford University Press.
Von Albrecht, M. (2006). *Vergil: Bucolica, Georgica, Aeneis. Eine Einführung*. Heidelberg: Winter.
Wankenne, A. (1970). 'Aristée et Orphée dans les Géorgiques'. *LEC* 38: 18–29.
Wardy, R. (1988). 'Lucretius on what Atoms are not'. *CPh* 83: 112–28.
Waszink, J. H. (1966). 'Horaz und Pindar'. *A&A* 12: 111–24.
Webster, T. B. L. (1964). *Hellenistic Poetry and Art*. London: Methuen.
Weinstock, S. (1960). 'Pax and the "Ara Pacis"'. *JRS* 50: 44–58.
Wender, D. S. (1969). 'Resurrection in the Fourth *Georgic*'. *AJPh* 90: 424–36.
West, D. (1979). 'Two Plagues: Virgil, *Georgics* 3.478–566 and Lucretius 6.1090–1286'. In D. West and T. Woodman (eds.), *Creative Imitation and Latin Literature*. Cambridge: Cambridge University Press, 71–88.
West, M. L. (1978). *Hesiod: Works and Days*. Oxford: Clarendon Press.

White, K. D. (1967). *Agricultural Implements of the Roman World*. Cambridge: Cambridge University Press.
—— (1967/8). 'Virgil's Knowledge of Arable Farming'. *PVS* 7: 11–22.
—— (1970). *Roman Farming*. London: Thames & Hudson.
—— (1973). 'Roman Agricultural Writers I: Varro and his Predecessors'. *ANRW* 1.4: 439–97.
Whitman, C. H. (1958). *Homer and the Heroic Tradition*. Cambridge, Mass.: Harvard University Press.
Wilkinson, L. P. (1945). *Horace and his Lyric Poetry*. Cambridge: Cambridge University Press.
—— (1950). 'The Intention of Virgil's *Georgics*'. *G&R* 19: 19–28.
—— (1956). 'The Earliest Odes of Horace'. *Hermes* 84: 495–9.
—— (1963). 'Virgil's Theodicy'. *CQ* 13: 75–84.
—— (1969). *The Georgics of Virgil: A Critical Survey*. London: Cambridge University Press.
—— (1970). 'Pindar and the Proem to the Third Georgic'. In W. Wimmel (ed.), *Forschungen zur römischen Literatur: Festschrift zum 60. Geburtstag von Karl Büchner*. Wiesbaden: Steiner, 286–90.
—— (1975). *The Roman Experience*. London: Elek.
—— (1982*a*). 'The Georgics'. In E. J. Kenney and W. V. Clausen (eds.), *The Cambridge History of Classical Literature II: Latin Literature*. Cambridge: Cambridge University Press, 320–32.
—— (1982*b*). *Virgil, The Georgics*. Harmondsworth: Penguin.
Williams, F. J. (1978). *Callimachus: Hymn to Apollo*. Oxford: Clarendon Press.
Williams, G. (1968). *Tradition and Originality in Roman Poetry*. Oxford: Clarendon Press.
Williams, R. D. (1979). *Virgil: The Eclogues and Georgics*. New York: St. Martin's Press.
—— (1983). *Virgil: The Eclogues and Georgics*, 2nd edn. New York: St. Martin's Press.
Wimmel, W. (1960). *Kallimachos in Rom: Die Nachfolge seines apologetischen Dichtens in der Augusteerzeit*. Wiesbaden: Steiner.
—— (1973). *Hirtenkrieg und arkadisches Rom: Reduktionsmedien in Vergils Aeneis*. Munich: Fink.
Woodman, A. J. (1975). 'Questions of Date, Genre, and Style in Velleius: Some Literary Answers'. *CQ* 25: 272–306.
Wormell, D. E. W. (1971). 'Apibus quanta experientia parcis: Virgil Georgics 4.1–227'. In Bardons and Verdière (eds.), 429–35.
Ziolkowski, T. (1993). *Virgil and the Moderns*. Princeton: Princeton University Press.

Acknowledgements

Permission to reprint the following items is gratefully acknowledged:

M. S. Spurr, 'Agriculture and the *Georgics*', *Greece and Rome* 33 (1986), 164–87.

R. F. Thomas, 'Prose into Poetry: Tradition and Meaning in Virgil's *Georgics*', *Harvard Studies in Classical Philology* 91 (1987), 229–60.

R. Rutherford, 'Authorial Rhetoric in Virgil's *Georgics*', in D. Innes, H. Hine, and C. Pelling (eds.), *Ethics and Rhetoric: Classical Essays for Donald Russell on his Seventy-Fifth Birthday* (Oxford: Oxford University Press, 1995), 19–29.

M. Gale, 'Virgil's Metamorphoses: Myth and Allusion in the *Georgics*', *Proceedings of the Cambridge Philological Society* 41 (1995), 36–61.

R. Jenkyns, '*Labor improbus*', *Classical Quarterly* 43 (1993), 243–8.

M. C. J. Putnam, 'Italian Virgil and the Idea of Rome', in L. L. Orlin (ed.), *Janus: Essays in Ancient and Modern Studies* (Ann Arbor: University of Michigan Press, 1975), 171–99.

P. R. Hardie, 'Cosmology and National Epic in the *Georgics* (*Georgics* 2.458–3.48)', in *Virgil's* Aeneid*: Cosmos and* Imperium (Oxford: Oxford University Press, 1986), 33–51.

L. P. Wilkinson, 'Pindar and the Proem to the Third Georgic', in W. Wimmel (ed.), *Forschungen zur römischen Literatur: Festschrift zum 60. Geburtstag von Karl Büchner* (Wiesbaden: Franz Steiner Verlag, 1970), 286–90.

R. F. Thomas, 'Callimachus, the *Victoria Berenices*, and Roman Poetry', *Classical Quarterly* 33 (1983), 92–113.

J. Griffin, 'The Fourth *Georgic*, Virgil and Rome', in *Latin Poets and Roman Life* (London: Duckworth, 1985), 163–82.

Passages cited

Greek

Aesch. *PV* 353: 124 n. 86
  369–73: 116
Anth. Pal. 7.274: 199 n. 36
  9.713–42: 196 n. 29
  11.25.3: 214 n. 82
App. *B Civ.* 3.49 ff.: 35
  4.5 ff.: 35
  4.85: 36
  5.13: 36
  5.18: 34
  5.19: 35 n. 53
  5.27: 36
  5.33 ff.: 36
  5.49: 36
  5.56: 35 n. 53
  5.74: 35
  5.80: 35 n. 53
Apollod. 1.9.12: 122 n. 80
Ap. Rhod. *Argon.* 1.54: 192 n. 11
  1.728–9: 219
  1.725–6: 219
  2.1231–4: 66
  4.1280–7: 116 n. 63
Arat. *Phaen.* 16–18: 164
  45–8: 108 n. 37
  100 ff.: 163 n. 4
  110–11: 85 n. 9
  133 ff.: 152 n. 16
  462–544: 108 n. 38
  462: 108
  529–33: 108
  976–81: 70
Ar. *Lys.* 729: 52
  Ran. 543–5: 52
Arist. *Hist. an.* 5.19: 222 n. 115
  Poet. 1448b23: 199 n. 37
  Rhet. 1393a23-b4: 84 n. 7
  1394a5–8: 84 n. 7
Artem. 5.83: 230 n. 18
Athen. 196a–206c: 217 n. 93
  196f: 221 n. 108
  197b: 221 n. 108

Bacchylides *P. Oxy.* 2364 (addendum): 183 + n. 5

Callim. *Aet.* fr. 1.16: 199
  fr. 1.17: 187, 201
  fr. 1.22: 206 n. 57
  fr. 7.11: 216
  fr. 24–5: 193 n. 16
  Dieg. fr. 31 b–e: 197
  fr. 44–7: 193, 210 n. 70
  fr. 57.4: 221
  fr. 65–6: 222 n. 112
  fr. 66: 216
  fr. 76–7: 195 n. 24, 205 n. 55
  Dieg. fr. 77: 205 n. 55
  fr. 84–5: 190, 195 n. 24, 196
  fr. 98: 195 n. 24
  fr. 100: 197
  fr. 101: 197
  fr. 110: 190
  fr. 110.7–8: 212
  fr. 110.54–8: 213 n. 74
  fr. 114: 196
  fr. 114.8: 197
  fr. 118: 198, 200
  fr. 118.2: 198
  fr. 118.3: 198
  fr. 118.4: 199
  fr. 118.6: 199
  fr. 118.7: 199
  fr. 177: 189, 209 n. 67
SH 254.25–32: 213, 222, 223
  25–31: 217
  26–31: 217
  27: 220
  29: 220
  30: 220
  31: 222 n. 115
Iamb. fr. 194.58: 195 n. 23
  fr. 194.82: 125 n. 89

Callim. (*cont.*)
  fr. 196: 197
  fr. 197: 197
  fr. 199: 197
  fr. 202.47 ff.: 200
  fr. 202.56–7: 200 n. 42
  fr. 202.63–8: 199
  fr. 202.66: 200
  Hec. fr. 248: 210 n. 68
  fr. 253.10–12: 218
  fr. 253.12: 222 n. 115
  fr. 256: 211 n. 71
  fr. 260: 125 n. 89
  fr. 260.41: 125 n. 89
  fr. 269: 125 n. 89
  fr. 339: 208
  Carm. ep. et eleg. min. fr. 383: 214 n. 82
  fr. 383.11–19: 213
  fr. 383.12: 215 n. 85, 216 n. 89
  fr. 383.14: 214
  fr. 383.15: 214
  fr. 383.16: 215 n. 85
  fr. 383.17: 215 n. 85
  fr. 384: 195 n. 24, 196, 197, 202
  fr. 384.44–5: 198 n. 33, 216
  fr. 384.57–8: 202, 203
  fr. 384.59: 202 n. 49
  Frag. gram. fr. 457–9: 192 n. 11
  Frag. inc. sed. fr. 520: 216 n. 88
  fr. 532: 216 n. 90
  fr. 547: 216
  fr. 596: 193
  fr. 640: 216
  fr. 666: 195 n. 24, 196, 197
  fr. 672: 216
  fr. 758: 195 n. 24
  Epigr. 21.4: 187 n. 21, 201, 203
  27.2–4: 199
  Hymn 2.47–9: 191
  2.48: 192
  2.105: 187 n. 21, 201
  2.113: 202
  4.304: 206 n. 57
Callixenus of Rhodes *FGH* 627 fr. 2: 217 n. 93
Cass. Dio 48.8.5: 36
  48.13: 36 n. 55

  51.22: 185 n. 13
  53.1: 185 n. 14
Chrysippus *SVF* 2.649: 108 n. 38
  2.1172: 103 n. 23
  2.1181: 103 n. 23
  2.1183: 103 n. 23

Dicaearchus *ap.* Porph. *Abst.* 4.1.2: 106 n. 32
Dio Chrys. *Or.* 36.33: 170 n. 21
Dion. Hal. *Ant. Rom.* 2.34: 199 n. 37
  Comp. 16: 198 + n. 35
  Dem. 58 fin.: 90 n. 22
  Thuc. 24: 199 n. 36

Empedocles fr. 105: 172 n. 26
  fr. 129: 168 n. 17
  fr. 132: 168 + n. 17
Epicurus, *Ep. Pyth.* 86–8: 101 n. 17
  KD 11: 115 n. 62
Eratosthenes fr. 16: 108 n. 35
  fr. 16.15–19: 108 n. 36
Eur. *Bacch.* 72 ff.: 169 n. 18
  Chrysipp. fr. 898: 89 n. 20

Heraclit. *Quaest. Hom.* 48–51: 108 n. 38
  76.1: 166
Hdt. 2.105: 214
Hes. *Op.* 11–26: 103 n. 25
  15: 103 n. 25
  42–6: 102 n. 21
  44: 102 n. 21
  46: 102 n. 21
  50: 102 n. 22
  113–14: 102 n. 20
  117: 102 n. 20
  299–301: 102 n. 18
  311: 103
  327–37: 113 n. 53
  382: 146
  415–16: 112 n. 50
  465–78: 113 n. 53
  516: 113 n. 51
  582–8: 113 n. 53
  618–94: 85 n. 9
  639: 146
  640: 146
  fr. 234: 101 nn. 14 and 15

Passages cited

[Hes.] *Sc.* 140: 219
  141–2: 219
  142: 220 n. 104
Hom. *Il.* 1.259 ff.: 84 n. 7
  2.459–63: 125 n. 89
  4.275–81: 111 n. 46
  16.384–93: 112 n. 50
  16.384: 112 n. 50
  16.385: 112 n. 50
  16.389–92: 112 n. 50
  16.765–70: 111 n. 46
  16.765: 111 n. 45
  18.571: 214 n. 84
  18.595: 214 n. 84, 215 n. 87
  Od. 4.441–6: 51 n. 18
  4.441–2: 51 n. 18
  5.291–6: 111 n. 45
  7.86–111: 215
  7.96–7: 215
  7.105–11: 215
  7.107: 214 n. 81
  7.109–10: 214 n. 83
  11.19: 109 n. 42
  14.404: 211 n. 71
  14.408: 211 n. 71
  19.226 ff.: 219 n. 99
Σ EV *ad* Hom. *Od.* 8.63: 91 n. 26
[Hom.] *Batr.* 7: 124 n. 86
[Longinus] 9.11: 84 n. 8
  9.14: 84 n. 8
  15.4: 84 n. 8

Maximus of Tyre 12.1: 183 n. 4
Mosch. *Eur.* 37–8: 219
  43: 219

Nic. *Ther.* 528: 85
Nonnus, *Dion.* 17.51–4: 209 n. 67
  17.52: 210 n. 68
  17.55: 210 n. 68

Panaetius *ap.* Cic. *Off.* 1.11–13: 103 n. 23
  2.15–17: 103 n. 23
Paus. 8.1.6: 106 n. 32
Philo *Quis Rer. Div. Her.* 147: 108 n. 38
Philostr. *Imag.* 10: 199 n. 40
Phld. *De mus.* 90 K: 199 n. 40
Pind. *Isthm.* 2.1: 187 n. 20

5.38: 187 n. 20
8.61: 187 n. 20
Nem. 1.7: 187 n. 20
1.8: 186
4.17: 209 n. 66
5.1: 196 n. 27
7.70–9: 186
8.21–2: 187 n. 23
10.20: 187 n. 23
10.42: 209 n. 66
Ol. 1.27: 185, 192
1.54–60: 188
1.115–16: 186–7
2.95: 187 n. 23
3.6: 186 n. 18
3.13: 186 n. 18
6.1–5: 182, 183
6.1–4: 186
6.1–3: 195–6
6.22: 187
6.27: 186
6.75: 187 n. 23
8.55: 187–8 + n. 23
9.10: 184
9.43–6: 101 n. 15
9.81: 187 n. 20
Pyth. 1.20 ff.: 188
1.85: 187 n. 23, 201 n. 45
3.113: 186
4.81: 186
6.5–18: 186
8.32: 187 n. 23, 188
8.72: 187 n. 23
10.65: 187 n. 20
11.29; 187 n. 23
11.54: 187 n. 23
fr. 124: 187 n. 20
fr. 137: 169 nn. 18 and 19
Pl. *Ion* 534b: 230 n. 18
Phd. 69c8–9: 170 n. 24
Resp. 365b: 183 + n. 4
Plut. *On Inoffensive Self-Praise*
  539b-d: 91 n. 23
  541e: 91 n. 23
  542ab: 91 n. 23
Polyb. 2.41.9: 244
  6.65.5: 237 n. 35
Posidonius *ap.* Sen. *Ep.* 90: 103 n. 23

Strabo 2.2.1–2: 108 n. 38
   4.4.4: 166 n. 12
   5.2.1: 29 n. 40

Theoc. *Id.* 1.32: 219
   1.56: 219
   1.146: 230 n. 18
   15.78–86: 219 n. 102
   15.78–9: 219 n. 102
   15.126: 52
Theophr. *Caus. pl.* 2.4: 69
   2.5.3: 77
   Hist. pl. 2.1.1: 72
   3.1.14: 72 n. 46
   4.4.2: 51
Thuc. 2.47.4: 122 n. 79
   3.37.1: 84 n. 7
Timagenes 88 *FGH* T3: 247–8 + n. 53
Timocreon *PMG* 731: 202 n. 47

Xen. *Lac.* 13.5: 199 n. 37

Latin

Apul. *Met.* 11.23: 168 n. 14
Augustus, *Res gestae* 15.3: 37
   16.1: 37
   25.1: 35 n. 54
   28: 37

Caes. *B Civ.* 1.18.4: 33 n. 48
   1.24 ff.: 34
   1.24.2: 33 n. 48
Cato, *Agr. praef.*: 42 n. 65
   1.2.7: 53
   2.2: 32 n. 46
   2.3: 32 n. 46
   6: 69
   8.2: 29 n. 41
   10–11: 78
   28.2: 17 n. 13
   37.3: 32 n. 46
   39.2: 32 n. 46
   40.1: 17 n. 14
   49.1: 17 n. 13
   61.2: 17 n. 13
   91: 55
   129: 55
   Orig. fr. 1: 244

Catull. 1.2: 198 n. 36
   64.31–44: 218 n. 97
   64.49: 219–20
   64.50–1: 219
   64.50: 218
   64.51: 218 n. 97
   64.228: 191 n. 10
   64.265: 218
   64.267–77: 218 n. 97
   64.267–8: 218 n. 97, 220, 221
   66.54–8: 213 n. 74
Cic. *Att.* 13.38.2: 183 n. 4
   Brut. 294: 199 n. 36
   Cato Maior 51–60: 83 n. 5
   De imp. Cn. Pomp. 16: 35 n. 53
   De or. 2.22: 83 n. 5
   3.43: 90 n. 21
   3.137: 233
   3.185: 199 n. 36
   Div. 1.101: 116 n. 63
   2.43: 117 n. 67
   Fam. 7.33.2: 199 n. 36
   10.32.5: 247 n. 51
   Fin. 1.14.46: 166 n. 9
   2.45: 245
   Mur. 83: 245
   Nat. D. 2.5: 118 n. 68
   2.6: 116 n. 63
   Or. 20: 199 n. 36
   Phil. 14.32: 245
   Rep. 2.2.3: 244
   Rosc. Am. 15: 30 n. 43
   20: 30 n. 43
   Sest. 138: 245
   Tusc. 1.11: 118 n. 68
   1.48: 118 n. 68
Columella 1.3.10: 30
   1.7: 32 n. 46
   2.2.13: 34 n. 52
   2.2.25: 42
   2.4.11: 19 n. 18
   2.10.9: 18 n. 17
   2.12.7: 28
   2.17.4: 26 n. 33
   2.19.2: 27 n. 36
   2.20.4: 27
   3.1–5.7: 20
   3.10.20: 41
   3.11.4: 33

Passages cited

3.13.8: 32 n. 46
3.13.12: 32 n. 46
4.11.1: 41
5.8–9: 20
5.8.1: 20
5.9.6–7: 17 n. 14
5.10.6–9: 16
5.11.1: 63
6.27.7: 19 n. 18
7.1.2: 25 n. 31
8.2.7: 34 n. 52
10.308: 29 n. 41
11.1.12: 32 n. 46
11.2.44: 34 n. 52
11.2.90: 32 n. 46
12.3.6: 32 n. 46

Enn. *Ann.* 432–4: 111 n. 45

Hor. *Ars. P.* 139: 134
    291: 199 n. 36
    323 ff.: 231
    465: 172 n. 26
  Carm. 1.37.31: 184 n. 11
    3.4.73: 124 n. 86
    3.6.38–9: 29 n. 40
    4.2.27: 230 n. 18
    4.15.5: 39 n. 62
  Epist. 1.19.44: 230 n. 18
    2.1.156–7: 231
  Sat. 1.3.9–11: 170
    1.10.65: 199 n. 36
    2.1.12–13: 174
    2.1.71–4: 83 n. 5
Hyg. *Astr.* 2.24: 213 n. 74

Isid. *Etym.* 11.3.13: 124 n. 86

Juv. 13.54–5: 106 n. 32

Luc. 5.597–677: 111 n. 45
    8.867: 229 n. 15
Lucr. 1.1–20: 114 n. 55
    1.10–11: 100 n. 11
    1.44–9: 98 n. 8
    1.62 ff.: 169 n. 20
    1.62–79: 116 n. 65
    1.63: 178 n. 38
    1.66: 178 + n. 38
    1.67: 106 n. 30
    1.71: 106 n. 30
    1.75–6: 100 n. 13
    1.75: 178 n. 39
    1.78: 169 + n. 20
    1.115: 109 n. 40
    1.117–19: 184 + n. 12
    1.117–18: 178
    1.117: 178
    1.119: 146 n. 13
    1.123: 116 n. 63
    1.146: 169 n. 20
    1.188–90: 118 n. 69
    1.199–203: 118 n. 70
    1.208–14: 105 n. 29
    1.211: 105 n. 29
    1.212: 105 n. 29
    1.214: 105 n. 29
    1.250 ff.: 89 n. 20
    1.250–64: 100 n. 12
    1.250–1: 113, 114 n. 55
    1.256: 114 n. 55
    1.271–6: 111 n. 44
    1.273–5: 111 n. 46
    1.277: 101 n. 17
    1.280–94: 116 n. 63
    1.313–14: 100 n. 11
    1.400–1: 107 n. 34
    1.410: 107 n. 34
    1.494: 101
    1.586–7: 100 n. 13
    1.595–6: 100 n. 13
    1.722–5: 116 n. 64
    1.736–9: 117 n. 66
    1.744: 119 n. 72
    1.803–11: 114
    1.805–11: 114 n. 55
    1.808: 119 n. 72
    1.820–1: 119 n. 72
    1.884: 116 n. 63
    1.921 ff.: 165, 177
    1.922–5: 124 n. 85, 164–5
    1.923: 172
    1.924: 165 n. 7
    1.926–50: 22 n. 25, 97 n. 7
    1.926–7: 124 n. 85
    1.927: 167
    1.938: 165 n. 7
    1.945: 165 n. 7

Lucr. (*cont.*)
1.947: 165
1.1052–82: 109 n. 41
1.1065–7: 109 n. 41
2.14 ff.: 169 n. 20
2.114: 107 n. 34
2.116: 111 n. 46
2.203–9: 116 n. 63
2.233–4: 105 n. 29
2.263–5: 119 n. 72
2.465: 101 n. 17
2.569–80: 115 n. 61
2.600: 121
2.652–4: 114 n. 56
2.700–6: 118 n. 70
2.707: 118
2.817–25: 118 n. 70, 125 n. 89
2.991–8: 100 n. 12
2.991–7: 113
2.991–3: 114 n. 55
2.994: 114 n. 55
2.997: 114 n. 55
2.1016: 119 n. 72
2.1105–74: 99 n. 9
2.1116–17: 99 n. 9
2.1144–5: 99 n. 9
2.1150–74: 100 n. 12
2.1157: 105 n. 29
2.1158: 105 n. 29
2.1160–3: 105 n. 29
2.1161: 105 n. 29
2.1173–4: 107 n. 34
2.1174: 107 n. 34
3.2: 106 n. 30
3.6: 122 n. 82
3.9: 106 n. 30
3.25 ff.: 169 n. 20
3.25–27: 109 n. 40
3.29–30: 167
3.65: 105 n. 29
3.91: 169 n. 20
3.211: 162 n. 3
3.247: 101 n. 17
3.288–307: 119 n. 72
3.294–8: 116 n. 64
3.296–306: 118 n. 69
3.316: 101 n. 17
3.458: 107 n. 34
3.939: 162 n. 3

3.978: 109 n. 40
3.1071–2: 169 n. 20
3.1072: 107 n. 34
4.1–25: 97 n. 7
4.22: 230 n. 18
4.35–45: 116 n. 63
4.129–40: 118
4.168–73: 111 n. 46
4.276: 108 n. 36
4.547–8: 119 n. 72
4.577: 107 n. 34
4.580–94: 97, 116 n. 63, 121 n. 76
4.638–41: 119 n. 72
4.678–83: 119 n. 72
4.710–21: 119 n. 72
4.711: 125 n. 89
4.732–48: 118
4.759–67: 116 n. 63
4.902: 107 n. 34
4.984–1010: 119 n. 72
4.1194–1207: 119 n. 72
5.7: 169 n. 20
5.9–10: 105 n. 30
5.14–15: 106 n. 32
5.20–1: 180 n. 42
5.26: 121 n. 76
5.30: 121 n. 78
5.33: 121
5.58: 100 n. 13
5.78–90: 115 n. 62
5.88–9: 100 n. 13
5.110–45: 114 n. 56
5.110–13: 117 n. 66
5.113–21: 116 n. 65
5.120: 124 n. 88
5.142: 100 n. 11
5.195 ff.: 108
5.195–234: 111 n. 47
5.206–17: 105 n. 29
5.206–11: 100 n. 11
5.206–7: 105 n. 29, 107 n. 34
5.210: 105 n. 29
5.211: 105 n. 29
5.213–15: 107 n. 34
5.213: 105 n. 29
5.215–17: 105 n. 29
5.215: 101 n. 17
5.252: 101 n. 17
5.272: 108 n. 36

Passages cited

5.306–17: 107 n. 34
5.308: 107 n. 34
5.389: 101 n. 17
5.405–8: 97–8
5.405: 121
5.411–15: 101 n. 16
5.487–8: 101 n. 17
5.509–33: 101 n. 17
5.545: 100 n. 13
5.575–6: 101 n. 17
5.580–704: 101 n. 17
5.611: 101 n. 17
5.644: 107 n. 34
5.650–9: 109–10
5.656–65: 101 n. 17
5.699–700: 165 n. 6
5.737–47: 110 n. 43
5.737–40: 114
5.751–70: 115 n. 63
5.751: 165 n. 6
5.780–820: 113
5.780–2: 114 n. 55
5.783–805: 114 n. 55
5.806: 114 n. 55
5.818–20: 114 nn. 55 and 59
5.826–36: 100 n. 12
5.855–77: 118
5.878–924: 118
5.890–900: 121 n. 78
5.923–4: 100 n. 13
5.925–6: 101, 114 n. 55
5.934: 106 n. 32
5.939–42: 106 n. 32
5.965: 106 n. 32
5.1002–3: 165 n. 6
5.1006: 105 n. 29
5.1078–82: 125 n. 89
5.1084–6: 125 n. 89
5.1086: 125 n. 89
5.1091–1104: 104 n. 27
5.1161–1240: 97
5.1185: 169 n. 20
5.1186–7: 97
5.1191: 116 n. 63
5.1218–35: 113 n. 51
5.1244–9: 101 n. 17
5.1250 ff.: 104 n. 27
5.1250–1: 104 n. 27
5.1252–7: 101 n. 17

5.1266–8: 104 n. 27
5.1283 ff.: 104 n. 27
5.1295: 106 n. 32
5.1297–9: 104 n. 27
5.1350–3: 104 n. 27
5.1361–78: 104 n. 27, 106 n. 31
5.1416: 106 n. 32
5.1427: 114 n. 55
5.1435–42: 104 n. 27
5.1452–7: 104 n. 27
6.1–6: 123 n. 85
6.27: 166 n. 9
6.39: 169 n. 20
6.48–91: 115 n. 62
6.51–5: 113 n. 51
6.52–3: 111 n. 46
6.64–5: 100 n. 13
6.96–101: 111 n. 44
6.97–8: 111 n. 46
6.115: 111 n. 46
6.129: 115 n. 63
6.140–1: 111 n. 46
6.148–9: 112
6.155: 115 n. 63
6.189: 107 n. 34
6.218: 115 n. 63
6.247–8: 116 n. 63
6.253–61: 111 n. 44
6.253: 111 n. 44
6.255: 111 n. 46
6.256: 111 n. 46
6.259: 111 n. 46
6.275: 111 n. 46
6.276: 111 n. 46
6.278: 112
6.288: 115 n. 63
6.291: 111 n. 46
6.330–1: 111 n. 46
6.357–78: 111 n. 44, 114
6.363 ff.: 111 n. 46
6.365: 112
6.379–422: 111 n. 48
6.379–86: 115
6.428: 111 n. 46
6.493: 101 n. 17
6.535–607: 116 n. 63
6.535: 165 n. 6
6.577: 165 n. 6
6.616–22: 101 n. 17

Lucr. (*cont.*)
  6.638: 108 n. 36
  6.639–702: 115 n. 63
  6.680–93: 116 n. 64
  6.681: 117
  6.703–11: 101 n. 17
  6.738–829: 119 n. 72
  6.749–55: 125 n. 89
  6.753: 125 n. 89
  6.754: 121
  6.830–78: 101 n. 17
  6.858: 101 n. 17
  6.943: 101 n. 17
  6.962: 101 n. 17
  6.1016: 101 n. 17
  6.1044: 107 n. 34
  6.1106–9: 100 n. 13
  6.1179: 122 nn. 79 and 81

Macrob. *In Somn.* 2.10.6: 106 n. 32
  Sat. 5.17.1–2: 233 n. 26
  5.22.9–10: 67 n. 43
Manilius 1.1 ff.: 166 n. 10
Marcus Aurelius p. 62 van den Hout: 83 n. 5
Mart. 9.43: 210 n. 69

Ov. *Fast.* 1.295 ff.: 166 n. 8
  1.307: 166 n. 8
  5.35–6: 57 n. 25
  Met. 2.547: 125 n. 89
  8.699–700: 211
  Pont. 1.1.6: 170
  1.1.9: 170
  1.1.14: 170
  1.1.29: 170
  1.1.35: 170
  1.1.45–8: 171
  Tr. 1.1.11: 198 n. 36
  1.2.17–32: 111 n. 45
  4.7.11–18: 118 n. 68

Plin. *HN* 1.1–22: 42 n. 65
  8.167: 25 n. 31
  8.196: 220 n. 108
  11.58: 229 n. 15
  11.75–7: 222 n. 115
  14.20–76: 23 n. 28
  14.49: 16 n. 10

  17.8: 21
  17.49: 24
  17.128: 24
  17.201: 24
  18.35: 30
  18.120: 18 n. 17, 24
  18.161: 27
  18.178: 29 n. 40, 42
  18.182: 33
  18.187: 26 n. 32
  18.242: 19 n. 18
  18.295: 27 n. 36
  36.53–4: 199 n. 36
Porcius Licinus fr. 1: 231 n. 21
Prop. 3.1.1–4: 205
  3.1.3: 206
  3.1.8: 198 n. 36
  3.1.9–11: 206–7
  3.1.9: 206
  3.1.17–18: 206
  3.1.20–1: 207
  3.1.24: 206
  3.1.38: 206 n. 57
  3.2.1–2: 207
  3.2.5: 207

Quint. *Inst.* 2.4.7: 199 n. 36
  2.8.4: 199 n. 36
  2.12.8: 199 n. 36
  2.17.21: 82 n. 2
  10.4.4: 199 n. 36
  11.1.3: 199 n. 36
  12.10.17: 199 n. 36
  12.10.50: 199 n. 36

Sall. *Cat.* 3.2: 202 n. 48
  9: 244
  52.23: 244
  Iug. 6.1: 203 n. 50
  10.2: 203
Sen. *Agam.* 465–97: 111 n. 45
  De ira 2.23–4: 247–8 + n. 53
  Epist. 24.18: 118 n. 68
  82.16: 118 n. 68
  86.14: 17 n. 12
  86.15: 14 + n. 1
  86.17–18: 17
  86.19: 16
  90.28–9: 167 n. 13

Passages cited

Q *Nat.* 1 prol. 3: 167 n. 13
  7.30: 167 n. 13
Serv. *ad* Verg. *Ecl.* 10.1: 194 n. 19, 246
  Verg. *G.* 2.121: 222 n. 115
    3.2: 191
    3.7: 193 n. 17
    4.1: 194 n. 19, 246
    4.219: 228 n. 9
Serv. Auct. *ad* Verg. *G.* 1.146: 131 + n. 6
  3.391: 67 n. 44
Sil. *Pun.* 7.395: 207 n. 60
Stat. *Silv.* 1.2.253: 208
    3.1.17–19: 211
    3.1.29–31: 210
    3.1.49–50: 211
    3.1.82–3: 210
    3.1.135: 211
    3.1.140–3: 211
    4.6.51: 210
    5.3.156–8: 208
  Theb. 4.158: 209 n. 67
    4.159–64: 209
    4.161: 209, 211
Suet. *Aug.* 18.2: 40 n. 64
    32.1: 40 n. 63
    42: 40 n. 64
    66.2: 248 n. 48

Tac. *Ann.* 4.35: 247
Tib. 1.7.28–9: 220
  2.3.2: 136 n. 15
  2.3.49: 136 n. 15
[Tib.] *Panegyric to Messalla* 12–13: 208

Varro, *Ling.* 7.36: 116 n. 63
  Rust. 1.1.2: 52
    1.1.10: 44 n. 5
    1.2.3: 37
    1.2.6: 37
    1.5.2: 23 n. 28
    1.7.5–10: 69
    1.8: 20
    1.9: 69
    1.13.6–7: 42 n. 65
    1.16.3: 29 n. 41
    1.17: 32 n. 46
    1.17.3: 32 n. 46
    1.19.1: 30 n. 43
    1.22.1: 27

1.23.5: 26 n. 33
1.29.2: 42
1.30: 17 n. 14
1.36: 32 n. 46
1.40.5: 19 n. 18, 61
1.41.6: 18 n. 15
1.50: 27
1.51.1–2: 55–6
1.52: 27
1.54.1: 20
1.54.2–3: 20
1.55: 20
1.69.3: 42 n. 65
2 *praef.*: 42 n. 65
2.2.4: 48 n. 15
2.2.10–11: 48
2.4.1: 53 n. 20
2.4.3: 53
2.4.7: 52
2.5.2: 53 n. 20
2.5.14: 58
2.7.2–6: 65
2.7.8: 51
2.7.9: 60
2.7.15: 27 n. 37
2.10.6: 52
2.10.8: 34
2.10.1: 34 n. 52
3.1.1–5: 42 n. 65
3.2.13: 21
3.6.10: 29
3.16.5: 228
3.16.7: 230
3.16.30: 229 n. 15
Vell. Pat. 2.89.4: 39 n. 62
Verg. *Aen.* 1.25: 158
  1.29: 158
  1.55–6: 157
  1.81–123: 111 n. 45
  1.278: 240
  1.289–90: 170 n. 23
  1.430–6: 239 n. 37
  1.456: 220 n. 104
  1.494: 220 n. 104
  3.539–43: 143
  3.570 ff.: 188
  4.68–73: 235
  4.412: 134 n. 11
  4.657: 235

Verg. (*cont.*)
  4.697: 158
  5.59–60: 170 n. 24
  6.109: 171
  6.276–7: 131, 146 n. 11
  6.277: 105 n. 29, 131
  6.463: 236
  6.601–7: 188
  6.693: 171
  6.707–9: 239 n. 37
  6.716: 171
  6.756: 238
  6.809: 170 n. 24
  6.817–23: 237
  6.847–53: 232–3
  7.41–4: 204 n. 54
  7.371: 120 n. 75
  7.483: 233
  7.501–2: 235
  7.506–8: 234
  7.521: 234
  7.523 ff.: 234
  8.85: 170 n. 24
  8.327 ff.: 145 n. 10
  8.364–5: 239
  8.500–1: 159
  8.612–13: 220
  8.618–19: 220
  8.624: 220 n. 103
  8.728: 157
  8.730: 220
  9.62: 103 n. 24
  9.86: 170 n. 24
  9.598 ff.: 239
  9.774–7: 236
  10.104–13: 131 n. 8
  10.111–12: 131 n. 8
  10.112: 131 n. 8
  10.113: 131 n. 8
  10.324–7: 236
  10.727: 103 n. 24
  10.809 ff.: 235
  11.709: 158
  12.13: 170 n. 24
  12.250: 103 n. 24
  12.827: 239
  12.938: 235
  12.945: 158
  12.946–7: 158
  12.951–2: 157–8
Ecl. 2.13: 50
  2.69–72: 241
  3.94: 227
  3.110: 231
  4.6: 152 n. 16
  6.3–8: 204 n. 54
  6.3: 197, 206 n. 57
  6.10–11: 84 n. 8
  6.64–5: 177
  7.17: 241
  8.15: 49
  8.52–3: 62
  9.27–9: 70
  10.50–1: 207 n. 62
  10.55: 207 n. 62
  10.69: 130
G. 1.1–5: 87
  1.2: 24
  1.5–6: 174
  1.27: 181
  1.41: 86
  1.43 ff.: 25
  1.43–203: 99
  1.43–4: 114 n. 57
  1.45: 24
  1.46: 100 n. 11
  1.49: 27
  1.50–61: 26
  1.50–1: 26
  1.50: 27
  1.53–4: 100 n. 13
  1.56: 86
  1.60–1: 100 n. 13
  1.63: 86, 114 n. 57
  1.71: 25
  1.74–5: 25
  1.75–6: 22
  1.79–81: 83
  1.79–80: 51–2
  1.80: 25, 27 n. 35
  1.84 ff.: 29
  1.86–93: 101 n. 17
  1.88: 101 n. 17
  1.89: 101 n. 17
  1.90: 101 n. 17
  1.93: 101 n. 17
  1.95: 26
  1.97–8: 42

Passages cited

1.101: 82
1.104: 24
1.108: 24
1.111: 26
1.112–13: 27
1.118–59: 99, 128
1.118–49: 54
1.118–21: 104–5
1.118: 102 n. 21, 105 n. 29
1.119: 105 n. 29, 134 n. 12
1.120–1: 105 n. 29
1.121: 103, 112 n. 49
1.122–3: 105 n. 30
1.124: 102 nn. 20 and 21
1.125: 105 n. 29
1.127–8: 75–6, 76, 102 n. 20, 105 n. 29
1.128: 105 n. 20
1.130: 106 n. 30
1.133–45: 135
1.133–4: 76, 104 n. 27
1.133: 77
1.135: 102
1.136–45: 102
1.139: 104
1.143: 104
1.144: 104 n. 27
1.145–6: 76, 102, 103, 128–37 *passim*, 146 n. 11
1.145: 57
1.146–7: 136
1.147–59: 136
1.147: 136, 137 n. 16
1.148 ff.: 136
1.148: 33 n. 51
1.150–4: 105 + n. 29
1.153: 105 n. 29
1.159: 33 n. 51
1.164: 27
1.176–203: 107
1.176–86: 54–5
1.176–7: 83, 107 n. 34
1.178–9: 27, 56
1.181 ff.: 134
1.181: 57, 59 n. 28, 134
1.184–5: 57, 124
1.193: 24, 85
1.197–200: 107 n. 34
1.197–9: 107 n. 34

1.197: 24, 26, 85
1.204–351: 99
1.210: 32 n. 46, 82
1.215–16: 14, 18
1.222: 125 n. 89
1.231–56: 107
1.237–8: 108 n. 36
1.240–3: 109 n. 39
1.242–3: 109
1.243–6: 108
1.246: 125 n. 89, 126
1.248: 109 n. 42
1.249–51: 109 n. 41
1.257: 86
1.259 ff.: 32 n. 46
1.264: 32 n. 46
1.270–1: 27 n. 35
1.271: 33 n. 51
1.276–86: 124
1.278–80: 57
1.284: 83 n. 6
1.287: 32 n. 46
1.291–6: 29
1.291–2: 32 n. 46
1.299: 32 n. 46
1.305–6: 33 n. 51
1.307–9: 33 n. 51
1.311–34: 111, 114
1.311: 112 n. 50, 114
1.313: 113 n. 54
1.316–18: 24
1.316: 32 n. 46
1.318: 85, 111 n. 46, 113
1.319–21: 111 n. 46
1.319: 111 n. 46
1.320: 111 n. 46, 112 n. 50
1.323–4: 113 n. 54
1.323: 111 n. 46, 112 n. 50
1.324: 111 n. 46
1.325–27: 112 n. 50
1.326: 113 n. 54
1.327: 111 n. 46
1.328–33: 112
1.328: 111 n. 46, 112 n. 49
1.329: 111 n. 46
1.330–1: 111 n. 46, 112 n. 51
1.330: 113 n. 54
1.334: 111 n. 46
1.335: 86

Verg. (*cont.*)
  1.343: 86
  1.353: 112 n. 49
  1.383–5: 125 n. 89
  1.383: 125 n. 89
  1.388–9: 125 n. 89
  1.388: 103 n. 24, 125 n. 89, 134 n. 11
  1.389: 125 n. 89
  1.390–2: 70, 125 n. 89
  1.390: 32 n. 46
  1.399: 125 + n. 89
  1.404–9: 122
  1.410–23: 89 n. 20
  1.415–23: 125 n. 89
  1.415: 89 n. 20, 125 n. 89
  1.448: 85 n. 10
  1.456–7: 84–5
  1.459: 86
  1.469–88: 38
  1.471–3: 115–16
  1.471–2: 85
  1.477–83: 116 n. 63
  1.501–2: 87
  1.502: 85, 117
  1.503 ff.: 87
  1.503: 85
  1.505–6: 239
  1.506–8: 38
  1.512 ff.: 142 n. 9
  2.1–135: 46
  2.1–8: 46
  2.1: 83
  2.7–8: 124 n. 85
  2.9–34: 46, 73
  2.9–21: 73–4, 75
  2.10–11: 76
  2.18: 125
  2.22–34: 74–5, 75
  2.22: 76–7
  2.23–31: 75
  2.28: 17 n. 14
  2.30–1: 17 n. 12
  2.32–4: 62, 77
  2.33–4: 19 n. 18
  2.33: 62
  2.35–46: 46
  2.35–6: 82
  2.42: 91
  2.47–72: 46, 73
  2.47–60: 73–4, 75
  2.47: 76
  2.56 ff.: 23
  2.58: 14, 16, 17–18
  2.61–72: 74–5, 75
  2.61: 77
  2.62: 32 n. 46
  2.63–8: 75
  2.63: 18
  2.69–72: 62, 77
  2.71–2: 62
  2.73–82: 46
  2.78–82: 77
  2.80–82: 77
  2.83–108: 46
  2.89 ff.: 23
  2.94–7: 23
  2.95–6: 86
  2.102: 86
  2.109–35: 46
  2.113–35: 23
  2.113: 23
  2.129: 46 n. 13
  2.130: 51
  2.131: 45
  2.135–9: 143
  2.136–76: 37, 38, 139
  2.140–2: 144
  2.143–4: 140
  2.143: 140 n. 4
  2.144: 140
  2.145–8: 142
  2.149–50: 140
  2.151–4: 140
  2.151: 140 n. 4
  2.153: 140 n. 3
  2.154: 140 n. 3, 146 n. 13
  2.155–7: 37
  2.155: 141 + n. 7
  2.157: 141, 142, 149
  2.158: 141 + n. 7
  2.159–60: 82
  2.159: 142 n. 8
  2.160: 141
  2.161–3: 156
  2.161–4: 141
  2.161: 147 n. 14
  2.162: 141 n. 6

Passages cited 279

2.165–6: 141, 147
2.167–9: 142
2.167: 142
2.169–70: 142
2.170–6: 88
2.170–2: 89
2.170: 142
2.171–2: 143
2.172: 139 n. 1, 149
2.174–6: 144
2.174–5: 140
2.174: 142
2.176: 23, 89 n. 21, 145, 146 n. 13, 174 n. 30
2.177–258: 26, 78
2.177–224: 69
2.177: 83 n. 6
2.192 ff.: 84
2.198–9: 24, 69
2.198: 90 n. 21
2.203 ff.: 26
2.205–6: 27
2.207–11: 123
2.211: 123 n. 83
2.222–3: 24
2.224–5: 69, 70
2.252–3: 85 n. 10
2.259–419: 19
2.259–87: 71
2.264: 32 n. 46
2.279–83: 71
2.288: 83
2.290 ff.: 24
2.315–45: 19
2.323–45: 111
2.325–7: 114 nn. 55 and 56
2.325–6: 89 n. 20, 113 n. 54
2.325: 113 n. 54
2.327: 113 n. 54
2.328–35: 114 n. 55
2.328: 114 n. 55
2.329: 114 n. 55
2.330: 114 n. 55
2.331: 114 n. 55
2.332–3: 114 n. 55
2.333: 113 n. 54
2.334–5: 114 n. 55
2.336–42: 114 n. 55
2.343–5: 114 n. 55

2.343: 114 n. 57
2.345: 83, 114
2.346–53: 46
2.354–61: 46
2.361: 24
2.368–70: 71
2.380–96: 124 n. 85
2.388: 87
2.393–4: 84, 86
2.412–13: 29
2.412: 78
2.416: 29 n. 39
2.417: 32 n. 46
2.420–5: 19
2.420: 78
2.425: 78
2.433: 86
2.436: 27 n. 35
2.454–7: 79
2.455–7: 123 + n. 85, 151
2.455: 123 n. 84
2.458–3.48: 161–81 *passim*
2.458–9: 87, 154 n. 19
2.460: 152
2.461–2: 147
2.463: 147
2.464–6: 151
2.464: 147
2.467–71: 151
2.469: 151, 152
2.473 ff.: 139 n. 1
2.473–4: 152
2.475–94: 87
2.475–86: 88
2.475: 87
2.478: 153
2.479–80: 153
2.481–2: 153
2.485–9: 152
2.486–7: 84
2.490–9: 237 n. 34
2.490–4: 94
2.495–8: 149
2.496: 150
2.501–2: 148
2.503–4: 148
2.504: 149
2.507: 147
2.510: 150

Verg. (*cont.*)
  2.518: 27
  2.532–5: 149, 237 n. 34
  2.532–3: 238–9
  2.536–40: 145
  2.536: 148
  2.541–2: 155, 187
  3.1–48: 88, 182–8 *passim*, 190–205
    passim
  3.3–9: 90
  3.8–9: 206
  3.9: 206
  3.10–11: 206
  3.10: 207 n. 62
  3.11: 87, 206
  3.12 ff.: 90 n. 21
  3.17–18: 206–7
  3.19–20: 212
  3.24–5: 224 n. 120
  3.37–9: 207
  3.40: 207
  3.41: 39, 89
  3.43: 207
  3.46 ff.: 89
  3.49–71: 47
  3.49–50: 184, 203
  3.64: 65
  3.66–8: 86
  3.72–94: 47
  3.72–208: 27 n. 37
  3.85: 121 n. 78
  3.89–91: 65
  3.90: 120–1
  3.92–4: 66
  3.95–6: 92
  3.103: 86
  3.105: 65
  3.113–17: 123 n. 85
  3.115–16: 66 n. 41
  3.118: 65
  3.133: 27, 28
  3.143–56: 58
  3.145–56: 66
  3.149: 121
  3.150–1: 59
  3.152–3: 66, 120
  3.152: 121 n. 76
  3.153: 121 n. 76
  3.154: 120 n. 75

  3.176: 27
  3.177: 55 n. 23
  3.210: 120 n. 75
  3.212–13: 68–9
  3.216: 65
  3.244: 121 n. 78
  3.245–66: 67
  3.248: 53 n. 22
  3.250: 86
  3.251: 51
  3.253–4: 68
  3.255–6: 53 n. 22
  3.258–63: 67–8
  3.258: 68
  3.259–60: 68
  3.264: 68
  3.266–8: 60, 121
  3.266: 67, 121 n. 78
  3.269–75: 19 n. 18
  3.269–70: 68, 124 n. 85
  3.272: 114 n. 58, 120 n. 75
  3.284–94: 88, 124 n. 85
  3.284: 91
  3.285: 84
  3.286: 83
  3.287–90: 49 n. 15
  3.288: 82
  3.289–90: 83
  3.291 ff.: 174 n. 32
  3.291–3: 124 n. 85
  3.294: 87
  3.295: 85
  3.300: 85
  3.306–7: 52
  3.322–38: 47–8
  3.324–5: 49
  3.326: 49
  3.329: 85
  3.331: 49
  3.332–4: 50
  3.338: 125 n. 89
  3.340: 84 n. 8
  3.384–413: 46
  3.384: 83
  3.391–3: 67
  3.408: 86
  3.419: 59 n. 28
  3.420 ff.: 86
  3.420: 82

Passages cited

3.421: 103 n. 24
3.435–6: 85
3.440: 85
3.441–4: 59 n. 27
3.458–9: 59 n. 27
3.468–9: 92
3.471: 59 n. 28
3.479: 59 n. 27
3.497: 53 n. 22
3.498–514: 47, 121 n. 78
3.500–1: 59 n. 27
3.511–12: 59 n. 27
3.511: 121 n. 78
3.512–14: 121 n. 78
3.513: 85 n. 10
3.514: 61
3.515–30: 47
3.515: 86
3.520–2: 49
3.525: 76
3.526 ff.: 141 n. 5
3.534–5: 29
3.549–50: 66 n. 41, 123 n. 85
3.550: 122 n. 79
3.554–5: 59
3.563–6: 64
3.566: 59 n. 27
4.1: 231
4.3: 83
4.15–17: 122
4.72: 230
4.86–7: 229
4.90: 229
4.106–7: 92, 229
4.116–48: 88 n. 13
4.125–46: 29
4.125–7: 24
4.133: 29 n. 41
4.137: 125 n. 89
4.139–41: 29
4.147: 91
4.149: 240
4.156: 228
4.158: 228
4.160: 126
4.170 ff.: 229
4.173: 117 n. 67
4.177: 228

4.184: 228
4.185: 228
4.188: 230
4.197: 86
4.198 ff.: 231
4.201: 228
4.204: 228
4.208–9: 240
4.210–12: 230
4.210: 228
4.218: 228
4.219 ff.: 176
4.228: 83 n. 6
4.232–5: 125 n. 89
4.239: 86
4.246–7: 125
4.251: 86
4.264: 85
4.300–1: 239–40
4.315: 86, 87, 239
4.359 ff.: 184 n. 9
4.415–31: 51 n. 18
4.415–8: 51 n. 18
4.431: 51 n. 18
4.464 ff.: 241
4.465–6: 240
5.471 ff.: 241
4.487: 240
4.511–18: 123
4.511–15: 91–2
4.528–58: 241
4.538: 241
4.540: 241
4.542: 240
4.544: 241
4.550–62: 241
4.559–66: 87, 242
4.559–60: 83, 90
4.560–2: 180–1
4.560: 246
4.561: 145
4.562: 181
4.565: 90
[Verg.] *Catal.* 5.12: 164 n. 5
Ciris 81–2: 77
386–90: 241
Moretum 15–16: 28
Vitr. 8.3.21: 122 n. 80